The Kazakh Spring

How can a deinstitutionalized protest movement disrupt a solidified, repressive, and extremely resilient authoritarian regime? Using the context of the Kazakh Spring protests that started in 2019, Diana T. Kudaibergen focuses on how the interplay between a repressive regime and democratization struggles defines and shapes both. Combining original interview data, digital ethnography, and contentious politics studies, she argues that the new generation of activists, including Instagram political influencers and renowned public intellectuals, have been able to delegitimize and counter one of the most resilient authoritarian regimes and inspire mass protests that none of the formalized opposition ever imagined possible in Kazakhstan. *The Kazakh Spring* is the first book to detail the emergence of this political field of opportunities, which made it possible to rethink political limits in Kazakhstan, essentially toppling its long-term dictator in the unprecedented mass protests of Bloody January 2022.

Diana T. Kudaibergen is a political sociologist. She teaches sociology at the University of Cambridge, where she is also a fellow at Homerton College.

The Kazakh Spring

Digital Activism and the Challenge to Dictatorship

DIANA T. KUDAIBERGEN
University of Cambridge

CAMBRIDGE
UNIVERSITY PRESS

Shaftesbury Road, Cambridge CB2 8EA, United Kingdom

One Liberty Plaza, 20th Floor, New York, NY 10006, USA

477 Williamstown Road, Port Melbourne, VIC 3207, Australia

314–321, 3rd Floor, Plot 3, Splendor Forum, Jasola District Centre, New Delhi – 110025, India

103 Penang Road, #05–06/07, Visioncrest Commercial, Singapore 238467

Cambridge University Press is part of Cambridge University Press & Assessment, a department of the University of Cambridge.

We share the University's mission to contribute to society through the pursuit of education, learning and research at the highest international levels of excellence.

www.cambridge.org
Information on this title: www.cambridge.org/9781009454223

DOI: 10.1017/9781009454230

© Diana T. Kudaibergen 2024

This publication is in copyright. Subject to statutory exception and to the provisions of relevant collective licensing agreements, no reproduction of any part may take place without the written permission of Cambridge University Press & Assessment.

When citing this work, please include a reference to the DOI 10.1017/9781009454230

First published 2024

A catalogue record for this publication is available from the British Library

Library of Congress Cataloging-in-Publication Data
Names: Kudaibergen, Diana T., 1986– author.
Title: The Kazakh Spring : digital activism and the challenge to dictatorship / Diana T. Kudaibergen.
Description: Cambridge, United Kingdom ; New York, NY : Cambridge University Press, 2024. | Includes bibliographical references and index.
Identifiers: LCCN 2024001513 | ISBN 9781009454223 (hardback) | ISBN 9781009454261 (paperback) | ISBN 9781009454230 (ebook)
Subjects: LCSH: Political participation – Kazakhstan. | Protest movements – Kazakhstan. | Social media – Political aspects – Kazakhstan. | Authoritarianism – Kazakhstan. | Kazakhstan – Politics and government – 1991–
Classification: LCC JQ1090.A91 K83 2024 | DDC 323/.042095845–dc23/eng/20240222
LC record available at https://lccn.loc.gov/2024001513

ISBN 978-1-009-45422-3 Hardback
ISBN 978-1-009-45426-1 Paperback

Cambridge University Press & Assessment has no responsibility for the persistence or accuracy of URLs for external or third-party internet websites referred to in this publication and does not guarantee that any content on such websites is, or will remain, accurate or appropriate.

*Dedicated to Qazaq Koktemi
and to everyone who continues to fight for democracy
in Qazaqstan*

Contents

List of Figures	*page* viii
List of Tables	ix
Acknowledgements	x
Introduction	1
1 What Is the Kazakh Spring?	35
2 Who Are Oyan, Qazaqstan?	60
3 Deconstructing *Vlast'*	98
4 Performing the State, Performing the Protest	134
5 Generation Q and Decolonizing Alash	169
6 The Public Square and the Body under Authoritarian Pressures	194
7 Queering the Public Sphere	220
8 Making Sense of the Bloody January 2022 Mass Protests With Marlene Laruelle	244
Conclusions	275
References	288
Index	301

Figures

2.1 Beibarys Tolymbetov and Asya Tulesova at the Almaty Marathon, 21 April 2019. Photo courtesy Suinbike Suleimenova *page* 66
2.2 'The Constitutional Banner', protest act by Qazaq Koktemi, 29 April 2019, Almaty. Source: Qazaq Spring activists 69
2.3 Qazaq Koktemi and Viktor Tsoi at Tulebaika, downtown Almaty: '[We demand] Changes'. Source: Qazaq Spring activists 81
3.1 Astana dweller Nesipkul Uyabayeva protested against the demolition of her house by covering it with ninety-one posters with Nursultan A. Nazarbayev's portrait. © Svetlana Glushkova, RFE/RL 108
4.1 'What to take to the rally': card produced by Oyan, Qazaqstan. Source: Oyan, Qazaqstan 146
4.2 Mural wars in Almaty: the Qazaq Koktemi art collective strikes with the 'Cancel Elbasy' campaign, May–June 2021. Source: Kazakh Spring activists 167
6.1 Qazaq Koktemi December 2020 protest banner. Source: Qazaq Spring activists 213
7.1 One of the participants in the 2021 Almaty Women's March. Her poster reads 'I don't want flowers for 8 March. I want equal rights every day!' © Petr Trotsenko, RFE/RL 226
7.2 Feminist artist Zoya Falkova at the 2021 Almaty Women's March with her legendary art object 'Evermust' protesting against domestic violence. © Zoya Falkova 242
8.1 Geographical distribution of protests in Kazakhstan, January 2018–June 2021 250

Tables

8.1 *Forbes*' ten richest people in Kazakhstan, 2021   *page* 249
8.2 Preliminary findings on the January 2022 protest groups   259

Acknowledgements

No one writes a book alone. For this manuscript, I am indebted to many amazing people who shared their wisdom with me. I want to thank my co-authors – the activists who shared their experiences and whose interviews the reader can hopefully hear while reading this book: Medina Bazargali, Suinbike Suleimenova, Saule Suleimenova, Assem Zhapisheva, Fariza Ospan, Dimash Alzhanov, and many others who preferred to remain anonymous. Without them, this book would not be possible. Every word in this book is dedicated to them.

I want to thank John Haslam and the whole team at Cambridge University Press for taking such good care of this project, and the two anonymous reviewers who offered a lot of food for thought and excellent points for making the manuscript better. I hope one day we can go for a coffee and discuss authoritarian regimes even more. I am indebted to Marlene Laruelle and Laura Adams, who read earlier versions of the full manuscript and offered helpful advice and encouragement. The last chapter of the book is a slightly reworked article I co-authored with Marlene Laruelle, which was published in *Post-Soviet Affairs* in April 2022, right after the Bloody January protests. Working with Marlene is always a pleasure, and I am incredibly indebted to her for her mentorship over the years. I also want to thank Taylor and Francis for their permission to reprint the article here as Chapter 8. In the Sociology Department at Cambridge, I want to thank Professor Manali Desai, who encouraged me to pursue this project and offered a lot of helpful advice for developing it. I received so much support and great advice during these years from my supervisor Dr David Lane, Prof Hazem Kandil, Prof Monica Morena-Figueroa, Dr Ella McPherson, Dr Ali Meghji, Lara Gisborne, and many of my colleagues. I am very grateful to them for their advice and support. My friends at Homerton College were my integral support system. I am especially indebted to Fernanda Gallo, who powered me through the editorial process, and Marta

Magalhaes-Wallace, who always inspires me in all questions of good writing and good ethnography.

My friends and colleagues offered much support throughout. I want to thank Botakoz Kassymbekova, Assel Tutumlu, Asel Doolotkeldiyeva, Erica Marat, Nodira Kholmatova, Gulzat Botoeva, Zarina Mukanova, Askhat Akhmediyarov, and Aigerim Kapar for support, inspiration, and encouragement along the way. In Almaty, the home of Saule Suleimenova and Kuanysh Bazargaliev was a space of inspiration and endless discussions that in many ways inspired me to write this book. I want to express my gratitude to the whole team at the Tselinniy cultural centre in Almaty, who became my friends, who supported my forthcoming book project on protest art that will hopefully be out shortly. Jama, Alima, Adiya, and Bart offered warm companionship and discussion points that enriched my thinking along these two big strands of my research. My students in Cambridge offered a wonderful space for discussions and questions that helped develop this book in many ways. Finally, God bless my favourite band, The Killers, whose songs kept me going even in the darkest times. They were great company in a cold Cambridge library or in the quietness of my apartment.

I am indebted to my family for their endless support and care. My father, Prof Turarbek Kudaibergenov, provided me with many sources and ideas to develop this book, but most importantly his text messages at any point of the day, checking in on me and my writing, greatly encouraged me, and his example as a tireless writer and researcher continuously inspires me in my own work. My mother, Raushan Ibragimova-Kudaibergenova, became my true editor and co-writer and followed every step in developing this project. Our long conversations about my writing and about my arguments helped hugely in shaping this manuscript. This project would not have been possible without my parents' unconditional love and support. Karima, Kaisar, Mansour, and Luna always offered good company and joy between writing and researching sessions. I want to thank my brother Kuanysh and his wife Marzhan, my aunts, and my cousins for their huge support and many laughs at family dinners. Special thanks to my sister-cousin Malika and my aunts Roza and Maskhuda Ibragimovas for their support.

Introduction

Honesty is essential. We don't have this honesty [as a concept] in Kazakhstan, in the public sphere, and there is never sincerity [here]. It [lack of sincerity] happens because everything that the regime [*vlast'*] transmits [in its messages] – there is no honesty in that. And in general, people got used to the fact that honesty as such does not exist [in Kazakhstan].[1]

Nothing is more characteristic of the totalitarian movements in general and of the quality of fame of their leaders in particular than the starting swiftness with which they are forgotten and the startling ease with which they can be replaced.[2]

In reality, Qazaq Koktemi [the Kazakh Spring] is more about the Prague Spring and about the fact that spring is, first of all, the period of renewal. [President] Nazarbayev left in spring ... When I say that I do not believe in revolution, I am not saying that we should not protest at rallies [*vyhodit'na mitingi*] – rallies are important and necessary. I should underline that I said this [laughs]. I believe in rallies [*ya veru v mitingi*] because rallies are the only [means] that we have left right here, right now. All I am saying is that we cannot change the whole system in one second; until we reach the critical mass, and even then, we need to understand what we are doing it [revolution] for. Because that same Kyrgyz [revolutions] or Ukrainian scenario [Euromaidan] simply does not apply or fit us, *we need to find our own path to how we will do it* [revolution].[3]

In early January 2022, the oil-rich state of Kazakhstan saw the biggest mass protests in its recent history and was shocked again when the protests were violently repressed. Thousands of people marched in the streets demanding political changes, the resignation of the government,

---

[1] Interview with an anonymous Oyan, Qazaqstan and Qazaq Koktemi movement activist, 22 July 2020.
[2] Arendt 2007: 407.
[3] Interview with Assem Zhapisheva, Oyan, Qazaqstan, and Qazaq Koktemi movement activist, 24 June 2020.

the return of the democratic constitution, and the improvement of economic conditions. The reason for the protests was not just the hike in LPG gas prices as many in the foreign media reported. This was only a trigger, a bitter joke that, in the gas- and oil-rich country, gas prices depended on corrupt networks of export and import controlled by the highest echelons of the autocrats. The disjointed groups of protesters occupied central squares in almost all the major cities of Kazakhstan, a vast country whose borders stretch from Russia to China. The crowds of protesters chanted 'Leave, old man!' (*Shal, ket!*) at Nursultan A. Nazarbayev, who remained the self-proclaimed leader, the Father of the Nation (*elbasy*), and controlled the authoritarian regime in Kazakhstan for more than thirty years. He killed off the most viable challengers to his power, co-opted or repressed those who were less dangerous to his rule, and suppressed any popular uprising, often leaving a bloody trace and dozens of dead protesters. The tragedy of Zhanaozen protests in 2011, where officially seventeen people died but unofficially many more deaths, tortures in prison, and grave injuries were unaccounted for, was a case in point. Many Kazakhstanis still remembered the horrible scenes of riot police shooting unarmed people in this small town in western Kazakhstan, the heart of the oil and gas industry, in December 2011. Eyewitnesses used their smartphones to film the scenes, and the videos quickly spread on social media. Eleven years later, the protest started off again in Zhanaozen. But this time, people in every major city all across the country answered the call to stand in solidarity with Zhanaozen and the start of 2022 marked the biggest protest and one of the most tragic days of Kazakhstan's modern history.

The January 2022 protests, also known as Bloody January (*Qandy Qantar*) claimed more than 238 lives when Nazarbayev's successor, Kassym-Zhomart Tokayev, announced that he had given the order 'to shoot without warning' and called many ordinary citizens among the protesters 'terrorists' who threatened peace and stability in the country.[4] Before we get into the complex story of what the Bloody January protests really represented – according to various commentators a failed revolution to remove the corrupt autocratic regime or a failed coup from rival intra-elite competitors – we first need to

---

[4] www.wsj.com/articles/kazakhstan-leader-gives-security-forces-order-to-shoot-without-warning-11641548642.

dwell on how the *political* was understood in Nazarbayev's Kazakhstan.

Nursultan A. Nazarbayev, an old Soviet-made politician, 'the party's soldier' as he once called himself, ruled Kazakhstan from 1989, while it was still part of the Soviet Union, up until January 2022, when he finally announced that he was stepping down fully from all of his political positions amid the mass protests. The streets spoke: 'Leave, old man' (*Shal, ket!*) was a ubiquitous slogan of the mass protests. Nazarbayev's career was no different from any textbook autocrat's – he quickly took over control of key state institutions, co-opted rival elites, staged and rigged elections where he won over 90 per cent of the vote, and at the end of his career engaged in a ridiculous cult of personality, issuing a series of films about his life from childhood in a poor family to his role as a young communist leader and to what he thought was the throne of an irreplaceable dictator. He failed in many things along the way, and one of them was that no matter how hard he tried, he could not find the secret to immortality. Hysteria around his succession took over Kazakhstan in the early and turbulent 2000s with the rise of the young technocratic opposition, the Democratic Choice of Kazakhstan movement (DVK), who once served as Nazarbayev's loyalists and were an integral part of his regime. Young economists, engineers, ministers, media managers, and charismatic mid-level politicians announced that they wanted to free Kazakhstan from autocracy and change the regime from within. They too failed, and the movement quickly disintegrated into smaller units of intra-regime political opposition. But their quick and spectacular moment of resisting Nazarbayev opened up Pandora's box for the last decade of the bloodied dictator's rule.

The truth was in plain sight – the aging dictator was a ticking bomb ready to explode the whole country. Geopolitical rifts that followed Kazakhstan's history for centuries continued to press the issue even more. On the one side, there was Russia, with its bloodshed in the first two Chechen wars and the rise of Vladimir Putin in the early 2000s. On the other side, there was China, which required sustainable diplomatic and economic relations but posed a continuous danger. The events of 9/11 brought more American influence to the region as a whole and put further pressure on Nazarbayev to democratize. The question of succession filled the air with unbearable heaviness. People discussed it openly, as it posed a lot of internal threats – from intra-elite conflict to potential civil war. Nazarbayev often dodged the question of his potential successor, claiming that he was in good health and did not plan to depart. This prompted even more rumours, anecdotes, and conspiracy theories about the dictator's health. At one point, conspiracy theories reached boiling point, alleging that there was no place on Nazarbayev's aging body that was not affected by cancer, as rumours spoke of all types of diagnoses, none of them officially acknowledged or disproved. Questions of Nazarbayev's succession would have caused even more bizarre developments than serious media discussions, books published on potential scenarios, and coffee-shop buzz about what healer Nazarbayev used to prolong his life – except that his successor was there all along.

Kassym-Zhomart Tokayev, a product of Soviet elite distillation, was the son of a relatively famous writer, and family ties paved his way to a successful career as a Soviet diplomat. He studied at the elite MGIMO institute in Moscow, spoke six languages (among them Chinese, which was quite handy), and travelled the world on different diplomatic postings. In the early 2000s, when the DVK movement announced their programme of democratization, Tokayev was prime minister and the first person from the regime to denounce them publicly. In breaking-news style, he spoke on state television asking President Nazarbayev to sack the government and eliminate many of the DVK leaders' positions, essentially throwing them out of the regime and leaving them with no political capacity. This historic event put Tokayev on the map as Nazarbayev's biggest loyalist, as a person without a political 'team' lobbying for its group interests,[5] and as his future successor. Tokayev also gained the colloquial name of *Kinder Surprise*, a type of toy soldier who could deliver any action, any speech

---

[5] Most of the Kazakhstani political commentators continuously viewed the autocratic regime as a conglomerate of different elite groups or 'teams', for example, Massimov's team, Tasmagambetov's team, and so on. By this logic, each team had strong group ties and was collectively fighting for a better position within the regime. However, this often overlooked powerful loners such as Tokayev, who refused to join any of the teams or groups of influence or to connect with anyone in the long term and instead focused on sustaining his career and loyalty only to Nazarbayev. The focus on the strict collective interest of the teams or groups of influence also overlooked the fluidity of these relations, where not every allegiance was set in stone and where each member could easily switch teams or leave the team altogether when they felt it would better serve their interests.

to protect the autocratic regime, even if it went against the country's interests.

In late March 2019, Nazarbayev, the eighty-year-old dictator, appeared on state television with an unexpected speech.[6] With his usual mechanical voice and expressionless face,[7] he announced that he was stepping down from the presidency without citing any clear reason. He mentioned that 'it wasn't an easy decision' and that he was happy that he could serve the country for thirty years as its first (post-soviet) president.[8] Nazarbayev announced that, according to the constitution, the speaker of the senate of the parliament would take over the position of interim president before the new presidential elections. Was it any surprise that Kassym-Zhomart Tokayev, the lone loyalist to Nazarbayev, was serving as the speaker of the senate right at this time and that he was not elected to this position by the citizens but was appointed to this key position by Nazarbayev himself? Nazarbayev paved the way to the consolidation of his rule and wanted a smooth transition first to Tokayev and then to a successor from his closest circle, potentially even a family member. After all, he had a huge family; but too many of his relatives were entangled in corruption scandals or did not have any political capital or popularity among the voters. Neither did Tokayev. But he was loyal, and loyalty is the main currency in Nazarbayev's supra-presidential system. This move allowed Nazarbayev to remain in power while changing the guard in the

---

[6] In this narrative of aging Soviet-educated dictators, 'state television' is an actor in its own right. A handful of well-sponsored television channels dominate the Kazakh airwaves and are available for free across the whole country. In the age of social media, Netflix, and mobile Internet, few people of the younger generation watch television, but as in Russia, where state television dominates the older age group, the Nazarbayev regime was never too quick to write off the powerful tool that state television presents in terms of propaganda. The total Internet blackout during the January 2022 protests made state television the only viable channel of information for many citizens for a short period of time of less than a week. In times of crisis, state television plays a crucial role in brainwashing and propagating regime-led ideas.

[7] Some commentators stated that Nazarbayev in his speech sounded like the late Soviet leader Brezhnev, who also stayed in power until an advanced age, and like aging Russian leader Boris Yeltsin when he resigned in 1999.

[8] Nazarbayev took special pride in his status as first president, which was mentioned in all official documents and commemorative rituals of his legacy. A lot of his critics claimed that Alash Orda leaders of the early 1900s pro-independence movement, and particularly Alikhan Bokeikhanov, were the first presidents of Kazakhstan.

institutions. When he stepped down as the president, he still remained a lifetime chairman of the country's security council and 'advisor' to the president and the parliament. He moved to the Library of the First President in Astana, the capital city that was swiftly renamed Nur-Sultan, and continued to control the web of autocratic governance as a shadow leader. This was a period of dual leadership – of President Tokayev and of the 'librarian' (*bibliotekar'*), as Nazarbayev was dubbed colloquially.

Nazarbayev was often called a 'wise leader' by some of the sympathetic commentators in the region. The myth of his politics of stability and multi-vector foreign policy sustained the facade of a successful dictator, while people inside the country suffered from widespread corruption, lack of effective governance, and the absence of viable channels for electoral participation. There is no such thing as a successful dictator, and Nazarbayev was no exception to the rule. Nazarbayev carefully calculated and controlled the threat to his rule from within the regime by co-opting and enriching his closest competitors – Imangali Tasmagambetov, Umirzak Shukeev, Karim Massimov, and others. He chose a successor who could not threaten his position as the Leader of the Nation (the self-fashioned title of *elbasy* that he adopted). Nazarbayev created the political field in Kazakhstan around the closed-off elitist circle of the regime and imbued it with so much power over decision-making that he overlooked the non-elite players who could easily disrupt the balance of the regime. One of the biggest mistakes he made was also to believe that he still retained wide popular support. Zhanaozen in 2011, street protests against local currency devaluation in 2014, land protests in 2016, and mothers' protests in early 2019 were symptoms of the imbalance in relations between regime and society that he believed he had locked down so well. The mass protests of January 2022 were a long time in the making but in the end represented a countrywide rage against the dictator and the corrupt system he had built.

The protestors were not stopped by the cold winter days of early January 2022. They openly demanded the complete removal of Nazarbayev and his authoritarian elites. Protestors raged against any physical reminder of Nazarbayev's cult of personality – they ripped off the street signs with his name on them, set the official party buildings bearing his name (the Nur-Otan party) on fire, and even toppled his monument in Taldyqorgan, the regional hub of Nazarbayev loyalists.

In the chaos of violent mobs and burning buildings, crowds of people cheered the downfall of the statues and chanted '*Shal, ket!*' – Leave, old man! Go away, Nazarbayev! National flags waved above the squares, and activists, peaceful protestors of *Qandy Qantar* (Bloody January) quickly wrote down political demands – we want democratization! It was a revolution that took to the streets, but it was also a revolution that was quickly stolen.

Bloodshed followed instantly, and the protests were violently suppressed at the expense of hundreds of civilian deaths. As the dead bodies of protestors piled up on the streets, the incumbent elites panicked. President Tokayev immediately sacked the government, removed Nazarbayev from his lifelong position in the security council, and introduced curfews to fight the alleged 'terrorist attack'. The regime could not afford to call the events of Bloody January 'protests' because the violence was so unprecedented – and because this same brutality and violence demonstrated the failures of the fake political transition to the post-Nazarbayev era after 2019. So President Tokayev claimed that the insurgencies were organized by 'specially trained groups' – the claim that is yet to be proved by a transparent investigation that many activists demand till this day. The regime's violent suppression of its citizens with the help of the Collective Security Treaty Organization (CSTO) troops, among them 3,000 Russian elite forces, contrasted with the legendary photograph of the 6 January Almaty protestors' handmade banner: 'We are NOT terrorists, we are ordinary people.' The early January days of violence coincided with a mass communication shutdown that echoed *1984*, where the only source of information was the state television channel asking citizens to remain indoors. Propaganda overlapped with fake news and conspiracies that quickly spread. The country, so dependent on its internet connection, was cut off from all forms of communication apart from occasional mobile coverage for days until 'order was restored'. However, as the this book will demonstrate, the January 2022 protests were only possible because of the structural changes that the Kazakh Spring brought with its three-year-long protests, contestations, and change of discourse since March 2019. The story of January 2022 cannot be understood without the continuous cycles of contention that preceded it and that allowed the possibility of a radically different future, where fears of repression could be diminished to the point that people normalized the thought that protests were possible. Protests became part of the people openly speaking up against the regime, criticizing presidents, and demanding further democratization.

The Argument

How can a deinstitutionalized protest movement disrupt a solidified, repressive, and extremely resilient authoritarian regime? In this book, I argue that often unexpected ways of political contention successfully shape the regime, its elites, and its forms of oppression even under the most authoritarian contexts and repressions. In doing so, various protest groups can push the limits of the regime's established political rules. The tug of war that emerges is between the authoritarian regime (including its competing elites, law-enforcement apparatus, and bureaucracy) and the field of protesters. The latter may not always represent a unified party or leadership but must be united by the same values and/or political goals. The success of the field of protesters depends on their ability to disintegrate regime capacity by attacking the main facets of authoritarian politics – staged and uncompetitive elections, laws that expand presidential powers, and the unified single-party approach of the authoritarian leadership.[9]

In this book, I use the context and temporal development of the Kazakh Spring protests (2019–) to focus on how the interplay between the repressive regime and pro-democracy protest movements defines and shapes both. Combining original interview data, digital ethnography, and contentious politics studies, I argue that the new generation of activists – the likes of Instagram political influencers and renowned public intellectuals – can delegitimize and counter one of the most resilient authoritarianisms and inspire the mass protests that none of the formalized opposition ever imagined possible in Kazakhstan. The Kazakh Spring activists managed to do so by radically changing the limits of what is possible within the established frames of regime opposition, which mainly relied on formalization and lack of electoral participation, and regime–society relations, where the regime failed to deliver on its promises of economic prosperity for all. In doing so, the Kazakh Spring formed as a new political field where different actors

---

[9] See Bunce and Wolchik 2009; but see also Isaacs 2010 on the importance of the one-party structure of authoritarian rule in Kazakhstan.

sought their own positions and discourses that managed to unleash the potential for major contention between society and the regime.

The book's biggest contribution is the framework of the formation of political fields under autocracies where contentions can open space for new fields beyond the rules established by the authoritarian regimes. These new fields successfully manage to produce new actors, new strategies, and new imaginations of the limits of the political. The testing of this framework in different authoritarian regimes can result in diverging outcomes – a more repressive response to dissent (Belarus), the regime's search for alternative legitimation and enemy-image construction at home and abroad (broadly speaking, Putin's politics in contemporary Russia before and during its full-scale invasion of Ukraine in February 2022), or the regime's total collapse and the re-emergence of new forms of authoritarian politics where the regime is openly responding to and is shaped by this new political field (Kazakhstan). This book provides a very detailed and chronological approach to explaining how this framework worked out and shaped Kazakhstani politics, leading to the political demise of the country's long-term dictator Nursultan A. Nazarbayev. His once-uncontested and solidified rule defined the very principle of doing politics and positioning oneself within the regime in Kazakhstan (Cummings 2006a, 2006b; Dave 2007; Fauve 2015; Isaacs 2010a, 2010b, 2011, 2013, 2014; Laruelle 2004, 2014, 2016, 2018, 2020, 2021, 2022; Laruelle, Royce, and Beyssembayev 2019). His once-omnipotent cult came crashing down with the wave of discontent that had built up over the years and culminated in the tragic but also important mass protests in January 2022. The book provides a chronological and rich empirical explanation of what led to these tectonic shifts in one of the most resilient and durable authoritarian regimes and theorizes what we can learn from the complexity of regime–society relations in non-democratic contexts.

This book is the first attempt to elucidate and illustrate the Kazakh Spring – Qazaq Koktemi[10] – as a field that has changed the way the political is understood and practised in Kazakhstan. In doing so, it

---

[10] Qazaq Koktemi is the original Kazakh name for the Kazakh Spring, and it is the way my interlocutors referred to it. Often in our interviews they would just say 'Koktem' (spring). I use this concept and its English translation, the Kazakh Spring, interchangeably in the text to keep the original concept unseparated from its translation.

offers a contribution and rich contextualization to the growing 'living archive of social movements'[11] and unravels the complex working of protest movements in societies with heightened authoritarianisms. The theoretical framing of the conceptualization of political fields and regime–society relations allows us to test the Kazakh Spring as a political field where different actors – from pro-democracy movements to queer feminists – find a space to contest the regime and the dictator. The famous slogan 'Leave, old man!' (*Shal, ket!*) translates well across these different groups and actors, across class, gender, ethnic, and other identifiable distinctions. In this book, I argue that the Kazakh Spring (Qazaq Koktemi) was able to shape the popular ideas and concepts that citizens had about state, regime, and their own position and participation in this paradigm of power relations.

The only way to achieve 'participation' or open engagement with the regime was at the level of unsanctioned activism or through the type of political acts conceived by the ruling regime as 'illegal' – unsanctioned rallies, unapproved protest-art actions, and subsequent court hearings and trials of activists as a result of these actions. In other words, the activists, and the authoritarian regime, had to engage on the level of confrontations where the Qazaq Koktemi activists questioned the whole paradigm of the 'rules of the game' set out by the regime. These rules are inevitably illiberal and authoritarian, even though they include a sophisticated and complex web of legal rules, law-enforcement institutionalization, and the forms and styles of authoritarian governance. By the last, I mean the type of systemic political decision-making where key powerful positions are occupied by the regime elites according to their 'selection' rather than 'election'. Thus, the focus on the interplay between the repressive regime and democratization struggles allows us to highlight and carve out processes, practices, styles, and discourses of the regime and its effects as well as of the new type of activism and confrontation of the Kazakh Spring phenomenon.

The key aim of this book is to focus on ways of analysing power, and I see the root in finding the rules that govern its existence – its edifice, practice, discourses, understanding (Glasius 2018), and its meaning as well as its effects on people (especially when thinking about authoritarian power). Thus, my thinking on authoritarian power pushes me to

---

[11] Gómez-Barris 2018: 2.

encapsulate it in the genealogy of the regime and the specific rules of the regime's existence and practice, to see how this power is contested and questioned. This is why Kazakh Spring's approach to the deinstitutionalization of their activities and the consistent refusal to formalize in the political field where authoritarian regime rules predominate is so important but also possibly dangerous. Deinstitutionalization of movements and actors strives for further democratization but also can influence spontaneity of activism and protesting repertoires that other actors (e.g., the regime) continuously appropriate in their own interests. For example, the rise of the traditionalist voices on social media who attack and harass LGBT activists or their agenda is a key example of how this is problematic.

I am inspired and moved by the necessity to provide rich answers to the questions of *what* happens when new protest waves emerge and *how* these waves happen and change political dynamics. In doing so, the book contributes to the call to study everyday authoritarianism ethnographically and detail the dynamic complexities (see Glasius 2018; Przeworski 2022; Wedeen 2019) that play a crucial role in routinizing authoritarian norms (Wedeen's work is an exemplary testament to that) and making them even more powerful. Under these conditions, activists and scholars must engage with questions of how we can reshape the normative approach to authoritarianisms and pave the way to further democratization even under the extremely difficult conditions faced by civil society and the totality of repressive tactics. My research on emergent protests in post-Nazarbayev Kazakhstan, in particular, was guided by the following questions: what did Qazaq Koktemi bring to the political dynamics of Kazakhstani authoritarian contexts that was not there before? How did Qazaq Koktemi shape and how does it continue to shape and rethink the idea of the state, the regime, and its influence over citizens?

In this book, I demonstrate (1) how the protest wave reveals the hidden or less visible ways of doing authoritarian politics under certain regimes; (2) how these new protest waves emerge and what makes them possible; (3) what are the ways, contexts, and other local factors that make possible such radically visible and sudden waves of protest as those of the Kazakh Spring; (4) how relations and discourses are produced and worked in this particular field; and, finally, (5) how this protest wave pushes the regime to change its tactics. I believe that the example of the Kazakh Spring (Qazaq Koktemi), as a field that has changed the way the political is understood and practised in Kazakhstan, is a very useful and illustrative manifestation of this change.

The Kazakh Spring – or Qazaq Koktemi in the local, Kazakh language – is not an identifiable party or movement, but rather it kicked off as a slogan, a hashtag, and the overall meaning-making theme of the protest that started in the spring of 2019. It represents the complexity of the important temporal divide in the Kazakhstani political field and later, its reconfiguration. It separates the before and after and provides an important ideological and forward-looking demarcation for all the movements, people, and discourses that became part of it. In other words, Qazaq Koktemi is a new field, a space where meaning, positions, discourses, and knowledge are produced, reproduced, circulated, and contested, and where actors are positioned with their share of different capitals (economic, cultural, symbolic, social, etc.). I use a Bourdieusian understanding of the field as a terrain of struggles, as a 'network, or configuration, of objective relations between positions' (Wacquant and Bourdieu 1992: 97). Bourdieu's definition of the field allows us to analyse the positions and practices of different actors and to introduce different characters engaged in the contention – movements, activists, journalists, and regime extensions such as the police. Bourdieu argued that:

These positions are objectively defined, in their existence and in the determinations they impose upon their occupants, agents or institutions, by their present and potential situation (*situs*) in the structure of the distribution of species of power (or capital) whose possession commands access to the specific profits that are at stake in the field, as well as by their objective relation to other positions (domination, subordination, homology, etc.).[12]

As a field, Qazaq Koktemi facilitates the production of a more or less coherent meaning and values that define all of the people and movements that operate within this field and claim its meaning, status, and positionality. The Kazakh Spring can also be conceptualized as a new part of the civil sphere – 'a world of values and institutions that generate the capacity for social criticism and democratic integration at the same time'. In doing so, the civil sphere 'relies on solidarity, on feelings for others whom we do not know but whom we respect out of

---

[12] Wacquant and Bourdieu 1992: 97.

principle, not experience, because of our putative commitment to a common secular faith' (Alexander 2006: 4).

Thinking of the Kazakh Spring as a shift in doing the political but also a civil sphere imbued with solidarity and a common call against injustices is a lot closer to its nature and origin than evaluating it according to models and statistics of a 'successful revolution'. Such 'success' usually implies the forceful removal of the autocratic leader, that is, the president, but not always the removal of the regime and its meaning-making and normative infrastructure. And this is what the activists of the Kazakh Spring acutely understand – they are in this revolutionary moment for the long run. They understand that it will take more than just defining the post-Nazarbayev era and dismantling his cult of personality, as happened during the January 2022 protests and its aftermath. What activists of the Kazakh Spring acutely understood even before the mass protests was that it would take a radical change of the 'system': redefining power relations and the understanding of *vlast'* – the regime politics and the regime's field of power. The Kazakh Spring is about protest and framing collective solidarities that take a long time to build, but also, more importantly, it is about establishing and nourishing a pro-democratic value system that many of my respondents see as the only way out of the authoritarian limbo.

There are a lot of links between the Arab Spring and the Kazakh Spring, even though Kazakhstani activists themselves speak about a concept of 'spring' that is closer to the Prague Spring. My respondents among the many makers of the Kazakh Spring view it as a process of gradual liberalization, with further politicization and involvement of different societal groups who can engage in the processes of political meaning-making alternative to the dominant authoritarian regime. As such, it is a very inclusive process that invites many different groups and ideologically divided collectives. The purpose of the Kazakh Spring is to incentivize political change and allow further democratization while at the same time giving a platform to a plurality of voices, opinions, and plans for change. Over the course of my study, I have seen how many people get involved in this overall process, feeling that this is a way for them to speak up and be seen, be heard. At the same time, many of them sustain their institutional identities as part of the projects, communities, and, in some cases, even political parties from which they emerge. This fluidity and pluriversal approach to doing the political allows the avoidance of ethno-lingual and class-based distinctions that came to the fore in how the regime assigned blame for the January 2022 mass protests, when a lot of the unofficial discourse covered it as 'Kazakh-speaking lumpen destroying Almaty's city centre'.[13] Kazakh Spring activists aim to push the agenda beyond just the central cities of Almaty and Astana, as many of the activists themselves come from various regions of the country; for years, they aimed for protest to take over each regional city and town.

The Kazakh Spring is also a prolonged process, and it is still continuing at the time of this manuscript's completion. However, one similarity with the Arab Spring is striking – when dictators fall, the dictatorships endure; revolutions emerge as a fervent movement but then are stolen by new dictators who are sometimes even worse than their toppled predecessors. The complete fall of Nazarbayev after the January 2022 protests did not mean the complete fall of the regime. Russian troops landing in Kazakhstan as part of the unprecedented CSTO operation to suppress the mass protests gave Tokayev important leeway to establish his rule firmly and without the old agreements binding it to Nazarbayev and his circle of elites. Tokayev managed to imprison some of Nazarbayev's old elites, along with hundreds of ordinary citizens who were tortured by the police to 'confess' to their supposed terrorist acts and confirm the regime's dominant narrative about the protests. But Tokayev failed to prosecute Nazarbayev and his family, even though he openly announced the return of all the assets the family of the first president stole from the country (making them billionaires). Just like the verse of the new popular song by Daiynball, 'shal kettip bara zhatyr [barattyr] ... Tigr, diplomat, orator. Qazaq eline plus bir dictator!' – 'The old man (*shal*) is gone, Tiger [the term local propaganda used for Tokayev after the January protests], diplomat, orator. The Kazakh people are getting one more dictator!'

---

[13] Official rhetoric still largely places the protestors in the southern part of the country (where violence prevailed) within the organized crime or 'extremists and terrorists' discourse. In late spring and summer 2022, state media started broadcasting documentary films about looters and criminals who took over central cities, most notably Almaty's rich central quarters, and in the interviews with supposed eyewitnesses strengthened the narrative that these were internal migrants (*prieszhie*) from nearby villages who aimed to destroy the city. Scandal broke out when one of the local media rumored that the editors called the Almaty protestors a slur denigrating rural ethnic Kazakhs, referring to the 'riot of the Kazakh lumpen'. Many civic activists, including those from the Oyan, Qazaqstan movement, opposed and criticized these narratives.

The Interplay between the Regime and the New Protest Field

Many commentators stressed the dependent temporality connecting the resignation of the long-term dictator and the emergence of the new wave of contentious politics (Ibadildin and Pisareva 2020; Tutumlu and Rustemov 2021, for example). But this dependent temporality needs to be addressed with a nuance of how and why Qazaq Koktemi became a *new* phenomenon in these contentious politics.

The classical definition and contextualization of social movements that emerge argue that 'contentious politics is triggered when changing political opportunities and constraints create incentives for social actors who lack resources on their own' (Tarrow 1998: 2). And this in part explains why Qazaq Koktemi was confused with the social movements it has inspired, namely, the Oyan, Qazaqstan (Wake up, Kazakhstan) movement, which no doubt emerged at the moment of political opportunity but was embedded in the networks provided by the Qazaq Koktemi (I discuss this process in detail in Chapter 2).

In this book, I argue that the redrawing of political opportunities after President Nazarbayev's departure in March 2019 were indeed so significant that it allowed the complete rethinking and reshaping of the previous political rules of the game when it came to contentious politics. However, the old guard of political opposition to the regime and the groups and movements that had been in operation since the late 1980s were not ready to adapt to these new conditions. And thus they failed in the face of the tremendous window of opportunity (the formal departure of Nazarbayev) for which they all had waited so long. In these conditions, previously unknown young activists, now politically engaged actors, entered the scene to (1) rethink the limits and discourses of political competition while addressing the deeply seated framework of regime–society relations (instead of the state–society relations in democracies); (2) challenge and expose the lines of difference between the state and the regime, which often are perceived as one and the same; and, essentially, (3) change the rules of the game within the political field by influencing the change of values and engaging more citizens in the protest movements. This is why Qazaq Koktemi is a completely new but also a very important and innovative phenomenon in the studies of Kazakhstani politics and contentious politics under authoritarianism in general. It sheds more light on how, while the elites within the regime regrouped and focused too much on the internal logics of regime survival from within,[14] they did not anticipate how this regrouping left the thriving field 'below' the intra-elite level ready to engage in this regrouping of power positions as well. In other words, the ruling elites of the Nazarbayev regime were too preoccupied with what would have happened to them and their positions within the political field of this same regime rather than thinking outside its limits and looking beyond the field they were engaged in.

This is what I call *authoritarian myopia* – the inability of authoritarian elites to adequately assess or even make sense of the social reality beyond their own position in the field that is the intra-elite authoritarian regime – for example, all those political elites participating in the actual political decision-making whether through formal or informal channels of doing politics.[15] Driven by the intensity of their competition within this field, they are unable to respond to the calls or claims of citizens who supposedly provide the capacity for these elites to occupy the positions of the field they find themselves in. In other words, the

---

[14] For the classic definition of the fragility of authoritarian rule shaken by intra-elite coups and vicious competition, see Svolik 2012; Bernhard, Edgell, and Lindberg 2016.

[15] I am a proponent of viewing the regime on different levels of its power operation, which I conceptualize in separate fields. In my previous work, I discuss the term nationalizing regimes to demonstrate how the highest political decision-making in any given state and regarding the nationalizing process of nation-building happens within the frames of the political and ruling elites, who find the discursive consensus on the main facets of this field (Kudaibergenova 2020). In this particular case of authoritarian myopia, I am conceptualizing the regime as a field of ruling elites (whether officially in political office or not) who have actual power (within their own limits, of course) over the political decision-making in the country. In another instance, I conceptualize the regime as an overall discursive field governing actions through the production of meaning, authoritative discourses, and appropriate behaviour (Kudaibergenova 2021). When talking about formal and informal channels of doing politics, I agree with scholars such as Juan Linz (2000), who conceptualized various types of authoritarian regimes where political decision-making is not always transparent or done entirely through formal procedures. This does not mean a complete disregard of the formal institutions that dictators need to maintain their rule (Gandhi 2008); rather, it positions power relations within the regime in a more nuanced way, where levels of power and decision-making are spread in the locus of power (e.g., family, dictator's closest circle) and then only in distinct institutions. There is a very strong school of neopatrimonialism led by Henry Hale in post-Soviet politics, for example, that discusses autocratic regimes as patron–client relations (see Hale 2014, for example). For me, the terminology of regime and power relations is close to the patron–client paradigm but is also expandable in the form of discursive power and competition.

people and the citizens provide the capacity for the existence of the political community known as the Republic of Kazakhstan, which becomes the host for the field known as the Nazarbayev regime, where each of the bargaining political elites found themselves on the eve of 19 March 2019 when their patron officially resigned from his position.

Unlike the elites within his own regime, Nursultan A. Nazarbayev was acutely aware of the necessity of responding to the social reality in which he operated as the president. Even though elections were staged and rigged throughout all of Kazakhstan's independent history (see Isaacs 2011, for example), and thus citizens were deprived of their direct right to choose those who govern them, Nazarbayev was aware of the importance of listening to the voices of these deprived citizens. The Archive of the First President of Kazakhstan in Almaty has a collection of historical files and minutes of the meetings held in the presidential administration in the 1990s. This was the time when Nazarbayev formed a number of internal committees (most of which still followed the Soviet model of institutions and approach to dealing with the population)[16] and stressed the importance of surveying social attitudes and catching the waves of social unrest and discontent. Piles of carefully drafted reports and surveys circulated in the administration, often with Nazarbayev's personal comments and notes on the pages. Take, for example, the archival report Nursultan A. Nazarbayev received and then addressed to Nurtay Abykayev[17] about the 'Socio-Political situation in the Republic' on 5 February 1991, where he evaluated the situation with intra-ethnic relations as 'ambiguous' and thus problematic:

> If the working people [*trudyashiesya*] in the absolute majority are guided by their everyday experiences and are included to resolve the arising contradictions by increasing the common welfare [*obshee blagosostoyanie*], on the basis of the good internationalist traditions that have developed in Kazakhstan, then intelligentsia, especially those who are part of certain political movements, often dramatize them. Here is where the myths about certain 'downtrodden' nations are coming from, and here is where [other rumors] about the mass outflow of the so-called Russian-speaking

---

[16] On the persistence of Sovietized approaches to politics, see Tutumlu and Imyarova 2021.
[17] Former head of the National Committee for Security (KNB).

population from Kazakhstan, the discrimination of the rights of the indigenous people [come from]. But, as sociological poll results demonstrate, the percentage of those dissatisfied with the living [conditions] in Kazakhstan according to these reasons [mentioned above], is very low (from 2% to 7%). At the same time, the number of those who wish to leave the republic exceeds the number of those dissatisfied [*nedovol'nie*]. The ecological state of different regions, the deterioration of the financial situations of some of the categories of the population, the fear of unemployment and of interethnic conflicts [happening in] neighboring republics and other reasons play an important role here [in the decisions for outmigration].[18]

Whether it was in President Nazarbayev's speeches,[19] in his programmes and initiatives,[20] or in his internal communication within the presidential administration (available to us through the archival minutes), it was fashioned as if all of these discourses represented his personal touch and omnipresent watchful eye. President Nazarbayev became the prime locus of the nationalizing regime I described elsewhere as 'personalized'[21] or Nazarbayevite, and he created the kind of discursive field of almost appropriating all of the political will and power within the state solely to himself (Ambrosio 2015; Anceschi 2017; Ibadildin and Pisareva 2020; Isaacs 2010; Kudaibergenova 2020). Or at least this was an attempt to present it as such by the regime. This is why, when many deprived or discriminated groups of people went to protest against unjust moves to remove them from their houses or cut social welfare to mothers and families with multiple children (*mnogodetnie*), they went to the presidential palace, Ak Orda, or addressed their letters directly to Nazarbayev himself, even after he officially resigned from his presidency.[22]

Even though these ubiquitous protests, especially those protesting inadequate welfare provision and cuts, do not represent coherent or institutionalized protest groups, their voices and their responses to the power axis are key, as they represent the systemic approach and dependency on Nazarbayev, whose power and discursive body became

---

[18] 19971b, Op.1, F. 7, Archive of the first president of Kazakhstan, Almaty, Doklad Prezidentu N.A. Nazarbayevu 'Ob obshestvenno-politicheskoi situatsii v respublike' (perepravleno na rabotu N.Abykayevu), 29 April 1991, p. 12.
[19] Insebayeva and Insebayeva 2021; Kudaibergenova 2019; Laruelle 2014; Tutumlu and Imyarova 2021.
[20] Kudaibergenova 2015; Kulsariyeva 2014; Nazarbayev 2014.
[21] Kudaibergenova 2020.
[22] See a report on these events at www.exclusive.kz/expertiza/daily/124400/.

the end point of political decision-making in itself during his thirty-year rule. Of course, in reality it is not like that, but as a trend, letters to Nazarbayev overshadow important institutions (whether democratic or not), laws (whether working or not), and formal procedures that are established in place to make the actual state work. And this is what is at the heart of the regime–society relations framework – people feel like it is not the state, but rather the regime, that is accountable for their demands, letters, and discontent.

Kazakhstani politics have been built on the cult of Nazarbayev, who was seen as the father of the nation but also the father who was supposed to take care of every little problem – from welfare payments to impoverished citizens to the large-scale laws and economic programmes that were supposed to make all Kazakhstani citizens prosperous by 2030 – although it has not been successful (Kudaibergenova 2015). Regime–society relations explain the dynamic where the authoritarian cult (as in the case of Asad in Syria or Putin in Russia) or authoritarian norms guide socio-political aspects of everyday life. These include the basic ways and principles of how to behave and what to say that form the corpus of views and norms of what is *appropriate* under any given authoritarian regime (see Kudaibergenova 2021; Wedeen 1999), creating the specific regime of truth connected to its local contexts, for example the Nazarbayevite regime of truth in Kazakhstan. Regime–society relations is a useful tool in explaining how and why authoritarian rule can be normalized on an everyday basis as something routinized and hard to change.

Furthermore, regime–society relations guide the norms and understandings (to build on Glasius 2018) of how things ought to work on the larger political plane, for example, within the state. It dictates how governance is done and what is expected from each individual citizen for the achievement of the vision of the collectively aspired good life. Too often what is asked of the citizens in these conditions is total obedience to the regime's governance and formal and informal rules in return for often fictional and unattainable visions of the bright future the regime paints for its subjects. But this normative order of things and this deeply seated understanding of *appropriate behaviour* (obedience) guide people's everyday lives and their values and aspirations, making the authoritarian regime durable from within.

Regime–society relations can be shaken out of this balance as long as large groups among the public realize that they are not gaining from the status quo and resort to mass protests (as discussed in the final chapter). The logic of regime–society relations, however, is hard to break down, as it is rooted and routinized as a 'normal status quo' that some citizens view as set in stone – that some form of authoritarian rule is inevitable or that it is the only way to sustain the country's stability and save it from rampant civil war.[23] But before this happens, the public needs to form alternative way of thinking and imagining the post-regime reality. As I discuss in this book, Nazarbayev's rule was routinized so deeply in people's perception of the political that they found it hard to imagine the post-Nazarbayev era. His cult and normative aspect of his regime were so deeply rooted in people's everyday lives, perceptions, and their aspirations for the future (encapsulated in their understanding of political and economic stability) that they dreaded drastic changes such as the overthrow of the regime and required time to get used to a post-Nazarbayev alternative. The Kazakh Spring was instrumental in providing this alternative and more democratic outlook on how Kazakh politics could work without Nazarbayev.

It was not surprising then that, when the system so concentrated on the role of Nazarbayev's presidency (as an institution and powerful discourse) had to move on from this status quo slowly but surely, it experienced tremendous levels of stress from within and lost track of what was going on outside of its own frames. And this is where an interesting puzzle, already explored extensively in the literature of contemporary authoritarianisms, emerges in Kazakhstan as well. It is the puzzle of to what extent intra-elite authoritarian regime depends on the combination of formal rules and informal practices (Gel'man 2015, 2016; Hale 2014; Ledeneva 2013; Urinboyev 2020). Students and teachers of authoritarian regimes explored in great detail the ways formal institutions (Boix and Svolik 2013; Gandhi and Przeworski 2007; Gandhi 2008), legal systems and the understanding of law and illegality (Botoeva 2019; Urinboyev and Svensson 2013), and formal procedures, albeit not open and free elections, can coexist with

---

[23] Nazarbayev used civil war as the most fearful outcome of political instability ever since his rise to power in the late 1980s. He helped build the strong discourse of valuing an illusory sense of 'stability' – the fact that the country was relatively peaceful even though there were on-and-off conflicts (between different ethnic groups) that were quickly contained and which he avoided discussing in public.

different levels and degrees of authoritarianism (most notably in Isaacs 2011; Wedeen 1998, 1999, 2009).

Resilient authoritarian regimes depend on their ability to suppress dissent and opposition by co-optation or complete coercion of rivals, the provision of welfare, and a coercive system in order not to be contested from below. Against them stands the challenge of contentious politics. The emergence of social movements and contentious politics depends on political opportunities and existent social networks capable of constructing new meaning and new solidarities (della Porta and Diani 2001; Tarrow 1998). This relationship between the ruling authoritarian regime (and its elites) and the response from diverse social groups from below demonstrates an important interplay and the way that both of these key players reflect their actions and production of meaning on each other. I would argue that in the post-Nazarbayev era, not everything in the dynamics of power and discursive production depends on the single figure of the dictator, even though the regime attempts to portray it as such and normalize the type of discourse where 'Nazarbayev is everything and everywhere'. The limits of the political are expandable, and many more actors from within the regime – for example, police and other law-enforcement agents (discussed in Chapters 3, 5, 6, and 8), civil activists, anonymous social media channels, and social movement groups – occupy their share of the political will, even if beyond the limits of formal political field, for example, in informal institutions. Even though Kazakhstan continued to exist under the shadow of Nazarbayev, often in bronze,[24] his role diminished after his resignation, and, following the January 2022 protests, the Nazarbayev regime collapsed. As the country is preparing to get rid of the Law on the First President *elbasy* that once solidified Nazarbayev's position within the state for life and prohibited any slander of his name in public, the January 2022 protests demonstrated how many people en masse opposed his cult of personality. They toppled his statue, got rid of his name from his institution, and demanded a full-fledged anti-corruption investigation into his and his family's assets.

---

[24] Monuments of the former president continued to emerge in different cities of Kazakhstan, most notably in Astana, where there are already four of his statues in public places such as parks and museums, but also in other cities – in Almaty, in the park of the first president, and in Taldyqorgan, the central city of the Almaty region. However, there is no clear evidence of 'popular support' for these monumental projects, which remain largely initiatives led by regime functionaries.

Qazaq Koktemi: Changing the Rules of the Game

Qazaq Koktemi is a completely new political field because it is identified by (1) lack of formalized oppositional parties; (2) continual outbreaks of protests and ongoing activism instead of previous protests and rallies that were rarer and coincided with specific dates and commemorations; (3) protestors that are made up of non-elite groups; (4) protest groups that aim to organize their movements and rallies across all Kazakhstan and not just in the two major cities of Almaty and Astana (Nur-Sultan); (5) creative and new approaches to protest; and, perhaps most importantly, (6) shifts in collective identities and protestors' agendas and values. Let me address these key elements to situate this field better.

Qazaq Koktemi was an important shift because it speaks against all of the established ways of doing politics. The field in itself is not dependent on coherent and stable structures of political parties or organizations and instead proposes an approach that is a lot more fluid and flexible. People who want to be part of Qazaq Koktemi prefer to call themselves activists, protestors, or active citizens, not members of the formal opposition. The Kazakhstani political field was dominated by the 'opposition' that came from the regime itself, and young activists from the Qazaq Koktemi and Oyan, Qazaqstan movements do not want to be associated with this tainted concept. Many of them expressed the idea that they do not wish to be linked with the 'sell out' opposition and thus need to create their own language for their resistance.

This disassociation plays on different levels – from choosing different tactics for protests and ditching the 'opposition' tradition of protesting only on specific dates of commemorations and instead deciding protest dates by general vote among the groups to the complete denial of any connection to opposition leaders of the past. For example, Mukhtar Ablyazov and his DVK movement, which is now prohibited in Kazakhstan, used rather destructive tactics to claim ownership of any political protest in Kazakhstan by announcing it online as his protest or sending his activist with posters to any rallies organized by Oyan, Qazaqstan or someone else. But Qazaq Koktemi and Oyan, Qazaqstan activists immediately resist all attempts to associate their movement or slogans with those of Ablyazov, as many of them consider him 'as much as a product of Nazarbayev regime as anyone currently sitting in the parliament or enriching themselves from the regime-facilitated corruption'.²⁵ When one activist was called the 'flag-bearer' of the DVK and Ablyazov's opposition agenda, she said that it 'shocked' her and that she 'didn't want to represent DVK, I didn't like, and I still don't like their rhetoric. I understand that any activism is important, but I don't quite understand their agenda – they are here and there but nowhere really, and I don't like and don't support Mukhtar Ablyazov at all'.²⁶

In order to avoid this open appropriation of their activism and the limelight that Ablyazov and the old opposition steal from them, all activists within the Qazaq Koktemi field follow a strict branding strategy for their message, from the places where it is published down to the smallest details in design – font, colour, themes – and in their discourses and messages. A lot of it is also heavily supplemented with distinct hashtags, which are tools still not known to the old guard opposition. Also, whenever other politicians or political entrepreneurs try to appropriate their messages for their own gain, all these attempts are negated and made public. This way, the Qazaq Koktemi protestors make a clear demarcation that none of them had a public connection with the regime or came from inside the regime, as Ablyazov and most of the old guard opposition did in the 1990s and the 2000s when they were close allies of President Nazarbayev himself.²⁷

Another feature of Qazaq Koktemi movements and protests is that they attempt to form contentions outside the major hubs of Almaty and Astana. The two major cities play an important symbolic role as the country's past and current capitals, but Qazaq Koktemi activism spreads more to the regional hubs, for example, Shymkent and Karaganda, and the Oyan, Qazaqstan movement assists and encourages the formation of its groups in cities outside its main centre in Almaty. The field of activism remains very open also due to the established infrastructure of social media presence and constant channelling via social media and communication. For example, Oyan, Qazaqstan has an open chat on Telegram social media where anyone can join the conversation, and most active members have their own Telegram channels as well as active communication on other social media platforms (discussed in Chapters 3 and 4).

---

²⁵ Author's interview with Oyan, Qazaqstan activist, anonymized.
²⁶ Author's interview with the Qazaq Koktemi activist, July 2020, anonymized.
²⁷ See Junisbai and Junisbai 2005.

As I will discuss in Chapters 1 and 2 in more detail, Qazaq Koktemi was born out of the network of young contemporary artists and activists in Almaty, which explains why their protest remained very performative and inspired by their art practices. In Kazakhstan and most of Central Asia (apart from Turkmenistan), the contemporary art field remains a space for socially conscious and socially responsible art production, which is often open to political discussion and critique under the auspices of political art. The makers of the Qazaq Koktemi and Oyan, Qazaqstan are the latest generation of this contemporary art wave. They are more tech-savvy, mostly fluent in English, educated abroad, and come from families and circles with established cultural and social capital. Many of the activists whom I interviewed behind the scenes of the Qazaq Koktemi were my acquaintances, respondents and friends from the time of my art fieldwork that I began with local contemporary artists in 2011. This in part explains two important things – their creative and innovative approach to protest by incorporating visual language (posters, protest street art, performances in courts, etc.) and my access to these very closed and anonymous communities.[28] I discuss this creative approach in more detail in Chapter 2.

The inception of the Qazaq Koktemi field also offered new collective identities and values brought along with the movement for democratizing Kazakhstan anew. They rethink the ideas of civicness, patriotism, and individual contribution to the state rather than the regime, which allowed them to criticize the regime–society framework as the biggest obstacle to democratization. Instead, they vouch for the elites' accountability and call for the Nazarbayev clan to stop considering the whole state of Kazakhstan as their own commercial enterprise from which they constantly extract resources. The slogan 'Kazakhstan without Nazarbayevs' precisely speaks of that idea and of building a more potent civil society and civic culture that can hold the government rather than the regime accountable to society. This rethinking of regime–society relations was not a new idea, as it circulated in the opposition's language throughout the 2000s – the decade when Nazarbayev solidified his rule – even before Nazarbayev's rule was

---

[28] The emergence of Qazaq Koktemi coincided with one of the most intense art fieldwork periods I was conducting for my book manuscript on protest art in Central Asia.

substantially questioned in the 2010s by labour unions in western Kazakhstan and economically disadvantaged groups of people who sought to profit from Nazarbayev's promises of a prosperous Kazakhstan and wanted to cash their cheque right away in the form of additional welfare payments or land ownership (e.g., *dol'shiki*, Shanyrak dwellers, etc.). The Kazakh Spring managed to shift these discourses of literally 'consuming the state' and mirroring what Nazarbayev's inner circle had been doing for the thirty years of his rule – extracting, corrupting, and robbing state resources for their personal gain. Instead, they called for citizens to be responsible and accountable for the state they live in and to demand the better governance they deserved as citizens.

This shift in how politics was perceived was remarkable given the regime–society relations that kept the regime in place as a normalized and routinized order of things. The waves of protests during the Kazakh Spring from March 2019 were dedicated to electoral reform and the openness of governing structures. In January 2022, these slogans became loud and clear. The more organized protestors in western Kazakhstan demanded the complete removal of the regime and the introduction of democratic norms and open, contested elections, while the less organized groups of protestors in Almaty demanded similar changes but under the slogan 'New Kazakhstan without Nazarbayev and his old elites'. So the public responded clearly to the shifts in framing the political and valuing their freedoms above the stability of the political regime. This is one of the biggest lessons to learn from the January 2022 protests for the political actors in Kazakhstan.

The Tokayev regime's swift response to this shift was the constitutional referendum and the slow removal of Nazarbayev from the key positions he acquired during his thirty-year rule, including the cancellation of the Law on the First President (discussed further in Chapter 1) that was instrumental in extending Nazarbayev's institutionalized powers. Moreover, Tokayev's regime also proposed a state programme borrowing from the demands on the streets, calling it 'New Kazakhstan' (introduced in March 2022). This interplay between the regime, which has to quickly adapt and respond to the claims and slogans of civil society, and the sporadic protesting groups is a significant shift for Kazakhstani authoritarianism and a conceptual insight for the study of non-democratic politics. As a conceptual insight, it demonstrates that authoritarian regimes and the realities they create are dynamic, complex, and often contradict their own rules of the game, but they are also highly attentive and responsive to the voices of the new and highly globalized civil society. The globalized outlook of the Kazakh Spring activists is something inescapable, as they are the generation that is more fluent in global social media networks than in the old Soviet 'authoritative' language[29] of the sort that the old guards (of both regime and opposition) continue living in.

What to Expect from This Book and Why You Need to Read It

This book is about a contemporary revolutionary moment, a type of temporal snapshot of the tectonic shifts of post-Sovietness. I perceive post-Sovietness not only as a space (geographical, cultural, discursive) with all its powers and inherent post–Cold War marginalization but also as a moment in history that is rapidly dying with Russia's colonial war in Ukraine. The Nazarbayev regime was in power as the dominant facet of post-Sovietness, but the emergence of Qazaq Koktemi and protest movements within it signals important changes in that powerful discursive axis. In explaining this argument of the new revolutionary wave, I in no way aim to evaluate it, and I certainly try to avoid applying the templates of 'success' or 'failure'[30] that are often ascribed

---

[29] See Yurchak 2006.
[30] Echoing the voices of the many colleagues and friends who sustained the Bloody January protests in diaspora (most notably in Berlin and Paris) and fully acknowledging the input of all those who fought for democratization (and not the violent mobs), I prefer to call this phenomenon a 'stolen revolution'. This way we can pay tribute to all those who went to the squares to voice their civic position and all those who tragically died fighting for freedom. I also believe that the Bloody January protests have many different narratives that happened in parallel to one another – there were organized crime groups who successfully hijacked the peaceful protests and perpetuated violence; there were also looters and criminals who took advantage of the chaos and broke into banks, restaurants, and shops (in an organized or sporadic manner); finally, there were peaceful protestors and those protestors who were so outraged that they resorted to different forms of violence, for example, storming official buildings, setting cars and public buildings (Nazarbayev's party headquarters, local municipal offices, Nazarbayev's monuments) on fire, or demanding the immediate demolition of these objects. Our story of these tragic days in early January 2022 needs to be researched and written from all of these different standpoints, and I hope there will be more work emerging on these themes soon (especially Daniyar Moldabekov's book on Bloody January told from an eyewitness perspective, soon to be published in Kazakhstan). The story of the

to other similar waves of protests, for example, with the Euromaidan in Ukraine, Bolotnaia and consequent marches in Russia, the 2020 stand-off in Belarus, or the array of Rose, Orange, and Tulip Revolutions prior to that. In fact, I am trying my best to avoid these simplifications that certainly were written with the best intentions to make sense of the complexity that post-Sovietness[31] represents as a phenomenon perhaps still less known to us than the Soviet Union itself used to be.

My aim is to focus on the description of the complexity on the ground, to tap into the abundant field of thoughts, aspirations, values, visions, and creative forces that drives many of my compatriots to imagine an alternative to the regime they never existed without. Many of my respondents were born during Nazarbayev's rule and never experienced the full social and political reality *without* him until very recently. Their voices, agency, and literally their bodies were embedded within this discourse of Nazarbayev's Kazakhstan. Yet it does not stop them from radically reimagining it. On the contrary, they take their resistance stance from this embeddedness within the dictatorship.

The solid authoritarian rule born out of and established on the ruins of the very distinct empire that appropriated communist ideals and made millions (including my respondents' parents) live in the unknown utopia is a complex world of its own. Add globalization, rapid neoliberalization, the opening of borders, access to global dialogues through education, social media, and the almost-complete negation of the conventional media by this generation of independence, and you will get a conglomerate of even more complex yet exciting identities, ideas, movements, and actions. Thus, the Kazakh Spring/Qazaq Koktemi is a product of diverse networks, complexities, and temporalities – of the Soviet and post-Soviet, global, neoliberal, nationalist and historical, decolonial and queer revolutions and dialogues. Above all, it is a phenomenon that is in constant conversation and dialogue with other global movements and protests waves happening due to the similar and acute realizations of inequality, lack of freedom and

---

stolen revolution that this book is partly telling is told from the narratives of those who started it as a peaceful manifestation of their civic and political positions and who refused violence.

[31] I continue to view this term critically but here it is written to simplify the historical process – 'post-soviet' here means 'post-1991' period in Kazakhstan. I fully acknowledge the limitations of this term.

representation. Thus, this book is not only about the Kazakh Spring or Kazakhstan per se – it is also about the global trends and responses to the growing inequality and disempowerment highlighted even more through the autocratic context.

Another thing that the reader should keep in mind is that this book is written through the numerous accounts of those who protested openly on the streets or met in private settings under strict security and anonymity measures. A lot of these interviews are anonymized for the security of my respondents, who were willing to talk despite the very real dangers and uncertainties of the repressive machine that they face. My aim was to write out the processes from the perspectives not only of the eyewitnesses but of the makers of the revolution at its inception. Thus, the book follows numerous and often long narratives from the direct speech of the actor. I combined these interviews with archival data and the interviews I collected in 2012–14 and 2015–19 fieldwork with the opposition old guard and their reflections on their time. I believe this combination of narratives and reflections is useful, as it demonstrates Kazakhstani politics as an ever-changing field even though it is often seen as 'stagnant' to outsiders, as much as an ocean once seemed 'pacific' to its explorers but in fact was far from it.

This book is written from the position of fieldwork at *home* – I am no alien to the Kazakh steppe or its Alucobond urban jungles. On the contrary, as a writer and researcher, I am the direct product of that space and a particular Kazakhstani time in the 1990s and the early 2000s, being a child of independence myself. While my fieldwork and connection to the circles of activists in Kazakhstan lasted for several years for the project on art activism that I commenced in 2011, I started consciously collecting interviews with the Qazaq Koktemi and Oyan, Qazaqstan and other protest movements activists from January 2020 until 2022 with some reflections in 2023, and I closely followed the development of protests from March 2019. That said, I was never part of the Oyan, Qazaqstan movement, although many of my friends and acquaintances were, which made my access to the interview pool much easier and allowed for the establishment of the needed trust in the interview process. This trust I was very careful not to abuse. Many more books should be written on Indigenous methodologies and on the ways researchers can and should approach sensitive contexts, clauses of confidentiality, and discussions of some of the most horrific moments of activists' lives – of the mental and physical torture by the

What to Expect from This Book

repressive regimes they live and operate under. And thankfully, many of these books have already been written, and I have followed their words of wisdom.[32]

Along with thirty interviews,[33] I conducted digital ethnography from the start of the Qazaq Koktemi in March 2019 until late 2022 (post-January protests). Digital ethnography is the method of gathering data in the form of the study of social media pages, commentary, and visual and textual content online. It also can involve online interviews, where 'in digital ethnography, we are often in mediated contact with participants rather than in direct presence' (Pink, Horst, Postill, et al. 2016: 21). Almost all my interviews with activists were conducted online through their preferred social media platforms – often with the heaviest encryptions and security – but some also on Zoom. I have also studied the Oyan, Qazaqstan Telegram chat, which I joined in April 2020, numerous Instagram accounts, including Rukh2k19, the official account of the Qazaq Koktemi, and Oyan, Qazaqstan's official Instagram account, and diverse social media accounts of all my respondents and many independent media outlets. Our interaction also included live stories on Instagram, when in the summer of 2020 Oyan, Qazaqstan activists hosted several live Q&A sessions with anyone interested in their activism. I have analysed the August 2020 televised trial of the activist Asya Tulesova and participated in chat and Zoom discussions with activists about the trial. This digital ethnography was in part dictated by the tactics of the Qazaq Koktemi field, where most of the activists preferred to communicate their messages online where state censorship could reach not them but also where many of them could remain anonymous due to personal choices and circumstances. In other words, the context of the 'digital revolution' that Qazaq Koktemi proposed also pushed me to move

---

[32] Smith 2021 in particular was a very useful guide. See also Denzin, Lincoln, and Smith 2008.

[33] All of the interviews were conducted with the consent of the respondents; some of them were interviewed twice, and I have written notes and transcripts of all the recordings. Due to the start of the pandemic, some of the interviews were conducted online via Telegram and other platforms, some over Zoom. For the purposes of confidentiality and due to the risk of further harassment of the activists, I anonymized most of the interviews, although some of the incidents (imprisonments, attacks, police harassment) would be familiar to those who were closely following the events. All interviews were transcribed and translated solely by me to avoid any breach of privacy.

fieldwork online. In August 2021, in July and August 2022, and again in January 2023 (for the first year anniversary of the Bloody January protests), I returned to Kazakhstan and met with many of my respondents in person to discuss some more details of our interviews and to confirm their choices for full or partial confidentiality in the final publication.

In the book, I took the approach of describing and analysing the complexity in the words of those who make it happen but also analysing the contexts in which this complexity happens. Telling the story from a participant's own perspective and in their own words does it more justice and allows for further evaluation of these positions and meanings in the future when everything will eventually become history.

Telling this story from an eyewitness perspective, the book consists of eight chapters, following the logic of the way Qazaq Koktemi developed in the first three years of its existence. Following the January 2022 mass protests, which I studied closely and actively commented on, I added the final chapter (co-written with Marlene Laruelle) to focus just on these events and their aftermath. In some ways, these chapters also follow a chronological development of events and the contexts that influenced them.

In Chapter 1, 'What Is the Kazakh Spring?', I contextualize the authoritarian systematization of the political field that made it so inaccessible to the non-regime elites and newcomers. I argue that this context of authoritarian rules of the game negatively influenced the established opposition and the regime elites on the eve of Nazarbayev's resignation. None of them were ready to react to such drastic changes in the political field. As a result, the established and formalized opposition disintegrated following a number of scandals, and the remaining politicians from the opposition had to comply with the populist calls to sustain their potential electorate. Within Nazarbayev's regime, the elites remained stagnant and disoriented; they focused too much on what was happening within the regime itself and did not manage to meet the growing societal discontent and protests. These conditions, on the one hand, left newly elected President Tokayev in an uneasy situation where he continuously had to deal with crises. But on the other hand, this type of intra-elite concentration within the regime offered a unique opportunity for new unknown political forces to emerge in the public sphere. This is how the Kazakh Spring was born as an alternative political field of opportunities.

In Chapter 2, 'Who Are Oyan, Qazaqstan?', I discuss how the protests of April 2019 initiated by the Kazakh Spring activists led to a growing sense of injustice and the necessity to protest even more. This chapter is devoted to the contextualization and explanation of why and how the protest movement of Oyan, Qazaqstan emerged in the corridors of the courts on the days of the activists' trials. The paradox of the authoritarian regime is revealed in these contexts. Still unable to adapt to the new conditions or see how the socio-political landscape has changed since Nazarbayev's resignation, his authoritarian regime machine continued to operate in the same repressive manner by arresting and harassing the dissidents and protestors. Unlike previous periods, protestors' arrests fuelled even more unrest and led to the organization of the protest movement Oyan, Qazaqstan, which publicly launched their programme to democratize Kazakhstan in June 2019.

In Chapter 3, 'Deconstructing *Vlast'*', I dwell on regime–society relations instead of the classic 'state–society' relations. In doing so, I argue that in the perceptions of many citizens under authoritarian conditions, the state and political power or regime (*vlast'* in Russian) is represented by the authoritarian regime and its main dictator. I further contend in this chapter that to analyse these relations between the regime and wider society, we need to study how these power relations are perceived, understood, and practised in a given case. Thus, the chapter represents an in-depth analysis of activists' and citizens' perceptions of their positions vis-à-vis the regime, the lack of the rule of law, and overall conditions of socio-political insecurity. In these conditions, the dictatorial 'stability' of everyday life and the established system of values under dictatorship – for example, economic capital, certain incentives to normalize corruption, and so on – represent a crucial backbone to regime stability, where coercion is not the prime and immediate mechanism available to the autocratic elites. The logic of the Kazakh Spring and Oyan, Qazaqstan activists is to fight against institutionalized authoritarianism and this embedded system of authoritarian values and perceptions of 'power' (*vlast'*) as something embodied in the figures of autocrats. This shift to fighting against authoritarian values and perceptions on the meaning-making level is a very new feature of the protest waves of the Kazakh Spring, and it potentially makes it more viable and sustainable.

In Chapter 4, 'Performing the State, Performing the Protest', I discuss the digital revolution context of the Kazakh Spring. In the absence of viable and independent media (print, radio, or television), the protestors had to move their communication, outreach, and engagement entirely online. Kazakhstan is one of the most digitalized post-Soviet nations and enjoys many Instagram (up to 9 million users out of the total population of 17 million) and other social media users. The Kazakh Spring managed to politicize this social media landscape and help the emergent protests even on less politicized platforms such as Instagram. The first pandemic year, subsequent lockdowns, and the full-fledged public health crisis, growing corruption, and the resulting highest peak of mortality in the summer of 2020 exacerbated the digital revolution in Kazakhstan. Political protestors were involved in creating online databases for Covid deaths that the state tried to hide and created the space not only for digital national mourning but also for online investigations of the corruption associated with the Covid crisis. I argue that through these processes, Kazakh Spring activists were able to unite many citizens who felt angry and disoriented by the circumstances of this crisis. This chapter also focuses on the online trial of activist Asya Tulesova in August 2020, which had to be held on Zoom due to the lockdowns. Tulesova was arrested in June 2020 during an unsanctioned rally, and her public trial (which was live-streamed on YouTube) inspired further digital and in-person protests and calls against injustice and the inadequacy of the law-enforcement agencies. In this chapter, I argue that the events of the summer of 2020 led to the strengthening of the Kazakh Spring and the creation of the imagined digital community in Kazakhstan, where bonds and feelings of collective solidarity were formed through social media and online channels.

In Chapter 5, 'Generation Q and Decolonizing *Alash*', I discuss the use of language, colonial heritage, and the rethinking of its legacy in the context of the nationalizing regime imposed by Nursultan A. Nazarbayev. I argue that the constructed divide between the Kazakh- and Russian-speaking political audiences no longer works as a divide for the Qazaq Koktemi activists, who are actively embracing bilingualism not as an unattainable aspiration but as a living reality of post-independence. Qazaq Koktemi activists can be also dubbed 'Generation Q' as they strive to return to the Latinization of the Kazakh language (given that Q represents the Kazakh language sound 'Қ' better than the Stalin-era established Cyrillic script). In this

What to Expect from This Book

chapter, I also discuss how activists read decolonial theory and use it in their activism, why their main slogans, names, and titles of their projects come from the oeuvre of the Kazakh pre-Soviet movement of *Alash* and its writers – for example the 'Oyan, Qazaq' poem of Myrzhaqyp Dulatov – and how these well-known discourses are changed and adapted to the contemporary Qazaq realities. I also discuss how Qazaq Koktemi as a field allows us to rethink the nationalistic stigma that remained a Soviet legacy.

In Chapter 6, 'The Public Square and the Body under Authoritarian Pressures', I return to the symbolic importance of Brezhnev Square in Almaty and the 1986/2011 commemoration of the victims of the Soviet- and Nazarbayev-era violent crackdowns on the protests. The December 1986 protests in Soviet Alma-Ata and the violent repression in December 2011 of the long stand-off in the labour dispute in the industrial oil town of Zhanaozen remain focal points for the claims of the Qazaq Koktemi activists, who were able to reshape the old opposition's agenda over these events. In this chapter, I make the body and the public square the prime focus of the discussion. Oyan, Qazaqstan activists stress that the unsanctioned December rallies in the same square in Almaty are one of their principal events of the whole year, planned in advance. They view it as a crucial representation of the physical protest. Through these rallies though, they also fall victim to the regime's unchanged tactics of violence and control over the body. I focus on the inhumane aspects of the police tactic of kettling, used against activists in public rallies in 2021.

In Chapter 7, 'Queering the Public Sphere', I discuss the important shift to queering and discuss how queerness and 'gender equality' become the new and acutely visible paradigms of the Qazaq Koktemi. Never did any movement pay so much attention to this agenda. And rarely in the contemporary history of Kazakhstan did protest movements call out openly the double oppression of the regime, through its patriarchal and authoritarian nature of governing. In this chapter, I also focus on the ideas of class inequality. Dwelling further on my argument about Qazaq Koktemi representing the fading of the post-Soviet era, I also analyse in detail the women's rally of 8 March 2021 in Almaty and the many actors united behind it in the call for de-Sovietizing and de-stereotyping this important day of mobilization. I believe that the 2021 Women's March in particular opened many eyes to the fact that there is a vibrant plurality of views and activist forms within Qazaq Koktemi and that these forms are no longer chained to the old paradigms of the 'gender' question à la Nazarbayev, with tokenism towards female politicians and persistent sexism in the political domain.

Chapter 8, 'Making Sense of the Bloody January', that I co-authored with Marlene Laruelle, is fully dedicated to the January 2022 protests. The chapter focuses on the detailed accounts of what triggered the mass protests and on the intra-elite problems that exacerbated the problems of inequality.

1 | *What Is the Kazakh Spring?*

While dictatorships are 'regimes in which rulers acquire power by means other than competitive elections' (Gandhi 2008: 7), very few dictators have total power over their own regime. Furthermore, they need to invest in co-optation, repression, and a sustainable image of the totality of their rule. This is why the resignation of Nursultan A. Nazarbayev was surrounded by an atmosphere of anxiety in certain social groups. For more than three decades of single-handed rule, President Nazarbayev was able to create a working ethos among the elites within his regime that associated almost all political decision-making – apart from those decisions he did not want to be associated with, such as the mass killings of protestors in Zhanaozen in 2011[1] – with his person and his legacy. But this powerful discourse of the personalized regime is not something set in stone, especially after his sudden departure offered a window of opportunity for the Kazakh Spring protestors. Their demands were and remain to democratize Kazakhstan by getting rid of the undemocratic and unconstitutional laws and regulations on political parties and sanctioned rallies, as well as the law pertaining to the first president that virtually allowed Nazarbayev to remain active in politics until his death.[2] All of these

---

[1] The tragedy of Zhanaozen remains one of the most secretive points of Nazarbayev's legacy and discourse. The long-term stand-off between oil-field workers and the authorities ended in bloodshed on Independence Day (16 December) in 2011, when official sources claim fifteen people died after police gunned down the demonstrators in the main square of the city of Zhanaozen; however, unofficial sources (e.g., the *Novaya Gazeta* investigation right after the clashes) claim at least sixty-five victims, and others estimate up to 100 victims, including children who were at the public square for the commemoration of Independence Day. But the regime officially settled on a narrative of fifteen deaths after protestors supposedly clashed with the police and the latter had to use guns.

[2] The law lost most of its components in the aftermath of the January 2022 protests, and Nazarbayev no longer enjoys the privileges it provided, such as sustaining his powerful position within the regime or the punishment of any insult to Nazarbayev, his image or his legacy.

laws and amendments legally institutionalized Nazarbayev as an omnipresent and sole leader even after his March 2019 resignation, because these regulations allowed him successfully to formally suppress any political competition. The calls of Qazaq Koktemi activists go directly against these regulations, including those that disallow the publication and dissemination of mocking portraits of the first president (especially images of the 2021 mural that pictures him as a clown, discussed further in Chapter 4).

As the former president officially departed the presidential palace, Ak Orda, he physically and symbolically remained the face of the city he built, Astana (from March 2019 until September 2022, the city bore his name – Nur-Sultan), as well as of the political scene he was supposedly leaving. But this change and the renaming of projects after him (including a major street in Almaty, another one in Taldyqorgan, which also hosted his monument) were not met with complete and full acceptance.

The process of 'Nur-sultanization' that started long before the 2019 resignation included consistent calls from parliamentarians to commemorate Nazarbayev's efforts in building an 'independent and prosperous Kazakhstan' (*uvekovechit'*). Monuments and city-planning projects aside,[3] the most important move to solidify Nazarbayev as a dominant discourse of the authoritarian regime in Kazakhstan was the 2000 law on his status as *elbasy*, the Father of the Nation, and the consequent amendments to the laws on public rallies and the formation of political parties. All of these laws allowed the strengthening of Nazarbayev's position as leader, even after his formal resignation from the presidency, and the simultaneous disempowerment of any formal opposition.

The 2000 law concerning the Father of the Nation (*elbasy*) and subsequent amendments to this law and to the constitution to support this special status for Nazarbayev prohibited the defamation of the first president. The law allowed him not only to be re-elected as the special advisor to the major political institutions (parliament, the security council) and thus to remain institutionally in nominal power but also to avoid all criminal, political, financial (anti-corruption), or other trials. Under the law on political parties, new political-party registration decisions are *de jure* solely in the hands of the Ministry of Justice,

---

[3] See Koch 2018.

which can take an indefinite time to make the decision even after all the formal requirements (collection of signatures, regional representatives, party convention, etc.) on the part of the party founders are complete. The amendments to various regulations on public gathering prevent potential protesters from organizing unsanctioned rallies, a move that has already landed many of the Kazakh Spring protesters in police vans and courtrooms. There is a significant problem with these regulations, as they contradict the constitution, which states the right of citizens to peaceful rallies. The regulations on rallies require the organizers to officially apply for a 'rally permit', and the local municipal office has all the power to decide whether the gathering should be approved or not. Thus, most of the rallies in Kazakhstan are considered 'illegal' by law but allowed and guaranteed by the constitution. This contradiction made police harassment of political activists a constant and mundane practice after Nazarbayev's resignation.[4]

These legal regulations defined the rules of the game at the level below the regime elites – at the level that could have served as a potential pool for the new types of political elites who could form coalitions in parliament to make alternative decisions and avoid authoritarian stagnation. However, this democratic strategy of elite circulation was shut down in the mid-1990s when the regime emerged as a supra-presidential republic,[5] and elite accession to power followed the logic of selection rather than election.[6] In combination, these rules created the sense that Nazarbayev and his regime was in Kazakhstan *forever*, and the key to breaking this enchanted circle was not the physical removal of one political body – that of Nazarbayev – but changing the rules of the game altogether. Changing the political system in Kazakhstan requires the total reform of the political institutions (including legislation) that were created to keep Nazarbayev's

---

[4] Police harassment was likely even before the resignation, but since the Kazakh Spring caused consistent street protests even during the pandemic months, police tactics had to adopt ways of taming the activists; I discuss this power play in Chapters 3 and 5. In some severe cases, this harassment unfortunately led to the deaths of activists, most notably Dulat Agadil in Astana. He was a known civil and human rights activist and died on 25 February 2020 after he was detained and beaten in police custody. The official forensic report stated that he died from cardiac arrest and that there were no bruises, although relatives' post mortem video showed bruises on his body.

[5] Cummings 2004, 2006a, 2006b.

[6] Laruelle 2012; Isaacs 2010, 2011, 2013 on party politics.

regime solidified in place and to eliminate all possible formal challenges to its reign. The institutionalization of the authoritarian regime, and the lack of an alternative political future with stronger anti-regime contenders to Nazarbayev's rule than the completely discredited and populist opposition, created the sense for some domestic audiences that Nazarbayev was irreplaceable. These same mechanisms now allow his successor, Kassym-Zhomart Tokayev, to consolidate his own authoritarian regime.

My numerous interviews with those who made Qazaq Koktemi possible – the activists, the protestors, and the tireless producers of anti-regime discourses – recalled how the departure of Nazarbayev was sudden and unexpected and even cheerful for a very few hours, before the next morning when 'everything remained as it was'. These interviews spoke of cheering and champagne popping, of calling each other and recording celebrations on their Instagram stories to be shared with thousands of people across the country and even the world. But as they woke up to the new reality the next day, they all acutely understood yet again that it was not at all about Nazarbayev:

[In the moment] it felt as if authoritarianism was over with the departure of Nazarbayev, but here, he left but nothing has changed. Hopes collapsed in 24 hours when [the regime] announced the new measures – that [President] Tokayev will for now substitute Nazarbayev and that there will be early elections. Everything [hopes for democratization] collapsed.[7]

Yet it was because Qazaq Koktemi activists were ready for the unexpected changes, even after Nazarbayev remained in close proximity to Ak Orda, that they were able to come together to oppose this new status quo and navigate the new tactics of protest. None of the previously existing political entities were able to adapt and offer new visions as quickly, and some even completely collapsed.[8] There were immediate waves of protests that, because of their unfamiliarity, the old regime was not particularly ready to face. The regime elites did

---

[7] Interview with a Qazaq Koktemi activist, 23 July 2020.
[8] Take, for example, the only registered opposition party at the time, the OSDP Azat/Akikat party, who found themselves in complete turmoil following news of the resignation. Unable to provide any coherent programme for the so-called transition of power, one public scandal after another followed for the party until it almost disintegrated in the autumn of 2019, ousting its previous party leader, Ermukhamet Bapi, and failing to stand in the parliamentary elections of January 2021.

not know how to battle with online memes and social media hashtag waves, including the popular #cancelElbasy and #shalket (literally translated from Kazakh as 'go away, old man'), and an online public that kept up the momentum of alternative (to the regime dogmas) thinking. And as the majority of repressive regimes are still figuring out how to tame the digital revolution, which turns out to be not as easy as closing down opposition or alternative press outlets,[9] the regime in Kazakhstan decided to continue with 'business as usual'. This included more repressions, intimidations, court trials of activists, and imprisonment for performances, for activism, and even for the 'empty' banner demonstrations (discussed in Chapter 2), proving the absurdity of such a repression strategy.

Political Opportunities in Historical Perspective

The contemporary Kazakhstani political field has seen several moments of tremendous shifts and changes in 'political opportunities'. These shifts allowed the formation of formerly strong opposition parties and movements immediately before and after the collapse of the Soviet Union in 1991. On the wave of perestroika in the late 1980s, new nationalist movements, ecological movements such as Nevada-Semipalatinsk, and alternative artistic communities such as Green Triangle emerged as new political forces (see Kuttykadam 2010; Sultanbayeva and Nuryeva 2016). Then was the period of the early 2000s, with the formation of the Democratic Choice of Kazakhstan (DVK) opposition movement led entirely by the political elites who were part of the Nazarbayev regime throughout the 1990s (Junisbai and Junisbai 2005). Finally, we saw the development of several contentious waves in the mid-2000s and early 2010s, largely fuelled by the financial crisis, housing, and land disputes (Alexander 2018; Caron and Malikova 2021; Dubuisson 2020; Jäger 2014; Satpayev and Umbetaliyeva 2015). Most of these parties and movements used the 'known repertoires of contention',[10] symbols and slogans that allowed them to stay on the centrist or right axis of the political demands – from calls for democratization to openly nationalistic slogans of Kazakhification.

---

[9] See Akhrarkhodjaeva 2017; Becker 2004; Heinrich and Pleines 2018; Reuter and Szakonyi 2015.
[10] Tarrow 1998.

Up until Nazarbayev's resignation and the prolonged deinstitutionalized protests and calls for fair elections within Qazaq Koktemi, most political opposition in Kazakhstan came from the regime itself, apart from several national-patriot groups and survivors of the Zheltoqsan mass protests of 1986,[11] who were largely marginalized. These were former ministers, governors, and even presidential advisors, who had become the main political players in the opposition field from the late 1990s to the mid- and late 2010s. They attempted to offer an alternative to Nazarbayev's personalized authoritarianism while they themselves originated from it and thus followed the blueprint provided by the regime. In other words, unable to change the rules of the political game, they continued to play by these rules by establishing opposition parties and trying to stand in the parliamentary and later even presidential elections, knowing in advance that they would lose.[12] In this process, the old guard of regime opposition also contributed to the loss of public trust in structured opposition such as political parties. Let me explain this in a short historical snapshot.

Some of the key examples of political opposition in Kazakhstan include former prime minister Akezhan Kazhegeldin in 1998[13] and former ministers and mayors of major cities who formed the DVK movement in 2001 (Junisbai and Junisbai 2005) and then created the initial Ak Zhol party in 2005. These included Galymzhan Zhakiyanov (imprisoned from 2002 to 2006), Altynbek Sarsembayev (assassinated in February 2006), Alikhan Baimenov (rejoined the Nazarbayev regime in 2006), businessman Bulat Abilov, and others. These opposition forces consistently attempted to organize in the form of a political

---

[11] These are activists from the December 1986 Alma-Ata (Almaty's Soviet name) uprisings against Gorbachev's unilateral decision to remove the Kazakh party leader Dinmukhamed Kunaev and appoint Russian Gennady Kolbin as the leader of the republic he did not visit even once. Many of the December 1986 protestors viewed this decision as colonial and anti-Kazakh. Their activism continued after 1991, when most of them became more nationalistically oriented.

[12] In its better years (mid-2000s and early 2010s), OSDP Azat actively discussed the possibility of nominating not only parliamentary lists for elections but also presidential candidates (especially Zharmakhan Tuyakbay, former prosecutor general), but their agenda remained largely stagnant until a majority of the leading faces of the party resigned from politics in 2013–2015. See some of their discussions about the parliamentary elections in Kazakhstan in 2011, for example, at https://rus.azattyq.org/a/osdp_azat_election_president_/2306945.html.

[13] Kazhegeldin resides in exile in the United Kingdom and is a frequent commentator on domestic politics in Kazakhstan.

party and gained a number of supporters, especially in the regions. But after two of its prominent members were assassinated – former regional governor Zamanbek Nurkadilov and former minister Altynbek Sarsembayev in November 2005 and February 2006 – and some members were imprisoned and others constantly harassed, the movement broke down. Alikhan Baimenov took over leadership of the Ak Zhol party and rejoined the regime by taking a position in the state's public administration unit, and then turning the previously opposing party into a typical loyalist of Nazarbayev's rule in parliament. The party is now chaired by Azat Peruashev, a long-term Nazarbayev loyalist. The valuable moments of political turmoil caused by the violent suppression of the opposition leaders were lost, and many potential voters felt like they were betrayed by elitist games once again.

The last 'opposition' party, which was chaired by the former prosecutor general, Zharmakhan Tuyakbay, OSDP Azat existed from 2006 to the late 2010s. OSDP Azat was one of the few opposition parties that was registered by the Ministry of Justice and today remains the only registered opposition party in Kazakhstan. Now renamed as the Social-Democratic Party Akikat (Truth), the party had a trail of conspiracies and scandals that associated it with the presidential administration, and many local observers questioned its true 'opposition' stance. This type of political opposition that came out of the regime was completely discredited during the last presidential elections in 2019, when long-term member of the 'opposition' and once a general secretary of OSDP Azat party, Amirzhan Kosanov ran for the presidency alongside Kassym-Zhomart Tokayev, and information was later leaked about his campaign's coordination with the presidential administration.[14]

---

[14] Kosanov publicly announced his defeat the day after the election and ahead of the official results published by the Central Election Committee, basing his findings solely on two exit polls. He also congratulated regime candidate Kassym-Zhomart Tokayev and expressed the view that the country 'required stability' and had to avoid post-election protests. In further addresses to the public, Kosanov condemned mass protests and in one of his interviews hinted that these protests were organized by the 'overseas opposition leader' (Mukhtar Ablyazov), even though many protestors took to the streets without supporting any political figure and my data demonstrates that the Qazaq Koktemi activists and other youth protestors were against any association with Ablyazov, calling him a 'regime oligarch'. Despite the voices of many independent observers (many of them young people), the election results were soon announced to be legitimate and lawful. More about the allegations of Kosanov's involvement with the presidential administration is available in

Amirzhan Kosanov, once a leading opposition politician and the only opposition candidate able to run in the presidential elections (albeit against Tokayev and not Nazarbayev in June 2019) quickly announced his defeat in the elections and endorsed Kassym-Zhomart Tokayev as the new president. This was happening while the streets of the major cities in Kazakhstan were flooded with unprecedented protest rallies and police violence, which Kosanov failed to address in June 2019 during one of the most intense periods of the Kazakh Spring.[15] Not only was this type of opposition discredited, but it was also dubbed with a colloquial term – *kosanovshina*,[16] the 'sell-out' or 'puppet' opposition of the regime, taking its name directly from Amirzhan Kosanov and the fiasco of the 2019 presidential elections. The local political concept of *kosanovshina*, disintegrated opposition, and growing distrust in institutionalized political opposition seen as 'agents of the presidential administration' are all signs of the failure of the elite-led opposition in Kazakhstan.

However, the story did not end there, as some young and ambitious opposition politicians, among them Zhanbolat Mamay, still hoped for the reorganization of the OSDP Akikat party. In September 2019, the then leader of the Akikat party Ermurat Bapi was removed from the party leadership, causing a public scandal. Bapi later revealed to the media that his plan was to resign anyway and to propose Zhanbolat Mamay as his replacement.[17] This move would have allowed Mamay to prepare for parliamentary elections in January 2021, since Akikat was already registered. But when these plans failed, Mamay and his closest activists (including his wife, the well-known political activist Inga Imanbay) called for the formation of the Democratic Party of Kazakhstan (DPK) in October 2019. Up until February 2020, when all of the DPK's attempts to formalize as

---

Sergei Duvanov's piece: https://respublika.kz.media/archives/2994. Kosanov denied the allegations.

[15] According to the 2021 report by the Oxus Society, Kazakhstan experienced an unprecedented number of protests between 2018 and 2020; out of 981 incidents in Central Asia, 520 took place in Kazakhstan (Oxus Report, p. 5).

[16] The term took on a life of its own amidst the post-election protests in June 2019, and many of my respondents repeated it. For further analysis on this term, see Sergei Duvanov's piece: https://respublika.kz.media/archives/2994.

[17] Ermurat Bapi was vocal about his removal and gave a number of interviews; see Radio Free Europe, Azattyq reports regarding this news at https://rus.azattyq.org/a/kazakhstan-political-party-osdp-2019-09-10/30157092.html.

Political Opportunities in Historical Perspective 43

a registered oppositional party failed, Mamay, a well-known Kazakh-speaking journalist and nationalist, was the most visible and vocal figure in the spectrum of the formalized opposition field. But when his attempts to form a party and follow formal (legal) rules of political engagement failed,[18] he took to the streets and became the country's most visible and vocal oppositional populist leader. Mamay was arrested following the January 2022 mass protests and was sentenced to a six-year suspended sentence for his participation in them;[19] his party remains unregistered at the time of writing.

It is hard to identify what exactly contributed to such a dramatic shift from the pro-democratization party following all steps for formal institutionalization to the anti-China rhetoric and populist calls to write off citizens' consumer debts for which Mamay started rallying after 2020, and especially during the difficult first year of the global Covid-19 pandemic in 2020.[20] The context of the pandemic and the total shutdown of all workplaces amidst lockdown left many Kazakhstanis in dire economic conditions. In this situation, Mamay's call to write off impoverished citizens' banking debts was met with fully fledged support, and the number of his supporters grew substantially.

In the midst of the trail of conspiracy theories and character assassinations linked to Mamay's possible connection to the presidential

---

[18] Activists from the DPK spent most of the autumn of 2019 collecting 20,000 signatures from their supporters and trying to organize party assemblies in the regions in order to meet Ministry of Justice requirements to formally register the new party. They submitted all of the documents in February 2020 and prepared for the organization of a major party convention as the final step of their formalization into a new political force, but their plans failed. Their supporters were harassed, detained, and not allowed to travel. The beginning of the Covid-19 pandemic also signalled further restrictions for gatherings in Kazakhstan, and seeing the obstacles to his formal party organization, Mamay called for unsanctioned rallies all across Kazakhstan on 19 February 2020 to protest against the harassment of DPK. During the press conference in Almaty, he said: 'We do not have any other choice. Because if we will try now to just have the party convention or collect the signatures [necessary for the party registration], this regime [*eta vlast'*] will not take it into consideration it seems. This is why we are ready to take it to the streets and force the current regime [*vlast'*] to register the Democratic party.' Quoted from https://rus.azattyq.org/a/30443038.html.

[19] Mamay was charged with spreading false information and organizing illegal gatherings, among other things.

[20] Mamay chose the writing off of consumer debt from the 'corrupt banking system' as one of the main slogans of his street politics. This is a populist yet popular move, since every third citizen of Kazakhstan is indebted to the banking system.

administration (*kosanovshina*), which numerous pro-regime Telegram channels spread from October 2019 throughout the difficult first pandemic years,[21] Mamay's active calls for public rallies and online presence remained a key issue in contentious politics in general. His protest activities also set him close to such pro-democracy movements as Oyan, Qazaqstan, for example, and other key figures in Qazaq Koktemi, most notably Asya Tulesova, who was arrested in June 2020 during one of Mamay's unsanctioned rallies in Almaty (discussed in more detail in Chapter 4).

Zhanbolat Mamay tapped into different fields of contentious politics, which highlights his aspirations and positions as more of a political entrepreneur than a political activist like Tulesova, for example.[22] In other words, Mamay sought political opportunities in all types of slogans and agendas without rooting himself in (or limiting himself to) one. He is often described as a fervent Kazakh nationalist, but a perfectly bilingual fighter for justice too, when calling for the immediate release of all political prisoners. He is also clearly a populist, with his agenda of claiming that the state should pay for all consumer debts owned by the 'corrupt' banking system that continuously harasses Mamay's electorate. But Mamay is equally close to the agenda of Qazaq Koktemi, with its calls for radical democratization and the eradication of Nazarbayev's authoritarian regime, though he does not openly support other agendas that come with such democratization, for example, support for LGBTQ rights in Kazakhstan.[23] Thus, he is not fully part of the Qazaq Koktemi field

---

[21] Kazakh Telegram, with its abundance of public and anonymous news and commendatory channels, political gossip, and conspiracy theories, quickly became a major hub for the spread of alternative information. Many channels are rumoured to have been sold off to pro-regime forces, for example, Salem media group, which leads the online provision of pro-regime content. One of the channels, now renamed Ak Ordinskyi Solovei (the Ak Orda Nightingale), often published articles about Zhanbolat Mamay's connection to the presidential administration, and other anonymous but pro-regime channels called him the 'product of Ak Orda', which amounts to *kosanovshina*. These rumours, however, were not confirmed.

[22] I share this argument with my colleague and co-author, Assel Tutumlu, with whom I spent numerous hours in 2020–1 discussing the outcomes of Mamay's populist agenda and the divisions in claim-making in Kazakhstani political fields. I am indebted to Assel for highlighting and pinpointing many of my and our common conclusions with her virtuoso political-theory mind.

[23] After the Women's March on 8 March 2021 that ended at the famous Chokanka (a street named after Chokan Valikhanov, a legendary gathering place for Soviet

but remains on its margins when it comes to voicing protest and calling supporters to the public square where Qazaq Koktemi activists (usually under the flag of the Oyan, Qazaqstan movement) often rally in close proximity. Many of them are united in protest for the sake of the protest, although the future may demonstrate how these two groups might coexist and collaborate as their key agenda points inevitably drift apart.

For a different outlook on the rules of the game set against those provided by the regime, I would separate Mamay's DPK from the Qazaq Koktemi phenomenon. While Mamay tries to balance three or four different agendas that often contradict one another, he does not completely fall into the paradigm of the Qazaq Koktemi. First, his internal decisions and possibly leadership attempts are guided by some of the remaining old guard of former Nazarbayevite elites (e.g., those who were working from within the regime in the 1990s and even 2000s). Second, even though he has been positioning himself as a 'street politician' since February 2020 and actively called for unsanctioned rallies before his sentence, his vision is still limited by the legacies of the formalized opposition he himself came from in the early 2010s. These include formal institutionalization of the opposition, participation in elections, and possible participation in the authoritarian parliament and other regime institutions. Third, his call for collective identity is based along the lines of ethnonationalist (Kazakh) claims and not a more unifying or post-ethnic, post-nationalist vision.

Inside the Kazakh Spring: The Chronology

The question that was on the mind of many Kazakhstanis on the eve of the launch of the Oyan, Qazaqstan movement was what made it possible precisely at that moment and what was necessary for its formation. This was the exact question I put to a number of the founding members of Oyan, Qazaqstan, so it is only fair to tell the

> and post-Soviet intellectuals of Almaty) location behind the Academy of Sciences building in Almaty, Mamay called on his supporters for the anti-China rally (against leasing Kazakhstani land to Chinese enterprises) to come to the same space but did not attend the Women's March himself. Mamay remains a fairly conservative politician with many traditionalist values, and he does not openly address the 'gender question', though some of the most notable Kazakh queer activists attended Mamay's rallies and support his call for protests. I discuss queering protest in Chapter 7 of this book.

story in their own words. Their temporalities were dependent on key events of the Qazaq Koktemi and the moments of their interaction with this phenomenon. Assem Zhapisheva, a renowned bilingual journalist and writer and a vocal activist, one of the frontwomen of Oyan, Qazaqstan and of numerous independent media projects, said that 'for me, it all started after the "You cannot run away from the truth" [a performative protest act at the Almaty Marathon in April 2019]'.[24] Many of those who took to the streets, who worked on the declaration and eventually formed the backbone of Oyan, Qazaqstan and Qazaq Koktemi, also expressed that they could no longer be silent about the injustices and failure of the rule of law under the Nazarbayev regime. Thus, they described this moment of protest as the moment of awakening and the need to act. In this section, I explain two key features of understanding these crucial changes. First, Oyan, Qazaqstan was embedded in the emergence of Qazaq Koktemi, even though the latter as a field encompasses a lot of other groups, activists, and key players whom I discuss throughout this book. Second, my approach to describing this reality is through the personal stories of those who made it happen. For each of them, the temporality of Qazaq Koktemi was and remains seen from the different angles that make up this complex puzzle. It is the pluriversalism of these voices and views that makes them so rich and authentic at the same time.

March 2019: Nazarbayev's Resignation and the Emergence of the Kazakh Spring

Many of my interlocutors remembered that the night of 19 to 20 March 2019 felt like a long, dark, heavy wave of anxiety. It was the only period when many felt like Nazarbayev was gone for good. After champagne bottles were popped and emptied and honking cars left the squares of major cities in Kazakhstan, the Instagram stories and WhatsApp group chats still buzzed with the most significant news – '*papa* is gone', 'I have never known another president, what is going to happen to us now?', 'I can't believe *Shal Ket* actually left!'[25] – and messages expressing mixed feelings along with conspiracy theories

---

[24] Interview with the author, 24 July 2020.
[25] This rather impolite Kazakh saying of 'Leave, old man!' became the angry slogan of late 2010s street protests calling on Nazarbayev to resign.

flooded the private and public social media accounts. Here is how one of my respondents, who was an active member of the performative activism group and later of Oyan, Qazaqstan, described it:

I was not in Kazakhstan at the time, and my friends sent me the link to the news [about resignation] via social media messengers. My first reaction was that it was a joke. Then I understood that it was *real*, and we all felt thrilled, and our friends [from other Commonwealth of Independent States countries] brought champagne. It was the feeling of happiness. Of course, I also felt some euphoria. I constantly checked social media [that night] and all these ten-second posts (live stories on Instagram) where everyone laughed and felt so happy. I know that in Almaty, there was a huge [spontaneous street] celebration dedicated to this event [the resignation], and someone even organized fireworks for the occasion. I know that in Almaty especially young people celebrated this occasion quite spectacularly. And in general, all 'critically thinking' people [in Kazakhstan] were very happy, I thought. Everything changed the next day when the capital was renamed [to Nur-Sultan], and then it was clear what course of development was taken and that there was no hope for [political] liberalization.[26]

The sequence of post-resignation events ignited so much anger that even the most experienced ideologues of the regime did not expect it. When Astana was renamed Nur-Sultan the next day, anonymous petitions and public protests ignited the physical and digital public space. 'We all felt so angry', remembered my interlocutors. 'Calling Astana *Astana* and not Nur-Sultan immediately became the sign of your civic position and duty even if before all these renaming projects few of us even liked the name Astana, and now we felt like we had to fight for it because it was part of our dignity that we were losing', said another anonymous source.[27] Moreover, as numerous residents of Astana replied in their Instagram posts 'We do not live in Nur-Sultan, we live in Astana!', an online petition was launched to collect signatures against renaming the capital city as Nur-Sultan.[28] Many residents were angered that the decision to rename the city was made without any consultation with them; some protestors believed that it should have been open to the public vote, and they felt that they were robbed of their dignity. When people started looking for ways to channel their

[26] Anonymous interview with the author, July 2020.
[27] Author's interview with anonymous activist of Qazaq Koktemi, June 2020.
[28] www.change.org/p/казахстанцы-против-переименования-столицы-казахстана-астаны-в-нурсултан.

anger about the decision and to find a way to respond to the regime, protest was inevitable. Initially, it started with online discussions and protests and then quickly moved to the streets, where people picketed. By 9 June 2019 – the day of the presidential elections – Kazakhstanis felt like the impossible was finally real; thousands of people marched through the streets of the central cities of Almaty and Astana demanding changes.

The Kazakh Spring was in full bloom but it did not yet unite people under a coherent umbrella of demands and slogans. The first waves of protests were sporadic but necessary to channel people's anger about staged elections. The emergence of the Oyan, Qazaqstan movement allowed the framing of diverse protest slogans into the more coherent democratization programme that they presented (discussed in Chapter 2). The first wave of the Kazakh Spring was largely leaderless, anonymous but also collective in its anger against the regime. It was an important first outburst of protests that set a precedent for many of those who feared coercion and sent out a clear message – the protests were finally possible. In a country where opposition leaders and activists were killed and imprisoned, where their family members were harassed, and where peaceful protesters were gunned down in December 2011 in Zhanaozen, the sudden emergence of political street protests was a tectonic shift. As one of the youngest protestors of Qazaq Koktemi told me, 'when I understood I no longer fear it [repression], I felt incredibly empowered'.[29]

Interestingly enough, these first mass protests created a window of opportunity for contentious politics even before the elections simply because the regime–society framework did not anticipate that people would get angry about the 'smooth' power transition from Nazarbayev to Tokayev. The regime's authoritarian myopia also did not anticipate that Kazakhstanis would not support the ridiculous moves to cement Nazarbayev's cult. Apart from the 'sell out' pro-regime politicians such as the twenty-five-year-old member of parliament Madi Akhmetov, who gained the status of a diehard loyalist for his speech to commemorate Nazarbayev by erecting his monument in June 2019,[30] there were mostly voices protesting against Nazarbayev's cult. Many of my

---

[29] Author's interview with Qazaq Koktemi activist, October 2020.
[30] https://ru.sputnik.kz/20210113/kazakhstantsy-protiv-madi-akhmetov-16016757.html.

respondents complained that the renaming of the capital city as Nur-Sultan made Kazakhstan appear to be a 'sultanistic' regime or a 'bizarre dictatorship', especially when they did not support the idea in the first place. Madi Akhmedov went on to make a successful career, nevertheless, and in February 2022, in the wave of anti-Nazarbayev protests, he voted as a member of parliament to circumvent Nazarbayev's institutional powers, namely his ability to influence law-making.[31] But for now, let us address what happened during these first weeks of the formation of the Kazakh Spring.

Facebookstan and Situating Kazakhstani Social Media as a Source for Collective Action

What is key in understanding the socio-political context of Kazakhstan is that the crushing force of authoritarianism[32] and the persistent attempts of the regime to suppress any form of dissent, mainly *institutionally* – through the closure of independent media, for example – led to increasing interest in social media. In the Kazakhstani case, this phenomenon was also given the name of *Facebookstan* and *VPN-stan*. Both concepts reflect the formation of the imagined digital community, where people who often do not know each other can interact in real time on the globally networked social media platform:

Facebookstan is a force of power; it is a possibility to disengage from your overstressed life and work and immerse yourself in a different world – posts, long reads and editorials, fights in the comments sections. Our culture of [online] commenting is rapidly developing – many people dispute their points of view with complete strangers in the online comment boxes [on Facebook, Instagram or Twitter under each post] . . . I read, I read a lot of things and comments on [Kazakh] Facebook. It allows me to keep my hand on the pulse and realize what is going on in the country in general and among my acquaintances in particular. Yes, certain fear from online politicization still remains because we come from our families who tell us not to

---

[31] https://exk.kz/news/121518/madi-akhmietov-progholosoval-za-sokrashchie niie-polnomochii-nazarbaieva.

[32] The process also known colloquially as *zarkuchivanie gaek* or – literally translated – tightening the nuts and bolts expresses the tightening grip on all institutional channels of dissent – from independent newspapers to independent NGOs – and the imprisonment of opposition activists.

write certain [critical] things [about politics] online, on Facebook [or any other social media, particularly popular platforms like Instagram and Twitter]. They transmit this fear to us and give us this feeling of insecurity because what they [our families] are trying to do is save us from the state [*oni hotyat obezopasit'nas ot gosudarstva*].³³

Facebookstan strikes as a force in crises when the official media cannot be trusted to provide objective or timely reporting on the events. Thus, Facebook discussions peak during significant events that require access to uncensored information – riots, unsanctioned rallies, imprisonments of activists, and extraordinary political events, as well as quite personal issues – the collective search for missing people and calls for justice for rape victims³⁴ or anyone who fell victim to an act that was publicly framed as unjust. Facebookstan is not a consistent phenomenon, but rather it develops in waves with the events and usually the social discontent that it has to respond to. Thus, the popularity of Facebook registrations among Kazakhstani residents or those who feel a connection to the country, who may reside outside its borders but still engage virtually, proliferates with time. As one of the analysts I interviewed described it, 'Kazakhstani participation on Facebook grew exponentially within 2–3 years before Nazarbayev's resignation and accounted for 6 million users on Facebook'.³⁵ Furthermore, 'with 10 million adult population in Kazakhstan, having 6 million of them registered on Facebook [and a bit more than 9 million on Instagram] makes it quite a mighty force'.³⁶

On 20 March 2019, Kazakhstanis turned to Facebookstan in yet another wave of crisis – trying to figure out what was going on and how to deal with the tremendous transformation of the possibly new post-Nazarbayev era. However, when Dariga Nazarbayeva, the eldest

---

³³ Author's interview with anonymous activist of Qazaq Koktemi, August 2020.
³⁴ Waves of rape and domestic violence condemnations raise significant surges in online protests. Some of the best-known (and tragic) instances include the group rape in the so-called Issyk (Esik in Kazakh) case near Almaty in 2016 and the group rape at the Talgo train in 2019. The Ne Molchi (Don't Be Silent) initiative plays an active part in mediating these and other gendered violence cases online and raises awareness about the injustices many rape survivors are faced with in the Kazakhstani legal system. During the finalization of this manuscript, the Kazakh regime opened several criminal cases against Ne Molchi NGO leader and feminist activist Dina Tansari, who was forced to leave the country.
³⁵ Author's interview, Oyan, Qazaqstan activist, 7 August 2020.   ³⁶ Ibid.

daughter of Nursultan A. Nazarbayev, was appointed as head of the senate the day after her father's resignation, hopes for the *post-* era were diminished. The problem with that appointment was that constitutionally the head of the senate can become interim president if the current president resigns, dies, or is impeached.[37] So this appointment raised fears that Nazarbayeva indeed was groomed to become the 'successor' of her father despite her political failures[38] and corruption scandals.[39] Dariga Nazarbayeva did not gain much public trust, and Facebookstan immediately responded with a protest against her appointment as a speaker of the senate. An anonymous user registered on Facebook under the name Akimat Astany (Astana's Mayor's Office) and started spreading the digital protest frame 'Nur-Sultan is not my capital, Tokayev is not my president, Dariga is not my Speaker of the Senate'. These digital frames can be replicated on the profile picture of any user on Facebook simply by following a two-step instruction from one's account, and within days the Kazakh section of Facebook was reframed to repeat the same message – 'Nur-Sultan is not my capital, Tokayev is not my president, Dariga is not my Speaker of the Senate'. And this was how the digital protest started – the simple Facebook frame allowed the expression of the anger thousands of Kazakhstani citizens felt.

---

[37] Constitution of the Republic of Kazakhstan, Part 3 on president, Articles 40–8.

[38] Dariga Nazarbayeva occupied a number of political positions, including the speaker of the Majilis, the lower chamber of the Kazakh parliament. In her role as chairwoman for social services in December 2013, she publicly called children with disabilities 'freaks' (*urody* in Russian) and suggested that teenagers should be brought to special institutions for children with disabilities in order to demonstrate 'defects' (in her words (and allegedly) caused by teenage pregnancies) instead of spending hours on sexual health education. This quote caused a major public outcry in Kazakhstan but did not lead to Dariga Nazarbayeva being stripped of her political positions. Full transcript available at https://rus.azattyq.org/a/kazakhstan-dariga-nazarbayeva-about-disabled-children/25198307.html.

[39] In 2019, Dariga Nazarbayeva and her eldest son Nurali Aliev joined the list of other corrupt post-Soviet elites on the United Kingdom's Unexplained Wealth Order (UWO). One of their properties in London at the time was worth 80 million GBP, but in April 2020 a high court judge granted the application to discharge UWO claims over the three properties owned by Dariga Nazarbayeva and Nurali Aliev. See also the Mayne and Heathershaw report on transnational kleptocracy and cases of explaining suspicious wealth in the UK where they discuss Dariga Nazarbayeva's and Nurali Aliev's case.

Artistic Underground and the Rise of Art Activism

Behind the scenes of online protests, young activists started gathering through their known networks of friends and acquaintances. These were artists, designers, curators, filmmakers, and journalists, who all shared the anger that the future of their country was decided without them. As one of the members of Oyan, Qazaqstan remembers, the days of the Nauryz celebration (21–2 March) in 2019 were filled with anger rather than despair – 'we felt like our vote was already stolen'.[40] The more they discussed, the more anger grew among them, and the more they grew in their desire to start doing something about it. Thus, when asked 'how did you become an activist?', most of my interlocutors mentioned these days at the end of March 2019 when the group of young artists and their friends gathered together to form what then became the 'You cannot run away from the truth' protest act at the Almaty marathon a month later, on 21 April 2019.

To the public watching from outside, the protest wave felt coherent and just 'young', though there were many different processes and actors that, as activists later reflected, *triggered* the creation of separate movements and groups. The story should be set straight, though: the 'You cannot run away from the truth' protest action was planned by an anonymous group of artists and activists and a politically minded community in Almaty. They also came up with the hashtag #QazaqKoktemi, which then became a concept of its own. In late March 2019, these people were gathering after the first spontaneous protests to discuss the situation. This is how one of the members of this first anonymous group remembered it:

It all happened quite unexpectedly. When Nazarbayev resigned from all his duties, Tokayev became the president, and then [Tokayev] announced the elections ... I remember how this move angered my friends and me. We immediately started gathering, organizing and it all just happened. But the main trigger [that led us to protest] was when Nazarbayev left, and they immediately announced the elections,[41] and we immediately understood

---
[40] Interview with Oyan, Qazaqstan activist, anonymous.
[41] Protestors explained one of the grievances later, at the trials of Asya Tulesova, Beibarys Tolymbetov, and Suinbike Suleimenova in late April and early May 2019 following the 'You cannot run away from the truth' protest act: they believed that two months' notice for the presidential elections was not enough time for real candidates to prepare for these elections. In other words, everyone was acutely aware that the June 2019 elections were staged and that there was

these elections would be unfair [not open and contested]. On the one hand, we all understood that, on the one hand, as if he [Nur-Sultan A. Nazarbayev] left, but on the other hand, it was clear that he was not leaving at all and that he was still able to influence political decision-making.[42]

These groups of people kept on meeting in private spaces – apartments and artists' studios. Participation was strictly controlled, and people were invited through trusted channels and networks, as other participants remembered, because this group of artists and activists had known each other for a long time, so trust was an important capital that opened doors to this community. They feared infiltrations from the secret police, since the protest action was prepared in complete secrecy for two reasons: (1) for the protection of all of its participants[43] and (2) because the protest action had to be entirely unexpected by the police and the regime, which is what eventually happened. Artists and activists followed strict security rules – they switched off their phones and left them outside their meeting rooms, so their discussions were not traceable or recorded and could not be accessed by the ubiquitous security forces. Their communication was also mainly in person, and initial digital chats were deleted for confidentiality and to prevent potential arrest implications for members who avoided publicity.[44] Meeting locations also often changed and were kept secret from outsiders.

This was a crucial initial moment in the formation of the new underground. Even though art activism had been a powerful space in Kazakhstan since the late 1980s and contemporary artists engaged strongly in sparkling political debates and political activism, the emergence of Qazaq Koktemi in these same art studios and homes of the

---

no hope to contest pro-regime candidates in what activists saw as the first window of opportunity for democratization.

[42] Interview with Oyan, Qazaqstan activist, anonymous.

[43] The arrests I describe in the next section (April 2019) happened unexpectedly and thus revealed some of the members of the group, but otherwise the protest planners did not plan or anticipate it.

[44] Many of my respondents later shared that on one occasion, an internal chat that was encrypted and to which only selected members had access became part of a secret file kept by the secret police (KNB). During numerous interrogations of different members of Oyan, Qazaqstan in 2021–2, the secret police officers revealed details of this chat to them but did not mention who gave them these details or how they were able to get hold of this information. This incident led to a serious internal discussion in the Oyan, Qazaqstan movement and further actions were taken to increase security.

older generation of artists and now their children was slightly different from the activism of the Green Triangle or Kokserek art groups in the late 1980s and 1990s.[45]

Qazaq Koktemi required action and deeper political engagement through *consistent* acts of insurgencies, protest, and performances in artistic and more political ways, for example, serving as independent election observers, writing texts, maintaining social media channels, and protesting on the streets. If the art activism I wrote about before engaged with a broader sense of the ideas of states and citizens in these frameworks and touched and continues to touch upon issues of identity, gender, religion, and other crucial self-identifying categories that were monopolized by the authoritarian state, but engaged with it mainly *artistically* and performatively,[46] then this generation of art activists merged with more non-artistic participants. This allowed them to expand the ways they were protesting and engaging politically. In other words, the emergence of Qazaq Koktemi allowed the breaking and shifting of the usual and very rigid categories of political engagement and cultural production by permitting artists to become political players without denying their embedded positions in the contemporary art field. And at the same time, it allowed all other participants – whether young politicians or activists – to shift and navigate their identities and positions freely within the field. Of course, many of them continue to suffer from the rigid framing from the outside the field – Aisana Ashim is often called a journalist because she is the head of many media projects, including The Village Kazakhstan, and co-producer of the Masa portal that I discuss in more details in Chapter 4. Suinbike Suleimenova is mainly considered to be an artist or film director, and other artists of Qazaq Koktemi also constantly stressed to me in our conversations that they are not just artists but also 'activists' and 'politically engaged citizens'.

Kazakhstani political art continuously attempted to push the limitations of its framing as just protest art against the state. For example, Askhat Akhmediyarov, perhaps the best-known contemporary political artist in Kazakhstan, did not view his art in purely artistic forms but argued for the necessity of viewing art practice as a socially engaged production of meaning. His 2016 performance 'Prayer', dedicated to

---

[45] See, for example, Kudaibergenova 2017b and 2018.
[46] Kudaibergenova, *Protest Art*, forthcoming.

the imprisoned activists of the land protests in western Kazakhstan – Max Bokayev and Talgat Ayan, for example – played on the shifting boundaries of art, the protection of human rights, and political protest. Bokayev and Ayan were arrested in May 2016 following the mass protests in Atyrau against the government's decision to sell or lease land to foreigners.[47] In his performance, Akhmediyarov painted the massive faces of the two activists on the surface of a field just outside Astana, calling for justice but also interacting with the idea of the 'land', which remains a contentious space and symbol in many areas and in anti-government and anti-China protests in Kazakhstan until today.

There is a crucial necessity to navigate these diverse forms of contentious politics, messages, and groups that often overlap or are used in the hierarchical analysis against each other. For example, it is important to highlight the significant contribution of the initial artistic voices (though they were largely anonymous) in forming the key events of the Qazaq Koktemi that allowed for the development of many movements, including Oyan, Qazaqstan. Later, this development allowed the activation of the famous political entrepreneurs – among them Zhanbolat Mamay and his DPK party and other players who took up this agenda of 'street politics' that Qazaq Koktemi made so popular. Social media played a crucial role in bringing them together through networks but also in shaping the dominant pro-democracy discourses of the Kazakh Spring, which allowed many dispersed and ideologically different groups to be united under one umbrella of making Kazakhstan a democratic state. The use of social media and its critical role in shaping and reinforcing these discourses went hand in hand with the key events that shaped the Kazakh Spring as a political field. I will discuss the key event of the Almaty Marathon, which led to the inception of the Kazakh Spring field, and then come back to the post-marathon chronology, court hearings, and the emergence of the Oyan, Qazaqstan movement in the following chapter. There, I build on the regime institutional interplay with the new emerging protest groups that formed literally in the corridors and open theatres of the courtrooms following the detention of the key actors of the Almaty Marathon art protest.

[47] Read more about the arrests here: www.ohchr.org/EN/NewsEvents/Pages/DisplayNews.aspx?NewsID=20990&LangID=E.

April 2019: The Almaty Marathon and 'You Cannot Run from the Truth' Art Activism

Events leading to the 21 April 2019 Almaty marathon were swift and intense for those who participated in the preparations for the 'You cannot run away from the truth' act. I will briefly outline the publicly available data about the events before turning to the interviews with the direct participants of these events, who will tell the story in their own words and from the excerpts of our interviews.

The 2019 Almaty Marathon was organized by a group of local sports organizations together with the city *akimat* (city administration) as a mass public event and to make Almaty a global city.[48] In the morning of 21 April 2019, major streets from the centre of the city – the Republican Square[49] – and from the former Furmanov (now Nazarbayev) Street to Al Farabi and Sain Streets were blocked for the marathon runners. The locations for the 2019 marathon were quite symbolic in many ways – they started from the now newly renamed Nazarbayev Street down to the major central square and the somewhat 'peripheral' parts of the city around Sain Street. In previous years, the same marathon was scheduled and looped around the Park of the First President (where the statue of Nursultan Nazarbayev is located) on the junction of Navoi and Al Farabi Streets, but the 2018 and 2019 marathons changed the course and the layout of the race. As a result, major city avenues were closed off and traffic was paralysed from the morning of 21 April. Many of the participants of the protest action told me that they had to find ways to reach the place where they agreed to spread four of their planned banners, and some last-minute changes eventually led to hiccups:

> *Diana T. Kudaibergen (DTK)*: Do you remember where you were when the marathon started, and the first arrests happened?
>
> *Anonymous*: I was a participant in this protest action. I held one of the big banners. There are several photos of the event, and on them, you can see different banners. I was holding one of them.
>
> *DTK*: But you weren't arrested, thank God. What happened? [The police] did not get to you? [*Oni ne uspeli?*]

---

[48] The organizers branded it as 'the annual international running competition' and 'the largest sports event in Central Asia' – see www.almaty-marathon.kz.

[49] The square where the December 1986 protests occurred and where all major protests and unsanctioned rallies usually take place.

Anonymous: Yes, they [the police] couldn't catch up [with us]. We were supposed to have three groups [of protestors]. But in the end, one group didn't come [*slilis'*] because we didn't expect that there would be so many [police] officers there – there was police [*menty*] there, secret police [*organy*] at the marathon. So, one group [of protestors] – mainly girls – their husbands prohibited them from participating [in the protest], they were worried for their safety, and they [female participants] said that they'd abstain from taking part (in the protest action). We didn't blame them – it was all in the moment [*eto takoi moment byl*]. Also, we were very scared, and at the beginning, we were panicking – should we open our banner or not? When we opened our Instagram and saw that Asya [Tulesova] and Beyba [Beibarys Tolymbetov][50] got arrested, we immediately decided that there was nothing to lose anymore and opened our banner. We stood a bit farther away, and they stood closer . . . we stood farther, almost next to Sain Street, and there were more of us [with the larger banner], and I think that law enforcement officers [*sotrudniki organov*] who stood close to us, well, they were younger, and there were few of them – they simply did not have as much power as their colleagues who arrested our friends [Asya, Beibarys, and Suinbike]. I think [this lack of police power] really saved us if, to be honest. At some point, one of the policemen just came up to us and told us to leave if we didn't want to get arrested. We stood there for forty minutes, we yelled our slogans [for open and fair elections], we took the photos, we've done all the *documentation* [of the performance], and that's when the policeman came to us and politely told us to leave now if we didn't want any problems. And we left. After that, we learned about all of the events that followed [arrests, trials of the activists].

DTK: Why did you choose the marathon for this action? Why banners [as a method of protest]? . . .

Anonymous: [We chose the Almaty marathon] because we wanted an event that received mass media coverage. We thought about what event to choose and then remembered the marathon, and immediately we started orienting [the message] around the context of jogging and running.[51] This is how the

[50] Asya Tulesova and Beibarys Tolymbetov held a smaller banner with the 'You cannot run away from the truth' statement and stood at one of the alleys away from the main avenue where marathoners were running. They were first harassed by the police officers while Suinbike Suleimenova (who was also arrested with them) took photos and videos of them at the close vicinity. See Figure 2.1.

[51] The main slogan of this protest act, 'You cannot run away from the truth', is a Russian saying, and, thus, in the interview my interlocutor used the interplay of words – running in a marathon and figuratively, running away from the truth by hiding from or avoiding dealing with the issue, in this context the issue of providing fair and open elections.

phrase came up – that it is something about the sport, jogging and 'You cannot run away from the truth'. Baurzhan[52] came up with this idea. Initially, we wanted to do everything completely different, and if to be honest, we thought we'd hang the banner on the bridge [the pedestrian crossing bridge across the major avenue], and we focused on the banner size precisely to fit the size of the bridge – it was a very large banner that we held. But every single bridge had CCTV cameras on them, and there were police officers blocking every bridge entrance. We did not manage to climb any of these bridges in the end, and we discovered it right on the day [of the marathon], so we had to improvise, and we stood and held our banner alongside the road.

DTK: it was probably a very fearful [moment]?

Anonymous: Yes, it was terrifying, but it was also a fantastic feeling because everyone was on edge, but we all were united by the common desire [to make a change], and these were such a long twenty-four hours. Back then, I didn't realize how strange the time passed [that day] because it was the day when guys were arrested, and within these twenty-four hours, they were tried though it was a Sunday, and that trial went for so long. And so many people showed up for the trial [of the arrested activists]. It was an incredible day. Right now, I remember that day [for the interview], and I am thinking – if this had to be repeated, would I do it again or not? But it was an incredible [experience].

DTK: How did these first arrests influence you all? These are usually the first acts of intimidation . . .

Anonymous: We got scared, but we continued to organize different [protest] actions. And already, at the end of April, they arrested Roma [Zakharov].[53] You do remember, but with a different banner . . .

DTK: He climbed the bridge [and got arrested], and only this way we found out some names from your largely anonymous protest collective, and we were all worried for him . . .

---

[52] There was no provision of the last name, just the forename. I keep the interview transcript here exactly as it was recorded. Later I found out that Baurzhan Sabitov who coined the slogan is a photographer and film-maker.

[53] Roman Zakharov is a well-known young contemporary artist in Kazakhstan. In the early hours of 29 April 2019, he was arrested in downtown Almaty at the bridge where he was lifting up another banner that now cited the Constitution of the Republic of Kazakhstan: 'The only source of the state power is people.' This banner protest was a response to the fifteen-day detention Asya Tulesova and Beibarys Tolymbetov had to serve following their post-marathon trial on 21 April 2019.

Anonymous: Of course, it [arrests] intimidated us, and they [secret police] started acting ... now they have a lot of information about each activist, but back then there wasn't so much information available, and we were more protected than we are now. But I think what really helped us then [at the end of April and throughout the May trials] was anger. We were very angered by the events that were happening – all these arrests, but there were many of us, and we felt the support and some collective unity. And then there were all these trials, this trial and this trial, Roma's trial. And when they [police and coercive judicial apparatus] saw how many people showed up for each trial and what [protest] reaction it caused and how many protests there were against Roma [Zakharov's] trial, they immediately released him. The prosecutor's office themselves changed their decision, and we understood that it was influenced by the social unrest.[54]

The performative act at the marathon had three banners and included more than twenty people who were actively involved in the performance. Four of them were arrested and tried on the same day as the marathon. These were the activists Tulesova and Tolymbetov, who held one of the banners and were detained for fifteen days, and Suleimenova and Nurbulatova, who were documenting the banner holding and the arrest. News of the arrests quickly spread on social media, and groups of activists and sympathizers started gathering at the downtown court where all four protestors were held.

What started as an explosion of different protests all across the country after many citizens felt like they were robbed of their right to decide the country's future after Nazarbayev's resignation soon found a way to channel the dissent. The grassroots organization followed existing networks of friendships and mutual trust. Activists, artists, and anyone who felt they needed *real* changes started organizing and reaching out to local NGOs, experts, lawyers, economists, and the like. A spark of indignation gave rise to the political movements that soon made the Tokayev regime quite anxious.

[54] Author's interview with anonymous Qazaq Koktemi activist, June 2020.

2 | *Who Are Oyan, Qazaqstan?*

The Oyan, Qazaqstan (Wake up, Kazakhstan) movement launched on 5 June 2019 through a press conference where they presented their civic declaration, just days before the first presidential elections post-Nazarbayev (9 June 2019). The group of young activists called themselves Oyan, Qazaqstan, taking inspiration from the famous 1909 poem Oyan, Qazaq, which was written by Myrzhaqyp Dulatov, one of the leaders of the Alash Orda political movement that stood in opposition to Soviet expansion in Central Asia and for independent Kazakh statehood.

Oyan, Qazaqstan as a movement presents an unconventional way of doing politics (for the Kazakhstani political field). There is no one leader, and decision-making in the movement is horizontal. Membership is fluid and mainly conveyed through online chatrooms, secret and heavily encrypted communication, confidential meetings and discussions in person, and the provision of complete confidentiality for each member who needs it. At the same time, Oyan, Qazaqstan presents itself as a platform for active political participation and activism however its members want to contribute. Throughout the course of its development, it gave a voice and platform to the emergent and very young new faces of civic activism in Kazakhstan. For example, Mira Ungarova – activist, feminist, and journalist, and a very active member of Oyan, Qazaqstan – started participating in the movement's activities while still a high-school student.[1]

The first press conference of the movement detonated like a bomb. While the protests in Almaty and Astana of the preceding March and

---

[1] She revealed this information in her numerous Instagram stories and live streams hosted by her and by Oyan, Qazaqstan in 2020. She also shared that some of her appearances at the unsanctioned rallies caused her issues with her school principal, since she was only seventeen when she started protesting. However, young protest is not new for Kazakhstan, and the December 1986 protests had many sixteen- and seventeen-year-olds rallying alongside other participants.

April spurred a deep sense of contentious atmosphere, few political analysts and watchers could anticipate the formation of the new movement. Besides, the conventional political field in Kazakhstan was traditionally divided into pro-regime and anti-regime forces and remained relatively stagnant on the eve of Nazarbayev's resignation – it produced no new names. The usual talk among the political analysts I interviewed in Almaty and Astana from 2012 to 2019 was about elite re-shuffling in Ak Orda, when one minister would move to a different cabinet, presidential administration, or the ruling Nur-Otan party (also captured by Isaacs 2011 and Laruelle 2021). And talk about the Kazakh opposition mainly included the same names and the same faces who had been in the political arena for at least two decades. From the likes of the late Kuanysh Zhasaralin to Amirzhan Kosanov, apart from the rare inclusion of new names who were mainly coming through the Kazakh ethnonationalist groups and Kazakh-language opposition media, these were the same old names. The exceptions were Zhanbolat Mamay and Inga Imanbay, the leaders of the Democratic Party of Kazakhstan (DPK) that formed at the end of 2020. In other words, Oyan, Qazaqstan emerged as a highly unexpected and, at the same time, very innovative political force because *oyanovcy*, as they were dubbed, immediately declared that they would not play by the established rules of the game. There was no talk and no expectation for them to formalize and form a party until the state underwent radical political reform. They did not come empty-handed. At the press conference, they presented their ideas for such reform. The text of the Oyan, Qazaqstan declaration stated that 'Kazakhstan requires the reform of the political system and the renouncing of the politics of repressions and restriction' and that it should be based on the following:

1. Respect for the fundamental rights and freedoms of all citizens and guarantee of political pluralism, as well as an end to political repression. Everyone should have the right to freedom of speech and expression, to receive and share information in any way, and to [have the right of] peaceful assembly and freedom of association. No person should be convicted or arrested for this [action].
2. All laws, including the Constitution [of the Republic of Kazakhstan] that impose restrictions on the citizens' rights and

freedoms, must be brought in line with international human rights standards and principles of the rule of law.
3. Transition to a parliamentary republic with separation of powers. A strong parliament forms the executive branch and represents the population through direct elections through single-member constituencies. The institution of the president should be deprived of expanded powers. Excessive power [concentrated] in one person's hands leads to abuse and authoritarianism.
4. Respect for the interests of the people on the local level [should be shown] through the introduction of a fully fledged system of local self-governance. [Members of] *Maslikhat*s [local self-governance institutions] should be elected according to the majoritarian system; their powers should be expanded. *Akims* [regional governors, mayors] at all levels must be directly elected [by the citizens].[2]
5. [Kazakhstan's] electoral system must be brought in line with international standards, and [it is our] country's obligation to hold open and fair elections in a democratic society.
6. Guarantee the independence of the judiciary and the rule of law by reforming the entire judicial system and abandoning the practice of the appointing of judges by the president. The classic model of the jury should be introduced, and the Constitutional Court should be reinstated.
7. Police should be accountable to society and parliament. The function of the police is to maintain law and order and fight crime. The police should not be used to suppress the rights and freedoms of citizens.
8. The introduction of the effective governance principle for all state institutions. The work of all state bodies should be transparent and

---

[2] *Akim* elections are one of the most heated issues in the opposition discourse. In the Nazarbayev regime, all *akim*s at all levels (from the smallest villages to the major cities such as Almaty and Astana) were appointed directly by the president, which ensured complete elite control within the regime from the regional to the central level. Oyan, Qazaqstan's calls for *akim* elections were not a new agenda and had actually been voiced as early as 2001 with the initial DVK movement, but the Oyan, Qazaqstan declaration allowed for these debates to resurface with a stronger and more visible agenda and discourse after Nazarbayev's resignation. Throughout 2019 and 2020, the regime and President Tokayev actually responded to these calls with his concept of the 'listening state' (*slyshashee gosudarstvo*), though no real changes towards democratization have yet been made (at the time of writing).

accountable to society. This is the only way to overcome the total corruption [in the country].
9. In order to reform the political system, separate powers between the branches of power, and introduce the system of checks and balances between them, an independent commission on political governance reform should be formed.[3]

The success of this movement lay not only in its innovative approach to self-organization and the right moment in the window of opportunity that Sidney Tarrow (1998) discusses as critical issues for the formation of social movements. The success of Qazaq Koktemi and Oyan, Qazaqstan also depended on two key additions to the status quo. First, they provided a completely alternative space for voicing discontent and engaging politically. Second, they provided a community voice that empowered every member who became part of the field (Qazaq Koktemi) or joined forces with any of the activities, movements, and rallies in any available way. The openness of such movements as Oyan, Qazaqstan, which proudly boasts of its complete refusal to have party memberships (*partiinyi bilet*) – the attribute of Soviet party institutionalization – allows anyone to join in and feel part of the politically innovative engagement. This openness was not available to the previous political setting of the opposition field that remained very structured and highly dependent on the personalities of the leaders – Zharmakhan Tuyakbai, Akezhan Kazhegeldin, and Bulat Abilov – and on the connection to the limited ideological agenda of the movements, for example, Kazakh ethnonationalists.[4] Oyan, Qazaqstan became a new platform for political engagement at the right time and for the right audiences – the educated, middle-class urban Kazakhstani millennials and Gen Z who preferred social media interaction to formal party conventions and state television.[5]

In face of the distrust of and despair in conventional political opposition groups and their actions, the new wave of well-educated groups of

---

[3] The Oyan, Qazaqstan political-reform declaration was published online and spread on the social media that the movement continues to use as an open channel of communication with its followers, listeners, and, eventually, with the regime itself. This declaration was also published on the *Vlast* media outlet website and is available in Russian at https://vlast.kz/novosti/33541-v-almaty-prezentovali-g razdanskuu-deklaraciu-oan-kazahstan.html, English translations provided by the author.

[4] See Laruelle 2016; Kudaibergenova 2016.   [5] See Kosnazarov 2018.

citizens, primarily English-speaking and those who had access to the global networks of knowledge, organized in a collective mode that empowered all of them in new ways. All of my respondents who took part in Qazaq Koktemi and Oyan, Qazaqstan expressed the view that before, they did not have a real chance of 'influencing politics' in a meaningful way. They did not trust the electoral process, could not vote for their representatives at the municipal levels, for example, directly electing the mayor (*akim*) of their city, and were not members of any political parties or movements. As a result, most of them did not know or have direct access to those who represented their district in parliament. The conditions of heightened authoritarianism left many citizens of Kazakhstan cut off and disengaged from politics. For years, many of my respondents described the Majilis (parliament) as a 'pocket parliament' unable to influence any real governance issues without the direct approval of President Nazarbayev himself. Thus, when Qazaq Koktemi started providing an alternative space for countering these injustices and allowing for significant and tangible change, it immediately attracted people who otherwise thought they could not make a difference.

The provision of anonymity played a crucial role in constructing these collectivities. People of different professions, skills, and positions within their social groups could unite anonymously under the banner of Qazaq Koktemi and express their dissatisfaction with current affairs through protest posters (see Figures 2.1 and 2.2), collective social media accounts, and donations. Every little contribution mattered to the larger cause where singular voices were united in one. Finally, the engagement allowed each participant to feel part of something bigger. As Dimash Alzhanov, one of the public figures of the Oyan, Qazaqstan movement (although he had exited the movement at the time of this manuscript's completion) explained to me in our interview, collective work within the movement spread across numerous fluctuating teams and groups. Within these teams, every participant could dedicate several hours of their expert knowledge in each field. Tasks included anything from designing the visual content for online dissemination to the writing of political texts:

> We have a lot of talented people. How does the process of work [within Oyan, Qazaqstan] work? Here is an example of the process: we needed a big socially interactive project and launched Oyan-Zhauap (Oyan-Answer) – this is

a Q&A about Oyan [Qazaqstan]. Anyone can ask us any question [online], and we answer these questions. The designer herself took charge of it, created content, she chose everything and told us everything will be done. We all said, 'Great! The [visual] looks great', and everything started working, the process was launched. If we need some political post or some [social media] algorithm to get highlighted, another expert in this field starts working on that task.[6]

Some local commentators have often discussed the emergence of Qazaq Koktemi and subsequently the Oyan, Qazaqstan movement as the rise of the 'creative class',[7] which is an explanation used for many other cases worldwide.[8] However, I am cautious of these approaches and divisions because this simplifies the complex positions and identities each participant decides to take – for example, one can simultaneously be an activist, a film director, a feminist activist, and a contemporary artist.[9]

In the following sections, I continue the genealogy of the Oyan, Qazaqstan movement and its embeddedness in the processes, narratives, and actors who made the Kazakh Spring possible. Following my interviews with eyewitnesses and the first members of Oyan, Qazaqstan, I argue that it was formed at the crucial intersection after the Nazarbayev resignation and on the wave of protests and arrests. These arrests, court hearings, and activists' detentions created conditions of such intense feelings of injustice that they moved many apolitical people and people who never were involved in activism to eagerly join forces to create the new horizontal protest movement. Thus, the trials of late April 2019 after the 'You cannot run away from the truth' action are so important to the analysis of the inception of Oyan, Qazaqstan.

---

[6] Interview with the author, January 2020.
[7] Members of Oyan, Qazaqstan were often criticized by pro-regime commentators and called 'Almaty coffee shop hipsters' as something offensive and far away from the 'public sphere' (quite ironically). More moderate commentators associated the Kazakh Spring with the outburst of youth educated abroad and mainly engaged in 'less pragmatic' spheres of everyday life, such as art. However, just because the public face of Oyan, Qazaqstan and the Kazakh Spring remained the face of the young Kazakh cultural elite, it did not mean that among them were and still are many no less creative people engaged in other spheres outside the art or media realms.
[8] The rise of the Occupy Wall Street and the artistic waves surrounding the Arab Spring are cases in point. See Huntington 2016; Loewe 2015; McKee 2016; Milner 2013; Ross and Rivers 2017; Shilton 2021.
[9] My prior research and fieldwork in Central Asia's thriving contemporary art, which I conceptualize elsewhere, demonstrated how artists serve as political activists at the same time. See, for example, the case of Askhat Akhmediyarov's political activism in Kazakhstan.

April 2019 Chronology: The Kazakh Spring Activists' Trials Begin

I consider what is happening now to be a crime – not my crime before the state, but the state's crime against me as a citizen of Kazakhstan, given that we have a Constitution that gives us freedom, such as freedom of speech.

Asya Tulesova's speech at the 21 April 2019 trial[10]

Following the Sunday, 21 April 2019 protest for open and fair elections, four activists were arrested and brought to the district police station in Almaty. These were activists Asya Tulesova and Beibarys Tolymbetov, who held one of the banners (see Figure 2.1), artist and director Suinbike Suleimenova, and Aigul Nurbulatova, who took pictures of the protest. Their trials happened on the same day, and all the arrested were found guilty. Aigul Nurbulatova and Suinbike Suleimenova (four months' pregnant at the time) spent hours in

Figure 2.1 Beibarys Tolymbetov and Asya Tulesova at the Almaty Marathon, 21 April 2019. The slogan on the banner reads 'You cannot run away from the truth' (in Russian) and hashtags 'I have a choice' (in Russian) and 'For fair elections' (in Kazakh). Photo courtesy Suinbike Suleimenova

---

[10] Full speech is available in all three languages (original Russian, in Kazakh, and English translations) at https://adamdar.ca/en/post/in-asya-s-own-words, published on 22 April 2019.

detention but were released and sentenced to fines. Asya Tulesova and Beibarys Tolymbetov received fifteen days of administrative arrest for the 'violation of the law of the Republic of Kazakhstan on the procedure for organizing and conducting peaceful assemblies, rallies, marches, picketing and demonstrations'.[11]

News of the activists' arrests immediately spread across social media, and groups of friends, acquaintances, and sympathizers gathered near the courthouse in Almaty. They recorded Instagram stories and provided live reporting from inside and outside the courthouse. Many of them repeated the slogans of the art protest calling for fair and open elections (*Adil Sailau Ushin*) and the release of the arrested activists, reminding their digital and real-time audiences that no one could 'run away from the truth'. Many of those who came to the courthouse were young people from the independence generation – all born in the mid- to late 1980s and the 1990s. Those who managed to get inside applauded every word from the activists. Suleimenova's and Tulesova's addresses to the court have been dubbed *Slovo Suinbike* (Suinbike's Speech) and *Slovo Asi* (Asya's Speech). These addresses were immediately transcribed and released online on such platforms as Adamdar.ca (run by a well-known Almaty writer and activist Timur Nusimbekov and his team) and instantly shared across Facebook, Instagram, Telegram, and other social media channels. The Kazakh public sphere was buzzing – 'You cannot run away from the truth'.

The activists' public trials brought unprecedented results – instead of intimidating and scaring away potential protestors, it united them. The story of the Oyan, Qazaqstan movement was born out of these early and sporadic days of the Qazaq Koktemi. It was formed entirely within the corridors and rooms of the courthouse that aimed to diminish the very idea of public protest. In the words of the founding members of Oyan, Qazaqstan, they met and decided to form an entirely new protest movement in the courthouse where Tolymbetov, Tulesova, Suleimenova, Nurbulatova, and later Zakharov were tried in the final days of the turbulent April 2019:

When we all came to these trials, some of us knew each other, and some didn't. So, we started introducing each other, meeting new people, interacting and everything just came about by itself – all this mutual help

---

[11] See https://adamdar.ca/en/post/you-can-t-run-away-from-the-truth-one-year-later for a comprehensive analysis of the events.

[*vzaimopomosh'*], some sort of solidarity [was formed]. Then we started meeting more often ... I had this idea for a long time, and I proposed to them [art activists and all those who gathered in the courthouse] to politicize so that this whole [protest] didn't just stay within the art field where the majority of the [Qazaq Koktemi] activists came from initially. I wanted this protest not to remain in some hybrid slogans but for this force to enter the political agenda that we had just started and were trying to form at the time. So, the idea came ... and we wrote the concept, better-said declaration where we listed all the main points [of Oyan, Qazaqstan agenda].[12]

The courthouse meetings provided the space for interaction, and for many, these were the first court hearings they had attended. By the following summer, court attendance became a new form of regular performance, since so many activists were arrested monthly and weekly (discussed in more detail in Chapter 5). Journalists and media activists Assem Zhapisheva, a well-known bilingual journalist, and Medina Bazargali, contemporary artist and a younger sibling of Suinbike Suleimenova, provided a word-for-word transcript of court hearings and recordings of the crucial moments. Bazargali's Instagram account attracted thousands of views and new interactions.

Outside the courtrooms, the protests continued, and on 29 April 2019, another activist and artist, Roman Zakharov, was arrested in Almaty for hanging the 'constitutional banner', which read 'The only source of state power are the people', citing Article 1 of the Constitution of the Republic of Kazakhstan (see Figure 2.2). In his own words:

We wanted to make this act [of the banner citing the constitution] anonymous. But in the end, it worked out completely differently because the power [*vlast'*] in the face of the judicial system and police helped us to speak up of the problems – about the fact that you can get imprisoned for citing the Constitution – it's nonsense, but it happened. It doesn't really matter what article of the Constitution was cited; it is about the fact that one got arrested for it.[13]

Zakharov's official conviction was for 'hooliganism', and he initially received a sentence of five days of administrative arrest. But word of his arrest spread quickly on social media and instantly incited outrage precisely because he was arrested for citing the country's constitution. Kazakhstan's daily news in that last week of April 2019 turned into the theatre of absurd – people were arrested for anything that looked

[12] Author's interview with Dimash Alzhanov, 17 January 2020.
[13] Interview with the author, 28 July 2020.

Figure 2.2 'The Constitutional Banner', protest act by Qazaq Koktemi, 29 April 2019, Almaty. Source: Qazaq Spring activists

suspicious or against the regime rather than against the law. However, Roman Zakharov was not the only person in charge of hanging the 'Constitutional banner'. Behind this protest was the same anonymous collective that organized the previous action, and Zakharov was there to 'support friends and speak up against injustices'. He mentioned that once the banner had been placed on the pedestrian bridge in the early hours of 29 April 2019 and he had gone down to take photos, he realized that one side of the banner was skewed and hanging down unevenly, so that photos were not perfect. He returned to the bridge to fix it.

All these small details of staging, documenting, choosing texts and citations, keeping the same font, and inserting the brand hashtag of Qazaq Koktemi revealed a very artistic approach to doing things professionally.[14] And the same approach to meticulous visual

[14] During my almost decade-long research on art communities in Central Asia, I spent long hours and often days in artists' studios, in the exhibition spaces and galleries, in the homes and workplaces of artists, curators, and art managers while conducting long interviews with them. Over the years of this meticulous

analysis, editing, and presentation then travelled to the Oyan, Qazaqstan movement once it was established in June 2019. Every text, whether on a banner or online on social media, has to follow strict and recognizable brand semiotics of colours, fonts, hashtags, and symbolism of naming. There was a fluctuation of people between the artistic field and what became the Oyan, Qazaqstan movement and back.

The openness of both the art field and the movement allowed constant debates, interactions, and sharing of expertise. However, the majority of outsiders view the political side of the Qazaq Koktemi as a primarily artistic protest that allowed the formation of the more significant social movement only peripherally, if was part of story at all. There are many reasons for this inadequate coverage in the press. Some academic debates are slowly emerging, as well as in the public discourse.

First of all, the artistic protest collective was formed and continues to thrive on their group anonymity. Only a few well-known names are out in public discourse because of police arrests (Suinbike Suleimenova and Roman Zakharov) or their active protest online (in the case of Medina Bazargali). Second, the artistic protest of Qazaq Koktemi was not yet framed properly as the force that stood behind the inception of the Kazakh Spring itself. And finally, the institutional viewpoint that continues to overwhelmingly influence the analysis of social movements and contentious politics paradigms is precisely focused on the structural formation of politically active groupness and sidelines the artistic part of the protest as a mere visual background or frame to the *real* revolution. The Arab Spring Graffiti discourses only started being picked up the debates a decade after the revolutionary wave, for example (Shilton 2021). The performative and visual sides of the protest are unfortunately still always not taken seriously by mainstream political science. These require in-depth qualitative analysis and careful analysis of the narrative approach to the movements. On top of that, artistic expression is seen as too emotional and less strategic.

> research (and often ethnographies of craft), I started learning these small but important points and especially artists' attention to detail, their discussions about the quality of materials, paint, parts of installations, down to the quality of environments (walls, galleries, texts accompanying art works) where art was exposed. My interlocutors viewed these things as 'insignificant' for the bigger themes of discourse I was trying to analyse, but this attention to detail caught me again when I interviewed artists such as Roman Zakharov, who is known for his impeccable craft and meticulousness when it comes to the smallest things.

In this analysis and through the focus on complexity, I aim to demonstrate how the formation of the social movement of Oyan, Qazaqstan was triggered and embedded in the first very emotional and spontaneous acts of artistic and performative disobedience. Artists spent days planning for the performances that started in March 2019 and continue today, as this manuscript is being finalized. They come up with new symbols and new stagings of the protest. They wrote 'Cancel Elbasy' on any public visual representations of Nazarbayev's cult, even before this became mainstream, and until today they keep the Qazaq Koktemi going through hashtags, ideas, and its spirit. In the words of Asya Tulesova, 'It was great not to be afraid, not to be afraid to shout, to say what we think'.[15] The genealogy of all post-Nazarbayev contentious politics is inevitably embedded in Qazaq Koktemi, as it opened the space for the revolution of minds and a possibility for actions. And as Roman Zakharov said to me in his interview, Qazaq Koktemi reflected and kept open a dialogue with the repressive apparatus of the authoritarian regime that tried to suppress the protest but, in reality, only influenced its viability even more. In the next section, I turn to the court hearings where Suinbike Suleimenova, Asya Tulesova, and Beibarys Tolymbetov were tried in April and May 2019. I contend that these court hearings united the critical mass of protestors who eventually formed Oyan, Qazaqstan in those same weeks of late spring 2019.

May 2019 Chronology: Trials of the Kazakh Spring Activists Continue

Asya Tulesova and Beibarys Tolymbetov were tried and convicted on the evening of the same day of their arrest on 21 April 2019 and were sentenced to fifteen days in prison. My respondents later revealed that the sentencing at the time felt 'shocking' and 'unreal'. The hearings also spurred a lot of conspiracy theories on the prosecution's side and a lack of independent reporting on the part of the media. Only Assem Zhapisheva provided day-to-day reporting directly from the court as an independent journalist, and the Adamdar.ca independent web portal published the court transcripts that I cite in what follows.[16] The attendees, activists who

---

[15] https://adamdar.ca/en/post/you-can-t-run-away-from-the-truth-one-year-later.
[16] The reporting from Tulesova's hearing was posted online the next day – 22 April 2019. All those who were not in Almaty at the time were dependent on

did not represent any media, recorded the hearings on their mobile phones and posted them on their own Instagram stories. So not only could those physically present in court be in the eye of the storm and have direct access to the information and the process but their followers too. The court hearings allowed the art activists to explain their agenda better. The courtroom became an extension of the stretch of the marathon course where the banners were exposed. Because the 'You cannot run away from the truth' protest act was staged as an artistic work open for deliberation, it did not provide a statement text. The activists' unexpected trial and their response to the judge and prosecution became *textual* accompaniments to the performance. Let us take the example of Asya Tulesova's hearing or, as it was dubbed, *Slovo Asi* or 'in Asya's own words' or, as I translate it here, 'Asya's Speech'.

'Asya's Speech' of 2019[17]

Asya Tulesova: I acted on my own conscience. Presidential elections have been announced for 9 June [2019], and I think it is an important moment in the life of every Kazakhstani citizen. We might finally hold open and fair elections. But unfortunately, our system is designed in such a way that we do not allow real candidates, the ordinary citizens, to have the opportunity to stand in these elections, which [the right and opportunity to run for office] I think is fundamental. Our flash mob [the protest act] was dedicated to this issue. Beibarys and I came out and said: 'Guys, let's all get together and organize independent elections.'

I consider what is happening now to be a crime – not my crime before the state, but the state's crime against me as a citizen of Kazakhstan, given that we have a Constitution that gives us freedom, such as freedom of speech. . . .

Judge Abraev: What is your goal?

Asya Tulesova: The goal is to attract people's attention to the necessity to unite and organize independent and fair elections. Any elections [should be fair and open] – the elections of the president of the Republic of Kazakhstan, [elections] of judges, and of course, elections of the *akim*s. We want for our executive power to be accountable to its citizens like it is supposed to be.

---

[17] the little news coming from the courtroom and turned to social media; state-owned media started reporting on these events only days later.
Since then, Tulesova was tried again in June 2020, where her court hearing was directly televised via YouTube and held completely online for the first time in the country's history due to the worst wave of the Covid-19 pandemic (I discuss the 2020 Tulesova court hearings in Chapter 3).

Prosecutor: From what you have just said, it turns out that this banner connects to politics even though before, you stated that [the banner] directly connected to the marathon.

Asya Tulesova: Of course. I think that this is a very witty banner.... It says: 'You cannot run away from the truth.' And people run from the truth. Even those who interrogated us were also participants in the marathon, as it turned out. And I think that in this outburst of energy, we forget about some of the fundamental issues that Kazakhstan is facing right now, for example, corruption. [There is] corruption in the law enforcement agencies or corruption in courts, and this same corruption impedes us from changing, enhancing, the air quality in Almaty.[18] [There] is a multitude of problems.

Prosecutor: Do you agree that your banner has nothing to do with sports and the [Almaty] marathon?

Asya Tulesova: It [the banner] is very much related to sports. As if it is saying: You can run, but sport won't substitute you with some ... I mean, sport is good, but sport and an active civic position are even better.[19]

Art activist Medina Bazargali, who was at the trial, remembered how one of the accusations against Tulesova and Tolymbetov was that their banner read 'The first president is the shame of the nation'. These accusations happened despite copious photographic evidence that there was no banner with that slogan anywhere near either activist nor anywhere at all.[20] Thus, the prosecutor's questions sounded silly to all those who had seen the banners:

---

[18] For years Tulesova was engaged in environmental activism and the launch of the AUA app that analyses levels of air pollution in Almaty. The name AUA stands for the Kazakh word that means 'air' (connected to air pollution in the city) but also to the wider connotation of 'environment'. With its quite symbolic meaning, when it launched, the AUA app tapped into many discourses of Almaty's problems with its environmental crisis and lack of good governance to deal with these problems. Tulesova even tried to run for the local municipal agency on this ticket but was denied her candidacy registration in 2016, claiming that she had a debt of 78 *tyin* – less than 0.0023 USD – in taxes.

[19] I quote this transcript from the Adamdar.ca website (available here in English translation: https://adamdar.ca/en/post/in-asya-s-own-words) and I used both original Russian language script and the translation into English in order to reach a third version with my own editing (I found part of the English translation provided by the Adamdar.ca website slightly inaccurate).

[20] Interview with the author, 27 July 2020.

Prosecutor: All right, but what does the external context of this banner mean?

Asya Tulesova: [cites one of the hashtags] 'I have a choice'? 'I have a choice' means that I have a choice. I want people to realize that they also have a choice, that we need to learn to build democratic institutions that would work. We need a good president who will be accountable to the people, who will also care about the quality of life of their people. These are simple truths. We are [standing] for simple truths, as I am sure you are too. You also [stand] for [the conditions] for your children growing up in a [environmentally] clean city. You stand for the justice that if Usenov[21] causes another car accident involving your son or daughter, he will get the [sentence for it]. Does that make sense? [*Ponimaete?*]. We are standing for these simple things. We are standing against corruption; we are standing against forcing poor [university] students to go and give up their votes . . .

Prosecutor: Let's get to the point . . .

At this point in the hearing, Tulesova took a breath and gave one of the most inspiring speeches of the Kazakh Spring:

Asya Tulesova: This is the point. And all of that is located in a single banner. Can you imagine? If we have an election, we want . . . to teach our students [critical] things and not just mindless voting for whom they are told to vote on command [*po ukazke*]. Let's teach our judges how to sentence those guilty and not just those they are ordered [to convict]. Let's teach our law-enforcement agencies not to persecute political activists but to defend the people, just to defend the people. Some people want to live, who want to build [their lives]. This is what our [protest] action with Beibarys was dedicated to.

And I am sure that each one of you, you, Mr Prosecutor, you, Your Honour, all the secretaries – you all want the same for our state. I am with you [in wanting this]. And everyone who came here today, they all want the same thing. And I also understand that right now is a difficult period. Still,

---

[21] Usenov or Usenovshina is a colloquial concept of unlawfulness. Its root lies in a deadly car accident when, in February 2014, Maksat Usenov, the son of a government official, caused a car collision killing one and injuring five. Further medical expertise proved that he was driving drunk at the time of the tragic accident. Since Usenov was not officially imprisoned for his crime, Kazakhstani society named the type of unlawfulness, corruption, and escape from legal trial for crime after Maksat Usenov, and so it became known as 'Usenovshina'. In her court speech, Tulesova was referring to the type of insecurity an average citizen experienced in Kazakhstan, at risk of becoming a victim of Maksat Usenov or of someone as privileged as him and to have no legal framework to protect them.

I also think that until we learn how to express our opinion and speak up honestly, openly, and directly about our goals, we will remain within the system [*sistema*] that will continue to devour us. We will just continue to rot away and lose our country. Does that make sense? [*Ponimaete?*].

[Ours] was a small banner. It was simply an outcry, a reminder, that people, we have a great beautiful country, let's develop it, let's make it beautiful, let us all collectively build it! Let's [allow] our students to invest in the [country's] progress, let them come out and protest, give them the freedom, let them make their own beautiful songs. Let's not be afraid to let our sons out of the house, fearing that maybe someday someone would steal his car mirrors and he would just be gone [dead] after chasing the thieves [who'd kill him].[22] Does that make sense? [*Ponimaete?*].

You also want this country. But until we start changing our decisions and building the [democratic] institutions we dream about, nothing will change. Each one of us makes these decisions on a daily basis on our own. And I am saying: 'Let's start making decisions, the right decisions that are based on honour.' We all grew up on these values that are … honesty, freedom, kindness, love, and knowledge. These are simple truths. When you leave the institutions that break you, you break your souls and mind, and you come home as completely different people. What you want for your children is a wonderful, wonderful Kazakhstan. Nobody wants to leave [emigrate from Kazakhstan] …

Judge Abraev: Asiya Tasbulatovna, let's get to the point.

Asya Tulesova: This *is* the point. This might sound naive, but this is precisely what this banner is all about. And Beibarys too, when he came out [to stand and hold the banner], he thought exactly the same. I just don't get it, and I cannot understand … it is so strange that [it happens] in our country that this boy [Tolymbetov] … he is only twenty years old. He is going to serve [his country] in the army, he didn't try to avoid it, he is

---

[22] Here Tulesova referred to the murder of Denis Ten, Kazakh ice skater and the bronze medallist of the 2014 Winter Olympics, who was killed in Almaty on 19 July 2018, when he was pursuing the thieves who stole side mirrors from his car. They stabbed him in the leg causing damage to one of the major blood vessels, and he died in two hours from massive bleeding. Denis Ten was only twenty-five and had promising career prospects as the country's leading ice skater. But above all, his death revealed the horrendous economic inequalities, impoverishment, and the levels of petty crime that the law-enforcement system was powerless to address. Ten's death caused public outrage across the country, where many commentators voiced the deeper-seated issues of overall state insecurity to combat crime levels and keep citizens from getting killed in a major city centre in broad daylight. Several protest waves following Ten's death called for the reform of the police system.

drafted, and he will join the army,[23] and he got sentenced to fifteen days in prison only because he said, 'Let's have open and fair elections.' ... I think we need to reach a moment when we need to say: 'This is it! From this moment, I will strive to live better.'

Judge Abraev: Does this banner have a political meaning?

Asya Tulesova: This banner is indeed political too.

Judge Abraev: This is a picket, a peaceful picket.

Asya Tulesova: What is a 'picket'? Give me the definition of a picket. I think that it is a flash mob.

Judge Abraev: A peaceful flash mob that raises political issues?

Asya Tulesova: Of course. Look, when I say that Almaty dwellers [*almatintsy*] require clean air [without pollution] – it is also a political issue. The air pollution problem in Almaty is a very political issue ... These basic issues – these are all political issues. Our whole life is about politics. Don't you get it? [*Ponimaete?*][24]

These court transcripts of direct speech allowed the formation of broader discourses circulating in these politically minded communities of activists. For example, Tulesova brought up in her address the issues of overall social and political insecurity of everyday life caused by the authoritarian regime – the dangers on the street and feeling and knowing that no state institution was there to protect the citizens. She brought up two of the most significant events that happened in Almaty, the country's major city, over the period of the last few years (prior to her own arrest). These were the car accident caused by the drunken driver Usenov, the son of the corrupt EXPO-2017 official, who walked free after the accident left one person dead and many injured, and the murder of Olympic ice skater Denis Ten. Tulesova

---

[23] Right after his arrest, Tolymbetov was drafted into army service and announced that he would serve. After another activist Alimzhan Isbassarov, was later drafted into the army immediately after his arrest for public activism, many commentators started speculating whether the army draft of young male activists was a regime tactic of intimidation. Tolymbetov served his obligatory year of army service in 2019 and upon his return from the army became an active and publicly visible member of the Oyan, Qazaqstan movement, launched his own Telegram channel, and remains an active political activist.

[24] I quote this transcript from the Adamdar.ca website (available here in English translation: https://adamdar.ca/en/post/in-asya-s-own-words).

was already known as a public activist before joining the Qazaq Koktemi. She was known for her environmental activism and her calls for the 'working democratic institutions' to solve all the problems she stated were part of her long-term and coherent agenda. But one cannot say that Tulesova was neatly placed within the political or activist milieu alone. Since her university years, she has been part of artistic circles, sang in a band, and was an active member of underground cultural movements and circles. Tulesova truly represented the face of this hybrid artistic-political conjuncture of Qazaq Koktemi.[25] However, there are very many faces of the Kazakh Spring.

These first trials of the young activists and artists were earth-shaking moments for the generation that grew up without first-hand memories of the repression of political dissent in the Soviet Union. On the contrary, this generation – open to globalized perspectives of democratic values (even from afar), who were frequent participants in their parents' political discussion clubs – was shocked by the arrests. In the case of Asya Tulesova and Suinbike Suleimenova, these were the arrests of well-known figures of the emerging artistic waves in Almaty. News of their arrests flooded major social media networks, channels, and social media platforms – the type of outreach strategy that set a precedent for all the subsequent arrests throughout the many months of the Kazakh Spring. And every arrest and every court hearing or post-arrest release started to have a critical performative and meaning-making aspect.

Suinbike Suleimenova recalled in her interview with me that she used her court appeal hearing on 17 May as a 'performance' where she could explain her actions in more detail and use it as a manifesto. Her decision to do so was inspired by what Tulesova turned her hearing into:

For me, she was like a heroine of an epic, and after that, people started calling her *batyr-qyz*.[26] She is truly a heroine of an epic, and that speech [she

---

[25] Tulesova has continued her political activism and at the time of the writing of this chapter remains active in diverse political debates, including a possible political party formation. After her arrest in June 2020 and subsequent trial, she was branded a *Batyr kyz* (literally female knight) and certainly became one of the main faces of the Qazaq Koktemi protests. Suinbike Suleimenova in her interview with me mentioned how she was inspired by Tulesova's improvised speech in court in April 2019; none of them had been prepared to be arrested so Tulesova completely extemporized her court speech.

[26] Loosely translated from Kazakh as a fearless female warrior.

delivered in court] in itself was like an epic as if she [Asya] is an *aqyn*.[27] She just used the art of improvisation. . . . That speech was so great – she nailed all of the points that we all thought about [*s yazika snyala u nas vseh*]. On top of that, her word [*Slovo*] was performed in that space, in that court, and to all those people, and we all wanted them to hear it. They wouldn't have heard it in any other situation, but it was amazing they heard it here. That is why we are all so grateful to her. I didn't manage to perform as she did in my first hearing, so I prepared for my speech during my appeal hearing. I couldn't improvise my speech into an epic [in the first hearing], but then I had time to prepare for the second one and managed. It was also quite inspiring, and someone was even filming because in the most crucial moment, when the punchline was coming – at that exact moment I paused for a specific period – precisely timed for the important moment [in a whole frame of the performance], and then a tear dropped from my eye . . . now that wasn't planned [*no eto bylo ne spetsial'no*]. And for me especially . . . I, of course, wanted at that moment mainly to keep my emotions at the minimum, but my tears just burst out. And this pause – it was good, I don't know. I took my appeal hearing as a performance because [I staged it] by wearing a huge gown, and everyone [Suinbike's supporters] had their mouths covered with a tape that had the '*uyat*' word [*shame* in Kazakh] written on the tape.[28] I hope it had an effect, but in any case, it was all directed at these people whom I mentioned in my speech [here Suleimenova refers to the actors of the police state]. These people put us in these conditions, divide us, and widen this incredible abyss between us [activists and the police state]. They try to throw us into this abyss with their actions, even though it is apparent that their actions are politically motivated. It is absolutely clear that their actions are aimed at censoring us, stripping us of our freedom. These actions were not planned like that. When we met as artists, we did not anticipate becoming the actors of these [protest] processes. We wanted to talk about the things that already have happened, and they [police state] only proved with their actions that everything that is going on with us is truly horrendous [police harassment and infringement of rights]. It turned out that with their repressions, they proved our words – 'You cannot run away from the truth', 'for open and contested elections' [*adil sailau ushin* in original Kazakh], and 'I have a choice' became the words that were on everyone's minds. I think, at the time, these slogans were simultaneously in the heads of the majority of Kazakhstani people. It was

---

[27] *Aqyn* is a traditional oral performer and singer, known as the 'steppe singer'. Aqyns, singers or poets, have transformed from the nomadic lifestyle to a more settled genre of improvised poetry production. For more context, see Salimjan 2017.

[28] See pictures from the trial at https://adamdar.ca/post/uyat-krupneyshiy-art-performans-protesta.

very interesting, exciting. Courtrooms became the spaces of a community coming together, the spaces of physical unity. It was very important that this [unification] happened offline and that online mediation also fuelled these processes further.[29]

Suleimenova was not wrong – the court hearings and the subsequent social media coverage of these hearings spurred a wave of protests online and offline. The so-called poster war started and was inspired by the 'You cannot run away from the truth' protest in late April in Almaty.[30]

The poster war was the war between police officers and young activists who used this new protest tactic. Because unsanctioned mass rallies are illegal in Kazakh law, protestors decided to rally alone. So the point was for one person to go to a major public square or monument (usually a monument to Kazakh poet Abay, which stands in almost every small town or village in Kazakhstan)[31] and protest with their poster. On 6 May 2019, Aslan Sagutdinov, a political activist from the western Kazakhstan town of Uralsk (Oral in Kazakh), decided to protest with a blank A3 poster in the public square. In his own words, he was outraged by the news about activists' detentions in Almaty and found the arrest for 'citing Constitution' absurd. However, day after day, the poster war became even more absurd. Sagutdinov was held in police detention and asked many of the usual questions – who he supported politically, what he was trying to do with an empty poster, the purpose of his action, and so on. Every police detention and every court hearing where activists were tried revealed one coherent aspect – the police state was crumbling in the face of a form of activism completely unknown to them. Many of the police

[29] Author's interview with Suinbike Suleimenova, July 2020.
[30] We can count 'You cannot run away from the truth' as the official inception of politically charged poster wars in Kazakhstan of the new Qazaq Koktemi era. However, another spontaneous poster wars started also in 2017, when Astana dweller Nesipkul Uyabayeva protested against the demolition of her house by covering it with ninety-one posters of Nursultan A. Nazarbayev's portraits. She later commented that her move was dictated by the fact that Kazakhstani 'bureaucrats are not scared of God' but are scared of Nazarbayev, and they indeed did not move to demolish the house while it had Nazarbayev's posters on it. See https://rus.azattyq.org/a/28477852.html.
[31] Abay is a symbolic signifier of Kazakhness. For protestors to choose Abay's monument as a main site of their political protest is also quite symbolic because the Abay monument is most likely located in the central part of any Kazakh city and because Abay himself was a rebel at heart.

officers who were arresting Sagutdinov had no idea what to do with him and how to proceed – what articles and what crimes to match his actions with if his poster was literally blank? But most importantly, the police were unaware of how their actions were viewed as a complete theatre of the absurd at home and abroad.

Following Sagutdinov's release from the police station, he became an internet sensation, with memes, videos, sharing of the photos of his protests, and calls for a flash mob picketing with blank posters widely shared online. Many followed the tropes of the 'empty poster protestor', and on 9 May 2019, another activist, Zhanbota Alzhanova, was detained and questioned for hours in Astana. Alzhanova posted a photo of her holding an 'invisible poster' (holding her two hands as if there was a poster in between them) on her Facebook page, adding to the Kazakhstani poster wars. Following this, she was arrested by two men who did not identify themselves and spent two hours at the police station without access to a mobile phone or a lawyer while she was interrogated. Upon her release, she immediately posted about it on her Facebook page.

While the police consciously used the only interrogative approaches they knew from the times of the Soviet NKVD (the People's Commissariat of Internal Affairs, the Soviet secret police of the 1930s), the protestors were finding new ways to channel their anger and frustration with the situation they found themselves in. When lone protests (*odinochnie pikety*) proved dangerous for the activists, anonymous actions would strike again. On 30 May 2019, anonymous Qazaq Koktemi activists displayed a banner reading '[We demand] Changes' (*Peremen*),[32] a famous song by Soviet rockstar Viktor

---

[32] The '*Peremen*' [Changes] song was first performed in 1986, and the original line goes: 'Changes! our hearts demand. Changes! our eyes demand. In our laughter, in our tears and in the pulsation of our veins: Changes! We are waiting for Changes!' My translation of the Qazaq Koktemi banner is slightly altered, as the message surrounding this protest action read more as 'We demand Changes', but the Russian '*Peremen!*' can be read via the original song citation as 'We are waiting for changes!' as well, depending on which line is chosen for the interpretation. The song itself is charged with heavy interpretations and became the song of the old and new revolutions; for example, it was the most cited and performed song during the Minsk rallies in August and September 2020. There are many interpretations of what the original meaning was. One of my colleagues, a music commentator, pointed out to me that the original '*Peremen!*' song was written as a critique of the stagnant kitchen clubs and quiet dissidence of the early perestroika period. The song was first performed in 1986 but gained

May 2019 Chronology

Figure 2.3 Qazaq Koktemi and Viktor Tsoi at Tulebaika, downtown Almaty: '[We demand] Changes'. Source: Qazaq Spring activists

Tsoi,[33] at his monument in downtown Almaty (see Figure 2.3). The communication remained anonymous, and the text explaining the protest move then appeared on the Instagram social media platform under the account of @rukh2k19:

We witnessed a lot of things in the 30 years of independence. We saw how the people [*narod*] were shot, how oppositions were killed, how prison sentences are given for nothing. We saw how whole districts were demolished, how children were gasping for air, how they killed the champion [Denis Ten]. We saw everything, but we haven't seen the changes. We have been waiting for the changes for 30 years, and now we need to implement the changes ourselves.

a new and more positive revolutionary aspect with the new waves of post-Soviet protests in Kazakhstan in 2019 and Belarus in 2020 and then in Russia during January 2021, where it was also performed as a protest song.

[33] Vikror Tsoi was the co-founder of the band Kino and until his tragic death in 1990 was considered the voice of a generation and the biggest Soviet underground rockstar. He also starred in the highly acclaimed 1988 film *The Needle* (*Igla*), directed by one of the legendary Kazakh New Wave directors, Rashid Nugmanov, which was staged in Almaty. People in Kazakhstan considered Tsoi one of their own because his father – an ethnic Korean deportee – came from Kazakhstan. So, dedicated Kazakh fans sponsored the Tsoi monument at the bohemian location on Tulebayev alley in downtown Almaty in memory of the protest underground years of the 1980s, in which the Almaty scene played an important role through artistic connections such as film director Rashid Nugmanov, artist Rustam Khalfin, archaeologist Alan Medoev, and many others.

What was crucial with this planned action was the interplay or the type of dialogue it was constructing with the police state by removing the physical bodies of the protestors from their purview and instead symbolically exchanging them with the bronze bodies of the monuments. This dialogue and mutual reflections on each other's actions defined the rise of Qazaq Koktemi and its tactics. As we will see from the following chapters, the police and other law-enforcement offices were slowly building their tactics in response to these new forms of protests (see Chapter 4 for Asya Tulesova's imprisonment in June 2020 and the kettling strategy discussed in Chapter 6).

By the end of May 2019, it was clear that a critical mass of protest feelings had concentrated online and in the streets. The online sphere was fuelled by messages, reposts, and buzz about the protests. People posted messages quoting 'We want changes' and 'I have a choice'. Meanwhile, several groups were working on distinct initiatives. The anonymous collective of artists continued to plan protest performances. The founding group of activists discussed and drafted the declaration and the launch of the Oyan, Qazaqstan movement. Moreover, actor Anuar Nurpeisov planned the video performance and the hashtag *MenOyandym* ('I woke up'). The releases of all three coincided and created a feeling that all participants belonged to the same coordination centre, which was not quite the truth.

The *MenOyandym* video launched on 29 May and featured many well-known faces of Qazaq Koktemi – Asya Tulesova, Suinbike Suleimenova, Assem Zhapisheva, Temujin Duysenov.[34] Each activist mentioned a fact about Kazakhstani political reality. For example, they said that 'I woke up in the country where the capital city can be renamed in one day without considering the opinions of citizens', or 'I woke up in the country where the Internet is blocked', 'I woke up in the country where I cannot afford to buy an apartment at 30', and so on. The video directly cited the reference to the 1909 poem 'Oyan,

---

[34] Temujin Duysenov came up with his own marathon that he titled 'From Nazarbayev to Truth', stemming from the ironic interplay of the street names in Almaty, the new (renamed) Nazarbayev Street in the central part of the city to the Pravda Avenue (the old Soviet name of the street, which translates as Truth). Duysenov ran this improvised marathon himself and proposed that others run it as well in a form of protest against renaming the old Furmanov Street in Almaty as Nazarbayev Street.

Qazaq!' by Kazakh poet and independence movement leader Myrzhaqyp Dulatov:

> Wake up, Qazaq!
> Open your eyes, wake up, Qazaq, lift your head,
> Don't waste your years in conscious darkness.
> Earth went from the feet, faith weakened, the soul is poisoned with disbelief,
> My dear, now is not the time for apathy.
>
> Oyan, Qazaq!
> Közindi ash, Oyan Qazaq, köter basty,
> Ötkizbey qarangyda beker zhasty.
> Zher ketti, din nasharlap, hal aram bop,
> Qaragym, endi zhatu zharamasty.

This was not the first time that Myrzhaqyp Dulatov's classical poem was cited in a movement or a protest action – it had been the flag-bearer of protest waves since the 1990s.[35] It did not quite belong as a slogan to any particular movement, rather it was shared among the many different groups that used it. Myrzhaqyp Dulatov remained an important historical figure for resistance and enlightenment, as one of the leaders of the Alash Orda movement who called for the independent statehood and modernization of Kazakhstan but who perished under the Stalinist repressions (Amanzholova 2013; Kendirbay 2020; Rottier 2003; Uyama 2000). Dulatov's message is also very much applicable to any situation of unjustness, because it calls for the necessity to wake and act on injustices. Thus, the video built on the background power of Dulatov's message. The story of what followed, however, was not pretty. Anuar Nurpeisov, who organized the video protest and disseminated it, then suddenly disappeared, prompting fears for his safety. He resurfaced six months later with a video confession of police pressure and a decision to abstain from the

---

[35] Dulatov and much of his oeuvre perished during the Stalinist repressions. He was rehabilitated alongside other Alash Orda leaders during the last period of perestroika. His poems reappeared in Kazakh print media (mainly newspapers) and were brought to life in Kazakh-speaking intellectual circles but quickly disseminated to the social and political groups. 'Oyan, Qazaq!' transformed from the initial slogan of a call for progress (and nation-building) to the different meanings of the post-Soviet ethnonationalist discourses and also the general, 'waking-up' moment in terms of political participation and democratization. With the Kazakh Spring, this same slogan changed to 'Wake Up, Kazakhstan' instead of just 'Wake Up, Kazakh'. I discuss this in more detail in Chapter 5.

political opposition.³⁶ The criticism was not directed so much to his decision to avoid protest or opposition activities but more because he used the video more to advertise his new business (lodging in Sri Lanka).³⁷ However, the video and the action became historic. Behind the scenes, Oyan, Qazaqstan was forming as a movement whose name was debated but eventually agreed on. Numerous anonymous activists were developing the civic programme for the movement and planned further actions when Nurpeisov left Kazakhstan following potential repression.

June 2019 Chronology: The June Presidential Elections and the New Observers

The launch of the Oyan, Qazaqstan movement was unexpected for the regime. At the same time, hundreds of activists sympathetic to Oyan, Qazaqstan and Qazaq Koktemi registered as independent observers for the presidential elections scheduled for 9 June. All the communication for these initiatives was done entirely through social media – Kazakh Instagram became a space for political streaming in spring 2019 and continues to shape this agenda in between TikTok dances and the latest fashion, gossip, and news, often overshadowing even the traditional Facebookstan. For example, some of the most famous political and opposition social media accounts such as ZaNamiUjeViehali [They [Police] are on their way to get us] has 124,000 public subscribers. Another protest account, rukh2k19, which positions itself as one of the many Instagram accounts of the Qazaq Koktemi, has over 30,000 subscribers. A popular anti-corruption account ProTenge has 55,300 subscribers, and the ZTB popular news channel has 1.6 million subscribers.³⁸

---

36 Right after the launch of the video, Nurpeisov disappeared from the online sphere, which prompted the campaign 'Where is Anuar?' (*Gde Anuar?*). He was silent for several months, and his video release about the details of his disappearance was very much anticipated. Thus, people felt disappointed that he used the opportunity not to speak up for politics but to promote his new business – a move that many activists viewed as insincere and a betrayal of the protest wave.
37 The very much anticipated video was released on 14 October 2019 on YouTube and is available here: www.youtube.com/watch?v=7W_mfRtvBsY.
38 However, the level of public subscribers only reflects the number of people who receive these updates without the fear of being tracked for following them; Instagram allows users to check content without subscribing, so the actual numbers for online engagement might be much bigger. However, these numbers

Social media has become an influential factor in protest waves and social movements (Ince, Rojas, and Davis 2017; Østbø 2017; Pearce 2014; Poell 2020) because it allows rapid access to censored information (Pearce 2014; Reuter and Szakonyi 2015). Moreover, social media allows dissemination from those who work without editorial board restrictions and those who are not dependent on advertisers, as major media outlets are.[39] Finally, social media is highly accessible and only requires a single device, usually a mobile phone, and internet access. It also becomes a source of self-liberation. As one of the protestors I interviewed revealed, she felt a sense of self-empowerment and liberation while sharing news about protestors' arrests, court hearings, and more planning for protestors. This is how she described it:

> These were the brightest moments when I mainly engaged with disseminating the information [about protestors' court hearings updates and more protests planned]. Because I think that the key thing back then [in April, May, and June 2019] was that many people lived in oblivion without having access to the information of what was going on, they did not have a trustworthy source of information. Back then, all I did was posting every day online about what was going on in courts. I posted and reposted all of the sources I could find and the ones I trusted. ... Then more and more people were sharing these [Instagram] stories and posts. ... At that time, people needed a trustworthy source of information. I felt a tremendous responsibility for it [sharing information from the source] and constantly sharing more and more information [online].[40]

---

are only available to the administrators of each social media account. For example, some people may not wish to subscribe to open opposition pages over fears of prosecution, as was the case with the social media account that published memes about Nazarbayev but which was deleted many times due to the infringement of the Law on the Father of the Nation.

[39] My sample interview with two anonymous editor of the Kazakhstani online portal, for example, revealed how many online media sources are dependent on *goszakaz* and how this is widespread knowledge in expert circles. *Goszakaz* is a budgeted project for publishing a number of pro-regime articles online. For many online media outlets, *goszakaz* and advertising remain the only source of income, as paid online media is not yet in vogue in Kazakhstan. However, both of the interviewees revealed that advertisers 'usually shy away' from the online media that is 'openly oppositional'. Thus, many online news and media portals in Kazakhstan have to depend either on *goszakaz* or remain less oppositional to remain economically profitable entities.

[40] Author's interview with anonymous activist of the Qazaq Koktemi, November 2020.

People started meeting online and offline and forming more stable networks. Courtroom meetings provided the necessary public sphere to start discussions about what to do next. This is how one of the participants of these discussions at the court, Assem Zhapisheva, remembered it:

> I spent one cold and rainy April day with a small group of people at the gates of the Almaty detention centre [*spetspriemnik*]. We were told that Asya and Beibarys were in danger, and we dropped everything that we were doing and came to the detention centre [where activists were held]. We did not have a specific goal in mind to organize a rally or to intimidate anyone. We stood there to help with anything we could do – [to offer] moral support to their parents. [Or to help] by reporting on the unlawfulness of the whole process; by calling human rights lawyers and lawyers or just in general, [to help] overcome the saddening feeling of disempowerment that was influencing [us] during these days. At some point, the car passing by stopped, and the fat driver squeamishly yelled at us, 'Go and work!' [*Rabotaite!*]. I don't know about the others, but this aggressive insult of the collective unconsciousness gave me some optimism – 'Go and work!' [as if] I heard, 'it will be long time until it changes, don't give up yet!'[41]

In these crucial moments of protests, the sense of the *collectivity* that many of these dispersed actors lacked emerged. It was a crucial moment for action:

> It was pretty clear at the moment from the very beginning since there was a capacity [to form a movement], and there was already a certain database or network [of activists] that has already existed. I mean that there were already people who were already visible and were important, [we knew some people] through some small projects, something else plus friends. And the flow of information that we started disseminating, we started gaining the power through the social media networks ... we realized [then] that we need to use this [power] more systematically and that we needed to start working in a more organized way. Within one to two months, we came up with [the Oyan, Qazaqstan declaration] – that's how much time was necessary.[42]

---

[41] Assem Zhapisheva's interview with the Village Kazakhstan on 30 May 2019, available in Russian here: www.the-village-kz.com/village/city/columns/5891-hipstery.
[42] Author's interview with Dimash Alzhanov.

In this moment of self-organization, Oyan, Qazaqstan felt like a breath of fresh air. This completely horizontal, de-institutionalized movement defied the formal rules of the regime. They announced that they did not have any plans to form a political party before the country democratized completely. They called for amendments to the law on mass rallies,[43] which required official approval for a planned rally, issued by the local municipality after the official procedure of filing the request. Anyone could become a member of Oyan, Qazaqstan and engage at any level and workload they preferred, with a provision of member confidentiality if necessary.

Most importantly, Oyan, Qazaqstan did not seek a monopoly over the protest agenda or to take over the Qazaq Koktemi discourses and field dynamics. The latter remained a field open to moulding and changing without being rigidly rooted in a specific wave or context or becoming dependent on one particular personality or leader. In part, it was achieved because all members of the field that Qazaq Koktemi became kept it separated from claims to leadership or ownership. Even Asya Tulesova, who had every chance to become the face of the Kazakh Spring, openly refused to take on that role. The Kazakh Spring has many faces, many of them covered by the secrecy and anonymity that must be respected, and who might come out in the public purview once they decide to do so.

9 June 2019: Election Day and the Street Protests

The first election day without *elbasy*, Nursultan A. Nazarbayev, on the ballot, was historic for many Kazakhstanis. The polling stations attracted an unprecedented number of international and local, independent observers.[44] Given the tremendous changes of the protest wave, many young people who were far from engaging with the

---

[43] The 'Law of the Republic of Kazakhstan on the Procedures of Arrangement and Holding of Peaceful Gatherings, Rallies, Marches, Pickets, and Demonstrations' (as of 17 March 1995) requires official approval for any rally organized on the territory of the Republic of Kazakhstan. In contradiction to this law, the Constitution of the Republic of Kazakhstan states that all citizens are entitled to the right of free assembly and rally. When Oyan, Qazaqstan activists protest, they appeal to the constitutional right instead of the law on peaceful gatherings, which they consider unconstitutional.

[44] According to the Kazakhstan's Central Elections Committee, there were more than 1,000 international observers.

political field started volunteering to be independent observers. I interviewed a number of those volunteers[45] who were also active online – they shared videos, stories from the polling stations, vote counting, and the final results. Even those who were not affiliated with any protest movements shared the view at the time that they were 'excited to be part of the process and to know that we contributed counting the votes without the usual deceptions'.[46] Was this sudden increase in activism and civic engagement part of the goals of the first wave of Qazaq Koktemi protests? I asked several eyewitnesses to recount the narrative of those days from their own perspective. For many of them, the electoral observation was an eye-opening experience to the ways regimes staged and operated elections to their own gain:

Elections were scheduled for 9 June, and we [within Oyan, Qazaqstan] started active preparations. Many people asked us what we could do in order to change the sequence of events? It turned out that there are many NGOs that work with preparing independent electoral observers. Many people started attending this [electoral] training, and it was easy because these were scheduled on the weekend so that we could go after work hours. It was essential to serve as an independent observer and broadcast the process live online on social media for all to see it. I served at one polling station close to the city centre, but the Internet was very weak that day because they were blocking it.

Through the live broadcasting, everyone could see what was going on at other polling stations, and we could see how our friends and other independent observers were working elsewhere. My polling station was quiet and calm, but other people asked for help directly online because they were circumvented in their ability to observe. Some people were told to sit in one place and observe only from there, others did not have access to the protocols, and some were prohibited from broadcasting live, and they announced that on their social media pages. At this moment, people quickly communicated with each other, and [independent observers] could go from one polling station to another to help out someone who was facing problems at their station. For example, my colleague [at the station] went to help Suinbike, and I decided to stay till my polling station was closed even though almost nothing happened at our end.

[45] My count of independent observers whom I interviewed was ten narrative interviews, of which four were not directly affiliated with Qazaq Koktemi. Most of these interviews took place in the summer of 2019 and 2020.
[46] Author's interview with anonymous political activist from Astana, August 2020.

Many people came [to the polling station], some people I knew. Some voters behaved strangely, and it was visible immediately. They quickly took the ballot [*bulleten'*], quickly voted, took pictures of their voting [for Tokayev] and left. Why were they doing it? Because then they had to send the photo of their ballots to their employer as proof that they had voted for Tokayev. Not only public servants did it – it's erroneous to think that only teachers are forced to vote as obliged [*kak nado*]. In reality, many private companies that are somehow affiliated with the regime are in the same space. Their employees also had to vote for Tokayev and then prove it by sending photos of their votes [via working chats on WhatsApp].[47]

It was also a moment of mixed feelings of hope, because it was the first time when a supposedly opposition candidate, Amirzhan Kosanov, was allowed to run for office, and of feelings of engagement. Many independent observers flooded the stations because they wanted not only to see the change but to be part of it:

> *Diana T. Kudaibergenova (DTK)*: [asking a question about post-election protests planned before 9 June]: How did you know that the elections would not be fair even though it was the first time without [Nazarbayev]?
>
> *Activist*: Unfortunately, in Kazakhstan, I cannot imagine the situation when we would have fair and open elections here.[48]
>
> ...
>
> *DTK*: What did you feel on the election day?
>
> *Activist*: In that moment, we all felt that we were part of some important process. We were all involved in the political process. For many, it was the first time they experienced something like this. Tokayev won at my polling station, but Kosanov was very close to the win as well – the discrepancy [in vote] was very minimal. It was the first time when the pro-regime candidate was winning the elections without the usual 90 per cent barrier [of votes for him]. We were all very inspired [*My vse byli voodushevleni*].[49]

For many of those who participated as independent observers, it was the first time they could feel their voice was counting, and it was also a way to engage with activism, seeing the tangible results through their work. In the words of Fariza Ospan, elections never lost democratic

---

[47] Author's interview with a former Oyan, Qazaqstan activist, 23 July 2020.
[48] Author's interview with anonymous Oyan, Qazaqstan activist, June 2020.
[49] Author's interview with a former Oyan, Qazaqstan activist, 23 July 2020.

importance to her, and seeing her vote stolen at the previous presidential elections led her to the fight that eventually made her one of the leading faces of the Qazaq Koktemi:

DTK: How did you become an activist?

Fariza Ospan: These were the 2015 early presidential elections, and I went to the polling station [to vote] in the evening because voting was open till 8 pm. I went at 6 pm, but they told me that someone else had voted for me already and counted my vote.[50] I thought to myself, 'Really?!' But at the time, I didn't know what to do in these situations, but I definitely knew that this was wrong. But that day, I just turned around and left. Then I started looking up different organizations online – those [NGOs] protecting rights, public associations, and this was how I found the Youth Information Service of Kazakhstan (MISK). I started coming to their events, I became their volunteer, and in that same year, in 2015, I graduated from the school of human rights and finished my first project against domestic violence.[51]

The electoral process and activists' engagement in it brought many systemic shifts in the minds of those who thought that no change was possible. When independent observers started pouring out photos and videos of electoral protocols from their stations all over Kazakhstan, demonstrating unprecedented numbers for the 'alternative candidate' Amirzhan Kosanov, Kazakh internet space was heated to the maximum despite the internet blockages. Photos and comments about the 'protest vote' remained sources of inspiration for a possible change even after the news of *kosanovshina* (see Chapter 1) flooded the Internet. In the context of distrust, Kazakhstani voters relied more heavily on personal networks and sources – WhatsApp groups and Telegram chats – and Facebook and Instagram kept on sharing the videos and news provided by ordinary people who witnessed the change at their polling stations. As many of my respondents later described it, the first post-election night felt 'euphoric', as for the first time in their life, they could feel a wave of possible democratization and unity with thousands of like-minded citizens whom they never met but whom they watched online.

---

[50] What Ospan described here was in fact a practice of the staged elections when those voters who did not show up to the polling stations automatically voted for President Nazarbayev.
[51] Author's interview with Fariza Ospan, November 2020.

The role and the impact of each independent observer stayed with many for months and encouraged them to continue working as electoral observers:

> *DTK*: Yes, there was euphoria after the initial vote count because people could see how Kosanov was winning at many polling stations 'for real' even though it was not the vote for him but the protest vote. But after the Central Electoral Committee announced the results [where pro-regime candidate Kassym-Zhomart Tokayev won with the official 71 per cent of votes], this euphoria must have been *en passé* ...

> *Activist*: For me, it was the feeling of excitement and inspiration that did not pass right after the elections – it stayed with me. It was the feeling and realization that I can contribute and influence political processes in my own country as a citizen and [it is] not just the state [*gosudarstvo*] that is completely alienated from people. I kept this feeling with me till today, and I plan to work as an [independent] electoral observer at the parliamentary elections [of January 2021].[52]

What is ubiquitous in the wake of any staged elections in authoritarian regimes is the tug of war between the incumbent regime and the international observers. Still, the stories of citizen engagement often fade or never appear in official reports of either side. As the ODIHR (Office for Democratic Institutions and Human Rights) final report on the 2019 presidential elections in Kazakhstan read, the OSCE (Organization for Security and Cooperation in Europe) observers (whose positionality and impartiality are usually unquestionable) had concerns about the local independent observers, even though there is no official OSCE or ODIHR procedure to check them:

> Several organizations deployed observers, including most notably Next.kz, 'Wings of Liberty' [*Erkindik Kanatty*], the Youth Information Service of Kazakhstan (MISK), and their civil society 'Echo'. In the run-up to elections, the observation platform *Amanat* announced plans to deploy observers in almost every polling station (some 9,000 observers). A considerable number of ODIHR EOM interlocutors questioned the independence of this observer group, citing political affiliation.[53]

[52] Author's interview with an anonymous activist, June 2020. [QL], anonymous.
[53] ODIHR Early Presidential Election 9 June 2019, ODIHR Election Observation Mission final report, November 2019, p. 21. Available at: www.osce.org/files/f/documents/2/7/434459_0.pdf. The problem with ODIHR reporting on independent observers is that the report lacked factual background to prove any affiliations, but with this statement and one more statement in the beginning of

My aim in writing out the narratives of independent observers is to demonstrate the type of opinions, moods, and feelings that were experienced on the eve of and after the election day. The voices and aspirations of all those who were engaging and felt the urge to continue their political activism were simply erased from the official discourse. My findings, on the contrary, demonstrate how this experience and engagement led to further politicization and activism in significant groups of those who were previously depoliticized – namely, the youth of Kazakhstan or the first post-independence generation. These were the prominent faces of Oyan, Qazaqstan, who spoke publicly, and at the time of the movement's presentation at the beginning of June, the oldest of them was in his early thirties and the youngest still in high school.

It is the practice of political engagement that I am interested in exploring because it is often overlooked or downplayed by the importance of quantifying the protest and the change of attitude rather than contextualizing it. This can be achieved only through the long narratives of those who take part in these interventions and protests, because these processes have a lot of closed networks where communication is private and trusted due to the pressures of the totalizing institutions of authoritarianism:

> In these political processes [at the beginning of Qazaq Koktemi] there was a lot of the personal [*bylo ochen mnogo lichnogo*] – all these groups and communities that sympathized with Asya [Tulesova] and Beibarys [Tolymbetov] saw in [activists' imprisonment] a very private reflection of the way their own rights were discriminated against. But participation in political processes [in Kazakhstan] is not safe. All these public interventions and actions, public engagement – it was all available as a visible protest; with all these *seruens* [walking protest] where people gathered to speak, communicate, but from the outside, they looked like some cultural events and not rallies. [Summer 2019 *seruens*] had songs, music, discussions, and walking tours in public spaces in different cities [of Kazakhstan] – *seruens* are still popular in different regions,[54] for example. Many people within the movement [of Oyan, Qazaqstan] wanted and still want to remain

---

the report they shed negative light on all independent observers in Kazakhstan without any provision of justifiable division or proof of any affiliations.

[54] My respondent here used the term '*v regionah*' which means in different regions of Kazakhstan, which is divided into fourteen regions and the three republican cities of Almaty, Astana, and Shymkent. I discuss this distinction between regions and central cities of Kazakhstan in the latter part of the next chapter, when I look at the phenomenon of Almaty protesting.

anonymous, and that's why we should not talk about them. Everyone discussed things in [private] chats and on the movement's platform on social media. ...

Oyan [Qazaqstan] became this type of movement because there was a lot of impulses. At the time, many different movements emerged and declared themselves as movements – Respublika, the Kakharman movement in Astana, but many later disappeared. Oyan [Qazaqstan] immediately did not envision itself as a political party, [we did not have] political ambitions – it was a community of people who wanted to change something. The [Kazakh] regime has its own parameters with which they evaluate different actors in connection to whether they 'threaten' or 'do not threaten' the regime itself and its stability. As soon as they [the regime] understood that Oyan [Qazaqstan] did not have political ambitions, then they positioned us according to the parameters 'does not threaten' and did not prohibit us but started repressing people from the movement directly, individually.[55]

The immediate post-election period was marked by several days of different protests and stand-offs, mainly in Almaty and some in other cities. These were spontaneous protests, when people took to the streets and to the main squares to protest. In the moment, the process looked very chaotic. People from different sides and groups protested and called for their supporters to join forces in specific parts of the city. All of that communication was done solely through social media. These were both private (chats, messengers, and private groups on WhatsApp, Viber, Telegram, and others) and public (mainly Instagram and Facebook) social media channels of communication. One of the biggest mobilizations caused by the famous Kazakh *aityshy*[56] Rinat Zaitov. Zaitov announced the protests and planned to organize his own movement in the wake of protests about the rigged elections. He was detained and interrogated at the police station in downtown Almaty, where several hundreds of his supporters gathered demanding his release. These were mainly Kazakh-speaking and nationalist-leading groups of supporters of Zaitov's *aitys* practices.[57]

---

[55] Author's interview with OQL, August 2020, anonymous.
[56] An *Aityshy* is an improvising poet who takes part in public *aytis* contests, which are traditional nomadic contests. See Dubuisson 2017 and Salimjan 2017 for more on *Aitys* and *Aityshy*.
[57] Different news agencies – for example, Al Jazeera – reported around 200 supporters outside the police station, but my respondents who were present at the mobilization reported up to 500 protestors overall, of all sorts (including those who knew nothing about Zaitov and his oeuvre).

That particular mobilization was widely broadcast and commented on online, as almost everyone gathered there had a mobile phone and mobile Internet. Many activists were communicating and asking each other for help and more information. In the late evening, Zaitov was released and addressed his supporters right outside the police station, asking them to calm down and go home. But the crowd, which consisted of mainly Kazakh-speaking men of various ages, were not ready to leave unheard. Their demands varied in voices, tones, and agenda – anything from supporting Zaitov to calls for justice, with openly Kazakh nationalist agenda and anti-regime slogans. The crowd was neither coherent nor organized – it was a spontaneous yet potent outburst of the protest mood that neither ordinary policemen nor Zaitov himself could tame. Protestors divided and moved down to Tole bi Street[58], where the whole perimeter was already secured by the special forces (*spetsnaz*) awaiting any protestors.[59]

The mobilization was brutally suppressed, and the most vocal activists were harassed by the police; many were detained, adding to the hundreds of already detained protestors in Almaty and Nur-Sultan (Astana) in the first three days post-election on 9 to 11 June 2019. With these coercive techniques, the regime aimed to suppress the protest wave completely by locating and identifying the leaders and

---

[58] As my respondents and some eyewitnesses of the protest noted, the whole symbolism of Almaty's downtown streets played an interesting role here. Three of the 'downstream' streets next to the police station where Zaitov was held are named after three of the Kazakh khanate's famous *bii* – a type of steppe judge – Tole bi, Kazybek bi, and Aiteke bi. These three figures were the symbols of the ethnonationalist history of wisdom and fair trials in the eighteenth-century Kazakh khanate. This whole nationalist symbolism and the belief in the 'steppe democracy' of the nomadic pre-colonial society played an important role for those protestors who associated themselves with Zaitov's Kazakh nationalist agenda and their search for justice.

[59] At the time, it was not clear who exactly was protesting and if the protest was at all organized by existing political forces. Because all of the communication happened online and thus required access to these special networks of information through WhatsApp groups or Instagram, different audiences were receiving different information. Those who followed famous Instagram blogger Madina Musina saw that she was with a group of Oyan, Qazaqstan activists, and those closer to the Kazakh-speaking content reported on the closest people in Zaitov's circles. Finally, there was also a lot of disinformation and fear spread in personal and private chats around the neighbourhood where the protestors were located at each moment to the effect that they were looters or dangerous people. Many Almaty dwellers received the information to stay inside and avoid clashes with the special police forces.

the main spaces of protest and suppressing them. Rinat Zaitov himself stopped broadcasting on any issue apart from asking his supporters to stop protesting and stay calm. The regime, however, could not completely suppress private online networking, as Kazakhstan had already turned into the 'WhatsApp nation' long before June 2019. Messages and conspiracy theories were spread on family, neighbourhood chats, and collegial communication and spread in a geometrical progression across the whole country and beyond. Anyone who had access to WhatsApp, in the villages, in the big cities, all over the country, had access to the buzzing online discussions. Just as in the case of the Arab Spring, access to mobile Internet and social media platforms became a viable platform for voicing protest moods and sharing information.

In these moments of distrust and disinformation, it was important for the new political actors to sustain the support and trust of their followers. To many, it meant a complete disassociation from previous opposition forces and names, especially a complete distinction from the DVK movement and Mukhtar Ablyazov, who was trying to use any opportunity to claim the protest wave.[60] For people inside Oyan, Qazaqstan, it was not a question of association with the regime or its 'inside-regime' opposition but a completely new direction for the reforms. In the words of Dimash Alzhanov, one of the leading voices inside Oyan, Qazaqstan, it was a crucial moment to explain to everyone that the new era of doing politics had emerged:

> DTK: What are your differences from the old opposition, the opposition that emerged and existed even before Amirzhan Kosanov revealed who he

---

[60] As soon as mass protests started in Kazakhstan, Ablyazov called on his supporters to join the protest actions at exactly the same locations but with their own banners. For many commentators, it created confusion as to who was supporting whom, and earlier on there were some unfortunate conclusions drawn that many protest movements were connected with Ablyazov, even though it was far from the truth. When I interviewed Oyan, Qazaqstan activists (former and current), all of them opposed any connection to the exiled oligarch, and some even became angry that they were associated with this name.
However, it did not stop him from discrediting almost any protest movement by trying to claim (similarly to ISIS tactics) that any contentious act was connected to him and his deeds. To many Qazaq Koktemi activists, such a connection was more than an insult – they took it as a direct attack on their agenda, as they wanted nothing to do with Ablyazov and his unknown goals (*neponyatnye tseli*). For example, some activists told me that, when during their arrests policemen asked them about their connection to Ablyazov, the activists took it as an insult.

was after the 2019 presidential elections? What is your difference from the opposition of the mid-2000s [when there was still public trust in that opposition]?

Dimash Alzhanov: You see, we don't aim to become part of the system ...

DTK: In your opinion, was the opposition always part of the system?

Dimash Alzhanov: No, but the way [the opposition] positions itself right now ... because oppositions were different. If you look at the time of the 1990s, the dissident times, then the emergence of [Akezhan] Kazhegeldin and then again, this attempt to enter the system [regime].

DTK: To reform the system from within?

Dimash Alzhanov: Yes, but I seriously doubt the ability of this regime to adapt, and to be completely honest, then maybe truly it requires a significant internal shock for this space of opportunities and changes to emerge [inside the political regime itself]. This is why our primary goals are to form a sustainable understanding of all these categories of rights and democracy. Because [ordinary] people still don't understand why the electoral system is needed, how it forms and influences the formation of parties and people's representation, and as a result – how it informs the decision-making within the state. This connection is completely absent [in public perception]. And we don't want to find ourselves in the situation again when interest groups are formed, the types of groups that you can hardly call parties no matter how institutionalized they'd be ... In other words, even if some opposition exists, it is a constant trade-off for [acquiring] the space and resources [from the regime]. But [the emergence of institutionalized opposition] does not mean more democratization, more procedural and rule-based practices. We [Oyan, Qazaqstan] are trying to move away from this trend to [explain] formal institutions and why these are needed in reality. Here we are also attempting to explain it to the public. I understand that these are very complex and amorphous categories. We ourselves are facing these problems because for the ordinary folk, it is easier to personify [and accept] the party with a specific person and live with these [authoritarian] categories rather than accept [political and democratic] categories. But we will see how it will work out, and this is why it is so crucial that we engage young people. If you noticed, we had a number of meetings and discussions just for these questions to be heard and for the people to get used to the level of these discussions or at least for them to start asking these questions. This is important because conventional media content is simply horrendous.

DTK: Yes, [the official media] is a controlled content that the regime wants and uses for its own goals – that's understandable.

Dimash Alzhanov: Yes. That's why we don't have the aim to fight for more extensive resources – we do not address this goal. Our goal is to try to break all these actions and the regime's strategy, to break it in order to leave this vicious circle of the limbo type that we find ourselves in at the moment and in order to have more opportunities and more space [for change], in order to provide journalists with more security in order to report on these issues, to give more content and dynamics to everything that is happening [in the country].[61]

This strategy of addressing the regime in its formalized and institutionalized practices to fight for more democratization was the type of political engagement and vision that differentiated the Oyan, Qazaqstan movement from many other emerging political forces. Oyan activists no longer believed in dismantling the regime by getting rid of several of its personalities or through their ability to enter the regime – these were the attempts of the old opposition, including Mukhtar Ablyazov's dreams of all-Kazakhstani revolution. Forces inside Oyan, Qazaqstan quickly realized the need to attack the regime through information wars and physical mobilizations where possible. Their street protests were calculated and varied, and they coincided with messages and discourses rather than dates per se. For example, while Oyan, Qazaqstan continued to protest on the symbolic day of 16 December, they expanded the agenda to claim that the Nazarbayev regime was just a revamped continuation of the repressive Soviet machine that killed protestors in December 1986 and then in December 2011 (discussed in more detail in Chapters 6 and 7). While Oyan, Qazaqstan became the hybrid public sphere with their significant online presence on social media platforms and secret chats, these discussions were and remain battlefields of opinions and are far from a coherent and smooth process of consensus. I discuss their strategies of re-imagining the political and their internal conflicts and developments in the next chapter.

---

[61] Author's interview with Dimash Alzhanov, 17 January 2020.

3 | *Deconstructing* Vlast'

The critical shift in doing politics in Kazakhstan came when activists changed their position on how they perceive the state. Unlike their predecessors or other commentators on dictatorships, people inside the Qazaq Koktemi field have very critical perspectives and understandings when it comes to dictatorial power relations. In their re-imagination of these relations, the locus of the problem is in seeing the state in a deep connection with the regime to the extent that these two distinct entities become one. My respondents from Oyan, Qazaqstan and in the Qazaq Koktemi field in general believe that the state needs to be saved from the regime, like a living body needs to get rid of cancerous cells, no matter how advanced their colonization of the body. In this chapter, I detail these complex power perceptions and relations to construct an argument about the importance of 'seeing the state' or, in other words, conceptualizing the force that protestors are fighting either against or for. The change of optics is crucial in their processes of contention. It is one thing to fight against police brutality in an autocratic context and to see the police as inseparable from the state and another to 'see' how the police are part of the regime and the two are simply occupying the state. The different perception of state allows many Kazakh Spring protestors to locate their strategies in fighting against the system and providing a democratic state rather than fighting against the regime-cum-state in its totality.

Who Is *Vlast'* Here?

There are distinct ways of conceptualizing governance under authoritarian and democratic contexts. In the former, governance is institutionalized formally (Gandhi 2008; Gandhi and Przeworski 2007; Gel'man 2015; Hale 2011), but decision-making within these institutions largely depends on the power of rulers who are not elected but selected. Many scholars studying post-Soviet Eurasia (which has somehow become a synonym for the authoritarian East and thus requires careful de-categorization)[1] pointed out its type of patron–client system where personalities play a crucial role (Fisun 2012; Gel'man 2016; Hale 2014). I find the way of looking at what power does to you (as a citizen) or from an everyday perspective is the missing piece in studies of authoritarianism. The genealogy and the guiding discourse that makes one protest or not protest is all encapsulated in the understanding of *vlast'* and how to relate to it.

In discussions with my respondents, this understanding of *vlast'* – translated formally as 'power' but also as the authoritarian regime – often appeared to define the complex state–regime–society relations in Kazakhstan. In one of the interviews, activist Medina Bazargali proposed differentiating between *vlast'* as a power capacity and *vlast'* as a negative connotation of the discourse of disempowerment that pushes citizens to view the regime as the ultimate power. For example, in describing the situation in the courtrooms, Bazargali described law-enforcement officers – all those wearing police uniform – as 'people who have *vlast'* [power as capacity], and they *know* that they have this power. They know that they can do whatever they want, and nothing would happen to them.'[2] People in Kazakhstan – and not only activists – have a very specific understanding of power as the capacity that law enforcement or any other 'man in uniform' can have by virtue of working within the system that in itself is also power – the type of power that the regime embodies (*vlast'*). *Vlast'* as disempowerment came from connecting or even equating state power to regime power and not seeing a way out of the vicious circle where the plural *vlasti* (the regime and, in another translation, people in the regime) create a perception of their totalizing form of power where no one else can change anything. This perception is very hard to fight against because the social reality is imbued with it, and everything around one's everyday life is a constant reminder of *vlast'* in the person of Nazarbayev. Qazaq Koktemi protestors themselves were battling with these complexities:

I recently read about this theme [of power] – stop saying *vlasti* [the power or authorities] because power [*vlast'*] is this concept that does not exist, and you

---

[1] As Juan Linz (2000: 50) wrote, 'unfortunately, we have to use names for realities that we are just attempting to define'.
[2] Author's interview with Medina Bazargali, July 2020.

need to mention the real names [of politicians]. When I say, 'the state', I, of course, first of all, mean the system that [Nursultan] Nazarbayev built. It is a clan-based system where there is no transparency, and everything happens behind closed doors, no one [among the power elites] can make decisions [on their own] – everyone is dependent on each other, and in the end, everyone depends on one person. Therefore we constantly have these never-ending and pseudo-political debates around *shaprashty* clans.[3] Do you know about this? About all these intra-elite struggles [*bor'ba*] and all these things? I mostly mean the system that this person [Nazarbayev] has built and [in doing so] I consider that given his [Nazarbayev's] old age, considering that even if he dies, this system won't collapse because it has its own internal mechanisms [that would ensure its continuous work]. In general, all post-Soviet states have these *systems*.[4]

Using *vlast'*, or *vlasti* in the plural, to explain their everyday life experiences, frameworks, and the navigation of their actions can be explained by the normalization of this powerful discourse. Michel Foucault's concept of 'discursive formation' conceptualizes it as different statements, symbols, discourses, and understandings surrounding a particular form and category that is normalized – for example, madness, sexuality, and so on. The same happens with the category of *vlast'*, which can be equated most directly to the regime but is often and quite incoherently ascribed to either specific, powerful people within the regime – the president or the main patron of the authoritarian system. *Vlast'*, or the plural *vlasti*, also can be used more ambiguously for anyone close to the regime but not clearly connected to it – for example, a famous oligarch who may or may not be directly connected to the regime.[5] As this book will demonstrate, many of the activists

---

[3] *Shaprashty* is one of the traditional Kazakh tribes within the Great Horde (*Uly Zhuz*). Kazakh is traditionally divided into tribes (and within them into sub-tribes); tribes then form three Hordes – the Great, Middle, and Small *Zhuz*. President Nazarbayev comes from *shaprashty* tribe, and the current president Tokayev comes from *jalayir* tribe, both of which are within the *Uly Zhuz* – the Great Horde. What my respondent refers to here is the commonly shared view that, under President Nazarbayev, most leading political positions were given to the members of his tribe, which eventually created the colloquial term *shaprashtyntsy* – the ones that come from *shaprashty* tribe – which instantly signifies their power position in the political and social contexts of Nazarbayev's Kazakhstan.

[4] Author's interview with Oyan, Qazaqstan activist in July 2020. This excerpt from our interview should be read within its historic context – when Nazarbayev was still in power (albeit in a position of the special advisor to the president and when he resided in his Library).

[5] Though it is often possible, see Cooley and Heathershaw 2017.

called law-enforcement officers and institutions *vlast'* as well because they considered them part of the regime system of coercion and oppression, but also operation.

So, this category of *vlast'* is a wide, encompassing one, though I mainly translate it as 'the authoritarian regime' in the contexts of this discussion. The interview with Assem Zhapisheva[6] demonstrates this normalization of *vlast'* as the effect and the operational explanation of the authoritarian regime. Our discussion was fruitful. Those existing within this system of knowledge might normalize it and work within its frameworks to explain their everyday reality. Fewer of them try to criticize not just the effect of *vlast'* on them but the whole concept at its core. Thus goes the argument Medina Bazargali made to me in an interview, claiming that 'using the term *vlast'* is making them [the regime] even more powerful' through the normalization of the language and perceptions of overpowering citizens in an authoritarian context. One item on the protestors' agenda is thus to break this vicious cycle and to disempower the *vlast'* by describing its inadequacy, unlawfulness, and, as a result, its weakness and fragility. Central Asian artists were better equipped with this critical understanding and apparatus, describing their respective repressive regimes as myopic and weak – almost like a raging bull, with all the power but lacking a sense of direction or wisdom.[7] The artists within Qazaq Koktemi thus were using the courtroom spectacles to demonstrate these fragilities and inadequacies, though they too were vulnerable to the widespread unlawfulness of the regime that went as far as kidnapping activists and intimidating them without their lawyers in police stations.

In describing the context of the emergence of Qazaq Koktemi so far, I have focused on the nature of authoritarianism and the regime dynamics with Nazarbayev's personalistic rule, the stagnant context

---

[6] In our later conversations, Assem shared a great idea of hers, that true decolonization would start in Kazakhstan once Nazarbayev's legacy had been destroyed, and the whole system he built would disappear, since he himself is the product of Soviet coloniality.

[7] In my forthcoming project on protest art in the region, I conceptualize how local contemporary artists envisioned Karimov's and Nazarbayev's regimes as old machines of repressions that were too slow and too large to fit the realities of ever-changing social relations. In one of the interviews in that project, Uzbek artist Vyacheslav Akhunov, for example, described the Uzbek regime (as he termed the state at the time) as a 'simulacrum' of state institutions working for the will and benefit of the 'mafia' regime. I discuss that further in my forthcoming book.

of the opposition field prior to his resignation, and the ways that Qazaq Koktemi was able to change the rules of the game that largely contributed to this stagnation. In this chapter, I present the way activists of the Qazaq Koktemi conceptualize the regime and its power and how and why this conceptualization influences their strategies and tactics of political engagement. I argue that the innovative approaches of Qazaq Koktemi are dictated by the radical shifts of perceiving the 'political' – the 'differentiation between government and the governed'.[8]

The activists pushed for a better clarification of these definitions of government and governed but also a clear distinction between the 'state' as a purely neutral and institutionally interwoven entity and the 'regime' – the group of autocrats who occupy the state. Thus, their call is for the saving of the state through the overthrow or eradication of the regime – from the removal of the literal bodies of autocrats in flesh and in bronze (Nazarbayev himself) to getting rid of the value system that these autocrats have brought up – widespread corruption, informalization of the political and everyday life, and the diminishing of the rule of law. This is the ethos shared by different actors within Qazaq Koktemi – bringing the state to the forefront of the agenda and saving the state from the figurative cancer that authoritarianism has become for the overall structure of the state. Thus, the Oyan, Qazaqstan declaration (see Chapter 2) reflects this ethos throughout the measures they propose but also in the closing paragraph that has guided their development since the inception:

> The historical moment is upon us today, the moment of truth and awakening when the free citizens [of Kazakhstan] need to claim back their lost rights and freedoms, [it is the time] when the state needs to choose the path of sustainable development in all spheres of life. ... We need to live in a democratic, independent and free country! Oyan! [Wake up!].[9]

The shift in 'seeing the state' from a different perspective and not completely encapsulating it in the regime alone allowed many of the activists and protests to go past the stagnant frameworks of opposition

---

[8] Defined succinctly by Anthony Giddens in relation to Emile Durkheim's political writings (1986: 1).
[9] Declaration available in Russian at https://vlast.kz/novosti/33541-v-almaty-prezentovali-grazdanskuu-deklaraciu-oan-kazahstan.html, English translations provided by the author.

political power figures and rather fight for extensive structural changes. The activists of the Qazaq Koktemi I interviewed were more acutely aware of the fact that the removal of one minister or one oligarch was not enough, as a whole new generation of autocrats was ready to fill the vacant space. In many ways, the long-awaited departure of President Nazarbayev, and seeing how it brought no changes but rather encouraged more sultanistic approaches to regime development, helped this new wave of protestors to 'wake up' and not rely on the sort of political chess game of the regime.

The removal of one figure in authoritarian regimes, even of the leading figure, does not always lead to its dismantling, even if it avoids worse scenarios when elite reshuffling might lead to coups and worsened repressive contexts. The Kazakh Spring learned lessons from the many other protests waves that happened long before it, including the most famous, the Arab Spring, which taught them that revolutions need to call for structural political transformations beyond the overthrow of the authoritarian regime. And as many of the activists in Almaty told me in the interviews, educating people to stand up for their rights, forming a civil society, and loud and widespread demands for functional institutions was and remained the only solution they saw in their attempts 'to change the system'. Now this approach was significantly different from that of the power-hungry opposition leaders of the mid-2000s, who wanted to use the protest as a way for them to negotiate with the ruling regime for better positions.[10] What Qazaq Koktemi and movements within it attempt to do is to change the way ordinary people perceive authoritarian power – *vlast'*. Activists, in their own and often differentiated ways (as I demonstrate through conflicts within Oyan, Qazaqstan later in this chapter), propose to save the state from the authoritarian regime by separating the two in a meaningful way.

---

[10] Even before *Kosanovshina* (see Chapter 1), the example of the prominent and well-spoken Alikhan Baimenov, who was part of the initial DVK movement and then a member of the ruling group of the oppositional Ak Zhol party, proved this case. Baimenov started a fully fledged campaign to stand in the 2006 presidential elections, divided the Ak Zhol party, and was rumoured to have eventually 'sold' it to pro-regime forces, leading to a major discrediting of the opposition forces at the time. Baimenov was then given a position in the presidential administration and now heads the Agency for Public Service. He denies all allegations against him.

Problematizing *Vlast'*

Thinking of regimes as 'the set of very basic formal and informal rules of choosing leaders and policies'[11] is a very useful outlook because it allows us to analyse them from the *how* perspective. It allows procedural and narrative-based approaches to the ways in which regimes are constructed in the first place and how these authoritarian entities survive over long periods of time. This procedural approach also helps to analyse and explain why people outside the regime – the 'ordinary folk'[12] who do not really have the possibility to engage in the election or selection process of the regime – then view it as absolute power – *vlast'*.

Vlast' becomes a monolithic image and a very concrete entity of power relations; it can be embodied by specific people – president, ruler, his family, as well as a local governor – and thus when embodied, it is also dispersed; essentially, *vlast'* is a reminder of the citizenry's disempowerment in the face of government that was supposed to work in their favour but instead works in favour of the few, the political elites in power.

I use the concept of *vlast'* in a relational manner – to describe a particular situation when one is subject to domination (e.g., police arrest or having to follow specific rules even if deemed undemocratic) or when one is living outside the circle of political power. In other words, authoritarian conditions do not allow people to directly elect their political representatives and to have significant involvement in political decision-making, and this condition of disempowerment makes them choose strategies of actively and symbolically disengaging themselves from the field of power. This is done through the language that describes the divide, the gap between the rules and the ruled. For example, there are significant differences between the ways people close to the regime used to describe President Nazarbayev in private discussions as '01' [*nol'-perviy*][13] and those for whom that level of

---

[11] Geddes, Wright, and Franz 2018: 5.
[12] As one of the former advisors to Nazarbayev once told me, this is how the elites label citizens.
[13] *Nol'-perviy* means the person who is the primary leader in the country, and the number zero before the 'first' highlighted the fact that there was no one above Nazarbayev formally (in the structure of the state) or informally (in a structure of inner-elite secret networks). My first encounter with this concept was through the discussions (and often brags) by secret police officers in Almaty in the late

connection was impossible and thus were distanced from the president through the cold distinction of calling him the *vlast'*.

This mechanism of 'seeing' power, state, regime, the president, or *vlast'* through a specific and locally established discourse of how one relates to the authoritarian power defines one's approach to living with it. Everyday life under authoritarian regimes is inevitably influenced by the conditions of authoritarianism, but each individual's *relation* to it and approach to living with it is different. These differences can be explained quite obviously by class or positionality in close or farther relation to the power elites, which I just described through the use of language identifying President Nazarbayev, for example. And this can be explained as a consequence of class and positionality because these differences will be related to levels of education, value systems, and access to specific communities. Take, for example, such a ubiquitous concept as 'fear' when describing authoritarianism. Do people fear the same thing and in the same way when facing real or imagined punishment from the authoritarian state? Do they structure their fear and the consequences of their actions (disciplining techniques) in the same way, through the same narratives? Or simply put, do we all, as citizens, fear the same thing when we fear the authoritarian regime? Fear is a great category to demonstrate this relational approach to authoritarianism, which differentiates on each level of the person and their community based on the above-mentioned influences. We fear differently because we are all afraid of losing different things and at different levels. Someone might fear losing a job whereas someone else fears repercussions (whether real or imagined) for their whole family.

I asked many of my respondents at length what kinds of fears they had when facing the authoritarian state machine, the violent *vlast'*, in the form of the arresting police or other members of law enforcement. Is bodily harm the first type of fear that one rationalizes? At what time does this rationality kicks in? The body does play an important role in

---

2000s. Before that, this type of fraternal concept of having a closer relationship to the regime and to the president himself was expressed through the nickname 'Nazik' (for Nazarbayev) in the mid-2000s, which was at first astonishing and then normalized in the form of anecdotes. For example, the punchline of one anecdote finished 'for the few it is Nazik but for the rest it is Nursultan Abishevich Nazarbayev'. Contrary to these personalized and private nicknames that were used by those who wanted to be seen as intimately close to the regime, those who wanted to distance themselves from it call Nazarbayev 'NAN' for short, or in extreme cases, *shal* (the old man).

fears and in calculating risks before engaging in a protest, and I discuss this in further detail in Chapter 6. But surprisingly, physical pain was not the first thing that scared my respondents. The realization of the possible danger and physical pain from protests came to some of them only when they saw police brutality in other cases, for example, in the Belarusian post-election protests that started in August 2020. But in other interviews, especially with people who were not activists or the 'usual suspects' at political rallies, fear of the post-protest contexts came from elsewhere – from the realization of how much they could lose in economic and symbolic capital if they ended up in court on political charges.

These disciplining practices of fear are constructed in relation to the regime's informal channels of repression. Simply put, it becomes commonly shared knowledge, which most people know about despite never having to experience it. For example, there was common knowledge among my respondents about the unlawfulness (termed locally as *bespredel*) of the financial police, which was used as an instrument of stripping people of their economic capital and estate – known colloquially as the *finpol bespredel*. Unlike any other law-enforcement agencies, the *finpol* (financial police) had a particular 'bad fame' among citizens. This discourse encompassed the following commonly shared knowledge: (1) this type of police rarely came after the poor but often targeted richer possible suspects; (2) *finpol* was an instrument of a particular elite group within the regime rather than a pure law-enforcement agency of the state; and (3) *finpol* rarely left their target without a substantial financial loss after their visit, through corruption, extortion, or blackmail, or a combination of all three.[14] As Erica Marat noted in her extensive study on post-Soviet police reform, 'predatory traffic policing, criminal police officers notorious for their own involvement in organized criminal activity, community policing that essentially spies on the population', represent 'lingering legacies of the pervasive and autocratic exertion of state power over regular citizens and politicized individuals'. Furthermore, 'the secret police and financial police are also central pillars of the Soviet and post-Soviet regimes' (Marat 2018: 61).

---

[14] This discourse was formed from a number of interviews, discussions, and deliberations throughout my earliest fieldwork in 2013–15, and this knowledge about the 'financial police' is a form of popular and widely known discourse.

The way this discourse on *finpol* and other *police bespredel* spreads, through webs of personal discussions, advice, and rumours spread in private chat rooms and groups shared with family, is an important source on the digital ethnography of authoritarianism. In one of those instances, I came across an upper-class milieu of families who owned elite apartments in one of Almaty's new districts. They made it into the news when they were protesting in the summer of 2020, in the heightened period of the pandemic, over an issue of access to basic utilities. 'What led you to the protest?', the journalist asked them. The major cause of discontent was the lack of access to basic utilities, even with the high cost paid for elite housing. Some protestors later revealed to their trusted circles that they were also protesting out of dignity and 'for their rights'. WhatsApp chats were bursting with texts of support and more demands until one of the protestors received a message from a relative from Astana.[15] The relative warned the protestor by mentioning that 'poor' protestors had nothing to lose, but the 'rich' or well-off protestors would have everything 'skimmed off'[16] (mostly liquid investments and bank balances) if they end up in a courtroom on the pretext of a real or fabricated 'political affair'. 'Do you want to lose everything?' was a rhetorical question that killed the discussion. In another instance, private WhatsApp group discussion offered a further rhetorical question, along the lines of 'how many of Nazarbayev's portraits are required in one place to solve the problem?', referring to the 2017 case of Astana dweller Nesipkul Uyabayeva (see Figure 3.1), who protested against the demolition of her house by covering it with the president's portraits and avoiding immediate demolition. The fear of losing capital or the position one holds in society is mixed in the upper-middle classes with the fear that their protest would be useless or that it would require a long-term and exhausting process.

The difficult question for the newly emerging political players within Qazaq Koktemi was that of engaging more protestors and educating

---

[15] The 'relative from Astana' (*Astanadagy baurym*) became a local concept with its own value. Not only did the Astana boom attract unprecedented levels of internal migration to the new capital, but it also influenced the creation of a specific milieu of people and culture. Living in Astana is viewed by some as a status upgrade, something to take pride in, and for others also the possibility of being close to the power centre and thus being well informed about the politics and news of the regime.

[16] The literal word used was *obez'zhiryat* – would strip off all capital.

Figure 3.1 Astana dweller Nesipkul Uyabayeva protested against the demolition of her house by covering it with ninety-one posters with Nursultan A. Nazarbayev's portrait. © Svetlana Glushkova, RFE/RL

more audiences despite the fears, the misconceptions, and the stagnation of the 'opposition' that preceded it. There was a shared ethos among all the players in the protest wave whom I interviewed. Oyan, Qazaqstan activists, for example, put considerable effort into analysing their obstacles:

Right now [January 2020], we are in the process of mapping out [target audiences]. We are testing, and we are analysing where [our messages] work or not. But we have met some obstacles – some groups of the society have a certain level of conformity that is really hard to overcome, and I do not know what kind of theory to use to explain it – people simply do not want to perceive this information. For them, this type of information about the rights, freedoms, [democratic] principles are significantly distorted. Naturally, the most well-informed audiences and the ones who are more active mainly on social media are young people, and there [our activism] finds a lot more responses. But we will see. We are trying to reach all sorts of audiences, and we are trying to make our content bilingual (Kazakh and Russian) – we are trying different formats.[17]

---

[17] Author's interview with Oyan, Qazaqstan activist, January 2020.

The movement had to come up with strategies beyond just protest for the sake of the protest. In the summer of 2019, after the presidential elections, Oyan, Qazaqstan started discussions about how to proceed with their activism. All of the people whom I interviewed for this research and who were active or former members of Oyan, Qazaqstan stressed that they valued the movement's horizontal organization in representation and decision-making. However, after the June 2019 elections, there were some crucial questions that shaped the movement's membership and allowed some of its members to choose varying paths. The biggest point of contention was about the strategy of engaging with the regime and democratization, and there were several visions and groups who lobbied for their agenda. One group propagated the necessity to continue working with the independent observers and prepare for the parliamentary elections, which are always announced in Kazakhstan prematurely and unexpectedly. As a result, this group of activists believed that the movement should have invested more time and resources into organizing and training independent election observers. This group also rooted for better institutional collaboration with existing NGOs and legal specialists. A second group within the movement, on the contrary, strongly believed that they had to take a hard line of not engaging with the regime until further democratization. This meant that they did not want to put everything on the line to 'prove that the regime staged another round of elections yet again'. Instead, this group proposed to invest more time in active protests and information campaigns. They drafted an outline of advice for protestors' starter packs on social media and got involved in more protest actions in different cities of Kazakhstan, including through the new strategy of *seruens*,[18] walking protests. The summer of 2019 was turbulent within the movement as it was drawing more supporters and dealing with its internal divisions. Key to further disintegrations within Oyan, Qazaqstan was the issue of dealing with *vlast'* – to engage with the regime gradually or to continue almost a partisan approach to street protests. After dealing with some rough edges and the departures of key members of Oyan, Qazaqstan (all of

---

[18] Roughly translated from Kazakh as 'promenade' or 'walking protest'. The idea of *seruen* emerged when police harassment against the protesters reached its peak and protest groups decided to change the rally – where most people usually stand in one place – to a walking tour, where people walked with posters told the police that they were engaging in a promenade (*seruen*ing).

whom nevertheless remained within the Kazakh Spring field and were active politically just outside Oyan), some middle ground was reached in 2020.

Emerging Protesting Tactics of the Kazakh Spring and the Regime's Response

Seruen – literally translated from Kazakh as walking – was a new strategy against the law on unsanctioned rallies that prohibits public assemblies without legal permission from the local municipality offices. Unsanctioned rallies were restricted in Kazakhstan throughout the protesting waves of the 2000s and 2010s, but by the time Qazaq Koktemi emerged, the protestors were not scared of selective detentions.[19] Instead of protest stand-offs, they invented 'walking protests' – *seruens*. From the outset, it looked like a large group of people walking and talking, listening to music and occasionally stopping to deliver speeches. But the whole idea of *seruen* is literally not to stand in one place and to deceive the police by making the rally 'mobile' – not a rally in form but a rally in content.

Seruens were introduced in summer 2019 to diversify big protest actions with continuous and visible smaller actions and in order to boost public participation in public places. Invitations for *seruens* were open to all and were widely circulated on social media. Participants were invited to join *seruens* to discuss the political situation in the country, and they became popular networking events. As one of the participants described it, the whole process left her 'inspired' and 'a part of something big and meaningful'.[20] *Seruens* allowed for quicker and more efficient communication and engagement of new members to the movement.

Seruens started inspiring new collective identities for a progressive, politically engaged, and alternatively thinking crowd that was often framed by their opponents as 'Almaty hipsters' – the frame that I discuss in the next section of this chapter. *Seruens* flourished in Almaty and in other cities of Kazakhstan – for example, in Karaganda, through the use of private Oyan, Qazaqstan encrypted

---

[19] Oyan, Qazaqstan activists frequently reminded me about the collective support that helped them get through the arrests and fines, collected through crowdfunding.
[20] Author's interview with Oyan, Qazaqstan activist, anonymous.

chats. At the time of the heated waves of protests after the presidential elections in summer 2019, it was important for some members of Oyan, Qazaqstan to incorporate the network of walking protests across Kazakhstani cities to address the critique that it was just a local, Almaty movement. Through *seruens*, they also managed to attract more members, though some of the founding members were leaving Oyan, Qazaqstan while staying within Qazaq Koktemi, and the confusion between the movement and the field of contentions left many observers puzzled. For example, Asya Tulesova left Oyan, Qazaqstan quietly at the end of summer 2019 but remained active within the protest field of Qazaq Koktemi. The departure of Leyla Makhmudova attracted more attention – she posted her official 'exit' message on all her social media platforms and asked journalists and commentators not to associate her public activism with Oyan, Qazaqstan anymore. This departure was shocking at first – Makhmudova was one of the first faces of the movement, who appeared at the joint press conference on 5 June and, as a popular feminist activist, was known for pushing a feminist agenda within Oyan, Qazaqstan and Femagora, another association connected to Qazaq Koktemi. Her departure marked a shift in the movement's strategy, because Makhmudova was one of the most active supporters of the independent electoral observers' strategy and invested a lot of time in building that programme from scratch. In her narrative, for her, the development of the movement coincided with important events:

Oyan is a movement with public actions, and it was important that we had to be visible and heard, although some wanted anonymity because everyone has their own risks. There were fears and risks, and these risks were individual-contextual (someone was losing clients at work, someone was losing work, and others were losing the support of their families). This [tradition of] tabooing political themes – we had to leave it behind. It was always considered dangerous and that all these attempts for political debates and contentions do not end up well and that the establishment [ruling elites of the regime] would just eat you up because it eats up all those who resist it.

The aim of the movement was to change that mindset. Leyla Mahmudova also mentioned how the experience of serving as an election observer inspired her, and many in her network found it elevating.

Before the [June 2019 presidential] elections, there was a question – what to do? Many activists questioned how they could change the situation. The most obvious answer was to become an electoral observer. There were also administrative observers of the independent observers. [Our] engagement in the political process and the counting of our own vote – that [was] our common civic contribution. There was a lot of solidarity at the time – even those Kazakhstanis who were abroad broadcast live [on social media] from the embassies. Facebook was always our political channel, and then it just became the mouthpiece of freedom. Social media works because of instant sharing – it would have been weird to expect some sort of electoral broadcasting from the usual media. Television wouldn't have done it, and expecting newspapers to do so was unusual and silly – these were released only after several days [post-election]. After the elections, I felt my own self-empowerment because I saw how my actions led not to something abstract but to real actions. Being engaged [in the political process] was a very important factor.

Through the [Qazaq Koktemi] actions and activities, civic consciousness started developing. It wasn't about emotions but about realizing yourself within the big state and [realizing] that you have the possibilities to change something. [It was the time] when civicness [*grazhdanstvennost'*] and dissent [*nesoglasie*] started emerging. The thing that was left was to stop being afraid of dissent and its consequences. In the summer [of 2019], there was a lot of mobilization. We discussed a lot inside Oyan, often through the chats, and there were [face-to-face] meetings. There were a lot of opinions about how to develop this civicness and how to change something in society. There were a lot of different opinions. Even at the beginning of the movement, there were a lot of voices and opinions about not making it public and maybe keeping it more anonymous. There were a lot of voices [opinions] about the [Oyan, Qazaqstan] declaration, and this is why it remained unfinished, I think, and it required a lot of work throughout the summer. In the summer [2019], there were all of these discussions, and inside the movement itself, there were a lot of different forces and debates; but we all believed that it had to be a democratic moment and that everyone had to speak up, especially because since the beginning of the movement it was agreed that it wouldn't have leaders. All of my plans for the parliamentary elections project diminished when the 'collective decision' was made not to take part in the big [and collective] initiative to organize and train independent electoral observers for the upcoming parliamentary elections. This decision and discussion that preceded it was done without me in August to September 2019, and in

September of the same year, I exited the movement officially. Before that, Asya [Tulesova] left it too.[21]

The project of training local electoral observers required long and coordinated training with various different organizations, and the group who supported this move within Oyan, Qazaqstan took it seriously. The debates on the other side concerned consistency with the initially declared message that the movement would not play by the 'established rules of the game' and thus would not support staged elections until alternative and independent candidates were allowed to run for office. But the majority of those voting and making decisions within Oyan, Qazaqstan believed that this moment was not coming anytime soon, and thus they voted to resort to fully fledged street protests on the day of parliamentary elections (discussed in Chapter 6).

What was seen from the outside was slightly different from what was going on inside the movement. Critics of Oyan, Qazaqstan, whom they already dubbed as 'Almaty hipsters' (discussed in the latter part of this chapter), rushed to form conclusions about the movement's collapse. After all, Leyla Makhmoudova was an active voice of the movement and of feminist civil society, and she was present at the Oyan, Qazaqstan press conference alongside political analyst Dimash Alzhanov, journalist Assem Zhapisheva, artist Suinbike Suleimenova, and economist Kassymkhan Kapparov. While there were important internal rifts and heated discussions about which direction to choose and the important departures of some of the key figures of Qazaq Koktemi – Asya Tulesova, Suinbike Suleimenova, Medina Bazargali – not all of these departures were as public, and all three mentioned that they were still part of the larger protest waves, just not directly associated with Oyan, Qazaqstan (though there was talk of them rejoining the movement later in the course of its development). This, for many of them, meant also continuing communication with other members but completely leaving the organization of the movement – the sphere some of them referred to as 'secret chats' or private, encrypted conversations in working groups where each member had to take the lead in managing a different project. Leyla Makhmoudova was part of the working group on training electoral observers, but when her proposal was voted on without her input, she decided to declare her complete departure from the movement:

[21] Author's interview with Leyla Makhmudova, 27 July and 11 November 2020.

We have done a lot of work in Oyan, [Qazaqstan] in order to train a lot more observers for the upcoming parliamentary elections and to research [the observers' work] across the whole country to use these numbers as representation and to demonstrate in detail what we are right about and what we want [*v chem my pravy i na chto my pretenduem*]. But Oyan decided to decline this idea in [early] September 2019, and this was the reason why I left the movement and declared it on all of my social media platforms. At that moment, I understood that people around me were not my companion-in-arms [*soratniki*] because they were not sharing my desires and aspirations for change, particularly that [political] aspect.[22]

Instead, the movement invested in more mobilization and protests on the streets and online. Their hard line remained to fight against the regime and its rules of the game and not to take part in formal political competition until further democratization and reforms they proposed were taken into consideration. Street protests that Oyan, Qazaqstan organized and framed around important state celebrations – for example, Constitution Day – reached more participants, who were drawn to the movement. Constitution Day was largely forgotten and diminished, but the Oyan, Qazaqstan protest action on that day brought more supporters to the movement. This is how a well-known fem-activist, Fariza Ospan, joined the movement and later became one of its leading voices:

I remember that I immediately thought that I trusted them [Oyan, Qazaqstan]. I saw them, and I read their civic declaration, and it resonated with me that they wanted political reforms. I thought about it too that truly in the context for women's rights – they [ruling regime elites] do not consider it as a danger to the regime and don't even consider it a political question even though it truly is. We can forever try to prove to our regime [*vlasti*] that a woman is a human too, that we need laws [on gendered violence], and that without the reform of the law-enforcement system – without making the judicial system transparent and fair, without police reform, nothing can be achieved because we see how the policemen treat women who suffered from gendered violence – domestic, sexual [violence]. Because the police do not want to investigate the [gendered violence] cases and that for ten years prior to [now], rape victims could actually reconcile with their rapists. Also, *vlast'* [regime elites] does not want to see women involved in politics because they see women only at home, in their kitchens, and they [regime elites] have very conservative views. I am tired of seeing all these male faces [speaking] on TV

---

[22] Author's interview with Leyla Makhmudova, 27 July and 11 November 2020.

and from the highest political positions, but that can be done only through reforms. I understood that [the need for reforms] resonated with me, and this is why guys [in the movement] and I immediately had a close connection. When I entered the movement ... it is like ... we do not have any hierarchies, we do not have any party membership [*partiiniy bilet*] in order to enter or leave the movement – and it is important to note that. I joined the movement during their march on 30 August 2019 [Constitution Day]. Then I saw how they are planning marches and protests. At the time [in summer 2019], they also launched *seruens*, and I saw how responsible they were about everything they did and how every one of them was so connected to the principles. It really connected me to the movement at the time, and it is still an important factor for me.[23]

The support and solidarity also played a crucial role for many members in staying close to the movement's values and collective identity. Two months after she joined Oyan, Qazaqstan, Fariza Ospan ran into problems at work. She wrote a story about a corruption scandal connected to Karakat Abden, who had written a book about traditionalist conservative views of how to be a Kazakh woman and who was accused of embezzling from a major state project.[24] Ospan, who at the time worked at an international organization, was forced to resign over her publication, and her colleagues did not support her:

At the time, it all felt very difficult because I didn't know where to find the support system, you know, the support, the rooting underneath your feet. And back then, guys from Oyan were saving me because they really protected me, and I understood back then that maybe I don't do enough for the movement, but I can rely on them in a difficult situation, and they'd help me. That was the moment when I started engaging more.[25]

Eventually, this dominant strategy of mobilization resulted in the formation of a more stable and consistent membership, where new members such as Fariza Ospan managed to replace the losses (albeit

---

[23] Author's interview with Fariza Ospan, November 2020.
[24] Karakat Abden received 197 million KZT in a tender to fund a school for Kazakh girls 'Kazakh kyzy' from 2016 to 2019. When Fariza Ospan published the short investigation about a potential corruption scandal around this school, she started receiving anonymous phone calls and threats to delete her post. More available at https://vlast.kz/novosti/36359-aktivistka-fariza-ospan-soobsila-ob-ugrozah-posle-posta-ob-institute-kazak-kyzy.html.
[25] Author's interview with Fariza Ospan, November 2020.

difficult losses) of the founding members and to keep the movement afloat. In other words, despite the fears of Oyan, Qazaqstan's supporters, the movement was not falling apart due to internal rifts and discussions that started to become more and more public after Makhmudova's departure. These questions about falling out were addressed in the Oyan, Qazaqstan public chat on Telegram and during live broadcasts with the movement's members on Instagram throughout 2020. The movement takes pride in its communication skills with members, law-enforcement agents, and the general public. They tried to address all the questions, but some members still wished not to make the internal fights public and mentioned how some of the members who left Oyan, Qazaqstan remained active within Qazaq Koktemi. For example, when Asya Tulesova was tried in August 2020 (discussed in the next chapter), many of the Oyan, Qazaqstan activists actively supported her even though the discussions behind her departure from the movement were not properly addressed by either side.[26]

One conclusion after the first spring was clear. Oyan, Qazaqstan activists believed that investing in continuous and varying forms of mobilization and protest was a more successful strategy. They also looked at the possibility of expanding their networks outside the central cities of Almaty and Astana to create more of a following from a 'regional' perspective. Over the period of their development, they used different strategies for which their online presence helped them greatly. Many activists also started creating their own civic engagement by creating different media platforms, which I discuss in the following chapter. For example, the Masa portal, dedicated to information about the overall rule of law, the BatyrJamal platform for the feminist agenda, and the Umytpa portal for counting and remembering those who died during the pandemic but were written off in the official statistics were media projects organized and led by Assem Zhapisheva and Aisana Ashim, both active members of Oyan, Qazaqstan. However, one specific critique of the movement has haunted it since the very inception of Qazaq Koktemi – how everything from the physical protest to decision-making remained

---

[26] During one of the Instagram 'lives' – live broadcasting with Oyan, Qazaqstan – Beybrys Tolymbetov, who did not leave the movement, was asked about Asya Tulesova's departure. He replied that Tulesova remained a part of the protest wave [within the Qazaq Koktemi field] and remained active whether she was part of any movement or party.

centrally in Almaty. I discuss the reasons for that development in the next section.

The Republic of Almaty, Its Hipsters and Coffee Shops: Situating the Public Sphere in the City That Has Seen It All

In this section, I discuss one of the main criticisms of Oyan, Qazaqstan's activism and explore the critique that they are mainly located in Almaty in relation to the regime's tactics to discredit the movement. Three things are crucial takeaways in this discussion – regime stagnation and authoritarian myopia as a predetermination for regime collapse; regime overlooking and misconceiving the centrality of Almaty, leading to the major problems in January 2022; and the strength of the new activists' approach to the challenges and criticisms of the regime. On the last point, I am specifically attentive to the ways activists were quick to adapt to the regime's criticisms and to the challenges they faced from the wider public. The tactical success of Oyan, Qazaqstan was in its rapid and informed response to criticism and in their consistent agenda for democratization. If there is a way to define this particular movement's success, then it is in their quick response and openness about their agenda, which they managed to communicate to a variety of audiences across different social and conventional media platforms.

Central to my analysis is the regime's response to the movement. I demonstrate how the regime remained locked in its own authoritarian myopia and old ways of doing politics when it first encountered Oyan, Qazaqstan and tried to attack them with old slogans that the young electorate immediately started making fun of (e.g., the coffee memes or the regime's inability to use the hipsters narrative). This outcome demonstrates how regimes can become incredibly fragile due to their stagnant outlook on political life that only reinforces the old elites' misconceptions of reality when they continue doing politics as if it were 1998. This demonstrates how authoritarian myopia is one of the most significant dangers for the regime. When the regime is no longer capable of responding to changing societal demands, it is deemed to face significant problems which was the case with Nazarbayev, who got lost in his own beliefs of the potency of his cult. In contrast to the old regime, new movements such as Oyan, Qazaqstan were incredibly quick and open with their agenda. They manoeuvred gracefully in the field, while the old regime was like a tank from the Second World War, a relic encrusted with layers of dirt and barely able to move. Because Oyan, Qazaqstan contrasted so much with Nazarbayev's immobile regime machine, they opened new venues for rethinking the political, where young and fresh faces could take over key positions and dominate the media sphere. Even if Oyan, Qazaqstan were not everyone's cup of tea (or coffee), their slogans landed well with overall societal discontent about the economic crisis, exacerbated further by the Covid-19 pandemic and lockdowns. By the end of 2020, 'Kazakhstan without Nazarbayevs' became a slogan that many took away from Oyan, Qazaqstan and made their own. Almaty, as the country's biggest city, its economic capital, and by all measures the hub of social inequality, became a hotbed of the movement's slogans about inequality and calls for regime change. In a nutshell, Oyan, Qazaqstan may have not entirely been responsible for the January 2022 mass protests, where Almaty represented the biggest space of contention, but it definitely inspired it. So, the regime's authoritarian myopia in criticizing Oyan, Qazaqstan for their focus on Almaty played out against them and toppled not only Nazarbayev's monuments but also Nazarbayev and his cult of personality. Thus, Almaty as a space that enabled contentions is a key player in these discussions, and its role cannot be overlooked.

Almaty is a historically important space for Kazakhstan's culture, political, and social life beyond just the usual debates and discussions about the city's economic centrality. Almaty is also a product of Soviet modernization and the rapid globalization of the 1990s. As a result, it became the central magnet for both neoliberal projects and leftist activists, the cosmopolitan hub for global players, and a unique space of some freedom of speech and freedom of conscience on the large canvas of the Kazakhstani dictatorship. However, it is erroneous to think of Almaty as the only hub of protests and social movements. Industrial disputes in Zhanaozen in western Kazakhstan or mine workers' strikes that are traditional to the central city of Karaganda, as well as the remaining infrastructure of Komsomol workers in different urban parts of Kazakhstan, remain active forces of contentious politics in the age of inequality and ever-growing economic crisis.[27] Many of

---

[27] The persistence of the Komsomol networks is well documented in literature on political elites in Kazakhstan (Murphy 2006 on the political elite and networks and Sharipova 2019 on the evolution of Komsomol and youth organizations to post-Soviet institutions). The key to Komsomol institutionalization was not so

these contentious centres also inevitably produce systems and discourses of political dissent. Mining-industry workers and pensioners' unions were some of the most vocal critics of the regime throughout the post-independence era.[28] These labour and class movements remain on the radar of contentious politics and discussions,[29] but for some reason, the regime does not place them within the same frame as 'political opposition'. And this is where the dividing line between Almaty dwellers and the rest really starts.

The Nazarbayev regime's strategies mostly focused on discrediting any opposition or dissenting voices to the regime and perfected these strategies over their long thirty years in power. In the past, the political opposition was discredited as 'thirsty for power' (for the initial DVK movement in the early 2000s) but incapable of governing. Then, the same opposition was branded as nationalist due to their close cooperation with some of the dissident groups that identified more as Kazakh national-patriots, though their agenda is so marginalized that these groups were rarely close to standing for office.[30] The regime used the discourse of framing Almaty opposition as detached from the people and too elitist at its core. The fact that Almaty remained the biggest and the richest centre in the country despite the gradual growth of Astana allowed the creation of this perception of disparity and inequality that later on played against all new movements that emerged in Almaty. Despite the reallocation of the capital from Almaty to the north of the country, Almaty did not lose its central place in the political field in

much its ability to parachute certain notable elites within Nazarbayev's regime to the top of their careers (e.g., Imagali Tasmagambetov) but in what Alexey Yurchak described as the post-Soviet transition of Komsomol to 'private firms and banks'. The Komsomol ethos and sustained network of members 'enabled them to devise, conduct, organize, guide, and represent complex activities of various people in the new context of quickly changing state ideologies, laws, rules, taxes, uncertainties, and forms of risk' (Yurchak 2006: 298). Even those members who did not make it into regime circles remained active in their respective cities and regions and continued to coexist, work, and construct their everyday life experiences through these contained networks of favours and collective (albeit often informal) mutual help and support. Their protest potential should also not be underestimated.

[28] The Pensioners Union *Pokolenie* (Generation), led by Irina Savostina, was once a vocal civil-society voice in the 1990s and early 2000s in Kazakhstan alongside the labour unions in industrial cities, for example, the miners' labour unions in Karaganda.
[29] See Satpayev and Umbetalieva 2015; Sorbello 2021.
[30] See Laruelle 2016; Kudaibergenova 2016.

Kazakhstan and continuously produced the space and capacity for new opposition to emerge. Other central and focal points remain important, with social unrest in the industrial west of the country, or the burgeoning overpopulated parts of the south with the emerging voices of the 'mothers with many children' (*mnogodetnie materi*) and their protests. The social inequality that the authoritarian regime itself produced continues to be the driving force for contentious politics all over Kazakhstan, but Almaty is the main focus of the regime due to its capacity to form bigger and stronger movements and their ability to be in dialogue with forces beyond Kazakhstan itself. This is why the regime continuously places Almaty in the public eye but frames it as an 'elitist' force despite the fact that the Almaty movements are a home for a number of activists from different regions and social milieu.

Take, for example, one of the videos that emerged after the 'Men Oyandym' (I woke up) video of June 2019, where many famous young activists were implicitly criticizing the Kazakh regime by calling out a lack of freedom of speech and a lack of democracy. Within a few days, alternative, pro-regime videos emerged to essentially start a campaign against youth movements. At the time, pro-regime ideologues could not even differentiate between the several dispersed groups and branded them all as part of an ambiguous youth movement. This included Anuar Nurpeisov, who never belonged to Oyan, Qazaqstan or any other groups but acted on his own; it also included all of the people he asked to take part in his famous video, and indeed any young protestor. But the criticism of pro-regime writers was aimed precisely at Almaty youth. One of their June 2019 videos, for example, said:

> All of these people [young protestors] are simply detached from the simple folk [*otorvany ot prostogo naroda*]. And their ideas won't take root even with democratic elections. These people declare that they are for democracy and the simple folk. But deep down inside, they hate this same folk [*narod*], belittling them in every possible way in their ordinary life. Why is the regime [*vlast'*] so merciless to particularly this party [*tusovka*]? From the regime's point of view, this party [*tusovka*] are the most ungrateful bastards, the biggest beneficiaries who condemn the regime [*vlast'*] who gave them everything while they sip coffee at Starbucks.[31]

---

[31] Cited at www.the-village-kz.com/village/city/columns/5891-hipstery.

The Republic of Almaty

The association with fancy coffee shops and Starbucks[32] was a direct connotation of Almaty's elitism that appeared in several media discourses during the elections. For example, candidate Toleutai Rakhymbekov from the Ayul party declared that he does not start his day with a cup of coffee but starts it with hard work. The coffee-shop drinker took on a negative connotation in official Ak Orda discourse as someone 'detached' from the 'simple folk' and living in the conditions of globalized possibilities the rest of Kazakhstan could not quite afford or have access to outside the major urban centres. This was a very generalized and rigid discourse about Almaty or other major-city activism, since coffee was popular in different parts of Kazakhstan before the introduction of Starbucks or other global coffee companies. In the words of Assem Zhapisheva, who herself was born in eastern Kazakhstan and not in Almaty:

> We should stop paying attention to the Ak Orda rhetoric on dividing people into lazy hipsters and the 'ordinary folk' [*prostoi narod*]. I will voice the unpopular opinion: the myth that there exists some regional life [in regions rather than cities of Kazakhstan] and that there are some special Almaty hipsters with hashtags 'you cannot run away from the truth' and 'men oyandym' (I woke up) is a completely wrong one. If we trust history and science, those who were called hipsters brought a complete change of systems and values in different [historical] periods.[33]

Zhapisheva's comment directly hit the dividing line that was abused by many Ak Orda ideologues, in which they tried to portray the 'ordinary citizen' as deprived of 'luxurious' habits such as spending time in coffee shops. For example, the above-mentioned pre-election video from Toleutai Rakhymbekov's campaign portrays supposedly authentic 'village people' who repeat a script along the lines of 'I do not start my day with a cup of coffee in a coffee shop but go straight to milk the cow' or 'every day I wake up early in the morning and don't drink coffee because I need to go and water the cucumbers in the field in order to get good harvest' and finishes by 'hello, city dwellers [*gorodskie*], in the

---

[32] Ironically positioned in this discussion as an elite and 'Western' coffee shop and a space of everything globalized. None of my interviews with activists took place in Starbucks but instead were mainly organized around independent coffee houses or exhibition spaces, some in the cheap (but delicious) *lagmanhana* small restaurant chains – but never at Starbucks.

[33] Cited in Zhapisheva's column at www.the-village-kz.com/village/city/columns/5891-hipstery.

aul [Kazakh village] everyone has long been awake, join us!'. The video appeared at the beginning of June 2019 with the hashtag 'men oyandym', which was used in the 30 May 2019 video by anti-regime activists who proclaimed that they 'woke up in the country where the capital's name can change in one day without asking the citizens'. The whole idea of the 'men oyandym' moment of awakening was highly contentious during the days leading up to the 9 June 2019 presidential elections, as it revealed the fake nature of the staged elections, which put up candidates who did not represent real competition to the regime candidate. A lot of these candidates became subjects of jokes and memes. For example, another presidential candidate, Sadybek Tugel, made low-quality videos of his raids of nightclubs in Astana, where he spoke to a group of young people about the negative consequences of vodka consumption and called on everyone to drink fermented horse milk, *kumys*, instead.

These attempts to discredit the new youth movements and activists with the tools of the previous century were very shallow and often hit the wrong spot – online communities would make fun of these videos and discourses instead of reposting them with support. One thing that they did highlight, though, was that by the time of the Qazaq Koktemi, Almaty had developed into a symbolic hub of dissidence in Kazakhstan, and it was not only centred around its traditional coffee houses on Tulebayev Street (colloquially known as Tulebaika) but also around the cultural circles that have traditionally flourished in this city.[34] The Soviet history of Almaty partly explains it, and further neoliberalization of the city in the post-Soviet era, despite the capital's move to Astana, also explains the continuation of Almaty's symbolic role in Kazakhstani politics. In the Soviet period, Almaty hosted the vast infrastructure of cultural institutions and was the centre of major publishing and art production for Soviet Kazakhstan.[35] In the 1990s, the city was a hub for rapidly emerging social and political movements. Several movements and parties such as 'Azat', 'Birlik', the social-democratic

---

[34] The historical development of the cultural networks in Almaty are well documented in Sultanbayeva and Nuryeva 2016, Kuttykadam 2010, and other volumes.

[35] I write at length about the networks and cultural production in Soviet and post-Soviet Almaty in my book *Rewriting the Nation in Modern Kazakh Literature* (Kudaibergenova 2017a) and in my subsequent articles on the role of contemporary art in Kazakhstan (Kudaibergenova 2017b, 2018).

party, 'Alash', movements such as 'Zheltoqsan', 'Memorial',[36] 'Shanyraq', and 'Democratic Union' as well as the ecological antinuclear movement of 'Nevada-Semipalatinsk' and the nationalist movement 'Kazakh tili' (for the provision of more Kazakhification) were active in Almaty at the time. And these organizations and movements were under the watchful eye of the regime, as seen in the 1991 report addressed to President Nazarbayev himself:

> It would have been not right to underestimate the work of [these movements and organizations], their ability to influence social perceptions. Moreover, it is important to pay more attention to the work of social movements that bring constructive meaning and [which already] received wide recognition. [According to the polling conducted], 'Nevada-Semipalatinsk' occupied the first place [in the rating of approval] and received 50–70% of approval votes from those polled, more than half of the polled population also highly acknowledged the work of the Communist Party of Kazakhstan and the third place in this rating is occupied by the 'Kazakh tili' [movement] that receive up to 40% [approval rate].[37]

During the turbulent time of the early 1990s, the Kazakh public sphere was located mainly in Almaty, where many of the popular political movements and alternative political leaders occupied public squares, in front of the parliament (locally known as the Old Square in Almaty) or in the famous Brezhnev Square, where the December 1986 protests happened. When the capital of the country was moved to what was then Aqmola, now Astana, the symbolic politics of contention did not shift away from Almaty. It took a long time for the pro-regime bureaucrats to move to the new capital, and the majority of the opposition forces remained in the 'southern' capital city. Big business also was slow to move up north, where the infrastructure was developing very slowly compared to the existing and comfortable conditions of Almaty.[38]

---

[36] Not the same Memorial as in Russia.
[37] From the report to N.A. Nazarbayev (and sent off to KGB chair N. Abykayev), about the 'socio-political situation in the republic', 1997b, op.1, F.7, from the Archive of the First President (29 апреля 1991 года Доклад Президенту Н. А. Назарбаеву (им же переправлено на работу к Н. Абыкаеву) «Об общественно-политической ситуации в республике», 1997б Опись 1, Фонд 7 – Президент КазССР) cited from p. 8.
[38] See Anacker 2004; Wolfel 2002; Koch 2014, 2018; Fauve 2015; Laszczkowski 2016; Bissenova 2017; Bekus and Medeuova 2017.

The duality of the Almaty–Astana political spheres is still at work today, and there is a type of competition between the two cities in terms of the impact they make on the overall Kazakhstani reality. But Astana remains largely bureaucratized, while Almaty managed to remain a political hub without the everyday presence of the pro-regime elites, including the president himself. One way to explain why there is such a great persistence of the centrality of these two cities in Kazakhstani development, in general, is the regime's input (including budgetary) into these cities, which also have the special status of 'republican cities'[39] and stand above any other administrative units, namely, the fourteen oblasts of Kazakhstan (those often mentioned in the discourses as 'regions'). Since the state invests disproportionally in these two cities, the rest of the resources are also spread disproportionally, so all of the pro-regime critique of the centrality of the Almaty public sphere is actually a direct consequence of the regime's politics. There is also a growing literature on the influence Astana is gaining as a magnet for internal migration in Kazakhstan.[40] And with its huge budgets for one megalomaniac urban project after another, it inevitably creates an axis of inequality between the overtly corrupt elites and the impoverished social groups who cause spontaneous yet continuous contentions and protests.[41] Finally, this duality of the two central cities can be summarized as a type of *neopatrimonial capitalism* (Isaacs and Frigerio 2018: 310) when an authoritarian regime coupled with rapid neoliberalization of the state create a system where financial stability depends on the incumbent regime.

Thus, the so-called hipsterization of Almaty's public sphere is the direct product of Nazarbayev's neopatrimonial capitalism. So, as a result, all those who criticized Oyan, Qazaqstan and other activists for being elitist groups and consumers of the globalized neoliberal order are actually criticizing the core of the system that Nazarbayev created himself. In the 1990s, then-president Nazarbayev built his whole platform around the discourse of 'first economic development and then political reforms' and his approaches to the developmentalist

---

[39] Shymkent is now also a republican city. [40] See n. 38.
[41] The Oxus Society Central Asia Protest Tracker is a good resource to map how protests are ubiquitous outside Almaty (most notably in the area of Astana and southern Kazakhstan); see https://oxussociety.org/viz/protest-tracker/.

paradigms of the neoliberal structure presented in the Kazakhstan-2030 state programme in 1997 and then in the Kazakhstan-2050 programme of December 2012. Both of these programmes became the blueprint of the country's rapid neoliberalization coupled with equally rapidly rising levels of corruption[42] and unequal development in the regional 'peripheries' of the country.[43]

What is even more ironic in this criticism of class inequality and the discussion of who has the right to represent whom is the Sovietized language and frameworks used in these discourses, which essentially become populist. Take, for example, the concept of *narod* – the ordinary folk – which is still often used in these divisive debates. It is one thing when this term is used by the completely politically marginalized Communist Party of Kazakhstan and another when this discourse is used in this Sovietized meaning by the leaders of the parties supposedly representing farmers, rural populations, or industrial workers and business owners for example, the Aul and Ak Zhol parties under the leadership of Azat Peruashev. These are pro-regime parties that are continuously selected and allowed to run for parliament and to represent citizens of Kazakhstan who know very little in reality about what these parties' programmes and political inputs are.[44] In the conditions of heightened authoritarianism that have divided the country into those 'close to the regime' and those outside the regime, discussions about class and inequality are incredibly important. These discussions are long overdue, especially in the light of the social crisis before and during the pandemic, with the mass protest of mothers and families with many

---

[42] The Transparency International 2020 Index ranked Kazakhstan 94th out of 180 countries, with a score of 38/100.

[43] Regional economic development remains highly uneven in Kazakhstan, where there are many regions and spaces without basic access to water and infrastructure. This is one of the reasons for the continuous contentious politics.

[44] Sociological polling before the January 2021 parliamentary elections demonstrated that an average Kazakhstani voter had mostly heard about the ruling Nur Otan party (50% of the surveyed respondents had heard about the party) and to the lesser extent about Ak Zhol (only 17% of respondents were aware of the party), Ayul (12% of respondents), and the new and still-unregistered Adal party (12%); an even smaller percentage were aware of the Communist party (8% of respondents). These numbers demonstrate overall political apathy and lack of awareness about the political process – only 14.9% of respondents to the survey stated that they were regularly following political news in Kazakhstan. For the results of the survey in Russian, see https://liter.kz/107467-2/.

children (*mnogodetnie materi*) but also the continuous social unrest in the sphere of housing, displacement, and overall unstable economic conditions for the ordinary citizens.[45] This ongoing moment of inequality, caused by the neopatrimonial capitalism of Nazarbayev's regime and its overspending on expensive yet economically inefficient projects such as EXPO-2017, created a sphere where anyone can be accused of classism. And this is where the criticism of Almaty hipsters sipping coffees in their fancy coffee shops and talking about politics came from.

My survey of Oyan, Qazaqstan activists did not reveal that any of them possessed major financial assets. A typical Oyan, Qazaqstan activist is actually not a native of Almaty (*almatinets*) and lives in a shared, rented apartment, works in a mid-level job in the service industry, obtained their education through a state scholarship at home or abroad (via the Bolashak state-scholarship programme), and has ties back to the community in the region they came from. For example, Assem Zhapisheva proudly represented her home region of Semey (Semipalatinsk in Russian) during numerous interviews on YouTube, Instagram, and in print media. Leyla Makhmoudova, an ex-member of Oyan, Qazaqstan, and Fariza Ospan are both natives of the southern city of Shymkent; several Kazakh-speaking activists come from different parts of the Almaty region. A number of well-known faces of the movement – Dimash Alzhanov and ex-members Asya Tulesova and Suinbike Suleimenova – are natives of Almaty (*korennie almatintsy*), but they revealed publicly and in interviews with me that they come from middle-class families, unlike the children of 'regime oligarchs' who are also visible in the Almaty public sphere but are investing in a different type of projects (including the media and entertainment spheres).

Hipster rhetoric aside,[46] there are bigger questions that Kazakhstan has to consider ahead of any future changes and reforms, and one of

---

[45] See Alexander 2018 and Yessenova 2010 on housing conflicts, and see Sanghera and Satybaldieva 2021.

[46] Rico Isaacs provided an interesting analysis of the Almaty hipsters in his 2019 chapter 'The Kazakhstan Now! Hybridity and Hipsters in Almaty' (Isaacs 2019), where he positioned Almaty hipsters as the hybrid identity of both globalized and localized identities and traits of urban consumption of global lifestyles and coffee shops. However, Isaacs's analysis was carried out before Nazarbayev's resignation and presented a rather generalized picture of the Almaty hipsters as 'interested in aesthetic consumption ... but not broader

these is the question of the centrality of Almaty. Numerous political analysts working on Kazakhstan domestically and outside its borders have long debated the successes of the localized revolution and its spread beyond Almaty's borders. The historical lessons of the December 1986 protests in downtown Soviet Alma-Ata demonstrated how such an uprising can be quickly subdued by specially trained riot-police forces.[47] The tragic events of December 2011 in the town of Zhanaozen and the neighbouring village of Shetpe also demonstrated swift repressive local forces that were not stopped by human losses – officially, sixteen protestors were killed by the riot police in Zhanaozen, but the unofficial count numbers more than a hundred victims. The trauma of the Zhanaozen crackdown affected Kazakhstani society for a decade and in many ways influenced the outburst of solidarity and protest with the western Kazakhstan dwellers at the beginning of January 2022, when mass protests first started there and then swiftly spread all across the country (see Chapter 8).

These historical and indeed tragic lessons have provided an important learning strategy for the activists behind the Qazaq Koktemi field and the Oyan, Qazaqstan movement. If in 2017–2018, some of the Kazakh political analysts did not share the view that Kazakhstan would see a fully-fledged revolutionary moment and agreed with the idea that the regime would change from an intra-elite coup rather than from the spontaneous protests, then their views changed rapidly when anti-regime protests rumbled around Kazakhstan since spring 2019 and continued to erupt throughout the pandemic years. In 2020–1, many of my respondents believed that fully fledged bottom-up revolution would require a consistent and stable infrastructure of networks and connections either in all regions of Kazakhstan or at least in the major

---

issues that would improve the lives of ordinary citizens' (238). This might be true of the upper-class children of the neoliberal reforms and their oligarch parents. For this stratum, the interest is perhaps in the 'aesthetic of consumption' through their control of mainly glamorous media content and restaurant businesses or some art galleries. But for the Oyan, Qazaqstan groups, the dominant agenda is precisely benefits and changes for 'ordinary citizens', as is seen through their media initiatives for gender equality (BatyrJamal), education (the Masa portal), and their socio-political protest agenda. Thus, the term 'Almaty hipster' requires further differentiation, not only at the class level but also in distinguishing the agenda they follow, which is not always just about individual interest.

[47] I detail this brutality in length in one of the chapters of my book *What Does it Mean to be Kazakhstani* (Hurst, 2024).

hubs to consistently push for the violent overthrow of the regime. But while the protest wave was building up through the dispersed social groups, such as mothers marching for better welfare provision or nationalist groups with anti-China rhetoric, their attempts were seen as by many (including pro-regime forces) as minuscule in number compared to the consistent and ideologically pro-regime police infrastructure.

Besides, a number of the protestors were regularly bought off by the regime, which was the case of the mothers with multiple children (*mnogodetnie materi* or *kop balaly ayelder*) who protested in different regions of Kazakhstan after the tragic death of five young children of the same family in a fire in Astana's outskirts in January 2019, which caused a major social backlash everywhere in the country at the time. The five siblings were left in their rented one-bedroom house while both of their parents had to work overnight to provide for the family, and the children died in a fire caused by the poorly installed heating.[48] Mothers' marches started first in Astana, where they protested against growing economic inequality in front of the Ak Orda presidential palace, and later spread in such regions as Shymkent, Almaty, western Kazakhstan, and elsewhere, where angry women demanded better living conditions for their children and families from the local governors. Eventually, the government had to implement social-policy campaigns but also make individual payments to most of the female protestors.[49]

This type of protest outburst was very different from what Qazaq Koktemi activists envisioned for changing Kazakhstan. Their aim is to claim back access to the public squares in order to raise more awareness about the undemocratic nature of the regime and to focus on the ways in which economic inequality actually originates in authoritarianism. Activists argue that the short-term buy-offs offered by the regime to

---

[48] See https://carnegieendowment.org/2019/02/08/tragic-fire-highlights-kazakh stan-s-social-problems-pub-78332 for the full report.

[49] These disputes were resolved locally through the local administrative channels paying 'financial help' one-off payments to families and, in certain cases, providing housing for those families who did not have a stable housing. However, this way out of conflict was not formalized in welfare policy. Welfare payments to mothers and families with multiple children were increased on average by 5 per cent in January 2021; payments vary depending on the number of children, starting at 46,000 KZT for four children to 186,000 KZT for sixteen children, according to the Ministry of Labour and Social Welfare.

spontaneous protestors from different economically deprived groups (mothers with many children, low-income groups, *dol'shiki* or those who invested in housing that was never built) are only a cosmetic repair to the fully fledged crisis of economic and social inequality Kazakhstan is already facing. Consequently, Qazaq Koktemi activists believed that their strategy to educate the masses was working as a first step towards engineering political change from below by demanding formal institutional reforms rather than an informal pay-off for several of the most vocal protestors from the low-income communities. Before the January 2022 protests and through their social media campaigns and physical mobilizations in the symbolic protesting spaces of Almaty – the squares, the self-organized marathon from Nazarbayev to Pravda Avenues (from Nazarbayev to the Truth),[50] they were trying to reinvent the city and rewrite its recent tragic histories while at the same time raising awareness.

Qazaq Koktemi initiated the process of claiming back access to the public squares, and the protestors did so through the shared ethos that the square already belonged to them by virtue of civicness and the constitution, which highlights a number of democratic doctrines such as the right to rallies, and the prerogative of human rights. The key thing that a lot of Qazaq Koktemi rhetoric brought was the return of the democratic values and norms written out in the Kazakh constitution that had been long forgotten. But the question they faced from 2019 to the very end of 2021 was whether the protest wave and the protest field, that emerge in Almaty due to its history and existing cultural infrastructure, could find supporters outside the physical boundaries of the central Kazakh city. This was the question I addressed to people inside the Oyan, Qazaqstan movement in 2020 and this is what they said:

Diana T. Kudaibergen (DTK): Do you feel that you [as a movement] work more for the Almaty [audiences], or do you think you are moving beyond

[50] This was an unofficial marathon proposed by Qazaq Koktemi activists after the old Furmanov Avenue in Almaty was renamed Nazarbayev Avenue in March 2019. Furmanov and Pravda Avenues were the old Soviet street names, but since the cityscape continued to exist beneath numerous layers of renamed and old street names, the organizers of this unofficial marathon played on this Sovietized post-Sovietness, hinting how Nazarbayev himself was embedded in the Soviet political experiences but also playing on the Russian meaning of 'ot Nazarbayeva do Pravdy' – running from Nazarbayev to reach the Truth.

the boundaries of the city's centrality [in Kazakhstani political and economic map]?

Dimash Alzhanov: It feels like we inevitably attract interest [from outside Almaty] because our movement has been associated not only with Almaty but also in other cities. Of course, there, for now, it works on the level of certain individuals – these are people who are interested and who have professional skills. And despite the fact that we are living in different cities, we still divide our roles through different locations, and this difference does not influence us (even though there is a three-hour difference with western Kazakhstan from Almaty) – people there also work with us on an everyday basis. But the overall central group [*kostyak*] is in Almaty, and you yourself understand the reasons for that. Perhaps this will not change in the nearest future.

DTK: What are the reasons for concentrating the major inception of Oyan in Almaty?

Dimash Alzhanov: First of all, the number of young people. [Then] Almaty is a lot more secure space [for political activism] because, in the region, the coercive apparatus is a lot stronger and is disproportional in power to what is going on in Almaty. There [in the regions] is not enough infrastructure of the civic organizations – there are no human rights lawyers, no lawyers, and no infrastructure from the organization that at least could cover it [in media]. And many activists in the regions feel very unprotected. The methods of coercion are also very different there – after all, it is a smaller provincial space and the police, secret police, try to target activists directly – they come to their universities, and people [activists] feel uncomfortable living and being in these targeted coercive conditions.

DTK: What about Astana?

Dimash Alzhanov: In Astana, we have several activists from the Nazarbayev University in our team, and they are openly supporting Oyan, Qazaqstan, and they cannot be de-registered from the university because it would cause a lot of scandal. If you remember, during last year's [Nazarbayev University] graduation, one of the students wrote 'Oyan' on her graduation cap [and posted it online]. So, we have our supporters in Astana. But Astana has its own specificity [as a space]; it is still a city of bureaucrats and officials, it is an administrative city, and in Almaty, we do not have as many officials. But Astana is our second biggest space where we can organize mobilization after Almaty.

DTK: What is the third city, if it is not a secret?

Dimash Alzhanov: I would say that for now, these two cities are more or less stable representatives for us.

DTK: What about Shymkent or Karaganda?

Dimash Alzhanov: In Shymkent, things work slightly differently, and even our relations with our activists there work slightly differently – there are a lot more informal networks there. Perhaps other cities do not have the same space as here [in Almaty], but we will work steadily to build it. There [in other cities], things work slightly differently.

DTK: Is the space here [in Almaty] ... does it provide this type of urbanized youth that is educated and had often studied abroad[51] – are these the people who form the major axis of the Oyan, Qazaqstan movement? If you had to draw a social portrait of *oyanovets*, who would it be?

Dimash Alzhanov: It would be not only those who studied abroad, it is not the necessary point, but yes, many of us received a Western education. The better way to put it, [Oyan activists] are the type of guys who have self-actualized already, they started their professional careers, and they have their own level of freedom, they are independent.

DTK: It is the youth [*molodezh'*] who has slept for a long time and now decided that something has to change ... ?

Dimash Alzhanov: Hard to say ... certain triggers reflect certain trends of perceptions in society. I do not think that our youth was 'sleeping'; it is just the change of the worldwide resonant public opinions that decreases the risk of repression. I think that over time more and more people would enter the category of protestors. As soon as people would see that repressions become more and more impossible or that the cost of the repression would be much higher for the regime, [more people would start openly protesting].

---

[51] The Bolashak state scholarship was launched in 1993 and since then has sponsored mainly postgraduate degrees. In 2005, it opened up to undergraduate levels of study and later included non-degree study trips for multiple months abroad. Over the years, thousands of Kazakhstanis got access to education abroad (including Russia) in all spheres of education, and a whole class of Bolashak alumni has formed among the political elites as well as in the private and public spheres. The overall number of all Kazakhstanis who have studied abroad, especially in Western Europe and North America is not recorded, since so many students self-sponsor their studies or obtain scholarships other than the Bolashak. Douglas Blum's study on return migration in Kazakhstan – *The Social Process of Globalization: Return Migration and Cultural Change in Kazakhstan* – is a good case study for the exploration of these claims (Blum 2016). See also Del Sordi 2018 on the influence of the Bolashak stipend.

DTK: So, you mean that people did not rally at the unsanctioned protests because they were scared of the repressions?

Dimash Alzhanov: Of course! If [the police] uses a very targeted coercive strategy like repressions in the university, then the person immediately leaves the rally. And here, the media understood that protesting content sells better, and this information finds its audiences even though it does not openly criticize certain people within the regime [*vo vlasti*], so it means that the regime cannot simply censor this information about the protests.[52]

The analysis of the Almaty public sphere that is inevitably connected to its special and perhaps central position compared to other cities of Kazakhstan and even Central Asia demonstrates a shift and critique of the neopatrimonial capitalism created by Nazarbayev. The system of Nazarbayev's regime was in deep crisis long before his resignation in 2019 and long before the outburst of mass protests in 2022. It has been in crisis for a long time. In the words of one of the political analysts whom I interviewed in 2012:

Authoritarians lead the country to that moment when they [dictators] no longer understand their people and people no longer understand the dictators – it is a mutual process. When I speak to our officials and colleagues within the regime [*vo vlasti*], I constantly tell them, guys, in that exact moment when you would establish full control [over the public], when you would tighten all the nuts, you would understand that you are not controlling anything. This is a paradox of any authoritarian regime. In the end, every time the regime [*vlast'*] would face new challenges and instead of democratically institutionalizing protest, it would [try to repress it], it would face this protest again and again. We are already at the point when the extremist underground is shooting the police, and it's only the beginning. So [the regime] should think about it [institutionalizing protest]. In reality, if you start thinking deeper about it, then you are getting sadder and sadder.[53]

Qazaq Koktemi was crucial in navigating these problems of the Nazabayev crisis and finding the right language and forms to address it. The old opposition spent enormous resources and time to find an alternative to the regime that could unite the people of different social

---

[52] Author's interview with Dimash Alhzanov, 17 January 2020, Almaty, Kazakhstan. Quite ironically, the interview was conducted in a coffee shop that was located on Nazarbayev Avenue.

[53] Author's interview with anonymous political activist, Almaty, summer 2012.

and even geographical stances. Inarguably, some of the breaking points for the mass protests such as those of January 2022 were lost by this same old opposition at the end of the 1990s and again in 2010–11. Unable to find popular support, some of them attempted to steal the agenda of the Kazakh Spring protestors, who finally managed to turn the tables. And the pro-democratic wave pays the price for its viability, as the performative and physical victim of police brutality and the inadequacy of the authoritarian law-enforcement system that I discuss in the next chapter.

4 | *Performing the State, Performing the Protest*

In this chapter, I discuss the interplay of relations between the protestors and law-enforcement agencies. In authoritarian systems, law-enforcement agencies and agents are a force of the regime rather than the state – they safeguard the order required for regime survival instead of focusing on social order per se. As such, they become part of the regime's system of controlling the boundaries and norms that define social reality, which inevitably becomes the authoritarian reality. The unconstitutional law on sanctioning peaceful and 'unapproved' or unsanctioned rallies goes hand in hand with law enforcement's repression of these rallies and the subsequent trial of the protestors. In this chapter and in Chapters 6 and 7, I build an argument that the public square where protest happens and the public court where trials happen are comparable to Foucault's 'scaffold, where the body of the tortured criminal had been exposed to the ritually manifested force of the sovereign'.[1] The sovereign, in this case, is a constructed figure or figures of the power vested in the regime – the imagination is really on the part of the actor who imagines; in this case, the judge, the police officer, or any other agent of the regime's law enforcement, is imagining the power (*vlast'*) for whom they are performing.

Since there is little 'justice' in these performed accusations, and, as the condemned say, it is rather 'the crime of the state' against them than vice versa, the trials and repressions demonstrate how the goal is not to establish lawful order but instead to establish an order that is suitable for the regime. Under Kazakhstan's conditions and the legacies of bloody and violently repressed protests in 1986 and 2011, the regime before January 2022 was fearful of an open and traumatic confrontation with the body of the protesting crowds. Thus, as I will demonstrate in this and in the two last chapters, trials and repression in this period

---

[1] Foucault 1977: 115.

before the January 2022 protests[2] were done in such a way as to balance the necessity of intimidating any further protestors and demonstrating the 'force of the sovereign' (dictatorship) as still potent against the need to not exacerbate the violation of human rights, which would lead to a significant state of victimhood on the part of the protestors. So the protestors had to leave the 'scaffold' bruised but not dead, fearful and defeated, while the Nazarbayev regime hoped to sustain its good image as the type of country that wants to join the club of the thirty most developed nations in the world. The aim of the regime was to tame the protest of the Kazakh Spring but to do so quietly, which, as we will see from what follows, did not always go as planned. One issue that the regime still cannot fully tame is the social media sphere, which remains uncontrolled despite the growth of bots, secret police profiling, and other tactical measures.

In this chapter, I argue that despite the shrinking of the public sphere and of channels for discussing and opposing regime coercion, Qazaq Koktemi allowed for creative and alternative approaches to debunking the effects of this coercion. My numerous respondents described their experience of living under an authoritarian regime as an effect of the totality of the state or regime coercion (described in the context of *vlast'* in the previous chapter). They spoke of potential fears and repercussions for their protest actions heard about from their parents and close friends but then described their own police detention and incarcerations as something completely unexpected and not as described. This experience of interacting with law enforcement and the coercive regime face to face proved to be very distinct for each of them. This, however, changed with the January 2022 protests that were locally dubbed as Bloody January (*Qandy Qantar*), to which I return in the final chapter.

In this chapter, I will present the accounts of pre–Bloody January coercion in more detail and use narratives throughout this and the following chapters to unpack the argument of how protestors viewed

---

[2] I suggest that these chapters, which recount the events preceding the January 2022 protests (covered in Chapter 7) should be read as historical material. The unprecedented violence of Bloody January 2022 divided history into 'before' and 'after'. In this book, I largely focus on the 'before', while in *What Does It Mean to Be Kazakhstani* I attempt to make sense of the horrors of what the long post-January brought to Kazakhstani society (see Kudaibergen 2024, especially chapters 5 and 6).

and continue to view law enforcement as a direct continuation of the authoritarian regime with its value system, mechanisms, and justifications for violence that are no longer legitimate. I also demonstrate how this de-legitimization and re-legitimization happens through the performative aspects of law, court hearings, and prosecution, using the case of Asya Tulesova's trial in the summer of 2020 for assaulting police officers during the unsanctioned rally in Almaty. I argue that this trial demonstrated three crucial shifts in regime–protestor relations.

First, the trial demonstrated the injustices and inconsistencies of authoritarian law-making and law-enforcement mechanisms. It was also done in a performative way[3] and televised live to demonstrate how many of the plaintiffs (police officers) could not answer direct questions about their own accusations in an open court. Second, the online trial coincided with online protests around the regime's inadequate response to the pandemic and saw the extent of the growing power of virtual communication that united a lot of people in the face of these injustices and problems. Finally, because the trial was televised on YouTube and held completely online (on Zoom) due to the conditions of the pandemic lockdowns, it transferred the regime's static approaches of control to a dimension where the regime could not dictate the narrative. The mediation of its practices got completely out of control and demonstrated the complete absurdity of the fabricated cases as well as the incompetence of most of the police officers involved. Long before the Depp–Heard televised trial that became a sensation in the United States, the Kazakhstani internet community turned the whole trial and its participants (apart from Asya Tulesova and her lawyers, who were considered local celebrities afterwards) into a major meme; prosecutor's and judge's quotes were ridiculed and pictures of police officers turned into ironic 'stickers' – online

---

[3] Due to the unprecedented conditions of the Covid-19 pandemic and lockdowns in Kazakhstan, the hearing had to be conducted online. Tulesova was given a separate interrogation room with a laptop and WiFi access in her prison to join via Zoom, while the team of her lawyers joined the same Zoom session from different locations. Under pressure from human rights activists and NGOs, and due to other complex and unprecedented reasons, the Zoom hearing was also broadcast live on YouTube and through MediaZone Central Asia social media accounts as well as the Facebook page of Bakhytzhan Toregozhina (the activist who was granted access to the online hearing).

communication tools similar to emojis – to make fun of the whole process.⁴

Had the police become an institution of fear or the butt of jokes? How did the open trial demonstrate the low level of police officers' preparation and their lack of work ethic? And most importantly, what does this institution of law enforcement tell citizens about the overall weakness of the regime? If, prior to the Kazakh Spring, detentions and court hearings after unsanctioned rallies used to scare people, then with the unprecedented wave of protests, new slogans – 'You cannot imprison all of us!' – emerged as a counter-force to these fears and tactics. After the incarcerations and tortures of January 2022, a new campaign to help the victims of torture emerged online under the hashtags of Qantar 2022 (the Kazakh *Qantar* translates as January), and I discuss this separately in the final chapter.

Prior to the 2020 protests and trials, some of the leaders of the then-OSDP Azat party (Bulat Abilov⁵ and Amirzhan Kosanov) resigned from doing politics publicly, citing their numerous detentions and possible longer sentences in prison as an explanation for such a sudden end to political careers. But in post-2019 Kazakhstan, the reality was such that the more activists were arrested, the more protest it caused. When every protest action ended up with police clashes and arrests, the remaining group of activists and protestors occupied spaces around police detention centres to force the police to release all those detained.⁶ Many of the protestors had not meet each other prior to coming to the squares, but their solidarity was growing stronger with each protest action. This, the emergence of the civil sphere, was something the regime did not anticipate at first when it continued to use the old ways of police harassment against the people.

The well-known expert on law-enforcement studies in the post-Soviet space, Erica Marat, defines police as 'a medium of state-society consensus on the limits of the state's legitimate use of violence'.⁷

---

⁴ See Huntington 2016; Milner 2013; Ross and Rivers 2017 on memes.
⁵ Following the January 2022 mass protests and the greater wave of contentions in Kazakhstan, Abilov announced his return to politics and the formation of a new party, which remains unregistered at the time of writing.
⁶ This tendency reached a boiling point when a famous *aqyn* (improvising singer) Rinat Zaitov was arrested in June 2019. See www.rferl.org/a/balloting-for-first-new-kazakh-president-in-three-decades-marred-by-hundreds-of-arrests/29990697.html.
⁷ Marat 2018: 2.

Furthermore, she argues that these reforms and consensus over what constitutes the police's 'legitimate use of violence against citizens to sustain public order' is not a static process but one that engages with constant debates and discussions with non-state actors about the state's monopoly over the legitimate use of violence.[8] In authoritarian contexts, these debates might have fewer established or open channels for negotiation, but that does not mean that these negotiations are absent.

Marat's well-documented analysis of five post-Soviet states and their similar police systems inherited from Soviet times demonstrates different tactics used by populations to oppose police brutality in Georgia, Ukraine, Kyrgyzstan, Kazakhstan, and Tajikistan. She writes that the population's desire to avoid contact with police and other law-enforcement institutions at all costs is one strategy. In fact, this is also the strategy that was adhered to in totalitarian Soviet times, when any law-enforcement actor was seen as a greater danger and more fearful subject than the public disorder that they were supposed to counter.[9] Kazakhstani citizens still lack trust in police and law-enforcement institutions and rely largely on their close informal networks to deal with problems and issues that arise, unless the problem involves a really serious crime or the necessity to contact the police.[10] This reflects the failure of the state, and the authoritarian system in general, to sustain not only the image but the real working of these institutions and to gain public trust in them. Another strategy she described was the use of mobile phones to document police brutality against the protestors, and this process of mirroring police action through mobile technology also allows the narration of the ways the authoritarian regime counters any protest:

Starting in the 2010s with the spread of video recording technologies, protestors have often used their mobile devices to document police actions.

The government swiftly reacts to any collective gathering for a common cause, usually with the Interior Ministry deploying armoured vehicles. Scores of protestors are arrested on the spot, while police personnel block access to the demonstration in case anyone else wishes to join it. Following the protest,

---

[8] Marat 2018, pp. 3–4. [9] See Yurchak 2006.
[10] The 2020 index of citizens' trust in law-enforcement agencies in Kazakhstan demonstrated that more than half the respondents do not trust the police and overall law-enforcement agencies (only 35 per cent trusted the prosecution office, 24 per cent trusted anti-corruption agencies, and 20 per cent trusted the so-called economic police).

the national government may issue a statement explaining why the protestors misunderstood the issue they were protesting and that their concerns have been taken into account. Those arrested are charged with misdemeanours and released.[11]

Since the advent of mobile technologies, the opportunity to televise protests and reveal the true nature of what is going on in the public squares shifted to anyone who has a phone. If, before, the protests were broadcast from the binary division of pro-governmental media outlets that either diminished or ignored protests altogether and the oppositional or foreign media that was seen as 'biased' against the regime, now the first videos of the 2011 Zhanaozen riots and of the police killing the protestors completely broke that old dynamic. First of all, the ability to televise is now within the power and in the hands of practically anyone with a smartphone. Second, this opportunity to broadcast allows complete freedom over the interpretation of content – videos from protesting squares or of police brutality require no reporting on the part of those who record and witness them. Finally, for better or worse in this instant mobile revolution, the first-hand content and videos of protests and police brutality spread rapidly through chat rooms, private communication, and trusted circles. And every new video created buzz in these smaller circles and communities. This is why the Tokayev administration's first move during the January 2022 protests in Kazakhstan was to shut down the Internet and all mobile connections at any cost. Kazakhstani citizens were cut off from any communication for days during the heightened clashes and killings of the protestors, and their only source of information was the state television that controlled the narrative. After the Internet was restored, during the second week of January, rumours and conspiracies spread all across the country. Many of my respondents among ordinary citizens (not activists) told me that they thought the January protests were a 'civil war'.

The protests that continued after the 2019 presidential elections and went on through the difficult first pandemic year of 2020 demonstrated how the new language of resistance occupied an important innovative niche with the use of social media, visual spectacles, and digitization of the community. This chapter is dedicated to the analysis of the digital ethnography of protests. It focuses on the different online initiatives

[11] Marat 2018: 159–60.

and case studies of group support and the first Zoom court hearings of Asya Tulesova's case in August 2020. In this chapter, I analyse how communities of activists engaged virtually, allowing Qazaq Koktemi to remain powerful without depending on the physical presence of its activists, but relying heavily on the production of meaning online. I first discuss the overall context of the social media landscape before turning to the ways activism exists online and to how televised trials expose the regime's inadequacy and weaknesses.

Qazaq Koktemi and Social Media

Understanding the rise of Qazaq Koktemi is impossible without the analysis of their social media engagement and without contextualizing it within the wider trend of further web-networking going on everywhere in the world. Even though some scholars, among them Manuel Castells, were fairly quick to weigh up the success of the Arab Spring on social networks and particularly on Twitter (2015), the growing online engagement is indeed not something to ignore in this decade. The top five global social media platforms in 2021 were Facebook (2.8 billion users), YouTube (2 billion users), WhatsApp (2 billion users), Instagram (1.074 billion users), and WeChat (1.24 billion users, with 45 billion messages exchanged on this app daily).

In Central Asia, Kazakhstan is the leading country for social media and mobile internet users. With over 87 per cent of internet users in the overall population of 18 million, Kazakhstan has 12 million social media users. Social media consumption increased expeditiously in Kazakhstan from 2020 by 26 per cent (adding 2.5 million users). The vast majority of these users (over 11 million) are using mobile internet for their social media presence, which is understandable since many messengers and platforms are meant primarily for mobile phone use. For instance, Instagram, as the most popular social media in Kazakhstan, is mainly accessible through phones and accounts for 11 million Kazakhstani users in 2021.[12] If we compare these numbers to other Central Asian republics, then only Kyrgyzstan, where half of the Kyrgyz population were social media users in 2021 – 3.2 million out

---

[12] Report available at https://datareportal.com/reports/digital-2021-kazakhstan. By 2023, the same data demonstrated that there were 17.7 million internet users (the population of Kazakhstan had grown to over 19 million people by then) and around 60 per cent of the Kazakh population were social media users.

of the 6.58 million overall population[13] – stands close in percentage numbers to Kazakh social media users. Eighteen million of Uzbekistan's 33 million population are internet users, but only 4.6 million of them were social media users in January 2021.[14] The least-networked online society is Turkmenistan, where only 33 per cent of the population use the Internet, with only 150,000 social media users,[15] where IMO messenger and Instagram remain the most popular social media platforms, and many users have to choose different VPN systems to connect due to state restrictions.

Why has Instagram become so popular and important for alternative political communication in Kazakhstan? Instagram is a visual-based social media platform that constantly offers new formats for engagement. It was launched in 2010 as a photo-sharing platform but quickly grew into the global neoliberal and influencing space for establishing trends on anything from consumption (fashion, travel, interior, food, etc.) to body and beauty standards.[16] It became popular in 2012. In Kazakhstan, Instagram is also highly political as a platform for political memes, video sharing, and content on everyday social issues and problems. In this space, the anti-corruption public platform (a type of Instagram group) ProTenge can be equally as popular as the so-called mummy bloggers talking and showing how to be a good wife and mother.[17] Kazakh Instagram offers a space for critique and opinion-sharing that is not openly and widely available elsewhere, because users can keep their profiles private or use different nicknames for their accounts and comment without revealing their identity. Different users can also engage with content by simply reading, watching, or listening to content but not subscribing to the public or the specific page where they seek this information. The popularity of Instagram is also

[13] https://datareportal.com/reports/digital-2021-kyrgyzstan.
[14] https://datareportal.com/reports/digital-2021-uzbekistan.
[15] According to the Data portal report for 2021: https://datareportal.com/reports/digital-2021-turkmenistan.
[16] See Cohen, Newton-John, and Slater 2017 on body image on Instagram.
[17] The popularity of such different segments on Instagram as the anti-corruption news portal ProTenge (57,000 public followers) and Happy Wife and Mom 'female club' (with 288,000 private followers) that shares anonymous and often problematic stories of married people seeking advice can be explained by different segments and interests of users. However, the level of 'engagement' with online content on Instagram – reposting, commenting, saving posts, and so on – demonstrates that many Kazakhstanis use social media as alternative sources of information-seeking.

explained by the variety of forms and genres of information sharing. There are reels – short videos (often duplicated from TikTok); stories – individual videos, texts, and photos shared by users for twenty-four hours only; and ordinary posts – in the forms of photos, videos, banners, memes, and also texts. Finally, because the average age of Kazakhstani social media users is thirty, and because Instagram is a highly popular platform for young people, in particular, it became a hit for Kazakhstani informal communication.

In my previous digital ethnography of Kazakh and Russian Instagram, I largely focused on gendered norms and power relations,[18] but since then I have explored issues of marriage and divorce, political memes, and, importantly, political mobilization of various opposition groups. President Tokayev uses Instagram as his active platform for communicating state programmes to citizens, and, equally, Zhanbolat Mamay uses it as a free media platform for his long speeches and programmes. Qazaq Koktemi and Oyan, Qazaqstan activists go further than that – they use a combination of different social media platforms where they are able to cross-post and cross-pollinate different audiences with the same messages. For example, Assem Zhapisheva has a YouTube channel for her Til Kespes Jok journalistic platform, a Telegram channel where she shares all types of news, opinions, and texts, Instagram, and a Twitter (X) account as well as Facebook. All of these platforms allow her to reach her own bilingual target audience and find new followers.

The question of how much impact this type of social media has on people will continuously influence research methodologies and outcomes for decades to come. Some findings demonstrate slight changes in opinions in the United States following the Black Lives Matter movement,[19] with 23 per cent of respondents shifting their views due to social media. The same report, however, mentions the overall negative view Americans have about social media. This analysis is further complicated by regional and country-based attitudes, and while in the United States, the perception is also divided by class, race, and ethnicity, in places such as Kazakhstan and Russia, this data is still largely unexplored. There is also a big difference between more democratic

---

[18] Kudaibergenova 2019a.
[19] See Pew Research Report, July 2020: www.pewresearch.org/short-reads/2020/12/11/social-media-continue-to-be-important-political-outlets-for-black-americans/.

and open systems where information is widely available and where citizens turn to social media for different reasons than places where access to independent sources of information is minimal. Social media remains the access gate to all sorts of information. There is simply a different type of social media consumption when it comes to authoritarian contexts, where public opinion can be imbued both with fears but also with distrust that inevitably leads to further social groupings, disintegration, and often conspiracies.[20] Within Oyan, Qazaqstan itself, there is a clear understanding of these social divisions and disintegrations because many of my respondents from the movement stressed the necessity to inform and attract as many as possible of the audiences who distrust everything – from the regime to its opposition.

The movement's strategy in this atmosphere of distrust and, as a result, political apathy is to turn to social media, which has already become a channel of information-sharing much more popular than the official Khabar media conglomerate with its significant annual budgets. The local term *khabarization* (*khabarizatsiya*) is used to ridicule the channel's way of presenting everyday life and news in Kazakhstan as if it is a parallel reality. The news creates a narrative of a peaceful and calm life by censoring the protests, labour disputes, and corruption scandals that happen in Kazakhstan on a daily basis. 'Instead, Khabar broadcasts happy people in the fields collecting the harvest', as one of my interlocutors commented by saying that *khabarization* is the parallel perfect world 'that exists only for Nazarbayev and his elites but not for ordinary people'.[21] One of the popular memes on the topic ends with the words: 'Switch on Khabar and let me doze off' – *vklyuchite Khabar i dayte mne zabyt'sya*. These conditions of dual reality and living in a situation where the whole population of the country knows that the official media does not report the truth but creates an invented country of peace and happiness where the biggest challenge are natural disasters (which official media cannot ignore) is the type of reality described by Lisa Wedeen in authoritarian Syria. In conditions where 'daily state-controlled newspapers in Syria are widely considered to be functional tablecloths, rather than respected records of current events', she wrote in 1999, and the fact that 'all Syrians are capable of

---

[20] On conspiracies in Russia and post-Soviet space in general, see Yablokov 2018 and Radnitz 2021.
[21] Anonymous interview with Oyan, Qazaqstan activist from the media sphere, July 2020.

reproducing the regime's formulaic slogans tells us mainly that the regime is capable of enforcing obedience on the level of outward behavior' (Wedeen 1999: 5). In authoritarian regimes, people are capable of living with a very balanced understanding that they are living in an authoritarian regime with all its negative consequences but also to balance it with the necessity of constructing their everyday life as best as they can. Thus, the knowledge of irregularity does not transfer to direct or public engagement with its injustice. Instead of condemning Khabar, people simply disregard it and seek their information elsewhere, often through trusted networks of family and collegial chats on WhatsApp or other messengers that serve as a digital sphere of connections and communication.

In these conditions, it was inevitable that Oyan, Qazaqstan activists, most of whom did not watch television but instead depended on their mobile internet for information, resorted to the type of digital activism they were used to. But in these approaches, they were following the template that everyone else around them used. In the words of one activist of the movement,

For us, it is about constructing communication – you are looking for your people. Then, in Kazakhstan, you rarely can rely on people physically protesting on the streets when you are going to protest against something, simply at rallies. There is an understanding that only 1% of those who announced that they would come to a rally actually show up. I think social media is a great tool and opportunity for all those who are still not ready to get out there and to claim their rights on the streets. So, for now, they can do it on social media by voicing their opinion. What is good about it [social media presence] is that it is something where you can develop your skills and considerably safely express your political opinion. For example, you can use the anonymous approach online or use other digital safety tools [for communication of your ideas]. But even if you are not making some super aggressive or strong announcements [about the regime], then you still can express your own opinion in a calm way and still find supporters. All accounts also have the statistics – they can see how many people support you [online]. You can see how many people like or follow you but also how many people read your content [without directly following the account], and this gives you an understanding of how many supporters you have. And also, when we have official media – this is official television and information that is broadcasted from there, but we only can find information that is actually factual and real and read this information on social media. And all those media that are adequate and independent are understandably based mainly on social media. So, it makes it clear that activism [in Kazakhstan] right now is not possible without social media. ... some of these independent or trustworthy media include Vlast' web portal [in Kazakhstan] and Azattyq; there is also Mediazona – they opened up their branch in Central Asia. There is also Kloop – a Kyrgyz portal – and we have Hola News. You can receive adequate information from them. In Telegram, there are a series of anonymous channels, and it is completely unknown who is editing and leading them, but there you can always find some sort of gossip and sort of political stuff you can read there as well [*okolopoliticheskie veshi pochitat' tam mojno*].[22]

Communication within Oyan, Qazaqstan is divided into two layers – the restricted one for the working group and the open one for any member of the public who has access to the movement's platforms and open chats on social media. Let me address these findings one by one. The working group of activists inside Oyan, Qazaqstan is a very secretive sphere, and it was something that many of my respondents were not eager to talk about openly. From their diverse comments, I was able to piece together a picture where the working group consists of around thirty to forty most active and trusted people at any time, and these people are divided into sub-groups based on their tasks. For example, one group might be tasked with working on preparing the visual aid for the protests on the ground and making unified font, colouring, and symbols for the movement on all physical posters.[23] Another group might be involved with legal aspects and preparing the quick info flyer for all those protesting at unsanctioned rallies (see Figure 4.1).

Because the movement is organized horizontally, each working group has a different leader for different tasks, and each group communicates with one another during planned meetings but also through

---

[22] Author's anonymous interview with Oyan, Qazaqstan activist, June 2020 [Q2].
[23] The importance of banners and posters largely increased after the initial 'poster war' in April–June 2019, when many protestors were harassed and arrested for holding even a blank poster, as was discussed in Chapter 2. The more Oyan, Qazaqstan protested in person in public spaces, the more they understood that their protest was appropriated by existing opposition forces, especially by the DVK group who tried to take away the speakers and microphones or who came to the announced meetings with their own posters. This explained why Oyan, Qazaqstan and the anonymous group of Qazaq Koktemi banner teams who continuously came up with different banners, graffiti, and other visuals throughout the course of the two years from 2019, focused so much on brand coherence. Font, colour, type of messages, and hashtags clearly separated these groups from everyone else protesting simultaneously in the same space but often with a quite distinct agenda.

Figure 4.1 'What to take to the rally': card produced by Oyan, Qazaqstan. Source: Oyan, Qazaqstan

heavily encrypted chats and platforms. Activists do not give up the spaces and names of the platform where they communicate due to the necessity of keeping their communication strictly private between those in each working group. As soon as someone leaves the movement or a working group for whatever reason, that person has to also leave the secret chat and lose access to the ongoing discussions and preparations for security reasons.

I still don't know, and all this time, I am still scared to speak about it all [respondent's activism in Oyan, Qazaqstan's working groups]. For example, yesterday or the day before that something has happened – someone made a video on YouTube, I think it was a Russian source, and they made a video using screenshots from one of our first chats [for Oyan, Qazaqstan activists]. In this video, one could see the name of the sender [in the chat], and some of our guys [within the movement] thought it was one of us who revealed and shared these screenshots, and this person was immediately removed from the secret chat following the security protocol. It is the right move – this was needed to be done because if his phone was hacked, if someone [completely outside the movement] got access, then it means [our member's] phone got hacked. Or there are other instances as well – if someone is arrested, the same thing happens, and that person is immediately removed from the secret chat because we cannot let others down. And now, this situation repeated itself again. I remember the time when we were all together, and I remember when this paranoia type of thing started. Some things I can talk about, but it is hard for me to discuss certain things without mentioning other people and their names, the names of people who were in the movement since the very beginning – this is very important. But it is impossible to mention their names without their consent, and it is more likely, that they might agree but not immediately. All this time, half the people [within the movement] agreed to publicity, but half completely disagreed with it [and wanted to remain anonymous]. That is why there is some problem with the description of the whole process and how it all started, but it has to be made without mentioning some names.[24]

Members of these working groups advocated for the necessity of encryptions and secret chats for security and organization but stressed that these chats were open to the wider following of the movement. The detailed procedure of entering these closed working groups is something that is dealt with within the movement and was explained to me as an internal process of selection and internal voting. But in order to seek a wider membership, the movement has to remain open to newcomers, and this is where they use other means of social media platforms. One of the biggest spaces for communication and interaction is the movement's Telegram chat, where more than 500 people are freely registered and can engage with each other, albeit many of the participants are communicating anonymously under Telegram nicknames. This is the second layer of the movement's communication. The chat plays a role of the gateway and a testing zone for the potential new members of the movement. This is where people can come to ask questions, report on protests in their city, discuss political issues, and communicate with Oyan admins about the movement. However, the decision to grant someone more access to the secured area of the movement happens in more private communication and often after the person has met the members face to face and some trust has been built.

---

[24] Author's interview with anonymous activist of Oyan, Qazaqstan, August 2020.

Digital Imagined Community United in Grief

The advent of the global Covid-19 pandemic changed the protest dynamics in Kazakhstan like everywhere else in the world in 2020. All of the rallies now became even more unsanctioned and even illegal due to the pandemic restrictions. However, despite the restrictive lockdown measures, the country experienced a dramatic outburst of infections and Covid-related deaths in the summer of 2020. The spread of the virus surged rapidly in June 2020 and continued its first deadly attack throughout July and August, leading to the virus's first significant blow. By 10 July, '54,747 COVID-19 cases and 264 deaths were recorded in the country'.[25] With the rather small population of 18 million (at the time) and the tightening conditions of the healthcare system's capacity to treat the severe cases, the situation was critical. On top of that, Kazakhstan suffered a significant economic blow. The World Bank Summer 2020 report on the Kazakhstani crisis stated that the country's 'GDP is likely to contract by nearly 3.0 per cent in 2020, more than double the rate previously envisaged in early March, as external demand and prices for crude [oil] potentially collapse more sharply and the mitigation practices last longer and hit businesses harder than envisaged previously' (Agaidarov, Izvorski, and Rahardja 2020: 20–1).

These conditions influenced growing feelings of insecurity and sent the country's population to constant applications for the meagre 42,500 KZT monthly welfare support payments (less than 100 USD). Protest feelings surged again when, on 6 July 2020, the official celebration of the Kazakh capital Nur-Sultan that always coincided with the unofficial birthday celebration for Nursultan Nazarbayev, who was turning eighty that year, were celebrated with pompous and expensive fireworks. People were angered all over the country, and this anger and criticism led to a number of cultural outbursts. Kazakh popular singer Dimash Kudaibergen wrote the following critical note on his Instagram account with 3 million people:

What were these fireworks supposed to honour??? The fact that we are in first place in coronavirus infections? People cannot find oxygen tanks, and in Astana, they are setting off fireworks! Carry on like this, and there will be nobody left to celebrate next year.[26]

[25] United Nations Kazakhstan: COVID-19 Situation Report No. 7 (10 July 2020).
[26] Cited from https://eurasianet.org/kazakhstan-nur-sultan-revelry-sparks-ire-as-coronavirus-crisis-escalates.

The popular Kazakh rappers Irina Kairatovna criticized the 6 July fireworks in their video '5 K', where people with oxygen masks, a pregnant woman, and others were dying from the fireworks. The visual and the video in general criticized many of the government's approaches to politics. They ridiculed the large-scale corruption, neglect, and failures of the anti-Covid measures that demonstrated that only the most powerful elites of the regime seemed to have access to the necessary oxygen masks, while dead bodies were piling up. The name of the song symbolized '5,000 KZT' as one of the most ubiquitous (albeit small) bribes.

The protest mood was everywhere on social media – people called for action, for the government to stop disguising the Covid-19 infections and deaths and to stop the mass corruption in the pharmaceutical sphere and in projects related to the so-called Covid hospitals.[27] The corruption scandals continued even after the former health minister was detained in October 2020 following corruption probes.[28]

During that tough summer of 2020, the Kazakhstani media space was overflowing with new details of personal tragedies, lack of oxygen provision for severe cases, and open corruption. One of these instances was the story from Shymkent of when the daughter of a patient who died from Covid-19 started an open campaign to sue the hospital for stealing her mother's private oxygen tank, which the family had bought on the black market at five times more than its usual price.

Different actors from Qazaq Koktemi got involved in this wave of mutual support for the digital 'imagined community' with solidarity and condolences over the deaths of relatives and loved ones. In messages, programmes, and initiatives led by different activists at this time, there was a deep sense of solidarity for each compatriot left in a difficult situation. This was how the Umytpa portal was launched, to document

---

[27] The BI group that won the tender to build additional hospitals for dealing with growing Covid-19 hospitalizations was involved in an alleged corruption scandal where they were probed for embezzling more than 9 million USD from the tender for the new hospitals. The scandal was branded in Kazakhstan as anti–Covid hospitals corruption: see https://ratel.kz/raw/skolko_esche_v_ka zahstane_modulnyh_infektsionnyh_bolnits. At the time of the writing, the anti-corruption law-enforcement agencies were still investigating this case. See also https://rus.azattyq.org/a/corruption-in-the-health-care-system-in-kazakhstan/3 0917536.html.

[28] https://thediplomat.com/2020/11/former-kazakh-health-minister-detained-in-c orruption-probe/.

the names of those who died from Covid-19 in Kazakhstan even though their deaths were often written off as pneumonia, accompanying underlying health conditions, and other reasons in order to flatten out the local pandemic statistics. *Umytpa* translates from Kazakh as 'Don't Forget' and was an initiative organized by six media platforms – Vlast' news portal, The Village Kazakhstan news portal, Mediazona Central Asia, Factcheck.kz, RFE Azattyq, and two Telegram and Instagram-based platforms Za Nami Uje Viehali and Til Kespes Jok, run by Assem Zhapisheva. In her own words, this is why they decided to organize this group initiative, which now includes over 500 names of Covid-19 victims with their dates of birth, occupation, and place of living:

> *Diana T. Kudaibergen (DTK)*: You are taking the lead with the Umytpa project that creates the database of those who died from Covid. Is this some type of an attempt to make statistics more personal?
>
> *Assem Zhapisheva*: Yes. First of all, it is a demonstration to the regime that we will not simply take [their lies] just like that. Because in the last past months [of summer 2020], it was impossible to reach some sort of open data on Covid infections. They constantly falsified statistics – they [the regime] started dividing between those with symptomatic and asymptomatic. And, secondly, I guess we are also tired because it is not happening for the first year. I remember in 2016 or 2017 ... our statistics committee used to send journalists statistical updates about the number of children born and those numbers of the dead, and this statistic was presented by each city. And when in 2017, there was another celebration of Astana's anniversary. A half-year before then, the statistics committee suddenly just stopped sending these reports, and this information disappeared from their website. Before that moment, Astana's population accounted for 800,000 people ... Journalists started sending requests to the statistics committee in order to find out what had happened, but they [in the committee] said that their system was glitching. ... And on 6 July, they started sending these statistical reports again, and their first report sent said that now Astana had 1 million dwellers. It was exactly on 6 July that year that Astana's millionth dweller was born. It was really absurd. First of all, so how were 200,000 people born [in that time]? Where did they come from? And we understand that this attitude is really about one person saying, 'I want 1 million people by this date [in Astana], I made this city into a capital city.' And the whole state apparatus basically lied to the whole country and kept the numbers hidden. And everyone swallowed it, and it happens all the time in all spheres. I remember how in 2008 when we had the [financial] crisis, all

journalists were forbidden to write that we had the crisis at the time, so we didn't have a crisis and then all of a sudden, the post-crisis period started. This total lie [existed for long], and they [the regime] got so used to it that the Covid-19 pandemic started to open it up. And if before these lies did not lead to something global, then now these lies create the situation when there are not enough beds in the hospitals, there are not enough meds, and there are a lot of different challenges because by hiding this data from the people, the system also hiding it from the regions. . . .

DTK: At Umytpa, you give a chance for people to talk about their relatives who died from Covid?

Assem Zhapisheva: Yes.

DTK: How do people react to it? It is understandable that they go to this website because they have specific goals. What are these goals? You communicate with them about these issues, so you know?

Assem Zhapisheva: You see, in reality, it is a very strange thing . . . people who sent their relatives' data, all of them understand quite clearly that right now there are a lot of applications that are frozen out there [in the database] because many people started fearing because they publish these details and then they would be sanctioned by the regime. . . . I am in charge of the Kazakh-speaking audiences on the website, and I constantly hear the same 'if the dead are already dead, then why bother? My relatives told me not to publish the name anywhere because then there would be problems' . . . It also happens like that because this is how the system is built, and people are scared . . .

Sometimes you call, and they calmly send you the details. Sometimes I called, and they told me, 'You know in my house [everyone] died.' With one woman I spoke to, she said her husband had died [from Covid], and then both of her parents died because they all lived together, and now, she was all alone in the big house. I just couldn't hang up, and we started talking. Then I asked her why she didn't report the details of her parents, but she said that her relatives did not allow her. And another woman said that in her circles, around forty people died from this virus among her friends and relatives because they were all in contact, and it goes like a snowball . . . I asked her why she only gave one name for the database, and she said that the relatives of other people who died rejected the idea of the database. They don't want to; they are scared. It is very emotional.[29]

Why did these stories and narratives matter at the time of the chaotic wave or what I call the Covid-19 summer 2020 in Kazakhstan? Because

---

[29] Author's interview with Assem Zhapisheva.

unlike the elitist view of macro-narratives where the state is constructed in a sense as a mass of anonymous and identifiable bodies and above all the only visible and important figure is that of the dictator, initiatives such as Umytpa spoke of personalizing the narrative and the tragedy. These were the meta- and micro-stories the 'state' – or rather the regime – was not interested in but also was actively suppressing in order to hide its major structural failures in addressing not only the pandemic but also the totality of the corruption that led to unfinished hospital buildings and skyrocketing prices for basic provisions of paracetamol and aspirin. The micro-stories, like one of the women who told Zhapisheva that half of her WhatsApp chat with her former schoolmates died from Covid after they all went to one wedding, were explicitly telling the story of personal tragedy but also the collective failure of the regime. So, when I asked her what the point of hiding these dead bodies of the state's citizens was, she described it as a paradox of Kazakhstani politics:

> This is the paradox. Because our state's client is not the person [*ne chelovek*], not the citizen, but its client is the regime itself [*vlast' sama*]. And when your client is the regime itself, you want to do everything in such a way to foremost make your client satisfied. And if the regime says, 'what the hell, I don't want to occupy fifth place in the global rating [of Covid mortality]', then [the state] serves the interest of the regime in the first place. What I want to say is precisely this – that the client [of the state] should be the citizen and for this service to be provided [to the citizen] in the first instance. ... Take, for instance, neighbouring Kyrgyzstan where they do not cheat with statistics, and they are in seventh place with Covid infections in the world, we are not far from that, but our statistics divide infected into those with pneumonia, symptomatic and asymptomatic and so on. ... The [state apparatus] client is the regime itself. If a given minister stomps his foot [*topnet nojkoi*], then the entire regime apparatus runs to implement [his wish] right away. Most important is for them [regime] to be satisfied ... this is why we have such a bad policy in social media with all these bots. These pro-regime bots are so obvious that they don't even hide. A lot of money is invested into these bots because some *agashka*[30] sitting in the Ministry of Information doesn't really care about the results [of this information policy], and to him, the most important thing is to have these 3,000 comments online. And no one, of

---

[30] A typical term for the 'patron'. Natsuko Oka defines *agashka* as 'an influential figure with strong personal connections enabling him to achieve objectives in informal ways' in her piece for the Global Informality Project available at www.in-formality.com/wiki/index.php?title=Agashka_(Kazakhstan).

course, would check these comments. If they had oriented towards the citizen as their client even in their perverted ideology, then they would have approached their information policy slightly differently, maybe even wiser.[31]

In her discussion of internet bots, Zhapisheva referred to people paid specifically to go around different accounts and posts on social media and target those people and posts that were negative or critical towards the regime and its health policy, for example. The aim of these bots was not only to discredit any critical positions but also to write about how great the regime was and how well they dealt with the problems.

They [bots] write these all the same comments on my and other people's posts [who are critical about the regime], something along the lines of 'And who are you?' [*A ty kto takaya?*], 'don't criticize our regime, our regime is the best regime in the world' [*ne rugai nashu vlast', nasha vlast' luchshaya vlast' na svete*]. These are bots, *nurbots*.[32]

When I asked Zhapisheva why she called internet bots *nurbots*, she replied laughingly that 'in our country, everything is "nur" and this is why "nurbots"'.[33] Indeed, from the ruling party, Nur-Otan to the capital's name, Nur-Sultan (now changed back to Astana), to the names of some banks and even the smallest kiosks in towns and cities across Kazakhstan the slogan *nur* (ray of light) is directly associated with the cult of *elbasy* – Nursultan A. Nazarbayev – in the best traditions of neo-sultanist rhetoric.[34] Zhapisheva's brief comments on the *nurbots* and the way the regime pays attention to the online and social media sphere are very important. After all, Assem Zhapisheva is not only a household name for bilingual journalism in Kazakhstan but also a big fish in the sea of different media and social media projects. With her own YouTube channel that attracted more than 108,000 open subscribers (by the end of 2023) and viewers and active Telegram and Instagram channels, she is also a co-founder of several media platforms such as Masa (which I discuss in the following chapter), BatyrJamal,[35] and Umytpa.

[31] Author's interview with Assem Zhapisheva.
[32] Author's interview with Assem Zhapisheva.   [33] Ibid.
[34] Applying Juan Linz's 'sultanistic' regimes formula but adapting it to the new contexts of global internet use and turning it into 'neo-sultanistic'. See Linz 2000. *Totalitarian and Authoritarian Regimes*. Boulder, CO: Lynne Rienner Publishers.
[35] This is an Instagram- and Telegram-based editorial portal dedicated to gendered issues, rights, information, and gendered violence. Their campaigns focus on

The proliferation of *nurbot* online campaigns demonstrates how the regime can no longer ignore the developing influence of the online civic sphere in Kazakhstan despite the blocking of the Internet[36] and the increase of the concept of *VPN-stan*. In this story, many would be interested in the ways we can calculate the influence of social media on ordinary Kazakhstanis and whether the Pew Research quantitative studies of social media attitudes are possible under a dictatorship where people are scared to report their relatives' and friends' deaths from Covid-19. Most importantly, we can conclude that social media presence allows ordinary Kazakhstanis to create forms of groupness and solidarity through different social media platforms (from chat rooms and messengers to Facebook and Instagram) and unite behind specific causes.

In this book, I discuss a number of these interrelated political activism campaigns, groups, and initiatives that are all enclosed within the Kazakh Spring field, but there are also numerous initiatives focusing on neighbourhood chat rooms and community-building projects, such as the Korsheler project, or on ecological activism, such as the 'SOS Taldykol' initiative in Astana or 'Save Kok Zhailau' in Almaty, and many more

---

gender gaps, female rights, and gendered violence, which received a lot of attention after the publication of open narratives by rape victims in May 2021. BatyrJamal has a fully fledged media team who interview and produce content with human rights activists and local feminist activists, of whom I write in more detail in the last chapter of this book.

[36] Internet blocking has been a very popular strategy for the Kazakh regime since Mukhtar Ablyazov chose his strategy of 'speaking' to Kazakhstani audiences through Facebook and YouTube social media platforms from 9 pm to 11 pm local Almaty time in roughly 2018. During that time, a lot of users complained about low internet capacity and no access to social media, including popular Instagram. This gave rise to VPN usage to bypass the government's internet blocking. Similar tactics but for blocking internet and cell phone coverage were then used for unsanctioned rallies and protestors, who could not access even basic local mobile network to call for help, and journalists, who could not instantly report the news online. Finally, after the 2019 presidential elections, there was a mass blockage of social media access, since a lot of reporting about vote count and subsequent protests happened on social media. At the same time, local journalists reported the costs for blocking one hour of social media usage in Kazakhstan. Factcheck.kz reported using the Cost Shutdown Tool (COST) that Kazakhstani state paid a total cost of 531,538 USD per hour to block the most popular social media – Facebook, YouTube, Instagram, Twitter, and WhatsApp in the country: see https://factcheck.kz/economics/26-mlrd-tenge-za-chas-blokirovok-socsetej-v-kazaxstane-mif-ili-pravda/. These costs infuriated many online users, who preferred for these budgets to be spent on infrastructure rather than blocking online dissent in the country.

different online solidarity movements and groupness initiatives. My aim is not to discuss all of them in their entirety here; my main focus in this book is to demonstrate how this specific case of political activism emerged in Kazakhstan and how it rapidly developed, taking the place of the previous and institutionalized opposition, now totally dismantled.

As a political sociologist, I am more interested in the tug of war between the regime through its elites, institutions, and indoctrinated officers (to which I turn in the next section) and the array of activists, who are more flexible in their field of Qazaq Koktemi. This tug of war demonstrates how rigid and clumsy the regime is when it comes to addressing the newest trends and technology. This rigidity is in part explained by the sole use by Nazarbayev's regime of instruments inherited from the Soviet totalitarian apparatus – intimidation, secret police, repression, and quiet establishment of a fearful atmosphere. The lack of significant non-regime competition left many of its officers incapable of adapting quickly to the change of environment and global trends. While Oyan, Qazaqstan, and Qazaq Koktemi activists can learn quickly from the Black Lives Matter and Hong Kong protest movements via instant access to global networks that all speak English, the only people within the regime apparatus who can do that are the so-called Bolashak generation of people in their mid-thirties and mid-forties who received their education abroad through the Bolashak state-stipend programme, some even in the elite schools of public administration in the United States, United Kingdom, and Singapore, but who are often as stagnant in their political views as their predecessors. This stagnation and rigidity were most clearly demonstrated through the clash of generations in the televised trial of activist Asya Tulesova in August 2020, to which I turn in the following section.

The Televised Courtroom in times of the Pandemic: Trial as a Spectacle

Abidulla? Abbidulla? – the judge asks again.
Abibulla, – responds [plaintiff] Abibulla.
Abidulla? – repeats the judge.
[I am] against. Abibulla, – repeats Abibulla.

From the Mediazona Central Asia transcript of Asya Tulesova's Zoom court hearing Day 1, 3 August 2020, 15:28 Almaty time

Activist Asya Tulesova was arrested on 6 June 2020 during unsanctioned rallies in downtown Almaty. Previously, the leader of the unregistered Democratic Party of Kazakhstan (DPK), Zhanbolat Mamay, had called for the people to protest outside the Abay monument in downtown Almaty on Saturday, 6 June 2020.[37] By then, it had become a tradition for the exiled former banker and Nazarbayev ally Mukhtar Ablyazov to call on his supporters to rally on the same day as other protests. Ablyazov's DVK movement is considered extremist under Kazakh law, and their protests attract more police repression than usual. This was the case on Saturday, 6 June, when the protestors were stopped short two blocks away from the legendary monument. The protestors were outnumbered by the police, who started pushing and arresting people randomly, Tulesova among them. When she attended the 6 June rally, she was already famous following her previous detentions and rallies, so the policemen attempted to detain her immediately during this rally. Different videos of the event demonstrated how Tulesova was dragged by the police officers; during the trial discussed in what follows, the prosecutor general claimed that she assaulted them.

The official press release from the Almaty police stated that Tulesova 'used force against the policeman' who was working at the time, and she was called into the police station for questioning and subsequently detained on 8 June 2020.[38] After the initial hearing on 10 June, Tulesova was charged and detained under Article 378, 'the insult of a government official' of the Criminal Code of the Republic of Kazakhstan.[39] Her first detention lasted for ten days but was then extended for the duration of her court hearings. In total, she spent almost three months in prison waiting for her trial and was released only after the verdict and a criminal conviction for 'insulting a government official' and 'using violence against a police officer', which after the trial placed restrictions on her movement for a year and a half.

[37] Abay Qonanbayuly is a famous nineteenth-century Kazakh philosopher. There are monuments dedicated to him in all cities of Kazakhstan, and there is an Abay monument in Moscow, where Russian opposition leader Alexey Navalny held his OccupyAbay rallies in 2012. The Abay monument in Almaty is a traditional place for unsanctioned and pro-opposition rallies because Abay was known for his criticisms of despotic powers.
[38] Press release available online in Russian and Kazakh at https://polisia.kz/ru/zh enshhine-udarivshej-politsejskogo-grozit-do-3-let-tyur-my/.
[39] In Russian, the article reads 'oskorblenie predstavitelya vlasti'.

The main evidence for opening the case against Tulesova was the video of her assault, which was heavily edited when presented in court.[40] In the words of Tulesova's lawyers, she was defending the elderly, who were ruthlessly attacked by the police officers. The group of police officers then dragged Tulesova to the nearby police vehicle to arrest her, but she returned to the street, and when she was standing next to another police officer, she was so angered that she removed the police officer's cap (*furazhka*). Six police officers filed the complaint (*zayavlenie*) and were present in the first Kazakhstani virtual court hearings that started on the 3 August 2020.

By the time of the court hearings, Tulesova had spent almost two months in police detention while numerous online campaigns called for her release.[41] One of the most notable was the Instagram-based activist platform Protest Körpe, which was launched online on 29 June 2019 in three languages (Kazakh, Russian, and English) and stated that:

PROTEST KÖRPE is inspired by quraq körpe, a type of Kazakh quilt. Like a quraq körpe, civic activism and protection of our rights depend on the voices and contributions of each one of us. In this work, each square on our 'collective quilt' is important to sew a new Kazakh reality.

We want a fair trial for Asya Tulesova, police that does not resort to violence, and just laws that respect peaceful assembly.

Join us – express your solidarity by creating a banner (on our website https://protestkor.pe) and joining our virtual protest![42]

The purpose of this initiative was to raise awareness about Tulesova's trial and to facilitate more public appeals to free Tulesova. Later, when allegations were growing around the edited video showing how Tulesova attacked the policeman, Protest Körpe used their platform as a way to show the longer video without the frames edited out where she was held by several police officers and forcefully moved to the police bus. This did not exclude the fact that Tulesova attacked the policeman, but the purpose of sharing the full video was to show the whole narrative and to stand against the

---

[40] Numerous online observers and Tulesova's own lawyers pointed this out on many occasions. Videos available at https://tirek.info/asiya-tulesova-ne-bila-politsejskogo-6-iyunya-2020-goda/.
[41] See Amnesty International, EUR 57/2531/2020, for example, available at www.amnesty.org/en/documents/EUR57/2531/2020/en/
[42] From the official Instagram account of the Protestor Körpe publication on 29 June 2020.

fabrications of the prosecutor's office. Protest Körpe raised the issue of law enforcement's manipulations and highlighted their distrust in the openness and fairness of the trial.

The court hearing was delayed till August 2020. In July 2020, Kazakhstan experienced the largest increase in the pandemic, with a record Covid-19-related death toll in Kazakhstan.[43] This raised more issues about the population's distrust in state institutions and their governing efficiency. Tulesova's supporters were very worried that in this situation she would be sentenced to the maximum of three years and that her sentencing would serve as an 'example' or as a precedent to intimidate and scare other activists. In these conditions, the rise of the Protestor Körpe and similar initiatives set an example of the ways civic activists could engage with their audiences online.

Protestor Körpe also called on its followers and their audiences to write appeals 'to the court, the President and the Human Rights Commissioner – three institutions whose responsibility is to protect human rights and uphold the rule of law'.[44] By 1 August 2020, the platform had managed to send 528 appeals in support of Tulesova and the announcement of her court hearing (3 August 2020), but most importantly, the platform was able to unite people as a politically minded community who continued to support Tulesova throughout her online hearings. Their written appeal read in all three languages as follows:

Let's celebrate. Thank you for your voice: please know that it matters. You might have left one comment. Or kept it all week. But every appeal is a mark of your care for Asya, for our political rights and our mutual future in Kazakhstan.

Every day we looked through comments and each time found new people who knocked on the Commissioner's inbox, joined the chain of comments on the Almaty City Court's Facebook page, tagged president on Twitter and

---

[43] The statistical committee of Kazakhstan reported that from May to July 2020 more than 57,000 deaths were reported, which was twice the number of deaths from the previous year. Due to the divided statistics for the Covid-related deaths, there was no clear indication how many people died from Covid or other causes. In July 2020, 28,000 deaths were reported, the vast majority of them due to Covid, even though other causes were often reported on the death certificates, for example, pneumonia or underlying health conditions such as heart disease that were exacerbated by the virus.

[44] From the official Instagram account of the Protestor Körpe publication on 26 July 2020.

Instagram,⁴⁵ or (alas, in vain) waited for someone to come up to the receiver in the Presidential Administration.

Every day there were more of us. And we felt like one united society, with hundreds of eyes and hearts, watching and demanding: with hundreds of arms outstretched to support. At such moments, we have no doubt that we will achieve justice in our country – right now for Asya, and later – for all of us, with freedom of speech, fair elections, the right to peaceful assembly and a just judiciary system.⁴⁶

As Kazakh Instagram accounts were filled with the Protestor Körpe filters and messages in support of Tulesova, she became practically the face of the Kazakh Spring. She united the community made up of all the groups of different activists and inspired change. Oyan, Qazaqstan activist Fariza Ospan, who was arrested in Shymkent for protesting against Tulesova's imprisonment, remembered her feelings around the Protestor Körpe and the subsequent hearing:

Of course, we are all trying to fight for the idea and not for the person [in all the activism]. But here what played out is that Asya is a good person and a nice girl, she has a deep sense of justice, and she really has done a lot of great things [environmental and civic activist projects]. That's why it was a double blow, and it was particularly sad that it had happened to her. How come? You know, had it happened to someone else, we would've stood up and protecting that person equally, we would have done the same [as we did for Asya], but here what also factored was that they claimed that supposedly she attacked six policemen. And you yourself understand that in the country where so much violence happens against women, here they tried to play it as if one woman committed a violent act against six men. It looked so crazy [*eto tak bredovo smotrelos'*]. I felt it back then, and I wanted to see it in order to feel the female solidarity, consolidation, for women to collectively respond to the accusations against her, against the allegation that she committed this crime; I wanted to see the response in rallies, with disagreement, with resonance, which ultimately happened apart for the rallies because I wanted to organize a series of picketing, but I couldn't do it. Regardless, I also saw, everyone saw how popular the online televised court hearings [for Tulesova's hearing] were and how many online comments there were on the court's webpage when Protestor Körpe joined forces and started documenting the hearings [in August 2020]. It was the time [of solidarity] when so many

---

⁴⁵ President Tokayev has official accounts on Twitter (with 190,300 followers) and on Instagram (with 1.8 million of followers) at the time of the Tulesova trial.
⁴⁶ From the official Instagram account of the Protestor Körpe publication on 1 August 2020.

people sent out letters asking to pardon [Tulesova]. It was really great to see how we all united and protected her.[47]

Fariza Ospan was abducted by unidentified police officers during her lone picket in support of imprisoned activist Asya Tulesova in her hometown of Shymkent on 6 July 2020. It happened in front of the city courthouse, but Ospan could not call the police because her abductors were the police. The news of her abduction was immediately shared by activists on social media thanks to her Instagram video (story) where she was seen screaming and kicking off the unidentified men, who were not wearing police or any other law-enforcement officers' uniform and who did not show her their documents. Ospan was held forcibly and assaulted verbally in one of the local police stations for hours while her colleagues and friends were calling all the police stations in Shymkent demanding her immediate release. She was eventually let go without any explanation or any apologies. In her interview with me, she mentioned that the activism behind Tulesova's court hearings left her reflecting on her own positionality in feminist activism and in regard to her own arrest:

This [trial] back then demonstrated to me that you cannot protect yourself, that you ... there was this feeling that if someone would attack you, then you just had to stand and endure the suffering. As patriarchy tells us, 'Women, endure' [*zhenshiny, terpite*] and endure violence, endure humiliation, you cannot do anything against it, and here the regime [*vlasti*] tells us exactly the same [through the court hearings and accusations]. I also felt it when I was picketing [in Shymkent] that I simply had to tolerate [injustice against me]. I had to tolerate and endure that they [policemen] were humiliating me. I had to tolerate how they forcefully threw me to the sofa because all you can do is stand still and be silent because you cannot say anything. Asya's case really influenced me that all I could say [to the policemen] that 'you do not have any right' [to do this to me], but it did not mean anything to them. This statement, 'you do not have any right', is simply a meaningless noise for them [*pustoi zvuk*], so what can you say? In the end, you just get tired of saying, 'you do not have any right' [*vy ne imeete pravo*], and you simply stand there silently, and you endure it. In reality, this is truly horrible. You understand that if you try to protect yourself in response [to what they do], even though it is logical for you to protect yourself in this situation – if they pushed you, then you should try to run away from this room, and even if you hit them [policemen],

---

[47] Author's interview with Oyan, Qazaqstan and feminist activist Fariza Ospan, 5 November 2020.

you need to try to run away, and you will still be right one in this situation because they are holding you illegally [*nezakonno*]. They didn't even tell you why they detained you, and they didn't offer you a lawyer; they threatened you that they would do something with you, and you have the choice to take it as a threat for your life and protect yourself. And even though the truth is on your side in this situation, the regime [*vlasti*] would still frame it in such a way that you [are guilty] and that you beat up the policemen. This is horrible. But the regime [*vlast'*] behaves this way[48].

The Protestor Körpe and activism around Tulesova's case during her hearings created a collective sense of injustice in different online and offline communities inside and outside Kazakhstan. It offered a type of discourse around the injustices of the authoritarian system beyond just the corrupt law enforcement, but with the realization that anyone could be tried by law even if they did not fall under the accusations provided in the 'open, transparent and not secretive court' as the judge Tasken Shakirov announced on the first day of Tulesova's hearing on the 3 August 2020.

Due to the lockdowns and the difficult epidemiological situation in Kazakhstan at the time, the hearing was for the first time held virtually on Zoom and was televised on the major media (Mediazona Central Asia portal) and social media platforms. I conducted my digital ethnography on each day of the hearing while connecting to the YouTube live broadcast and checking Facebook audiences who were also watching and commenting; and on one of the days, when the judge for some reason did not allow YouTube broadcasting, there was an unofficial Instagram live 'stories' broadcast on one of the Qazaq Koktemi accounts, where the live audience could not see the Zoom broadcast but could at least hear it. I also spoke to the people in the audience, and all of my discussions online at the time were connected to the trial.[49]

During the hearing, Mediazona Central Asia, Vlast.kz news portals, and many individual and group social media accounts also provided

---

[48] Author's interview with *Oyan, Qazaqstan* and feminist activist Fariza Ospan, 5 November 2020.
[49] During summer to late 2020, I was simultaneously conducting digital ethnography and fieldwork for this book and my ongoing art fieldwork with the community of contemporary art activists on Zoom and other communication and social media platforms. A lot of my respondents' lists were overlapping, since a great number of art activists that I interviewed during that time were also members of Oyan, Qazaqstan or were within the Qazaq Koktemi field or somehow connected to what was going on around Tulesova.

transcripts of the hearing. Those who did not have access to YouTube, Facebook, Instagram, or media portals could also follow updates on several Telegram channels connected to the Oyan, Qazaqstan and Qazaq Koktemi activists. As the hearings proceeded and news about this digital movement of online watchers spread, many more people joined in every day. In part, a lot of the interest came from the jokes and anecdotes about the policemen's accounts and the prosecutor's objections. Eventually, all seven of them became part of numerous memes.

Five policemen – Nurbek Temirkhanov, Ernat Sabalakov, Tlek Tulegenov, Ulan Abibula, and Taskyn Taldybaev – accused Tulesova of insult, and two – Nurbek Temirkhanov and Meiirzhan Turganbek – of physical violence.[50] All men were part of the group of law-enforcement officers who, in their own words, were called in the early hours of 6 June 2020 to police the unsanctioned rally in Almaty. One of the main pieces of evidence was the edited video showing Tulesova pushing the police cap off of one the policemen with her hand, and she is heard screaming, *Menty, menty, merzkie menty* (disgusting policemen). In this video, *menty*[51] is a colloquial term for policemen that has existed since Soviet times, but plaintiffs and the prosecutor took this term as an offence and argued that Tulesova should be charged for it.

What is crucial in this trial is the use of formal, legal rules and language by law-enforcement officers to justify the regime's undemocratic shutdown of the rallies. Even though their main goal was to sentence Tulesova to the maximum term of imprisonment, the process of the court hearings revealed an important dynamic of how the law-enforcement machine normalized and acquired authoritarian values, leaving no space for the considerations of freedom and civil rights. If Tulesova was or is guilty, she, like any other citizen of Kazakhstan, has to be tried accordingly. But the prosecutor's office relied on continued manipulations of the video, which was heavily edited, and of the plaintiffs' claims, where they were openly fed with answers to the questions raised in the open court. The court processes should be read as the regime's extended symbolic power to define the limits of the possible and the impossible but also to remind the new wave of protestors of the rules of the game, where intimidation and fear play

[50] See transcripts of the hearings at https://mediazona.ca/online/2020/08/03/asya.
[51] *Menty* (plural) or *ment* (singular) is in everyday use, but a more offensive term for the police in Kazakhstan and other parts of the post-Soviet space is *musora* (plural) – translated from Russian as 'garbage'.

a key role. If the courtroom is the symbolic scaffold from Foucault's conceptualization of disciplining and punishing – a space imbued with feelings of fear rather than justice – then the law-enforcement officers play the role of the regime's extended powers to define the meaning of this reality, where even the prosecutor has to obey and fervently support the legal rules of the regime in power (at the time, the Nazarbayev regime). Tulesova's court hearing demonstrates how the law-enforcement institutions, the plaintiffs – the policemen who accused her of violence – and the judge were co-producers of the regime's 'regulatory power' of norms and the behaviour that is expected of the law-enforcement officers, who side not with the state and its citizens, the law and its ideals of freedom and respect for human rights, but with the regime and its autocratic norms of punishing dissent.

In the institutional outlook, this finding is important to stress the deep connection between different state institutions, specifically law enforcement and the regime. In different types of authoritarian regimes, the police, for example, can be a strong contender for power claims within the regime. In Kazakhstan under Nazarbayev, though, the police and other law-enforcement institutions were in full compliance and obedience to the dictator himself. They proudly displayed his portrait in their offices, cited his words and his (often sexist) anecdotes, and felt like the highest goal of their service was to serve Nazarbayev himself. In this process, law enforcement disciplines the people but also disciplines itself by constructing the idea and value of directly obeying Nazarbayev and what they thought he liked and wanted. Lisa Wedeen followed Arendt in the discussion of the prevention or loss of 'personality' – 'a uniquely political self constituted through words and deeds' (Wedeen 1999: 45). The purpose of authoritarianism (Nazarbayev's notwithstanding) in preventing this *political self* is 'to destroy the possibilities for public expressions of contingency, frailty, and interpretative ambiguity, thereby fixing meanings and censoring facts in ways that silence or render irrelevant people's understandings of themselves as publicly political persons' (Wedeen 1999: 45). The law-enforcement officers' speeches and language in Tulesova's court hearing demonstrated that they had lost their political selfhood and taken on the authoritarian selfhood, where they obeyed the Nazarbayev regime without a single idea of contention or ambiguity. In this perception and embodiment of their own authoritarian selfhoods, they sought their positions of power, albeit often completely unaware that they had little to no chance of reaching the top. So, each one of them developed a level of subjectivity where they became their own 'small dictators' within the limits of their own positionality – as the chief prosecutor with his own limitations or as a policeman of the lowest rank who had power within their own families or unleashed violence when ordered to stop the protest.

This is why this trial was so significant for the civic activists and those who formed the new political field. Those who understood the Nazarbayev regime's rules of the game within the Kazakh Spring field immediately proposed law-enforcement reform, to make it an institution that secures citizens' safety instead of securing, producing, and reproducing authoritarian discourse and safeguarding Nazarbayev's rule. During the second trial day, prosecutor Kulanbayev read the following indictment for Tulesova's 'crimes' to legitimate the trial and its purposes, which served the authoritarian order more than anything else:

On June 6, 2020, Tulesova had a direct criminal intent aimed at inflicting violence not dangerous to health on government officials [*nanesenie nasiliya, ne opasnogo dlya zdorovia na predstavitelei vlasti*]. ... Tulesova went to participate in an unsanctioned rally. In order to prevent violation of order, measures were taken to prevent the demonstrators' breakthrough to the Abay monument.[52]

In the prosecutor's words, Tulesova then 'waved her hands' and tried to attack Nurbek Temirkhanov, the police officer who escaped the first blow but lost his police cap after Tulesova's second blow. According to the same indictment, she then 'began to publicly insult all of the victims by shouting at them "Bastard! Bastard! And you are bastard! None of you are worthy to wear the uniform! Vile cops"',[53] which in the original (Russian) language read '*Gad! Gad! I ty gad! Nikto iz vas ne dostoin nosit' formu. Merzkie menty!*'. The terms 'bastard' and 'vile cops' raised a lot of back-and-forth discussion

---

[52] Directly cited and translated from Russian (by me) from the official transcript published by Mediazona Central Asia, available at https://mediazona.ca/online/2020/08/04/asya-2.

[53] Directly cited and translated from Russian (by me) from the official transcript published by Mediazona Central Asia, available at https://mediazona.ca/online/2020/08/04/asya-2.

between Tulesova's lawyer team, which included the lawyer Djokhar Utebekov – who is famous for his social media presence and writing on legal injustices[54] – the prosecutor, and the judge.

The public trial resonated with the equivocal performance of proclaimed justice but was enveloped in injustice and was supposed to serve as an act of intimidation, though it turned into a theatre of the absurd. None of the plaintiffs knew how to answer the judge's or lawyers' questions and kept on disappearing from their individual Zoom screens – an unfortunate move for which they were constantly scolded by the angry judge. They mixed up their facts, and their record of events conflicted with each other. Tulesova's lawyers had to constantly raise the issue of plaintiffs sitting in the same room (which was prohibited) or getting hints and cues for what to say next from someone else. Thus, some of them kept on looking above the camera as if listening to someone standing in front of them while they kept their Zoom on mute. All the online audiences commented and ridiculed the prosecutor general's idea of *menty* as a 'bad word'. As one of the online watchers commented, 'It would've been hilarious if it wasn't so sad', but the whole court hearing just demonstrated how incompetent the law-enforcement officers were. The hearings became a spectacle of this incompetence, which also allowed the audiences to feel more solidarity and sympathy with Tulesova. And once again, Foucauldian analysis of the spectacle of punishment and conviction played out so well in the ways Kazakh authoritarian regime used this strategy.

The apportioning of blame is redistributed: in punishment-as-spectacle a confused horror spread from the scaffold; it enveloped both executioner and condemned; and although it was always ready to invert the shame inflicted on the victim into pity or glory, it often turned the legal violence of the executioner into shame. Now the scandal and the light are to be distributed differently; it is the conviction itself that marks the offender with the unequivocally negative sign: the publicity has shifted to the trial, and to the sentence; the execution itself is like an additional shame that justice is ashamed to impose on the condemned man. (Foucault 1977: 9)

[54] Utebekov was a very popular public figure on Kazakh *Facebookstan* before he joined Tulesova's trial as one of her three lawyers. At the time of writing in the summer of 2021, he was followed by almost 65,000 people (including his list of friends) on Facebook. He became highly popular for writing about numerous legal injustices and defending those left in these unjust situations.

Tulesova's trial was a spectacle of legitimate violence appropriated by the regime. Every piece fell into place – from the way the regime used formal institutions, such as the courthouse itself, laws, and legal rhetoric to punish and intimidate public activists to the ways the bodies of the policemen were represented as fragile in face of the 'attack' from a young woman. At a time when police officers were violently oppressing any act of physical dissent on the streets and looking for new strategies to tame the outbursts of protest, the claim that one woman could viciously attack and hurt six specially trained police officers sounded ridiculous. And thus, Tulesova's legal team's claim that she had never trained or got involved in martial arts or any type of sports inverted this overall narrative of violence. The people who watched the trial on the YouTube channel simply replied – 'Look, the king is naked!' – meaning that the regime itself was inadequate not only in its use of legal forms of intimidation and staging trials and convictions but also in the ways it crumbled in the face of new protest waves. Unlike the past opposition, the young activists were no longer scared of imprisonment; they knew how to build their legal protection and organize campaigns calling for justice, and that their individual cases were becoming more and more visible to the global arena.

To a regime that invests so much time and resources in portraying itself as a global and outward-looking member of the 'Western' club of leading nations, this blow to their facade of fake democracy became a complicated puzzle to address. Coupled with the regime's slow learning process, the rapid nature of the digital activism demonstrated more and more inadequacy. Regardless of the question of how many audiences were exposed to this new digital revolution, it quickly became part of the discourse and the alternative narrative to the spectacle of oppression in the Zoom digital court. In the words of the newest generation of TikTok and Instagram activists:

> I am still in active fight against all these injustices that seem so devastating and scary to me. I am engaging in resistance through the creation of [digital] masks. I think that [digital protests] with the use of masks [online] are the coolest contemporary digital protests. We just have done the [digital filter] mask with Protestor Körpe to support Asya [Tulesova]. This project with Protestor Körpe is so important because through this idea of quilting and the many pieces of quilt we also demonstrate how each person is contributing to [the protest] and how we all can make a common voice through one körpe. So, we collaborated and made a mask for the [Instagram] stories with them.

Figure 4.2 Mural wars in Almaty: the Qazaq Koktemi art collective strikes with the 'Cancel Elbasy' campaign, May–June 2021. Source: Kazakh Spring activists

Throughout the whole of last year (2019) I was engaged in making these digital protesting masks. And right now, I am learning from Exit Stimulation, who is the leading producer of these filters. This is an intense course. He opened this course to people of colour for free, I sent in my application and got in. It is great that we can learn from so many creators all across the globe.

I hope that after his course, I will be able to make even cooler and more professional masks [for protest online].⁵⁵

What these different online civic initiatives, like the Covid-19 database Umytpa, the news portal Masa, the Protestor Körpe initiative, and others, demonstrate is that the digital space became a type of civil sphere for Kazakhstani protestors, where the regime was still to learn how to sanction numerous elusive and rapidly changing strategies for protest, like this example of Instagram story filters or the strikes of anonymous art groups. These spaces enable new forms of engagement, cooperation, and solidarity. Instances such as Tulesova's televised court hearings and live streaming on YouTube where anyone can watch it also add to the processes and practices through which activists quickly learn and respond to authoritarian discourses, often in a creative way. For example, the poster wars of spring 2020 turned into mural wars in Almaty in summer 2021 (see Figure 4.2). I will come back to this mural in Chapter 6 when discussing the fixation on the physical body as a type of force and coercion by the regime. But before that, in the next chapter, I will first address the ways Generation Q in Kazakhstan continues to rethink national divisions.

⁵⁵ Author's interview with Medina Bazargali, November 2020.

5 | *Generation Q and Decolonizing Alash*

In this chapter, I address the question of nationalist frames proposed by the Nazarbayev regime in the context of the nationalizing regime and discuss how the Qazaq Koktemi field was able to push the limits of these frames. In my earlier works, I argued that Kazakhstani politics of nation-building and power relations among the elites can be better understood through the analysis of their power field, which I called the nationalizing regime (Kudaibergenova 2016, 2018, 2020). I defined the nationalizing regime as the power field 'formed of the most powerful elites who manage to control and impose the specific discursive and nation-building outcomes on the wider population, including ethnic minorities' (Kudaibergenova 2020: 7). I argued that the ruling ethos of the nationalizing regime in Kazakhstan was its dependence on the figure of Nazarbayev as the Father of the Nation and the actual nation-builder. Before Nazarbayev resigned, he embodied the nationalizing regime he constructed so meticulously by killing off and moving under his watchful eye any dissent to his dominant discursive field of harmonious, multi-ethnic yet ethno-nationalistically leaning Kazakhstan. However, the core problem of this nationalizing regime was that it 'performed' its power to a variety of audiences and groups.

All of the dominant discourses within the nation-building strategies that were controlled by the regime originated with the ideas and words of Nazarbayev himself or in the aura of his direct presence. The shared ethos among the regime elites was to construct or attempt to construct this discursive paradigm around Nazarbayev. The one thing they missed in their calculations was that, even though Nazarbayev's word became ubiquitous, it did not guarantee that power would be 'set in stone' – nor that it would be possible at all (see also Wedeen 1999 for a similar argument regarding Syria). To my numerous respondents, it was clear from the ubiquitous banners spread all over the cities, towns, and villages of Kazakhstan that depicted parts of Nazarbayev's speeches, state programmes, and portraits. In its ubiquity, the 'word of Nazarbayev' was empty of meaning. It did not incite more dominance but indeed produced diverse discourses, including ridiculing, countering, and resisting. As one respondent told me in an anonymous interview, 'if the state thinks they have the right to speak to us [through banners], then why can't we speak back?'.[1]

What Qazaq Koktemi was able to bring to the table was the shifting of this 'language', or what Michel Foucault called the regime of truth of the dominant discourse that is embedded in the structures of society. In the Kazakhstani case, this regime of truth was also heavily structured by the approaches of the political regime itself, which inherited the Soviet practice of divide and rule and slightly modified it. This precisely concerns the divisions into Kazakh-speaking and Russian-speaking political communities, used by former president Nazarbayev as a technique to invent his own 'legitimacy' by speaking to both of these audiences with the message the regime thought they wanted to hear, no matter how conflicting or incompatible these messages were.[2] The old opposition could not change this structure of doing politics à la Nazarbayev, despite acute awareness of how this divide was damaging political competition, disintegrating society, and leading the opposition to further marginalization because the regime was able to brand them as Kazakh nationalists (see Kudaibergenova 2016). For example, this was how the leader of the old opposition Amirzhan Kosanov (before his public discrediting) conceptualized and then confused this situation in his 2012 interview with me:

I always say that the regime [*vlast'*] considers this issue very primitively. It is the first thing that the regime does – it uses the linguistic division issue, especially before the elections. And the regime sometimes performs this two-faced Janus – to [ethnic] Kazakhs, it proclaims one thing in the Kazakh language, and to ethnic Russians, it says completely the opposite in the Russian language. But it is not right. I think that it is time for accepting national ideals in Kazakhstan not as nationalism with a negative implication but as a natural process of revival of the nation that for 70 years was

---

[1] Author's interview with anonymous activist of Qazaq Koktemi, July and August 2020.

[2] There is a growing body of literature on this division now, most notably in Marlene Laruelle's excellent analysis in her chapter 'Which future for national-patriots? The landscape of Kazakh nationalism' in *Kazakhstan in the Making* (Laruelle 2016) and in her book *Central Peripheries: Nationhood in Central Asia* (Laruelle 2021). Insebayeva and Insebayeva 2021 also touches upon this. I wrote about this tactic extensively in Kudaibergenova 2019, 2020.

oppressed under Moscow's [rule] when in Alma-Ata with its 1 million population there was only one school with Kazakh-language instruction. Of course, there were distortions. This is why I think that the regime [*vlast'*] needs to understand that not only non-Kazakhs but also all non-Kazakhs who are living at the same time as Kazakhs who do not know their native language due to objective or subjective reasons, they all are ready for this renaissance, the Kazakh renaissance. But again, it is important [to do this renaissance] without discriminating rights and freedoms of other citizens because this is very important. The regime [*vlast'*] uses the rise of national consciousness only in the type of cultural-spiritual sphere – in cultural [management], language, and history. And I always say, what about the economic and social sphere? For example, 90–95 per cent of *aul* [village] population are [ethnic] Kazakhs. It means that if we are reviving *auls*, then we are reviving Kazakhs, and it means that we are not just reviving the Kazakh language knowledge [which is the agenda of Kazakh national-patriots]. I have this forever dilemma with [Kazakh] national-patriots. They always tell me, Abike, you do not support us really. I tell them that they only speak about the language but what is the difference if an ethnic Kazakh who is a governor [Kazakh-*akim*], who knows the Kazakh language, would get a bribe from the hands of the ethnically Kazakh businessman who also knows the Kazakh language and the bribe would be in Kazakh *tenge*? Is that the rise of national consciousness?[3]

While opposition leaders at the time understood the game that the regime was offering and conceptualized it well in terms of the Kazakhified and ethnic-minority agenda, they actively supported and played by the rules of this game. For example, the majority of opposition politicians whom I surveyed in 2011–14 and even 2016 relied on the existing paradigms of Kazakh- and Russian-speaking socio-linguistic communities. They did not deny these categories, but they also did not try to reconfigure them by changing the discourse and narratives. Too often, they actually played on this division and thought of their potential (albeit weak) political agenda in terms of these categories, already proposed by the regime. In other words, they were not willing to change the rules of the game but exacerbated the unnecessary division, which got even more embedded and mystified.

The provision of socio-linguistic communities at least proposed the potential idea of blurring the ethnic lines that Nazarbayev was himself

---

[3] Author's interview with Amirzhan Kosanov, then one of the leaders of the opposition OSDP Azat party, Almaty, 20 September 2012.

eager to keep for ethnic minorities beyond the Kazakh–Russian divide through his own invention of the Assembly of Peoples of Kazakhstan, which he proposed to his administration as early as 1992. For him, the division into ethnic Uyghurs, Dungans, Ukrainians, Greeks, Uzbeks, Germans, Tatars, and other smaller ethnic communities served as the ideal of Soviet multiculturalism wrapped in the framework of *druzhba narodov* (people's friendship), and whether these ethnic groups wanted to be represented like this or not was a concern for the regime. This division into the '140 ethnic groups' of which Kazakhstan boasted also allowed the regime to navigate the Russo-Kazakh divide, which was a potentially dangerous affair in the late 1980s and after the collapse of the Soviet Union in 1991 due to the rise of what Soviet sociologists considered to be Kazakh ethno-nationalism after the events of 1986. Adding in the problems with northern Kazakhstan's regions bordering with Russia, which could still create a 'Crimea 2.0' scenario, these tensions on both sides of the ethnically divided groups caused a lot of headaches for Nazarbayev and his regime.[4]

However, the argument that Nazarbayev's strategy on the national question was influenced only by the Soviet legacy (see Dave 2007, for example) is too simplistic. The tools that the Soviet Nationality Policy provided came in handy when the regime elites understood that their resilience tactic should be based on the paradoxical balance of consistently dividing the population into rigidly defined and codified ethnic groups and fully controlling the production of the nation-building discourse (thus, the formation of the nationalizing regime) while at the same time blurring the socio-linguistic communities. The rigid codification of the Kazakh-speaking community defined it as a closed group narrowly oriented only to the agenda of Kazakh language and culture revival. This was the main factor in their disempowerment. As Kosanov mentioned in our interview, 'nothing would change if ethnic Kazakhs in villages would wear national clothes and speak only Kazakh' – this would not have led to an economic revival, since the narrow linguistically oriented ethno-politics and agenda of Kazakh national-patriots never provided a feasible economic-development (or political) blueprint. Caged in its own framework and its often aggressive claims to Kazakhify the public sphere, this group and its representatives continued to stagnate for more than thirty years while still

---

[4] Diener 2015; Faranda and Nolle 2011; Laruelle 2018.

depending on Nazarbayev personally to implement their agenda and cheering every state programme on the Kazakh language, even though each one of them kept failing (Fierman 1998, 2009; Yessenova 2005).

Meanwhile, Nazarbayev actively personalized his nationalizing regime by locating himself and his will at the centre of all conflicts and their solutions. He kept on promising inter-ethnic stability and harmonious ethnic relations to all minorities who feared the rise of Kazakh ethnonationalism while at the same time vouching for nationalistic slogans such as 'Eternal Nation' (*Mangilik El*). Some scholars erroneously took this agenda as a type of balancing of civic nationalism while missing the point that no illiberal regime can create a truly civic culture, especially when it is all framed and dictated from above, without any wider social contribution to the political agenda.[5] Instead, the regime actively dismisses propositions coming from the emerging civil sphere and continues business as usual. The problematic aspect of the former opposition is that it was aware of these rigid frames that contributed to authoritarian resilience in the 2000s but did not attempt to change them; instead, they often built their discourses around them. Here is how Amirzhan Kosanov thought about it in 2012:

I, as a Kazakh, feel offended when other Kazakhs tell me, 'There is no one else but the president [Nazarbayev]', but what about the other 10 million Kazakhs? Are they second class [Kazakhs]? We have to, and the president has to create a competitive sphere. There are a lot of intelligent people in the opposition; go and work with it! ... All I am saying is that we cannot develop based on this national question that the regime proposed to us and narrow it all down simply into spiritual-cultural and linguistic paradigms. The national

---

[5] That said, and adding to the fact that regimes of truth are never reigned over in totality by singular actors or singular forces, the discourse developed well beyond what Nazarbayev envisioned (I discuss this in my forthcoming work). However, there is a difference between a regime of truth in practice and the attempt of a nationalizing regime (a different species) to construct a narrative of its omnipresent power. I take the latter as the power field where establishment of dominant narratives is organized solely around the elitist field without any input from civil society or non-regime players. This logic makes the nationalizing regime a very closed-down mechanism, but its effects, in the form of the multiplicity of discourses and their reproduction (regime of truth), are something it can never even imagine fully controlling or dominating. However, in order to save face, the regime would struggle (albeit in a clumsy way) to establish the illusion of its dominance.

question cannot be very narrow, and it has to have a wider conceptualization, and I think that society is ready for that at the moment.[6]

My archive of political discourses and interviews also includes some wiser voices from non-Kazakh politicians and so-called minority elites. Here is an example of how one of them conceptualized the nationalizing regime and Nazarbayev's rule in it, also in 2012:

> It is clear that he [then president, Nazarbayev] does it in a very sly, feudal way – to yours and to ours [*i vashim i nashim*] but he does it very skilfully [*ochen umelo*]. I will repeat that he as a neo-feudal of the twenty-first century is a lot more progressive than the national-patriots who in reality, are his supporting system though they are very thick [*dremuchie*]. And he is this some sort of balance because one part of the society views him as a guarantor of the Kazakh national state-ness [*kazakhskoi natsional'noi gosudarstvennosti*] which in reality he is, and the other part of the society sees him as a guarantor and protector from open Kazakh nationalism. Here he is at the right place. But again, it is his positively balancing role, and it is clear. This role works only in the feudal system, in the system centralized on personal power. When we will start transitioning to democracy, even if it is going to be imitation democracy but we will nevertheless start transitioning towards it – it is inescapable ... Just like no country can close itself down to mobile networking and the Internet, then no country in the contemporary world can close itself down from the latest technologies like municipal elections or multi-party parliament. All of this will start happening at some point, and most probably, this will start happening in the nearest future. Then for sure, the main pressing question will be whose country is it? Is it the country of all citizens of Kazakhstan, or is it the country of Kazakhs who, thanks to their tolerant nature and hospitality and a set of all other reasons, agree with the fact that in *their country,* everyone else is also allowed to live and allowed to live well, but is it nevertheless the country of only one part of the population [ethnic Kazakhs]? This is the key question that will most probably define the political content of future Kazakhstan very soon.[7]

This reflection of the decade-long opposition practice in Kazakhstan (and not of the first DVK era of 2001, for example) is necessary to provide the base of where contentious politics were on the eve of the

---

[6] Author's interview with Amirzhan Kosanov, then one of the leaders of the opposition OSDP Azat party, Almaty, 20 September 2012.
[7] Author's interview with the non-Kazakh oppositional politician and former member of the Nazarbayev ruling elite, Almaty, 20 August 2012, emphasis is mine.

inception of the Kazakh Spring in 2019. The discursive divisions, the great power, and the grip of the nationalizing regime on the categories, codifications, and logics of group formation along national-ethnic lines were still in the hands of the ruling elites of the Nazarbayev regime. The old opposition was largely dismantled, although it was never able to provide an alternative agenda to the dominant discourse imbued and imprinted with Nazarbayev's own face and will.[8] The consistency of 'domineering discourse' under the name of Nazarbayev was necessary for the construction of the vision of 'normal state-building' for domestic and external audiences. Nazarbayev's personalized nationalizing regime also subdued any internal competition coming from within the regime with alternative voices (primarily leaning towards more ethno-nationalistic Kazakhness). But above all, the personalized nationalizing regime allowed Nazarbayev to remain the only contender for the political field – by embedding the sacredness of national sovereignty and prosperity with his own 'wisdom' and strong presidency (read dictatorship). And this explains why so many people within and outside the regime felt anxious once the guarantor of peace and stability in the country announced his overdue retirement.

Oyan, Qazaqstan and Qazaq Koktemi came to crash this invented power axis. First, they started dismantling the ideals of the sociolinguistic divides. Then, they proposed the complete rethinking and decolonization (in their own terms) of the old legacies and paradigms of the 'real fathers of the nation' – the early twentieth-century Alash movement leaders that the Nazarbayev regime was not so eager to put at the front of their nation- or state-building agenda. Yet, unlike Alash or Nazarbayev, this new generation of leaders shifted their ideas from rigid ethnicity more to groupness connected by values.

Though their process is still in development, it demonstrates how a type of *civicness* can trespass the rigid frameworks of ethnically divided nation-building but also show that there is no particular requirement for one dominant ideal of national identity or nation-building framework. In other words, because they are standing for the values of freedom, democratization, and pluralism, and against the clear-cut division of group interests between Kazakh- or Russian-speaking groups, their

---

[8] I discuss this approach in depth and in a more detailed historical manner in Kudaibergenova 2020 and partly in Kudaibergenova 2017a, especially in the last two chapters and conclusion.

vision is more flexible and accommodating. As I will point through the narrative in the remaining part of this chapter, this civicness was expressed in the initial discussions of how to name the movement; the majority of the members opted out of keeping the original 'Oyan, Qazaq' (Myrzhaqyp Dulatov's 1909 poem), but instead voted for Oyan, Qazaqstan to demonstrate more inclusiveness – something other scholars prefer to call 'Kazakhstani'. However, I will demonstrate that these two concepts are very different. Kazakhstani à la Nazarbayev is a late Soviet construct, whereas *Qazaqstan* is not only a post-Soviet phenomenon but also possibly a post-Nazarbayev and decolonized vocabulary.[9] What I mean by this is that some members of the movement consider Nazarbayev to be a direct product of the Soviet era and that his legacy (if any) also requires further decolonization. I discuss this phenomenon of 'Generation Q' in the latter part of the chapter.

Not Just the Name: On the Legacy of 'Oyan, Qazaq!', Masa, and Koktem

For any new movement that emerged in Kazakhstan, framing became a crucial problem for self-identification and the external gaze. The problem with naming and framing is that the regime is ready to discredit any new political force as overtly nationalistic and thus potentially at risk of throwing the country into inter-ethnic conflict or imbalance. Official and unofficial media rarely provide a nuanced and adequate analysis of the types of intra-ethnic conflicts that emerge with consistent frequency and largely due to failures in the regime's approach to the multiculturalism it boasts of. The February 2020 intra-ethnic conflict between Dungans and Kazakhs in Kordai on the border with Kyrgyzstan, which led to eleven deaths, 192 injured, and more than 20,000 refugees (mainly Dungans) moving across the border, was surrounded by secrecy, heightened police control, and an overall atmosphere of distrust. As one of my respondents, a political analyst, described it in 2012, the Nazarbayev regime plays the role of 'firefighter', not knowing exactly where the next conflict would emerge. But the tactics for dealing with these outbursts is rarely the Assembly of the Peoples of Kazakhstan but rather the repressive machine of the secret police, closed court hearings, and the overall secretive containment of

[9] I dwell on this distinction in Kudaibergen 2024.

the conflict. This is to say that the inter-ethnic stability that the regime made one of its main slogans in the 1990s usually exists on paper, but no single force (within the government or outside it) can guarantee that this stability will endure. However, the regime's favourite tool for discrediting opposition remained the Soviet strategy of blaming them for overt nationalism (*natsionalizm*).

There are many local debates in Kazakhstan among different groups and audiences about the importance or erasure of the memory of the Alash movement, which is tainted by colonialism, Soviet repressions, years in oblivion, and the difficult post-Soviet remembering. Some of the nationalist groups I have spoken to since 2011 lamented the fact that very few central streets in Almaty or Astana were named after the forefathers of Kazakhstan, and others criticized the lack of reinterpretation of the heritage of Alash. It was quite symbolic, then that it was only on 6 July 2021, during Astana Day (the official celebration of the capital even before the renaming) when President Tokayev unveiled the monument to Nursultan A. Nazarbayev, that the media followed up with the news that the capital also had also received a monument for the Alash leaders – Akhmet Baitursynov, Alikhan Bokeikhanov, and Myrzhaqyp Dulatov grouped together.[10] Decolonial scholar Madina Tlostanova writes that 'decolonization of collective and personal memory is an extremely difficult task in which decolonial art, problematizing the official versions of history can play a crucial role' (Tlostanova 2018: 120). This process, however, has been 'extremely difficult' not only in Kazakhstan but all over Central Asia, where the term 'decolonial' was often mistaken and taken for a complete erasure of the Soviet or Russian colonial pasts instead of the critical questioning of their legacy and remaining coloniality. Perhaps this is because:

It is a painful work asking for ruthless self-criticism. Paradoxically the colonized themselves often oppose this process. The surrogate of memory and the simulacrum of ethnic culture offered to the post-Soviet zombified nations, naturalize humiliation and cut off the ability to think critically. (Tlostanova 2018:120)

---

[10] One of the important critiques of the legacy of Alash leaders is that their discourse is always represented through super-masculinity. While there were important female (and perhaps even queer) figures in the movement itself and in other anti-Soviet and anti-colonial movements, these voices are largely silenced and remain underrepresented.

The decolonial school of thought emerged in Latin America with the critique of European hegemony that is rooted in colonialism but does not end with it, because the colonized continue to live within the frameworks that were introduced and naturalized by colonization. The coloniality of knowledge and the continuous existence of the formerly colonized people within the structures of imperial, Western, and colonial frames of knowledge and being is the main problem that decolonial thought deals with. In the words of Anibal Quijano, who coined the term 'coloniality of knowledge':

In the beginning colonialism was a product of a systematic repression, not only of the specific beliefs, ideas, images, symbols or knowledge that were not useful to global colonial domination, while at the same time the colonizers were expropriating from the colonized their knowledge, especially in mining, agriculture, engineering, as well as their products and work. The repression fell, above all, over the modes of knowing, of producing knowledge, of producing perspectives, images and systems of images, symbols, modes of signification, over the resources, patterns, and instruments of formalized and objectivized expression, intellectual or visual. It was followed by the imposition of the use of the rulers' own patterns of expression, and of their beliefs and images with reference to the supernatural. These beliefs and images served not only to impede the cultural production of the dominated, but also as a very efficient means of social and cultural control, when the immediate repression ceased to be constant and systematic.

The colonizers also imposed a mystified image of their own patterns of producing knowledge and meaning. At first, they placed these patterns far out of reach of the dominated. Later, they taught them in a partial and selective way, in order to co-opt some of the dominated into their own power institutions. Then European culture was made seductive: it gave access to power. (Quijano 2007: 169)

In the post-Soviet space, attempts at decolonization are still weak. Tlostanova (2018: 122) explains it by the way these movements 'are notoriously weak, demoralized and marginalized' but also because many in the post-Soviet space do not particularly see themselves as colonized or existing within the axis of the coloniality of knowledge. The persistence of the rigid 'ethnic' paradigm is one of the vivid examples of this continuous coloniality of knowledge, where 'ethnicity' itself was its instrument. However, because the dominant paradigm of thinking is that the Soviet Union was not an empire and not a colonizer in the given terms of coloniality, but, on the contrary, the Bolshevik rhetoric of decolonization and self-determination of formerly colonial people pervaded these countries, it provides a space for further debates on this issue. The point though is not to prove or set in stone that Soviet power was oppressive (which it was) but to be able to think alternatively and outside the stale frameworks that it has provided. The paradox of the early post-Soviet nationalist and independent movements was that they continuously abused the Soviet ethnic codification but failed to reinvent the Kazakhness they were all so eager to achieve. The decolonial debate was lost in translation, where provisions of the 'authentic' and pre-colonial heritage were taken for granted (and often constructed) without a critical reflection that, as Tlostanova and others mentioned, can be very painful. However, there are some attempts at decolonization in Kazakhstan, and they mainly come from the artistic field because:

Decolonizing memories and existence through art, entails a restoration of the artist's and the audience agency – their right and ability to finally make their own choices and decide what to remember and how; to realize who they are and why were we brought into this world. Such decolonial creative acts inevitably address the spatial and corporeal memory and the memory of objects constantly traversing and problematizing the boundaries and leakages between human and nonhuman, animate and inanimate. The decolonial cathartic power of art then is realized through resisting and re-existing moves as forms of embodied memories, evoking the most primal affects – sonic, visual, olfactory, tactile, causing uncontrollable avalanches of previously censored remembrances that stubbornly reemerge.[11]

Because the initial backbone of Qazaq Koktemi was formed of contemporary artists (of various ethnic backgrounds living in Kazakhstan), their urge for the decolonial agenda came almost naturally. On the eve of the inception of Qazaq Koktemi, I was conducting art fieldwork in Almaty and carried out several interviews where a number of artists from the decolonial movement. Some of them were erroneously criticized by those who took it as a nationalist anti-Soviet agenda. However, when the protest started forming, with all the banner wars, anonymous art acts, and the discussions that led to the formation of the Oyan, Qazaqstan movement, it was clear that, while certain people did

---

[11] Tlostanova 2018: 120.

not quite clearly settle on a definition of decoloniality, they were practising and constructing narratives that were decolonial.[12]

This was happening precisely because many artists and activists were enacting their performative critique of the Nazarbayev regime, which many of them still considered Soviet and thus containing the structures of coloniality. But because Soviets did not use the concept of race but instead used the concept of ethnicity and self-determination through codified ethnic groups, then repression happened along the lines of those who did not agree with the party's main line, written out as a canon in the Soviet Nationalities Policy. This is to say that whoever pushed the limits of this canon was immediately accused of bourgeois nationalism and often repressed for the same reason. Alash intellectuals and leaders were the first victims of these repressions, as their focus on the Kazakh autonomous state and national development was immediately condemned as 'nationalist'; as a result, they perished in the Stalinist NKVD torture camps.[13] Throughout the Soviet period, official Writers' Union discussions and other official art institutions did not mention their names, and certain Soviet Kazakh clergy (among them Sabit Mukanov) tried to erase the overall memory of Alash by calling them 'nationalists' or 'enemies of the state'. The rehabilitation of the whole array of these scholars, intellectuals, and political leaders in 1989 came as a shock for many people who grew up without knowing this part of the history.[14]

By the time the current generation of young Kazakhstanis emerged, they did not have an issue with addressing Stalinist repressions and atrocities – they grew up with a full awareness of what had happened and how it continued to happen, albeit with certain silences over the issue of the Kazakh famine of the 1930s, for example.

---

[12] During my 'post-January' fieldwork and discussions, it was clear that even those who used to criticize Kazakhstani decolonial art had changed their views and stopped seeing it simply as 'anti-Soviet' ideas and engaged in decolonial debates more actively.

[13] None of their bodies were ever recovered, and there are only approximate but not precisely known places of their mass execution and burial. Commemorative locations are also largely sporadic, with the central museum located at the former Karlag (gulag) territory outside Astana and in Dolinka (a former gulag) near Karaganda and in other smaller museums and places.

[14] I discuss this in Kudaibergenova 2017a.

As Assem Zhapisheva remembers, the term 'to awaken', or *Oyatu* in Kazakh, came to some of the members of the newly forming movement quite naturally:

In terms of *Oyan* this is exactly the kind of word [with the right meaning]. I always had the spot for the term 'Oyan' (to awaken from Kazakh) and 'Qazaqstan' really harmoniously fit with it. Even though, 'Oyan, Qazaq' is the initial concept, it is still about nationalism ... many of us do not believe that nationalism is the right path, and this is why Qazaqstan is a type of unifying base for all of us.[15]

Another member of the movement told me that:

I do not remember precisely who came up with this name [Oyan, Qazaqstan] but the reference was to Myrzhaqyp Dulatov and his 'Oyan, Qazaq' poem. I guess we wanted a type of name that could have connected to Kazakhness because this [Dulatov's] poem is a very sacred phenomenon. And I think it really influences people [on the emotional level]. But we changed it a little bit and made it into *Oyan, Qazaqstan* because we were always against nationalism ... we had the art group, and we were against [the ethnonationalist view] because we thought it had to be a different name and I remember that we did not quite like the idea [of keeping it only for Kazakhs]. Then someone wanted to use the hashtags *Qazaq Koktemi* more often and that was what we really aimed at. So, we decided [to divide the social movement and the protest wave itself]. And we decided to choose a different name [for the Oyan, Qazaqstan movement].[16]

This discourse of taking 'Oyan, Qazaq' as a very important and symbolic poem for Kazakhs and denationalizing it was also echoed by other members of the movement:

We precisely wrote it on our social media pages that we are reinterpreting it [Dulatov's legacy] in order to give it an adjusted meaning than the meanings that were used in the rigid 1990s when it all was understood mainly in nationalistic frames. But here [we aimed to show] that this meaning can be completely not about [ethnic] Kazakhs but about citizens and about Kazakhstan [as a whole].[17]

---

[15] Author's interview with Assem Zhapisheva, 24 July 2020.
[16] Author's interview with anonymous member of Qazaq Koktemi and the Oyan, Qazaqstan movement, June 2020.
[17] Author's interview with Dimash Alzhanov, one of the members of the Oyan, Qazaqstan movement, 17 January 2020, Almaty.

Many members recalled how these initial discussions were wholly 'democratic' and that 'everything was done for every voice to be heard', even though there was no clarity in the very beginning on how to proceed. Oyan, Qazaqstan, as much as Qazaq Koktemi activism, was developing sporadically, ideas were flying around and being discussed collectively. 'We do not have leaders' was the phrase that was constantly repeated as a way to express the view that they were very different from the regime-type institutionalization where one dominant party with its strictly vertical structure monopolized the political field (see Isaacs 2011 for discussion of the Nur Otan party).

It was clear that we wanted to understand who do we want to become [as an organization] – inside [the movement] there were a lot of discussions even to define the form of this movement, what type of movement is it, what does it mean to have a horizontal movement, where are we going, what are our aims, and do we want to become some sort of a registered and formal organization or not. We discussed a lot how we wanted to develop and into what – as a more or less stable 'organization' or a political party. Or do we remain as a movement and in this way, speaking with this language, *we would be able to decolonize the political sphere itself*, right? This was the moment when we understood that we are already a political unit, but we do not need to institutionalize or become some sort of NGO, a party or something else and to be part of all these structures or become the structure ourselves in order to have the right to talk about politics or in order to reform something. These were crucial and important debates that were constantly ongoing in the movement. . . . it was a constant discussion.[18]

The name Oyan, Qazaqstan stemmed from the reworked title of Myrzhaqyp Dulatov's poem, and the news portal Masa, which was launched by Oyan, Qazaqstan members Assem Zhapisheva and Aisana Ashim in August 2020 took its name from Akhmet Baitursynov's poem,[19] which was given a breath of fresh air in the symbolic politics that were no longer associated or owned by the post-communist nationalizing regime or its frames. These symbols inevitably had a type of connection between the movements that were more than a hundred of years apart – Alash emerging at the beginning of the twentieth century and active in the 1910s and 1920s and Oyan, Qazaqstan emerging in 2019–20. In one of the interviews, Assem

---

[18] Author's interview with Qazaq Koktemi activist, anonymous, August 2020.
[19] Both Dulatov and Baitursynov were leaders of Alash.

Zhapisheva bitter-laughingly told me that the politics of total repression and critique had not changed in those hundred years:

The funny part is that when Alash leaders were active they were constantly criticized for [Western lifestyles] that they drank tea, for example, [while Oyan, Qazaqstan activists were framed as coffee shop hipsters]. It was a hundred years ago, and I think, God, nothing had change since then! Also, they [Alash leaders] were criticized for wearing European clothes that were strange [for some] – all of this [is still repeating]. So, I just said [to critiques of Oyan, Qazaqstan], OK, Whatever![20]

Despite the criticism that Oyan, Qazaqstan activists are bringing Western values or are West-facing, there are many arguments for their embeddedness in the local, Kazakhstani context and politics. They discuss the necessity to elect *akims*, local governors who were appointed by the president at the time, or their activism is related to issues of Kazakh history and development rather than, for example, building a paradigm for an overall regional, Central Asian perspective. Through this type of localness and solidarity with the Kazakhstani rather than external civic sphere, they change the existing paradigm of the so-called *kumys* patriotism – thinking that all problems would be solved if everyone became a Kazakh ethnonationalist, wore Kazakh 'national' clothes, spoke the Kazakh language, and drank the traditional fermented horse-milk drink, *kumys*. In the words of Assem Zhapisheva, who herself shifted her YouTube and Telegram media channels completely to the Kazakh language broadcasting, the only solution to Kazakhstan's structural problems is further educational programmes and raising awareness about the human rights, freedoms, and citizens' constitutional rights for active political engagement.

All of my personal projects – the Masa online resource website,[21] my YouTube channel *Til Kespek Jok*, and my group work in the Oyan [Qazaqstan] movement – have one focus – education [*prosveshenie*]. I cover quite a lot of different problems, also considering that I am a fact-checker as well, so I try to tell my audiences some anti-conspiracy facts ... It starts with the smallest things and concludes with the bigger question – where do all these problems originate? Many people, due to different reasons or access to education and information, see only one side of the problem. When someone starts saying that this *akim* or the other *akim* is bad, then I reflect

[20] Author's interview with Assem Zhapisheva, 24 July 2020.
[21] https://masa.media.

from the position that it is not about 'bad *akim*' but from the fact that he was appointed here. In a year he can be moved or reappointed to another place and he doesn't really care about this city because he is not even from here, and before his appointment (as *akim*) he worked in some ministry and was in some other position but then he was told, now you will be *akim* in this place literally just a day before his official appointment [due to the authoritarian system where political elites are selected and appointment by the dictator rather than elected by people]. This is all about a typical *akim*. But if he was elected, if the city dwellers knew him and if he was connected to that community, then he would've tried as a public politician [to get re-elected] like it happens in the majority of [democratic] states. In these conditions, he would've invested in writing a development programme for this city, and then you would've voted for him [because] it would have been the responsibility and accountability directly to the people. But in the current status quo he is completely not accountable to the people, and he is only accountable to those who have appointed him to this position. [This system] works in such a way, that even if he was [a bad *akim*], then in a month he would be reappointed to another place – this is how it works.[22] With this *akim* accountability it is just one example that I have used but with every issue like that I try to analyse it systematically [for my audiences] so that people would see these issues systematically and that they would demand systematic changes. It is the same with police reform in Kazakhstan. When they say, here policemen have beaten up some people, I tell them that the problem is not in these specific policemen, but the problem is in the whole system, the issue is that we do not have service police . . . All of these problems are very systemic, and the pandemic clearly demonstrated how the whole [authoritarian] system [of governance] is the biggest problem.[23]

The decolonization of this system is the de-sacralization of the dictatorship and democratization, the establishment of the rule of law and

---

[22] To prove Zhapisheva's point, there were several scandals with the 2019 *akim* of Shymkent, who shared a personal video from London praising 'the system' for his successes on his personal (but public) Instagram. He then was sacked as the *akim* of Shymkent (on 30 July 2019) but reappeared in Astana as the advisor to the prime minister (on 13 September 2019). Another bureaucrat, Serik Abdenov, known for his media nickname *patamushta-patamushta* (translated from Russian as 'because-because', the phrase he used in a 2013 interview when he could not answer the question addressed), was sacked from his position as a minister of labour and social protection of the population. He spent less than a year on the job when he became an internet meme and was attacked during press conferences, but he shortly rose in the ranks of the national oil company KazMunaiGaz, where he was a vice-president (in 2016).
[23] Author's interview with Assem Zhapisheva, 24 July 2020.

provision of the human rights and freedoms that Oyan, Qazaqstan stated in their civic declaration. So, as Marlene Laruelle also writes, 'contrary to the national-patriotic side of the spectrum, this trend [of Oyan, Qazaqstan] is more liberal and cosmopolitan, seeking to articulate Kazakhness with globalization and ready to take from the West without "becoming" the West'. The movement's agenda is with the locality, in Kazakhstan:

> Even if it does focus on issues related to democratization and human rights, it would be premature or excessive to label Oyan, Qazaqstan a pro-Western movement, as it is mostly centred on domestic issues with no foreign policy strategy. But its political agenda is more or less clear: a parliamentary democracy, reform of the judicial system, the election of local *akims* to develop local governance, and the de-monopolization of the economy (Laruelle 2021 : 206).

Since this distinction between the national-patriots, the old opposition, and the new movements within Qazaq Koktemi is visible even on the level of structures and the rethinking of the meaning of these sacred symbols and legacies, how do these activists achieve their goals to rethink and de-Sovietize the legacy of the first nationalist wave of the 1910s and 1920s known as the Alash movement? First of all, they are aware of the negative nationalistic framing strategies, but they are also able to analyse them beyond these frames thanks to their education and critical thinking. After all, the Qazaq Koktemi wave is formed of the first post-independence generation, and they were not familiar with the type of Soviet authoritative discourse.[24] The new movement completely refused to play by the rules of the game established by the regime, which were almost identical to the Soviet authoritative discourse that Alexey Yurchak described in such a great detail:

> The uniqueness of the late-socialist context lay in the fact that those who ran the Komsomol and party meetings and procedures themselves understood perfectly well that the constative dimension of most ritualized acts and texts had become reinterpreted from its original meaning. They therefore emphasized the centrality of the performative dimension of this discourse in the reproduction of social norms, positions, relations, and institutions. This emphasis on the performative dimension took place in most contexts where

---

[24] In Alexey Yurchak's terms, authoritative discourse is the type of discourse 'whose meanings are not necessarily read literally ... to assert that citizens act "as if" they support' (Yurchak 2006: 16).

authoritative discourse was reproduced or circulated: in votes, speeches, reports, slogans, meetings, parades, elections, various institutional practices, and so on. It became increasingly more important to participate in the reproduction of the *form* of these ritualized acts of authoritative discourse than to engage with their constative meanings. It is crucial to point out, however, that this does not mean either that these ritualized acts become meaningless and empty or that the other meanings in public life were diminishing or becoming totally constrained. On the contrary, the performative reproduction on the form of rituals and speech acts actually *enabled* the emergence of diverse, multiple, and unpredictable meanings in everyday life, including those that did not correspond to the constative meanings of authoritative discourse. (2006: 25)

In Nazarbayev's system, which was also made up of many former Komsomol leaders[25] and their children who were born in the 1970s and 1980s – at the time of late socialism that Yurchak described so well – the performative obedience was almost the same as in the Soviet system. But I would argue that Nazarbayev's rule sustained itself in a hybridized form and selectively got rid of certain aspects of Sovietness while it took on (again selectively) many globalized trends in building his dictatorship. This is why many activists of the Qazaq Koktemi wave believe that Nazarbayev and his system need to be equally decolonized and, in some instances, even cancelled (discussed in the Chapter 6). Because these new political activists did not experience life under the Soviet authoritative discourse or under the post-totalitarian legacy, they were better equipped to detect the wrongs of this system and stand against it. As they said themselves, they refused to play by the rules of this regime:

We understood that we want to unite but not only among us but also to unite with people from other regions, to have more people, and we wanted to know each other [and communicate] face to face. In order to unite, we first needed to wake people up. *Oyatu* [to awaken someone] sounds very ambitious and maybe even a bit maximalist but considering how old Myrzhaqyp Dulatov was when he wrote his poem 'Oyan [, Qazaq'] or all these guys [in the movement]. I in no way equate what they [Alash leaders] did and what we are doing. These are completely different scales of course. For me these figures [Alash leaders] are sacred. This is why Aisana Ashim and I decided to call our new project, information portal, we decided to call it Masa because Akhmet Baitursynov had this collection [of poems] called Masa,

---

[25] Most notably, Imangali Tasmagambetov.

and it started with this particular poem [*masa* translates from Kazakh as mosquito]. It is what he said, the mosquito [public intellectual] would keep on biting the sleeping people [*narod*] until it wakes up. Before [the Oyan, Qazaqstan movement] all of my projects were related to education – I had the *Oyla* [education] magazine and I wanted to move in this direction further, this is why all these initiatives really hit me in the right places. We sat down [with the initial founders of the Oyan, Qazaqstan movement] and developed this [civic] declaration where we reflected on the main issues that need to change in Kazakhstan, we agreed that at our base we are not a political party. [We do not aim to be a political party] because in these existing conditions and with the existing political regime to organize a [politically institutionalized] party means to agree to play by the rules [of the regime], which we absolutely do not want to do. And for ourselves we have decided and accepted this philosophy that our movement needs to be useful to absolutely anyone who wants some type of changes [reforms] and when we achieve them, then [one can] join some parties, will stand in elections [*idti vo vlast'*] – this is the personal decision of every person. We reflected all of these principles [in the civic declaration].[26]

In seeking inspiration in rethinking or decolonizing the heritage of Alash, the Kazakh Spring activists hope to disconnect the routinized narratives established by Nazarbayev's personalized nationalizing regime. In other words, they seek alternative perspectives on thinking about Kazakhness or Qazaqstani beyond the frames, narratives, and codes provided by the Soviets and reproduced and exacerbated by the current nationalizing regime. The Kazakh Spring activists see these narratives when used by Nazarbayev elites as too narrow, undemocratic, and void of public discussion. What they propose instead is a type of plurality of views and of heritage that, despite its romanticizing, can be seen as de-Sovietized and de-Nazarbayevite. This leads to a peculiar situation where different actors within the Kazakh Spring field seek liberation from double dictatorship – from Nazarbayev's rule but also from the Soviet institutionalization of ethnicity and ethnolinguistic politics inscribed in what the activists intuitively feel as the 'coloniality of knowledge'. Naturally, to get rid of this framing, they go back to the type of alternative thinking that remained not only anti-Soviet but also de-Sovietized. So, in this sense, decolonization through Alash (rather than of Alash) is done in the conditions of finding alternative to Soviet categories.

[26] Author's interview with Assem Zhapisheva, 24 July 2020.

Generation Q

Generation Q emerged as a movement to decolonize the Soviet and post-Soviet rigid codifications of fixed ethnicity and divisions into socio-linguistic bipolar communities of so-called asphalt Kazakhs or all those who primarily speak Russian in contrast to those who predominantly speak only the Kazakh language. The problem with that division and the continuing usage of this framework for a population as diverse, flexible, but also globally networked as Kazakhstan is simply that they are instruments of the past century. The same authoritarian myopia of the regime that invested millions of taxpayers' money into the Bolashak international stipend to create a whole generation of English-speaking and Western-educated elites is pretty clear here. It seems that many of the old guard among the elites in the presidential administration missed the memo that even if two socio-linguistic communities may not communicate in one of their predominant languages, they no longer need or consider Russian the language of 'intercultural communication' or of the *druzhba narodov* (a Soviet term, people's friendship, where Russian was a *lingua franca*). The English language has steadily taken on the role of intercultural communication for those middle- and upper-class communities, especially in their online communication.[27] In fact, many Generation Q Kazakhstanis do not even know what *druzhba narodov* is, since it is not the highest trending hashtag on TikTok or Instagram, where Kazakhstan has the biggest share of subscribers in the whole of Central Asia (11 million on Instagram of the 18 million total population).

The average age of a Kazakhstani citizen is thirty – almost exactly the same as the independence of the country. Even though some scholars have attempted to coin the concept of the Nazarbayev generation, I prefer to identify young Kazakhstanis born after 1991 as the generation of independence. The generation of independence accounts for more than 6 million Kazakhstanis who were born during the period of

---

[27] When the audio-based social media platform ClubHouse became extremely popular (albeit not for long) in the post-Soviet space in February–April 2021, Kazakhstani segments had an equal share of both Kazakh- and Russian-speaking discussions and rooms where many were mixed and did not require cross translations. Some of the very popular mono-Kazakh-speaking discussions invited their participants to join conversations in English when they could not express their views in Kazakh. Author's digital ethnography of the Kazakhstani ClubHouse discussions 16 February–16 April 2021.

independence itself and sometimes also includes those who were born in the late 1980s. As Junisbai and Junisbai (2019) note in their sociological study of this young generation, most of them have a very distant idea of Sovietness, welfare, free education, and the Soviet ideological system as such.[28] They simply no longer comprehend the Soviet constructs of a singular 'ethnicity' and require new frames and meaning to go about constructing their everyday realities.

The Soviet Nationalities Policy was launched in 1924 to organize and distinguish different nationalities into culturally, linguistically, territorially, and possibly ethnically coherent groups. While the Soviet state showed a strong interest 'in the lengths to which it went to elaborate these new identity categories in the non-Russian periphery', the local intelligentsia, followed by political leaders and the local population, likewise embraced these efforts and contributed to the construction of their own identities and self-perceptions.[29]

According to Joseph Stalin's famous definition, national republics, and the titular nationalities (*natsional'nost'*) that constituted them, had to have a stable territory and population, as well as a common language and cultural background. These attributes and categories were shaped in the Soviet period to create a sense of group belonging to a specific territorial and national unit within the Soviet Union and then to construct a common sense of that national republic belonging to the Soviet Union. Soviet 'nationality' was therefore a project of territorial and cultural differentiation based on the institutionalized sense of ethnicity. As Ronald Grigor Suny explains:

The practice of fixing nationality in each citizen's internal passport on the basis of parentage rendered an inherently liquid identity into a solid commitment to a single ethnocultural group. Young people with parents who had different national designations on their passports were forced to choose one or the other nationality, which then became a claim to inclusion or an invitation to exclusion in a given republic. In some cases, people could opportunistically change their nationality officially, or change their names, to ease their situation in the national republics.[30]

---

[28] The same study (Junisbai and Junisbai 2019: 36) also demonstrates that this generation is a lot more receptive to democratic values of open and contested elections; up to 95 per cent of young people surveyed consider it as a value 'important for economic development of the country' and for the well-being of their families.
[29] Edgar 2006: 3.   [30] Suny 2001: 867.

Ethnicity inscribed in passports was adapted to local understandings of lineage and kinship but then abandoned in post-Soviet Kazakhstan. As Saule Suleimenova, a decolonial artist, mentioned in one of the discussions, 'this [nationalistic and ethnic] binary is already an outdated model'.[31] This is also reflected in Oyan, Qazaqstan rhetoric, where they use the trilingual system (Kazakh, Russian, and English languages) in their communication but rarely focus on why and how this happens.

> *Diana T. Kudaibergen (DTK)*: In Oyan [Qazaqstan communication] texts are constantly provided in both Russian and Kazakh [and often also in English] – is this the type of necessity to work with both audiences?
>
> *Dimash Alzhanov*: Yes, sure.
>
> *DTK*: And how many [predominantly] Kazakh-speaking supporters are in Oyan, Qazaqstan?
>
> *Dimash Alzhanov*: We never counted, but actually there are many of them. We have a lot of people from the regions and districts, so we have a lot of Kazakh-speaking guys, and we have people of different ages, [our movement] is represented by very, very different [categories].
>
> *DTK*: How do people from different regions get engaged [in the movement]? Do you have some specific channels of communication [in both languages][32] or do you meet in person?
>
> *Dimash Alzhanov*: Yes, we have different channels of communication. I won't reveal them [due to the security measures] but they exist.
>
> *DTK*: Your linguistic approach in the movement and its fluidity is pretty cool.
>
> *Dimash Alzhanov*: We all understand how important it is, and from the political point of view as well, you understand it. It is a very crucial moment, and we constantly engage with it.

Other members of the movement also criticized the Russian-speaking or Kazakh-speaking division but embrace the complex hybridity of

---

[31] Author's online focus group with Kazakh contemporary artists, November 2020.

[32] Later on, I followed up on this point to prove that communication is bilingual and is not complicated. Even the public chat of Oyan, Qazaqstan on Telegram simultaneously hosts debates and discussions in both Kazakh and Russian languages without stressing the differences between these audiences (e.g., no one is asking for translation, and the conversations immediately get comments and answers from different members).

linguistic and national attachments that can coexist and overlap with other identities – for example, queer identities (discussed in the Chapter 8). Qazaq Koktemi demonstrates how there is a considerate (though not yet dominant) shift away from Sovietized tactics and perceptions of national identity.

> *DTK*: You said that you don't like the division into Kazakh-speaking and Russian-speaking audiences, but it also concerns Oyan [Qazaqstan] and what is going on in the country. It is not clear who particularly made this divided paradigm so prominent, but it is definitely works for the regime's [strategy of divide and rule].
>
> *Anonymous Oyan, Qazaqstan activist*: Yes.
>
> *DTK*: Do you think this division really exists or is it ... ?
>
> *Anonymous Oyan, Qazaqstan activist*: It is like with inter-ethnic conflicts – people are accustomed to think that they live so badly because these Uyghurs, Uzbeks, or someone else do not allow them to live better. And they cannot understand that this division should not be made between them – between these people and Uyghurs, not between Kazakh-speaking and Russian-speaking, not between the urban and the rural, but they need to draw the dividing line between them and the regime. Because everyone is oppressed in our country without linguistic or national distinctions ... and those who are oppressing [us] precisely are the Kazakh-speaking men, well predominantly men. Let's not say the 'Kazakh-speaking' but just call them Kazakh-men in power – these are the oppressors. I constantly pay attention to that. I tell, 'this Uyghur did not do anything to you in your life. It is not the Uyghurs' fault that you are poor. Look at the Ak Orda instead. The [regime] is the reason why you are poor, and you don't have opportunities for social mobility in your life, and that is why we don't have [enough] housing in our country, and this is why you cannot find a job.' In general, I think that these divisions are not good because yes, it would be stupid of me to deny that certain groups exist, but we should not normalize this [interethnic] division. We need to normalize this division when it comes to the division between the state meaning-production apparatus and the citizens. We are finding ourselves almost constantly in the conditions of civil war when we do not have resources and they [the regime elites] have too many of these resources and when they [the regime elites] do not like something, then they rapidly can change the law, and we would not be able to do anything about it.[33]

[33] Author's interview with Oyan, Qazaqstan activist, July 2020.

The emergence of the Qazaq Koktemi as a field of rethinking the political in contemporary Kazakhstan allowed for the variety of existing opinions and discourses to emerge from the different, dispersed (and mainly online) spaces. Their contribution to rethinking the models of the nationalizing regime in Kazakhstan is the first significant attempt within the political field to directly oppose the narratives and discourses that the regime has continuously produced since the very first moments of independence. Their message about the inadequacy of outdated models of Soviet ethnic and ethno-linguistic divides as well as of the strategies of the personalized nationalizing regime is powerful and clear. It is the first strong alternative to the old ways of dealing with nation-building in post-independent Kazakhstan. The question still remains of how long it will take for Generation Q's ideas and alternatives to take root and to normalize a different type of reality, which would not be post-national but would precisely be post–post-Soviet. The question also remains as to where the fragile project of Kazakhstani decolonization will go and how it will develop. However, with the growing number of formal (Tselinniy Centre for Contemporary Culture[34] as well as Nazarbayev University School of Social Sciences[35]) and semi-formal (the Artcom platform[36] and other decolonial artistic initiatives[37]) institutions that contribute to the development of the decolonial school of thought in Kazakhstan will continuously contribute to the growing interest in this field. One thing is very clear with Generation Q – they are striving to become post-ethnic (beyond the Sovietized codification), but, at the same time, they do not intend to become post-national. Nation

---

[34] This institution with its own publishing house and capacity for a wide educational programme, already established itself as a leading institution in this sphere by publishing at least two books (one by Madina Tlostanova and one forthcoming under editorial leadership of Alima Bissenova) on the theme in Russian and planning the translation of these decolonial thought books into Kazakh.
[35] There are several initiatives within the school that teach both the post-colonial and decolonial thought, including Alima Bissenova's public classes on the subject.
[36] The Artcom art platform, established for research, education, and artistic dialogues since its inception in 2015, positioned itself as a fully decolonial art platform and has since engaged some of the leading voices of decolonial art in Kazakhstan and has brought many young-generation artists and researchers into its orbit.
[37] Most notably, decolonial artists Saule Suleimenova, Suinbike Suleimenova, and Medina Bazargali.

remains a unifying connotation for many activists despite the diverse tactics of protest (Chapter 6) and growing diversity of identities (Chapter 7).

This complexity, along with the looming questions of where the pro-democratic movements place Kazakhstan on the global map, remain key to defining their agenda in the wake of the January 2022 mass protests but are also complicated by major geopolitical conflicts and Russia's expansionist and colonial war in Ukraine. While Tokayev's statements against the self-determination of the self-proclaimed quasi-state territories of the Donets People's Republic (DNR) and Luhansk People's Republic (LNR) gain more popularity in Kazakhstani contexts, there are still large groups of people in Kazakhstan with a pro-Russian stance, which complicates the situation further. What was clear after the first months of the tragic and useless war in Ukraine is that the whole post-Soviet space,[38] along with Kazakhstan and Kazakh Spring voices, entered a major moment of rethinking its past, the colonial aspect and legacies of its present, and the difficult questions facing its post–post-Soviet or even anti-Soviet futures. These rethinkings are at the core of regime–society and civil society tactics and engagements, as the 'national question' remains even more dominant and defining for the political field in Kazakhstan, Russia, Ukraine, and the CIS (Commonwealth of Independent States) space than it was in the 1910s and 1920s when Lenin came up with the Soviet Nationalities Policy to resolve it. Unfortunately, the legacy of this policy will define ethno-political issues in the foreseeable future, with its risks to Kazakhstani territorial integrity, and thus will influence its political developments further.[39]

---

[38] I use this term here mainly for its historic connotations as I, along with other authors, oppose the usage of 'post-Soviet' to define this region and take active part in discussions to rethink this term. One solution could be to call this space 'post-Russian'.
[39] See Laruelle 2018 and Diener 2015 for context.

6 | *The Public Square and the Body under Authoritarian Pressures*

On 10 January 2021, police in Almaty used a different technique for fighting protestors – they resorted to public torture by capturing people in a tight circle in the main square of the city without allowing them to leave. This police tactic is known as *kettling* or 'trap and detain'. It was used during the 2020 Black Lives Matter protests in the USA and after the Navalny arrest in January 2021 in Moscow and St Petersburg to tame the crowds of protestors. The explanation for kettling is always the same – to keep order and calm the protestors – and even though the tactic is described as 'non-violent', it can lead to severe consequences for the protestors. When kept inside the kettling circle of police officers surrounding groups of protestors, people cannot easily escape, or in some cases, even move. Many protestors were kettled in Almaty without access to water, food, or bathroom facilities for hours.

What happened in the central square of Almaty during the very cold January day, with temperatures reported at –20°C (–4°F) was a case of state-approved torture of protestors by the specially trained law-enforcement forces (SOBR). The protestors were out in the symbolic Republic Square in Almaty that once, in December 1986, when it was called Brezhnev Square, had witnessed the violent repression of protest riots (Kuzio 1988; Olcott 1990; Paksoy 2016; Shelekpayev 2021). Some of the activists requested medical help but were not set free by the special forces. Calls for help spread quickly through social media networks – one of the activists needed a spare pair of shoes and warm socks because she had lost one of her shoes during the pushing and pulling, and another activist was injured by a falling icicle from a nearby rooftop; activists also called for the wider spread of the news and requested hot tea, even though mobile internet was partly blocked in the square at the time. Many of those who were first trapped in the Almaty kettling in January 2021 were frequent protestors at rallies, but even they reported inhumane conditions when special forces could change over every two hours and activists stood within the tight circle barely able to move.

In this chapter, I address the following questions in relation to the persisting protests and activism of Qazaq Koktemi. Why does physical coercion play such an important role in dictatorial politics? How do protestors respond to this paradigmatic strategy of the regime to continuously incite fear of fighting dissent? And where is the symbolic location of the physical body as a paradigm of the power axis? With that last question, I am particularly interested in exploring two sides of the body as a power-inflicted space. One is the body of the dictator, which is constantly imagined by his followers and opponents as the locus of power itself, and, for example, how the attempts of the 'Cancel Elbasy' campaign require the complete abolishment of this body and the discourses of power surrounding it. This is, of course, only an effect of authoritarianism, which is temporal and fragile because no man's power is total. And the second part of this discourse is the absence of the body of the protestor, which is connected to the 'Cancel Elbasy' campaign where a group of anonymous activists who represent themselves through the hashtag Qazaq Koktemi strike through banners. In these performative protests, the whole point of their success is to strike with a bodiless claim, where the text speaks its own powerful narrative with the total absence of the protestor's physical body. This also the principle of social media, where the digital body is never the same as the physical body and thus is less endangered.

The space of protest and repression plays an important role. As I discussed in Chapter 3, the authoritarian regime in Kazakhstan selectively uses direct exposure to its repressive tactics, but at the same time it also needs to tame the protests no matter how small or big they are, since the whole paradigm of the regime is obsessively constructed around high rates of approval. Thus, social unrest in Kazakhstan is something the regime tries to hide and mask. From the 1986 tragedy to the violent repression of 2011, the tactic of the regime elites (many of whom remained the same in this time span) is to deal with the protestors violently and directly – with the least number of witnesses. The legacy of Zhanaozen is a significant one – the real numbers of the victims are unknown, and the accidental witness videos that emerged demonstrated unprecedented violence, when people were literally gunned down in the public square where they were protesting. Since Zhanaozen, the regime has not become less repressive, but it avoided direct clashes and deaths (up until January 2022, to which I come back in the final chapter), so the tortures have become secretive,[1] repressions and intimidations of activists have moved directly to the sphere of their private lives (including such severe cases as revenge porn blackmail), and public confrontations – silent. Officers who carry out the kettling strategy – who publicly tortured activists in the public square in January 2021 and then again during the summer 2021 protests near the stadium in downtown Almaty (the DPK rally on 6 July) – prefer to stay anonymous by wearing black masks and stay silent without answering queries from the protestors.

In this chapter, I argue that kettling is only one strategy among so many ways that the regime is repressing dissent in the 'developed and stable' country of Kazakhstan. But the space of punishment – the body of the condemned or the square where they are repressed – remains closed off to public view. The repressive apparatus performs the punitive spectacle for the regime and not for the public. Through the theatre of kettling, the regime reacquires its power by stating (1) that disobedience to its own rules will be punished regardless of the formal legal procedures and (2) that these repressions not only demonstrate the ability of the regime to tame any resistance to its rule but also attest to its internal strength. What I see in this clear picture of what others call 'a police state' is the incredible weakness of the regime and its fear of appearing incapable of fighting off a group of coffee-house hipsters. Thus, kettling had (1) to be targeted at a specific group and (2) to demonstrate to the regime how the police apparatus is still mindlessly following all of the orders of the political elites and their norms and ways of doing politics; but at the same time, (3) this procedure had to be done away from wide public exposure in order not to reveal the regime's weakness. The regime did not want the Kazakh Spring to be seen as the straw that broke the camel's back.

---

[1] The case of the death of Dulat Agadil, who passed away on 25 February 2020 after his forceful police detention, is one of the most tragic contemporary reminders for any dissidents in Kazakhstan. The cases of people who died after their police interrogation after the 2011 Zhanaozen tragedy is another reminder. The death of Bazarbay Kenzhebay in Zhanaozen is a particularly symbolic reminder of the type of tortures and tragedies that happened behind closed bars during illegal interrogation marked by the police as necessary measures to keep order in the city.

The Body of the Protesting

It was around midday on a Monday when a large group of young people walked up to the central square in Almaty next to the Monument of Independence and in front of the local *akimat*, the municipal office. They carried large banners in their hands that read 'Kazakhstan without Nazarbayevs', 'Parliamentary Republic', 'We won't forget 1986/2011' ('Umyltymas 1986/2011'), 'Our freedom is stronger than your prisons'. Once they all gathered at the centre of the square and behind the monument to the constitution, which bears what is allegedly the imprint of Nursultan A. Nazarbayev's palm, they raised their hands to show palms covered in red cloth to symbolize blood. The protest performance was organized on the public holiday of Independence Day (16 December) in 2019, as a commemoration of the December 1986 protests and December 2011 Zhanaozen killings that happened on the same dates of around 16–17 December and have since played an important symbolic role in anti-regime politics and discourses.

The December 1986 protests were surrounded at first by heavy secrecy during the Soviet period because riots were severely repressed, and the real number of victims is still unknown. The initial discontent was caused by the removal of Dinmukhamed Kunaev – the long-term Kazakh Soviet leader – and his replacement by Gennady Kolbin, who had never visited Kazakhstan before his appointment. The issues of the ethnicity of both politicians (Kolbin as Russian and Kunaev as Kazakh) and the nature of the removal (Gorbachev famously made and finalized this decision within a meagre seventeen minutes) fuelled further conspiracies and gossip about potential inter-ethnic conflict. On top of that, the December 1986 protests were branded 'nationalistic' and as being organized by 'drugged' youth and alcoholics – the best Soviet propaganda could come up with.

For many years the question of December 1986 in Kazakhstan remained an issue of divisions (due to ethno-nationalist discourses) and claims of trauma and gave rise to numerous movements and political initiatives, most of which remained highly Kazakh-speaking. The problem with late Soviet and early post-Soviet Kazakhstan was the legacy of the Soviet sociological implosion of the division into ethnic Kazakhs and ethnic Russians and the creation of possible dangers and conflicts between the two ethnic groups in the wake of the

December 1986 riots. Right after these events, the Moscow-based sociology group under the leadership of D. Tolstukhin travelled to what was then Alma-Ata to conduct sociological research with a focus on potential inter-ethnic conflict between Russians and Kazakhs. The report was secretly published and distributed among the party's highest officials (and then kept in the archive where I found it years later). The report's findings were divided along the lines of the 'Russian population' and 'Kazakh population', where the former considered the December events as 'nationalistic in character' and the latter at the time supported the idea that the protestors 'rallied the interests of the Kazakh population'.[2] What was left out of these discussions was the brutality of the protest repression, which was picked up again as a discourse once the Soviet system was crumbling in 1990. This was the time when many of the movements were active and were demanding to make the December 1986 archives and information about perpetrators open.[3] However, the problem was that while 'this brutally candid evaluation of the December 1986 protests leaves no doubt why, among many other things, the task of moral regeneration carries utmost urgency for the Kazakhs, who are addressing it in a polyphonic choir of solutions' (Rorlich 2003: 160), these solutions for a long time remained very much stuck in Soviet nationalistic frames.

These frames provided strict black and white, positive and negative labels and nothing in between. Those who backed the 'Kazakh liberation' idea were branded as nationalist, and those who condemned the December 1986 protests were branded anti-patriotic. In the words of

[2] D. Tolstukhin, 1987. 'Obshetvennoe mnenie naselenia KazSSR', p. 7 [Public opinions of the KazSSR population].
[3] The KGB files, perhaps some of the most crucial evidence in this case, were burned(when the KGB officers reported to the December 1986 investigation committee chaired by Mukhtar Shakhanov in 1989). While working in the archives in 2016–19, I also could not locate the necessary files, and it was rumoured that some of the elites close to Nazarbayev had already ordered the destruction these files during independence. In my current work with many historical KGB files (mostly from the end of 1940s to the 1950s) that were made public in 2023, I find it hard to believe that the institutions of coercion that kept every small detail and interrogation file in their secret archive would burn a collection of files as powerful (for accusing Nazarbayev or any other political elites involved in the suppression of these protests) as these were. In my search for December 1986 histories, I read several official interviews with KGB officers who reported on the full destruction of these files.

the Kazakh opposition politician Zhasaral Kuanyshalin in his 2012 interview, the agenda of all those who united around the December 1986 discourse became 'preserved' in the time period of the late pre-independence and early independence years – between 1989 and 1996, which was 'the very short time on the eve and the beginning of independence'. He described this time as

> the years of the real 'Kazakh Thaw' that emerged after the wild rampant reaction in connection to the imperialist authorities' suppression of the Zheltoqsan uprisings of the Kazakh youth. In this period [of the Kazakh Thaw] there was a complete reign of a real 'revelry' of the rights and freedoms of the individual and citizen, pluralism – freedom of speech and diversity of opinions, rallies, meetings, and other attributes of democracy. A number of important [social] movements emerged at the time. . . . And it is no coincidence, and an extremely important point in my opinion, that precisely at this time the idea of the country's decolonization was put forward to the agenda as the main national-democratic idea. [Because] without decolonization both the full-fledged consolidation of the Kazakh society and the real restoration of independence and a truly independent development in the future of the former colony (as was observed, for example, in the Baltic countries) is simply impossible. . . . And the subsequent history of the country, unfortunately and indisputably, proved our point of view correct – since the new-old communist regime [of President Nazarbayev] that usurped power, only formally, i.e., de jure, proclaimed the independence of the republic, but de facto, from the very beginning he took the course of building a clan-oligarchic and comprador system of government in essence (although the regime itself, of course called and calls it differently).[4]

The 'decolonization' of the political sphere, which Zhasaralin spoke about in the 1990s during his active role within the Azat movement and in the 2012 interview quoted above, happened – and continues to happen – very slowly. The main problem with this slow approach is

---

[4] Zhasaral Kuanyshalin in an interview with Kenzhe Tatilya, 'The corridors of power lead to the dead end?', 30 March 2012, *Central Asia Monitor* newspaper. Zhasaral Kuanyshalin was a very active political activist and an opposition leader throughout Kazakhstan's independence. In the 1990s he was the first deputy to then popular *Azat* political movement and since 1994 to 1995 was a member of the Kazakh parliament (which historically considered by many local political analysts as the most 'democratic' period of the parliament). With the rise of the intra-regime opposition, Kuanyshalin was actively collaborating with the first *Ak Zhol* party (not the one under the current leadership of Azat Peruashev) and other oppositional movements.

that many of the old opposition forces and the so-called national-patriots continued to view the regime as vested with the ultimate power to make this decolonization happen. In their campaigns and claims, they are not very distinct from the impoverished mothers who go directly to the presidential palace Ak Orda to address issues of inequality to president directly.

The issue for Oyan, Qazaqstan was not to be tainted with these old politics and old agendas that remained stagnant and very much embedded in the Soviet and early Nazarbayevite periods of doing politics – dividing and ruling through ethno-linguistic communities, dressing old ethnic concepts of people's friendship into multiculturalism, and dividing the opposition. What did Oyan, Qazaqstan activists bring to the agenda that was new? How did they manage to rethink this prolonged history and lack of real data on what had happened in 1986 in Almaty and then in 2011 in Zhanaozen, when a group of protesting oil field workers were shot down by the police during the Independence Day celebration, officially killing sixteen people but unofficially hiding so many bodies?[5]

Oyan, Qazaqstan activists are not just 'youth' as the regime tries to position them; these are also people from different generations, including people in their fifties and sixties. As one of the leading voices of the movement told me, not all the younger-generation activists know anything about the politics and turmoil of the 1990s, nor do they know about the political killings of the old opposition, namely Altynbek Sarsembayev (February 2006) and Zamanbek Nurkadilov (November 2005). However, for all of them, the events of December 2011 in Zhanaozen served as a 'dividing line', the 'breaking point', as a 'maximum' they believe they no longer can tolerate. Thus, the commemoration of 16 December 2011 that coincides with the riots of 16–17 December 1986 became a major event for Oyan, Qazaqstan activists. The December protests were planned months in advance through the meticulous work of the movement, divided into groups

---

[5] One of the investigative journalists who managed to enter Zhanaozen within the days of police shooting, Elena Kostuchenko from Russia's *Novaya Gazeta* conducted two separate investigations (second when she came back almost a year later) and concluded that at least 64 people or more were killed. During her second trip to Zhanaozen she was searching for the anonymous graves but could not count them. See her second report in Russian at https://batenka.ru/protection/war/zhanaozen/, last accessed on 27 July 2021.

and sub-groups. Many of my respondents, who had not participated in any other rallies before and for many of whom the fear of regime oppression was yet unknown, expressed their excitement at being able to be part of 'something bigger' and making their voice 'heard'. The text for the December 2019 Oyan, Qazaqstan protests read as follows:[6]

We need to bring the end to the political violence of the state against its citizens. 33 years after the tragic Zheltoqsan events [December 1986] and 8 years after the violent shooting of the Zhanaozen protestors, we, young and free citizens [of Kazakhstan] will go to the historic square to commemorate the numerous victims of the authoritarian terror and to demand for repressions against Kazakhstanis to stop.[7]

And on 15 December 2019, the movement published another text to announce the goals of their rally:

We are organizing a peaceful rally on December 16 at 12:00 to demand the end of tyranny. We uphold our right to live in dignity in a democratic country and to choose our representatives in fair elections. We organize for freedom of speech and for peaceful assembly. This is what young people did in Almaty in December 1986, and what the workers of Zhanaozen did in 2011.[8]

The majority of my respondents from within the Oyan, Qazaqstan movement stressed how protesting, particularly in this public square in Almaty, was of crucial and symbolic importance to them. By accessing the 'historic' square with large rallies and branded banners, they were claiming their constitutional right to rally without special permission. It was also a visible reminder for their followers to construct a powerful discourse that these types of rallies were possible and were not always crushed. Oyan, Qazaqstan activists told me that before the pandemic they were using both online and offline sources (mainly rallies and *seruens*) as tactics to construct a powerful discourse around their demands and declaration for further political reforms, a move to a parliamentary republic, and democratization. Prior to the pandemic, there were also plans to organize the first political rave for the Oyan, Qazaqstan platform as a resistance to the police harassment of their

---

[6] The text was published online on the movement's numerous social media platforms on 22 November 2019 ahead of the protests to invite more activists to join them.
[7] Text available at https://adamdar.ca/en/post/miting-16-12-v-almaty.   [8] Ibid.

unsanctioned rallies. As one of the respondents told me, 'raves and *seruens* are distinct forms of protests but these are still protests' because these events allow for people to gather, 'network', and voice their demands, albeit not in the form that the police state were used to detect as 'hooliganism' and 'unsanctioned rally'. More *seruens* and raves were planned for summer 2020 and were intended to be open air, but the conditions of the pandemic and worsened epidemic situation in Kazakhstan had to shift these plans further (to summer 2021).

Since these unsanctioned rallies became more frequent in 2019, the police took time to adjust to the new type of opposition, since they did not know any other ways and categories of seeing and perceiving the 'enemy' when even journalists fell under this umbrella. Their tactics shifted to filming protestors and then individually attacking them in their work and home; some activists privately complained of interference in their personal life, of intimidation, and of blackmail concerning their partners. The police state has no other understanding of repression but attacking the personal body and repressing protestors in their private spaces. From making punishment visible in the same square in Almaty as in 1986 to now reviving traumas and demonstrating how the regime is really the same in its approach to punishing dissent – from 1986 to 2011 to 2020, the Nazarbayev regime's repressions demonstrated how Nazarbayev was an ugly hybrid of the Soviet repressive machine itself. But Oyan, Qazaqstan activists turned this strategy on its head when they brought their physical bodies to the arena of protests, much like the cases of art activism and performances (Lucento 2017). The example of Pussy Riot in neighbouring Russia comes to mind, when their bodies were also on display as the police state took their freedom and imprisoned them for the rather small protest (Bernstein 2013; Gapova 2015; Prozorov 2014). Why this is so paradigmatic of authoritarian regimes?

This is because in an authoritarian system the regime appropriates the state's monopoly over violence and builds its legitimacy around the conviction that the regime is, in fact, the state. As I analysed in Chapter 3, often the two concepts of regime and state are amalgamated and expressed under one idea of 'power' (*vlast*'). This is not matter of confusion but rather the concept that comes out of the lived experience of feeling the everyday oppression of the regime's illegitimate violence that can come at any time and in any form, simply because it is not sanctioned by anything else but the regime's internal logic. Since the individual citizens' bodies are under the control of the state, which is occupied by the regime, the regime can access that body through its own institutions – police, secret police, but also universities, schools, and workplaces. This constant interplay between the individual body and the repressive power of the regime is not something new for such regimes (see Arendt 2007) and definitely not a novelty for the activists who can easily conceptualize it themselves. Their experiences speak of the systematic abuse better than any other discourses:

> *DTK*: Where are citizens, people in this [authoritarian] system?
>
> *Assem Zhapisheva*: They are ... how to explain it better, they are more like masses, I think. Here they are mostly counted as statistics. In general, the relation of the [regime] ... let me still use the word 'state' in order to make this [explanation] faster, we can see [this attitude of the state] in a lot of things. We can see this attitude according to their [regime's] rhetoric; we can see this attitude in the way they [the regime] do not bother significantly about how the citizens would react to the decisions they [the regime] are making.[9]

Bodies of the citizens become the platform for the regime's intimidation of dissent and the creation of the type of public order that serves the power and durability of the regime itself. In this perverted social reality, 'the state in this initial belief being an institution designed to serve the common good, the government serving the good to the people' (Bourdieu 2014: 5) turns into an institution designed for the good of the regime alone but not the people. This echoes what Lisa Wedeen explored in Syria, where the authoritarian regime used bodily spectacles of its citizens as a public depiction of order:

> Applied to Syria, a broadly construed 'Foucaultian' approach suggests the ways in which Asad's cult is *effective*: First, orchestrated spectacles discipline the participants and organize them for the physical enactment of ritual gestures, regimenting their bodies into an order that both symbolizes and prepares for political obedience. Second, spectacles are not only a preparation for but also themselves already instantiations of political power. They dramatize the state's power by providing occasions to enforce obedience, thereby creating a politics of pretence in which all participate but few actually believe. Third, spectacles serve to anchor visually and audibly politically significant ideas and self-conceptions that might otherwise remain

---

[9] Author's interview with Assem Zhapisheva, 24 July 2020.

fluid and abstract. They ground political thinking in the images and symbols the regime puts forth, framing the ways people see themselves as citizens, much as advertising offers people a frame in which they imagine themselves as consumers. The cult, like advertising, is a mode of ambivalent interpellation, a way of 'hailing' spectators that is effective even if its claims are not taken literally. In Syria, spectacles combine the consensual desire for stability with images of Asad's omnipotence. In American advertising, desires for the 'good life', for love, comfort, wealth, and efficiency become moored to the acquisition of particular commodities. (Wedeen 1999: 19-20)

Nazarbayev was no different from Asad in practising the omnipresence of his discursive body in every aspect of political life – from the ideas of the prosperity of development to the provision of a safe and happy future. In the words of one of the anonymous members of the Qazaq Koktemi, it really echoed Asad's cult and slogans in Syria. In Kazakhstan,

[The regime speaks to the society through slogans like] 'Youth is our future'. These general phrases [sound as if they come] from the quotes of Kim Jong-il, something of that sort. [These are] some generalized slogans directed at our future wealth that we are about to achieve. If before we were waiting for communism, then now we are awaiting some amorphous happiness because we do not have a clear ideology and this ideology is centred around one person who says, 'soon, guys, we will start living'. It is, of course, absurd.[10]

In authoritarian systems, where 'regimented bodies are consistently mobilized to perform such gestures of symbolic order', turning the bodily agenda into the spectacle of disobedience despite repressive repercussions is the type of drastic shift that can lead to transformative changes. The logic of the regime is to reinforce its legitimacy through parades of obedience, where according to Wedeen (1999: 21)

In Syria, regimented bodies are consistently mobilized to perform such gestures of symbolic political order [participate in spectacles declaring love to Syria, etc.]. The trading children receive their membership in organizations modelled on paramilitary groups may indeed encourage self-discipline (it may still be too early to gauge the effects of such mechanisms). Insofar as spectacles act as instances of intervention, however, the body functions in them to *substantiate* rather than legitimate power. In other words, spectacles make power palpable, publicly visible, and practical. Bodies serve as the apparent and immediate site upon which participation is enforced. The spectacle shows that authorities are

[10] Author's anonymous interview with the Qazaq Koktemi activist, June 2020.

able to compel citizens to enact the choreographed movements that iconographically configure worship of the leader, representing his power body visibly (in the display) and tangibly (in each participant's body).

The disobedient body under authoritarianism becomes the space of iconographic illegitimacy and the spectacle of the regime's lack of real legitimacy or capacity to establish the type of order it strives to achieve – the order of the police state. As one of my respondents shared, 'once it becomes clear that the king is naked', the system loses its power. Now the price for such a claim is dear for the protestors, and they have to navigate risks as well as possible physical harm, as I discuss in the following section.

'You Run for Cover, but You Can't Escape the Second Attack'

When activist and member of Oyan, Qazaqstan Fariza Ospan was kidnapped from her picket in Shymkent on 6 July 2020, she told me it was the first time when she experienced 'real fear for my life'. Unidentified men caught her before she was able to unpack her banner (in solidarity with Asya Tulesova, who was imprisoned at the time in Almaty), and if it was not for Ospan's last-minute capture of her kidnappers on her Instagram story, her supporters would not have known that she had been attacked and detained. Instagram stories allow quick upload and public access to the uploaded content (photos, videos, texts, gifs), which the arresting police were not aware of at the time. As they dragged the twenty-five-year-old to the unmarked car, they snatched her phone and her banner. She screamed at the top of her lungs, but no one, not a single person on the overcrowded bus that stopped nearby, paid attention to the kidnapping.[11] Ospan did not know who the men were and where she was going, trapped in their car as one of them was holding her hands and the other one kept on searching her phone for the video she made of them; the third one kept on screaming at her and telling her to shut up. At the police station where she was delivered by her kidnappers, she was pushed and pulled.

They threw me to the sofa. One of them took my backpack and started inspecting it. I had a book about beauty in the backpack[12] and he asked me if

---

[11] Narrative from the author's interview with Fariza Ospan, 5 November 2020.
[12] Prior to her picket, Ospan prepared all the necessary things to spend 24 hours in a possible detention and this included in her own words, some person hygiene,

I considered myself ugly, I replied, 'no' and he said, 'well, in vain'. They asked me if I had a boyfriend and they told me, 'of course!' because who would date me, and they tried to offend me making some comments about my physical appearance and personal life, it is nobody's business. Then they asked me why I am still single, asked me my age and made comments that I am too old [for marriage] at 26. Then they said, 'I will now hit you and I won't get anything [punishment] for it.' I remember that they yelled at me so hard, I don't understand why I infuriated them so much.[13]

In a system where the illegitimate regime appropriates the monopoly over violence for their own good, the institutions of such violence play according to the rules the regime creates for them. This also explains why no police officer that ever inflicted 'too much' violence on their victims ever considered their acts as illegal. The rules of the game are such that whoever challenges the regime's power and legitimacy is subjected to violence, whether it is masked under the formal legal rules of unsanctioned rallies or the illegal rules of forceful detention, as Fariza Ospan's case demonstrated in all its ugliness and the straightforward belief that the policemen 'will not get anything for it' (*nichego mne za eto ne budet*). For this reason, activists had to find and expand their counter-strategies. Along with their collective solidarity and fighting for their supporters at police stations and detention centres, coming en masse to the court hearings, and protesting detentions, they also expanded their media presence, fighting in court against illegal detentions. And above all, they had to normalize the violence by exposing how ubiquitous it is under Nazarbayev's authoritarianism and how it can happen to anyone, regardless of their actions and intentions. This realization came to each activist after their first serious detention or encounter with the police, and each experience forced them to highlight how this violence was a built-in feature of the authoritarian regime. For example, this is how Suinbike Suleimenova remembered her detention in April 2019 after the Qazaq Koktemi's first strike:

I told [everyone in the team] that I cannot run and jump because I was pregnant, but I could coordinate things and tell people on walkie-talkie that there are policemen behind them or something else, some provocateurs.

---

a book and other personal things. She never gave the permission for anyone to inspect her personal stuff but the men who detained her did not ask for any permission.

[13] Author's interview with Fariza Ospan, 5 November 2020.

But everything turned out the other way around and it turned out that I became the action figure which wasn't very good because after [the detention] I fell sick with pyelonephritis, and it led to Tau [Suinbike Suleimenova's son] having some heart issues. I got sick because we were detained for five hours, and it was very cold there. They [policemen] did not give us anything – no water, nothing. We were left to sit there in this cold and then I got sick – I remembered it very well. But after that I didn't even think about it. I felt very upset about falling sick with this pyelonephritis, but when we started gathering and feeling this unity and some solidarity – it all spurred a lot of interest [and solidarity].[14]

The writers and the makers of the Kazakh Spring often underlined this paradox of the authoritarian system – where repression was supposed to intimidate and silence the protestors, it gave them strength to resist with even greater force and intensity. Protestors' detention led to more indignation and counter-resistance. Fear-inducing strategies that the regime used previously were not echoing with the same intensity as they did before. In other words, if before the opposition backed down from their activities for fear of further imprisonments, then Kazakh Spring protestors felt they could push the limits of this intimidation. With every small victory of fighting for their detained friends, they felt that the 'limits of the fear can be pushed further'. In the words of one Oyan, Qazaqstan activist:

We are trying to understand that here [in Kazakhstan] it is a different space. If they [the regime] maximize this fear, then nothing would come out of it. On the other side we understand much better now that a lot more is possible here [in terms of activism], and we also understand what is not possible. And there is a feeling that these are not the final boundaries [of the possible unrest].[15]

The protestors of the Kazakh Spring were more adaptive and creative in the face of the coercion that they knew was coming from the regime, while the regime's law-enforcement strategies for a long time remained inadequate and simply harassing and repressive. The activists of Oyan, Qazaqstan told me that they were actively watching and learning from the experiences of social movements and protest waves globally. They tracked police brutality in the United States after the killing of George Floyd and before that attentively watched the resistance techniques of the Hong Kong protestors.

[14] Author's interview with Suinbike Suleimenova, June and July 2020.
[15] Authors interview with anonymous Oyan, Qazaqstan activist, June 2020.

On the part of the activists, there is a constant learning from and sharing of experiences. Even during our interviews, some of them asked me for academic sources to read and adapt their practices more, to enhance ways of leading a movement, and to organize internal workings, or on how to address formal institutionalization under dictatorships. And on the other side of this conflict were the law-enforcement officers in all sorts of capacities – from the lowest-ranked police officers to the specially trained elite forces – who understood only the language of punishment and repression. The punitive spectacle à la Nazarbayev is about framing protestors as 'illegal' or going against local traditionalist values (see next chapter) and to harass them to the extent that they would fear to ever protest on the streets. In this relational approach between the protest and repression, the physical body and the private space of the protestor become the main space for law enforcement, where the regime can attack a given citizen by demonstrating that it has all the powers to get away with it. The repetitive 'I will not get anything for it' (*nichego mne za eto ne budet*) ethos that activist Fariza Ospan heard from her police kidnappers is repeated again and again in the protesting public squares in Kazakhstan (and similarly in Russia). Perhaps this is the frightening part of the regime – the widely shared ethos of unlawfulness and the atrocious power of the executors and prosecutors who believe that their power within the regime is above the law and above the citizen. Fear feeds this power as much as fear would feed a mythical monster, and this is the unspoken rule for a lot of post-Soviet dictators. Where the Nazarbayev regime has been cautious in recent years not to portray him as a bloodthirsty dictator, neighbouring regimes provide the type of fearful theatre that serves its purpose well beyond its borders:

The fear is, of course, existent. This fear particularly increased when I understood how dangerous my activism is and it happened this summer [2020] when I saw protests in Belarus and Kyrgyzstan. I saw how people die in real time. Before it was somehow different – I understood but I did not realize [the risks]. When I read the stories of the Okrestina rapes[16] in Belarus

---

[16] Here my respondent referred to the Okrestina Detention Centre in Minsk, Belarus, where mass repressive actions against detained protestors took place in
August 2020. Some reports cite more than 1,000 protestors seeking medical help after their detention, but Belarus officials deny physical injury, rape, and other cases of injuries to genital areas. For the reports, see Voices from Belarus (https://voicesfrombelarus.medium.com/including-genitals-51f3cca278f9), Radio Free Europe

and how women were hospitalized and kept in intensive care units for days after these violent rapes by the police officers. And if to be completely honest ... I thought to myself if it can be so atrocious, am I ready for it? Am I ready to fall sick at the rally [to catch cold during kettling]? Am I ready to physically lose something – an arm, a leg, an eye – at the rally? Because this was what had happened in Belarus. And that's when I felt the real fear, and I understood that before I didn't have this fear. It [the fear before] was somehow different – unperceived, it was there but I anyways went as if a tank, with my eyes closed [to it]. And now when I would go to the rally, I would realize what it can lead to.[17]

Physical coercion plays an important role in dictatorial politics precisely because of this logic of inciting fear to keep not only protestors and activists but also the rest of the population paralysed and away from any civic engagement that could kick the system out of balance. After all, the tendency in Kazakhstan is such that the regime has to respond to the demands of the activists and movements slowly but surely, no matter how small or vast these are. President Tokayev's move to the 'listening state' (*slyshashee gosudarstvo*) strategy in June 2020 was a direct reflection on the first year of the Kazakh Spring. In the strategy, he proposes that Kazakhstan is building 'an open state that is ready to engage in a constructive dialogue, react to the demands of its citizens in a timely manner'. In this new vision of the regime, the listening state is a state 'where society is engaged in the decision-making process, [and] makes the country into a strong and constantly developing state'.[18] In a nutshell, Tokayev's proposal for the 'listening state' is a better-developed civil society where different social groups have better access and space to engage with state institutions and bureaucracy consistently and effectively because 'the main goal of state institutions is the highest quality of the provision of the demands of its citizens'.[19]

This strategy was followed by the creation of the NSOD – the National Committee of Social Trust – a type of expert-advisory board comprised of predominantly pro-regime activists. Similar to other

---

(www.rferl.org/a/firsthand-account-of-torture-at-minsk-detention-center/30790313.html), and the BBC (www.bbc.co.uk/news/world-europe-53773534).

[17] Author's interview with anonymous Qazaq Koktemi activist, November 2020. After this interview, my anonymous respondent attended a number of rallies and organized one large rally in downtown Almaty.

[18] From the strategy2050.kz: https://strategy2050.kz/ru/news/kontseptsiya-slyshashchee-gosudarstvo-ot-slov-k-deystviyu/.

[19] Ibid.

committees of this kind, NSOD has little power to influence policy and instead mainly serves as a way to open a discussion space between pro-regime forces, the new opposition, and de-institutionalized groups. This discussion inevitably happened online – on Facebook, Telegram, and Instagram instead of in parliament or at least the ministerial corridors. In the words of the Qazaq Koktemi activists, NSOD became another 'pseudo' and 'hypocritical' change instead of the 'working law on elections or parties' that the activists demanded and rallied for. As a response to yet another 'cosmetic change', the Qazaq Koktemi continued to develop their strategy away from regime institutionalization, arguing that precisely this institutionalization of authoritarianism became a barrier to democratization. Protesting on the streets, despite their fears, the continuous coercion, calls to family members, and blackmail, became the only working strategy. They believed that making the protest visible both physically (with bodies in the public square) and online (with continuous information sharing and everyday practices of texts, videos, and manifestos) was and continues to be the only way to create a consistent movement to fight the regime in its core. In the words of Dimash Alzhanov from the Oyan, Qazaqstan movement:

DTK: How many times were you arrested?

Dimash Alzhanov: Three times.

DTK: But there are severe consequences after three detentions with 15 days in prison . . .

Dimash Alzhanov: If they arrest you [for 15 days]. But in my case, I was detained, kept at the police station, and then let go without any explanations. They didn't even make notes in their journal.

DTK: Do you remain in some [secret] lists [for surveillance]?

Dimash Alzhanov: Most probably yes.

DTK: If we come back to the turbulent June [of 2019] when a lot of people started participating in unsanctioned rallies en masse and there was a feeling that Almaty became the protesting centre but not only Almaty, Astana too. But Astana was in this role of catching up with Almaty [protests]. It seems that Astana always follows Almaty [in protest politics] and they are not in the avant-garde of it yet . . .

Dimash Alzhanov: For the reasons that we all understand.

DTK: But there [in Astana] is also some alternative discourse …

Dimash Alzhanov: You know, we were hoping. Even with [Nubulat] Masanov[20] in the beginning of the 2000s there was a discussion about the managerial revolution that happened in the 1970s and 1980s in the West. [We question] whether the sustainable state apparatus has formed, the type of the state apparatus that understands the demands of the state apparatus and the concept of democracy – but it hasn't happened yet.

DTK: But the interest is still alive because many people within this system want to get to positions of power.

Dimash Alzhanov: Yes, but if there is a sustainable space where you understand that perhaps this system of shifting positions is constructed especially from within in order stop these [intra-elite] protests from forming. Because so many years of [authoritarian] institutionalization should have led to somewhere. [Because] besides the necessity [for this system to exist for participating elites] or besides the possibility of corruption, [this system] forms some sort of class, even the whole city [of Nur-Sultan] appeared [from this practice].

DTK: Yes, there is perhaps a feeling that there is a new generation of [authoritarian] governors in Astana …

Dimash Alzhanov [laughs]: The first generation of Bolashak [scholars]?[21]

Our conversation on this issue ended with his insight and a paradoxical conclusion that while there is a possibility for change and reforms from within the regime, these possibilities are too uncertain and unstable. The regime gives no guarantees that one day it just would start dismantling the system on the basis of which it was built and existed for more than thirty years. Alzhanov was right to say that intensive institutionalization of the authoritarian system inevitably led to its internal strength and the building of the administrative class that is particularly loyal to the former president Nazarbayev himself. From within this complex administrative system, it looks like an upgraded bureaucratic-loyalist system, which the Soviets built with a single party (the one that Jennifer Gandhi (2008) called a perfect invention for

---

[20] Nurbulat Masanov was a famous Kazakh historian and an expert on Kazakh nomadism. He was also an active figure in the intellectual sphere where he contributed greatly to discussions on Kazakh nationalism and traditionalism. Along with other public intellectuals and activists, he was active in the Polyton discussion club.

[21] Author's interview with Dimash Alzhanov, January 2020, Almaty, Kazakhstan.

autocratic systems) and a dictum of the charismatic leader where the proto-ideology is built on the belief that he is the guarantor of everything happy and great happening in the country. While Qazaq Koktemi activists were neither hopeful nor patient enough for the system to start reforming itself from within, they started attacking one of its weakest links – they launched the campaign to cancel Elbasy, Nursultan A. Nazarbayev.

Cancel Elbasy and Qazaq Koktemi Bodiless Protest

On 1 December 2020, simultaneously World AIDS Day and the Day of the First President in Kazakhstan,[22] a group of anonymous activists placed a banner with the text '37.3 billion tenge for the name'. Two hashtags accompanied the writing on the banner, and these were #QazaqKoktemi and #Cancel Elbasy (see Figure 6.1). The banner was placed on Nazarbayev (former Furmanov) Avenue in downtown Almaty and, in the best traditions of the banner and poster wars with the #QazaqKoktemi hashtags (such as *Peremen!* and other performative acts since April 2019), was later accompanied by a text that was shared online on social media and by several independent news portals such as The Village Kazakhstan. The message for this banner stated that:

We did not forget how in March 2019 Kazakhstani government renamed the capital-city and central streets of the country without consulting with the opinions of the people (*narod*). According to different sources, more than 47.3 billion [Kazakh] tenge[23] has been spent already in the attempts to immortalize Nazarbayev's name. Today when he and his retinue are celebrating this day as a holiday [*prazdnik*], citizens who do not recognize it, are thinking about ways to put an end this cult of personality.

The Constitution of the Republic of Kazakhstan states that the only source of power [in the republic] are people [*narod*]. We believe that every citizen of Kazakhstan should have the opportunity to participate in the governance of state affairs and [that] our freedom of choice and freedom of speech should be respected. We also state that in our common home everyone is equal before the law and thus the law on 'The Leader of the Nation' should be annulled.[24]

---

[22] Public holiday in Kazakhstan celebrating Nursultan A. Nazarbayev's achievements and contributions to the country's development.
[23] Approximately 110,974,550 USD.
[24] Text available at https://www.the-village-kz.com/village/city/news-city/15067-47-billion-on-name-nazarbayevm.

Cancel Elbasy Bodiless Protest 213

Figure 6.1 Qazaq Koktemi December 2020 protest banner. Source: Qazaq Spring activists

This visual-performative and textual aspect of the protests without bodies was what the Kazakh Spring (Qazaq Koktemi) started with in March 2019 with the secret preparations for the 'You cannot run away from the truth' performative action in Almaty that I discussed in Chapter 1 and 2. After the gradual division into public and anonymous or confidential circles of activists, among them also many existing NGO players whom I consider more structured and institutionalized participants the field of Qazaq Koktemi expanded. This expansion still included an array of different players – from individual activists like Tulesova, who still take time to position themselves in the field, to activist-educational initiatives such as Femagora, who remain in the field of Qazaq Koktemi though not within its most visible and vocal movement Oyan, Qazaqstan. And to complicate things even more, within the Qazaq Koktemi field there is another player – the anonymous group of art activists who go by the same name of Qazaq Koktemi and strike with their anonymous and bodiless protest banners.

The chronology of this Kazakh Banksy-type group is as follows:

- April 2019, 'You cannot run from the truth'; Adil Saulau Ushin

- May 2019, *Peremen!* at the monument to Viktor Tsoi
- 1 December 2019, *El Basynnan Shridi*[25] [The country rotten from its head]
- 29 February 2020, portraits of Presidents Kassym-Zhomart Tokayev and Nursultan Nazarbayev with the writing 'Parasites who do not have an Oscar'
- 1 December 2020, '47.3 billion for the name'
- Finally, May 2021, the start of the 'mural wars', when the Qazaq Koktemi anonymous collective kept on changing the mural to Nazarbayev that spontaneously appeared at the intersection of Zharokov and Mynbayev Streets (see Figure 6.1); each time the wall was repainted, the Cancel Elbasy hashtags reappeared.

The campaign with the hashtag #CancelElbasy technically originated on social media right before the 1 December 2019 celebration of the First President's Day and as a resistance to what many art activists saw as a 'cult of personality'. However, this hashtag strategically appeared in the banner wars and then the mural wars only from December 2020, when the anonymous Qazaq Koktemi art collective decided to change their strategy and focus precisely on the idea of cancelling Elbasy while he is still alive. In this widespread trend for cancel culture, the anonymous activists seek 'power' (*vlast'*) over the dictatorship vested in the physical and metaphorical body of Nazarbayev himself.

The discursive power of Nazarbayev and his body is very similar to other authoritarian systems, and Lisa Wedeen's classical study on Syria is a clear template for such 'bodily authority building'. She discusses Asad's cult and its attempt to personify the state with his own physical body and personality:

On the level of representation, Asad's cult registers the paradox between state-formation and nation-building. On the one hand, Asad's cult, like monarchical cults in the West, works to personify the state, to set it above and distance it from society. The cult of Hafiz al-Asad, like former monarchical cults in Europe, can be taken to epitomize the attempt to distinguish between a sacred elite and the profane rest of the population. Power is

---

[25] In this slogan, there is an interplay of words with *El* – translated from Kazakh as people, nation, or country – which is also used in *Elbasy* – the Father of the Nation and in many of nationalizing regime's slogans and programmes, such as *Mangilik El*.

sanctioned by the ruler's sacred investiture, which functions to identify the mortal body of the leader with the immortal body of the realm. In Weberian terms, individual charisma imbues the office with extraordinary qualities, with the effect that the institutions of the modern state survive the demise of its founders. In the West, charisma became 'routinized', and legal-rational states adhering to rules and procedures succeeded those based on personal leadership and personal connections. A cult of Asad as superhuman positions him to perform this state-building function for Syria.

On the other hand, and in keeping with modern notions of equality and national identity, Syria's cult paradoxically narrows the gap between ruler and ruled. In the words of a broadcast on Damascus radio in 1980, 'In order to kill the revolution, they will have to kill the people, and this is impossible. They should know that Asad is no one, but one of you. Every citizen in this country is Hafiz al-Asad.' (Wedeen 1999: 16–18)

Thus, the symbolic location of the physical body as a paradigm of the regime's constructed power axis lies in the mortal body of the dictator, which they try to immortalize or mummify (like Lenin) after his death, and in the mortal body of the protestor, whom they try to tame with violence (physical and psychological). This is done in order to create the myth of shared belief that resembles what is known as the cult of personality. However, what I find problematic in the conceptualization of the cult of personality is the construction of its discursive power rather than detailed demystification of such a narrative (not a discourse) as weak and working only on the level of the most loyal regime elites or the most indoctrinated bureaucrats. As Wedeen writes, the regime aims to achieve the type of feeling as if:

Asad represents not just the extraordinary individual, the authoritative 'father', the 'knight' who can 'lead forever'. He is also the average Syrian, a 'man of the people', a brother among equals: 'Asad is no one, but one of you.' Can tropes that function rhetorically to identify an exclusive object of awe be reconciled with the inclusive rhetoric expressing the nation's doctrinal commitment to leveling distinctions in accordance with Ba'thism's socialist dictates? 'Every citizen in this country is Hafiz al-Asad.' (Wedeen 1999: 16–17)

But was every citizen in Kazakhstan Nursultan A. Nazarbayev? Doubtful. The rift of inequality that the pandemic bared across different socially vulnerable groups demonstrated how the myths of 'stability, prosperity, and strong presidency' under the Nazarbayev regime were a mere sandcastle. Very few Kazakhstanis could afford the type of healthcare, access to rapid vaccination once it was released, or even basic income needed to survive national lockdowns as the Nazarbayev family could. Yet in this protest there is a dividing line between Cancel Elbasy and growing social unrest fuelled by economic inequality. The former protest was flamboyant, if not from the position of the elite with abundant economic capital, but at least from the position of public intellectuals with abundant cultural capital. The Qazaq Koktemi collective's texts, banners, changing murals, and messages within the Cancel Elbasy programme are filled with a type of artistic performance quality, though they too find themselves at the economically impoverished end of the spectrum. But unlike those who protested and continue to protest on the streets under the populist agenda for writing off consumer debts to banks or seeking additional and spontaneous payments from the state,[26] the Cancel Elbasy protest is not demanding the redistribution of wealth to individual families. They fight for the redistribution of the investments spent on fighting protestors, censoring the Internet, sponsoring police, and investing in Nazarbayev renaming projects, to direct them to the infrastructure (health, education, and institutionalized welfare).

The reproduction of the Qazaq Koktemi collective's visuals and texts for their performative protest actions happens in the media sphere. Most non-state sponsored media sources, such as Vlast.kz, Mediazona, The Village, and others, as well as social media channels, reproduce what the anonymous collective publish on their Instagram account, rukh2k19, and the Ministry of Information and Social Development fights its spread. One of the ways the Kazakh government tried to prohibit the Cancel Elbasy campaign and the reproduction of the changed mural of July 2021, where the Father of the Nation was portrayed as a 'clown' (see Figure 6.1), was by citing the constitutional law 'on the First President of the Republic of Kazakhstan' or the so-called *elbasy* law. According to this law, which was first adopted in July 2000 and granted Nazarbayev the titles of the First President of

---

[26] I do not mention here the labour unions and those protestors in Zhanaozen who still find themselves in new labour disputes in the summer of 2021, with the legitimate demand for adequate pay for their risky industrial jobs. Spontaneous groups, on the other hand, demand the radical distribution of wealth, for example, payments to individuals and their families because they position themselves as people in need, but often bypassing the social welfare infrastructure already in place.

Kazakhstan and the Father of the Nation, only Nazarbayev has special provision for an unlimited number of re-elections and inviolability of his property, political status, and bank account. The same law, which was amended on a number of occasions over almost two decades, also provided a special status for Nazarbayev in the case of his resignation – he still retained the right to 'consult' the parliament and the next presidents, to take a seat at the Security Council, and, in general, remain quite active in the political life of the country. The 2017 provisions and additions to the Criminal Code of the Republic of Kazakhstan (Article 373) also directly affected the '*elbasy* law' because it prohibited any 'public insult and other encroachment of honour and dignity of the First President of the Republic of Kazakhstan'. This article has a provision that any public insults, including the 'desecration of images' of the Father of the Nation can lead to up to two years of imprisonment or 'restriction of freedom' with a fine or 'correctional labour'. Media outlets who are found guilty of 'public insult' or 'desecration of images' of Nazarbayev are prosecuted with a fine ten times higher and possible imprisonment or restriction of freedom for the duration of three years. Both the law on the First President and Article 373 in the Criminal Code related to this law cover Nazarbayev's 'closest family members' without specifying who falls under this category.

This explains why the Qazaq Koktemi collective's actions have to remain anonymous and bodiless. If their actions with textual effect – for example, banners citing the constitution or the play on words with 'El' (people, country in Kazakh) – were prosecuted on the basis of an accusation of 'petty hooliganism', then active use of the hashtag Elbasy and even a painting of Nazarbayev's face could land any of them in jail for two years, if not more. Independent media were also targeted for sharing images of the desecrated portraits of Nazarbayev, which made editors take the decision to blur the images on their websites. Other potential victims of Article 373 were several Instagram accounts, including those that directly focus on producing memes with Elbasy (e.g., @Elbasymemes_, which was previously closed and had to reopen in January 2020 and @shalmustbgone), but since these are largely anonymous, their creators mainly received threats and were forced to change accounts several times. The digital sphere that operates through easy access to social media platforms and uses the language of memes and short TikTok videos (or reels) and the discourse that is at once globalized but at the same time very localized (inclusive of an organic mixture of Russian, Kazakh, and English in the caption of the meme) remains a black box of riddles for the traditional police and law-enforcement agents in Kazakhstan. Meanwhile the Cancel Elbasy campaign operates via hashtags, videos, digital jokes (memes), and a combination of coined terms, for example, '*shal* must be gone', where the derogative word *shal* – the old man in Kazakh – equates to the Father of the Nation. There are no physical bodies of protestors in this type of anonymous protest; instead, it places all the focus on the body and image of Nazarbayev, his closest allies (including his younger brother Bolat), President Tokayev, and some local and foreign celebrities (trending Angeline Jolie, for example) to ridicule the idea of the dictator's omnipresent power. In fact, memes and an artistic type of inversion of these authoritative narratives turn around the idea that 'every citizen in this country is Hafiz al-Asad' or in this case, Elbasy. Not every *body* is imbued with this domination.

By way of conclusion to this chapter, what Oyan, Qazaqstan and Qazaq Koktemi activists are able to bring is the rethinking of the public square and public protest by transferring it to the symbolic body – both physical and metaphorical – of the oppressed and the oppressor. In locating 'power' within the locus of the body, they were able to offer a powerful critique of the authoritarian regime and to highlight how, despite the deep embeddedness of the regime within the state, the state still remains something that can be defended and returned to the citizens. Through the struggle of the body, the activists bring back to the fore the idea that the state is 'a field' where different actors can fight for its definition, redefinition, and powers. In the words of one of the best theorists of the state, Pierre Bourdieu,

The state, in other words, is not a bloc, it is a field. The administrative field, as a particular sector of the field power, is a field, that is, a space structured according to oppositions linked to specific forms of capital with differing interests. These antagonisms, whose site is this space, have to do with the division of organizational functions associated with the different respective bodies (2014: 20).

Qazaq Koktemi and Oyan, Qazaqstan were able to shift the existing frames of the political established by Nazarbayev's regime by questioning not only the legality and legitimacy of 'sanctioned' protests but also by questioning the whole premise that only the regime had full power over the state. Very few of the previous political forces that called themselves 'opposition' could achieve this shift in frames and discourses, since they did not believe that changing the system under the reign of Nazarbayev was possible at all; but they also were aware of their inability to mobilize large enough and networked enough groups of people to overthrow the regime. There is also a distinction here between the opposition coming from the regime itself and the Qazaq Koktemi phenomenon emerging on the margins of any regime power – in the stereotypical coffee shops, the new digital public spheres, and through the networks of higher education. Unlike the late Altynbek Sarsembayev, who was one of the ideologues of the early Nazarbayev era, very few of the Qazaq Koktemi activists have any type of insider access to the regime, but it did not stop them from analysing and cracking the system's code. What was important in this symbolic success was the ongoing network of activists, who were learning from other repressive regimes and staying connected to the global agenda. In the next and last chapter, I discuss how the protest became more transnational and how the agenda of the Qazaq Koktemi activists trespassed on one of the most persistent frames of the Nazarbayev regime – authoritarian patriarchy.

7 | Queering the Public Sphere

On 8 March 2021, five feminist NGOs and initiatives organized the first Feminist March in Almaty to be approved by the local municipality.[1] The organizers of the march had been fighting for this initiative for some time, and the march was the culmination of several years of unsanctioned public artistic actions, rallies, and clashes with the police.[2] A lot of protest against gendered violence and for gender equality is concentrated online, with initiatives such as Feminita, KazFem, SVET Foundation, and many more taking action and focusing grassroots activism entirely on social media platforms. Prior to the 2021 march, there were also many individual initiatives and activist voices. Among them, the best known are Arina Osinovskaya, Fariza Ospan, Dina Tansari and her Don't Be Silent (NeMolchi) initiative for the support of victims of gendered violence and rape, artist Suinbike Suleimenova and her initiative 0 Gender, and the UyatEmes sex-education platform in Russian and Kazakh led online by Karlygash Kabatova,[3] to name just a few of most outstanding activists' names.

In Kazakhstan, the gendered order of regime rhetoric and attention is organized in such a way that it mainly centres on women and family issues. The regime's paradigm is highly conservative and patriarchal – the list of prohibited jobs for women (the list includes at least 191

---

[1] This is the only way to organize mass rallies and marches in Kazakhstan. KazFem and other feminist organizations tried to organize more marches prior to this, but their attempts resulted in the detention of their members and police harassment.
[2] On 8 March 2017, KazFem activists tried to arrange the first Women's March in Almaty but were harassed by the police. They planned to organize a march every year to raise awareness about gendered violence and problems. In August 2017, fem-activists were arrested and later sentenced for 'hooliganism' for a performative action destigmatizing menstruation. In 2020, activists Arina Osinovskaya and Fariza Ospan were tried in court for their unsanctioned rally on 8 March 2020 in downtown Almaty. There were more repressive actions throughout, especially the 2021 imprisonment of Feminita activists Zhanara Serkebayeva and Gulzada Serzhan in Shymkent.
[3] See Kabatova's research piece, Kabatova 2018.

professions) is justified by the necessity 'to take care of the weak sex'– *slabiy pol* – as women in Kazakhstan are often defined. The state programme of gender equality is called the 'Concept on Family and Gender Policy in the Republic of Kazakhstan till 2030' and is connected to 'Kazakhstan-2050', the umbrella policy and regime vision on modernization and industrialization. The Concept on Gender Policy mainly approaches the issue of gender problems and challenges through the lens of the family. For example, the Concept focuses on the provision of social welfare and care to the family and regrets the increasing numbers of abortions (every fifth pregnancy in the country ends in an abortion) and childless families (the 16 per cent of families where one or both partners are infertile).[4] The Concept briefly touches on the gendered violence that became ubiquitous in Kazakhstan – according to the official statistic cited in the Concept, every third woman in Kazakhstan suffered from one or another form of physical and/or sexual violence.

The Kazakhstani law on gendered violence moreover has several major flaws that have been publicly criticized by activists, including the provision that the offender is subject to administrative and not criminal charges. Furthermore, none of the current laws, concepts, or state programmes on gender policy include the rights of non-binary, gay, bisexual, and transgenderpeople, as the state vision on the gender issue remains authoritarian-patriarchal. The focus of this authoritarian-patriarchal vision is on the conservative division into male and female (less-protected) groups, reproduction goals, and family issues, as well as the symbolic or cosmetic changes of counting the number of female 'representatives' in municipal and wider state institutions. However, what is missing from all these state programmes and rosy reports on achieving the United Nations sustainable goals for gender equality is actual power vested in these representatives and how much they can actually change the state's stagnant policy. Because regardless of how many flowery and happy reports are produced in regard to the number of women members of parliament or the consistently 'female' positions in the Ministry of Labour and Social Policy, gendered problems and inequality persist in Kazakhstan.[5]

---

[4] The Concept is available in Russian at https://adilet.zan.kz/rus/docs/ U1600000384#z14m.
[5] The 2018 Asian Development Bank report stated that 'Kazakhstan steadily reduced its Gender Inequality Index (GII) value from 0.405 in 2000 to 0.202 in 2015, bringing it lower than the 0.279 average for Europe and Central Asian countries'.

With growing insecurity and spontaneous mothers' street protests in major Kazakhstani cities, the text of the Concept on Gender Policy reads almost ironically, citing how 50 per cent of small- and medium-scale businesses are occupied by women in Kazakhstan. The problem with this type of statistic is that it often masks the deeper levels of unemployment, inequality, discrimination, and lack of health insurance. Every hairdresser or nail technician working in semi-informal conditions across different cities of Kazakhstan can be signed off as an 'individual entrepreneur' in these official statistics without taking into consideration their unstable income, lack of pension savings, absent health insurance, and long working hours. But these same statistics can count them as employed as long as they pay taxes on their 'business'.

As gender inequality persists and the regime continues to approach it blindly through the external frameworks of 'representation'[6] and 'welfare provision' and an internal focus on biopolitics and reproduction, alternative voices of activists emerge to battle this one-sidedness, as they view it, and to criticize it. The spectrum of feminist activism is very wide in Kazakhstan. It includes the fight for sex education and against the growing re-traditionalization; there is a strong civic lobby to criminalize domestic violence, and an array of NGOs, initiatives, and voices fighting for the inclusion of rights for all sexual identifications, orientations, and positions that commentators united under the umbrella of LGBTQ rights activism. In this chapter, I discuss this important shift in protesting that stands in direct opposition to the

---

[6] What I mean by this 'external' critique is that the regime aims to follow the United Nations sustainable development goals only through cosmetic approaches – they add more women to the leading party Nur-Otan or nominated a female candidate to run in the presidential elections for the first time in 2019 in order to construct 'perfect' statistics. However, because this gendered representation is done within the authoritarian-patriarchal system, women are not directly elected to their positions, and the logic of their selection to particular positions remains obscure. Moreover, this argument for 'women's representation' in politics is then used to fight off any alternative opposition from the feminist groups and candidates who want to stand in elections not for the prize of being the regime's 'window dressing' but for real involvement in politics. Besides, this type of selection of pro-regime female politicians leads to further sexism in the system, where women are seen as mere substitutes for 'soft' positions on committees for welfare or family relations but not considered for higher positions, for example, prime minister or even a city mayor (not a single Kazakhstani woman has so far occupied either of these positions).

regime's authoritarian patriarchy. Feminist movements and movements for LGBTQ rights allow a potential expansion of the rigid authoritarian-patriarchal dimension between male and female politics and representations. It was clear that Nazarbayev's regime and now Tokayev's regime continued to build a patriarchal system with traditionalist family values and consistent use of the discourse of women as 'mothers' and 'breeders of the nation'. This explains why 8 March remained a celebration of neoliberalism – the one day of the year where most flower sellers, the baking industry, and other celebratory sectors had their most profitable day. Feminist activists who fought for their right to a peaceful rally for years instead spoke of raging incidence of domestic violence, rape culture, and widespread gendered violence and discrimination that is embedded in the regime's authoritarian-patriarchal-traditionalist approaches to gender relations and values.

Women's March 2021

The date for the 2021 Feminist March was not accidental. International Women's Day was widely celebrated during the Soviet period as marking the liberation of women, and the celebration was continued in the post-Soviet period simply as the 'women's celebration day'. Surrounded by many sexist jokes about women receiving all the praise and flowers on the 8th and having to clean up and return to their household roles and unequal positions the day after, 9 March has been a contested territory for post-Soviet feminists for a while. As Xenia Udod writes following her interviews with KazFem activist Arina Osinovskaya, 'by marching down the Almaty streets the feminists had wanted to re-appropriate March 8 as their holiday, which has been established more than one hundred years ago as a platform to demand equal rights and opportunities for (Western) women and demonstrate their determination to become socially and politically engaged' (Udod 2018: 3). Many of the feminist voices wanted to remake the celebration away from a public holiday imbued with a neoliberal feast of flowers, pink cakes, and the reincorporation of sexist and gendered bias.

The slogan for the 2021 Women's March dealt particularly with women's rights and gendered insecurities in Kazakhstan. The authoritarian-patriarchal system led to many everyday aspects of gender discrimination and the normalization of sexism, gendered violence,[7] exacerbated patriarchal-traditionalist narratives on control, and scrutiny over the ways a 'real Kazakh woman' or a 'real Kazakhstani woman' should behave, live, and appear. Thus, the official organizing committee statement shared on social media prior to the march read:

> We, women of Kazakhstan, activists, feminists, human rights defenders, daughters, mothers, girlfriends, and wives. We won't allow anyone – neither politicians nor nationalists and traditionalists nor those who want to appropriate our March – to take away our voices, our platform and our ability to speak about our rights. To all those [who want to appropriate the march] we contend – 8 March is our day, and [Women's] March is also ours. [Kazakh] Feminists plan to organize these Marches every year. Get used to it.[8]

The 2021 Women's March in Almaty happened at a very heated moment in gender politics, as fem-activists and human rights defenders from all sorts of NGOs, grassroots initiatives, and de-institutionalized groups were discussing the decriminalization of the law on domestic violence and the rise of gendered violence against women during the pandemic in Kazakhstan. In 2017, the law on domestic violence was decriminalized and moved to administrative punishment, specifying that a first assault is only punished by a written warning. Given that so many acts of domestic gendered violence go without reporting, the 'victim' of the assault can find herself in greater jeopardy if she reports her abuser the first time and he walks free; he would only be sentenced to ten to fifteen days in police detention if the attack happened a second time. Critics of decriminalization reported on a number of high-profile cases where women were killed by their violent husbands after numerous attempts to report domestic violence to the police. Dina Tansari from the NeMolchi initiative,[9] which is very active online, in 2021 reported that her team received at least fifteen calls each day for help and support. Another staggering and alarming number was reported during the Women's March – fifty-six women were killed in

---

[7] Official statistics in Kazakhstan reports a very alarming situation where every third woman in Kazakhstan has faced gendered violence in her life, and every day in 2020 five women were raped in Kazakhstan.
[8] KazFem Instagram post from 6 March 2021.
[9] As I finalize this manuscript, Tansari and Ne Molchi Foundation are under attack from the regime, leaving the Ne Molchi founders no choice but live in exile. Many of the Kazakhstani citizens who donated to the foundation were called in by the police and asked about their payments and affiliations with the foundation.

Kazakhstan in domestic violence cases during the first year of the pandemic.

Calls for criminalizing domestic violence intensified in the winter of 2021 when more and more activists opened up public debates. These discussions were again located in the social media domain with the initial February and March 2021 boom of Clubhouse discussions and rooms, many of which were dedicated to heated debates about the law or numerous accounts of public cases of rape, gendered violence, and the deaths of women at the hands of their husbands in Kazakhstan.[10] The slogans and banners of the Women's March reflected these debates and read: '[If he] beats [you], then he should be imprisoned' [*Biet, znachit syadit*];[11] 'Today flowers, tomorrow you won't have a kidney' [*Segodnya tsvetochki, zavtra net pochki*];[12] 'We don't need flowers, I Iwe need safety' (see Figure 7.1), as well as the classic 'My body, my rules'.

The Women's March was organized by five local fem-initiatives that have been active in Kazakhstan since 2015–18. The organizing committee included the Feminita grassroots queer-feminist collective, KazFem radical feminists, FemSreda, SVET Foundation, fighting against gendered violence and offering psychological and legal help, and educational-research initiative FemAgora. Since the field of any type of activism is a public sphere, all of the organizers and 'public faces' of the march not only knew each other prior to the event but also had collaborated in the past and organized unsanctioned rallies for the same causes. They chose 'Rights and activism of different women' as their main theme for the 2021 march and announced that every year the march would focus on a specific agenda concerning the rights and conditions of Kazakhstani women generally, thematically organized around equality and provision of equal rights. This is why the LGBTQ

---

[10] Clubhouse is the social media app that allows its participants to form 'rooms' for audio discussions in real time. In February and March 2021, the app was very popular among Kazakhstani Russian- and Kazakh-speaking audiences. In early March 2021, there were at least two to three discussion rooms dedicated to the women's rights in Kazakhstan prior to the 8 March public rally. One of these discussions included a heated debate about decriminalizing the law on domestic violence, which coincided with the possible reworking of the law in parliament.

[11] The original Russian saying reads as '[if he] beats you, then [he] loves you' [*biet, znachit lyubit*] – the phrase that many feminist activists view as a patriarchal normalization of violence against women.

[12] In Russian, this slogan rhymes.

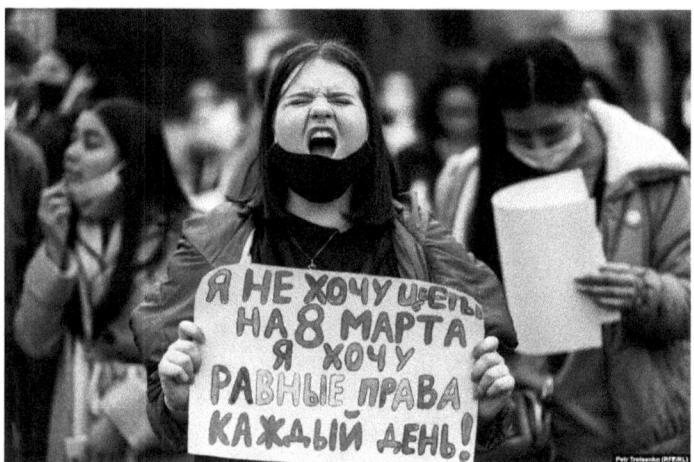

Figure 7.1 One of the participants in the 2021 Almaty Women's March. Her poster reads 'I don't want flowers for 8 March. I want equal rights every day!' © Petr Trotsenko, RFE/RL

agenda (not only in the form of flags at the march but also in the texts of the resolution and speeches of the activists) was highlighted as a crucial trend for this wave of feminist activism. Previous waves of activism in the gender sphere in Kazakhstan focused on economic rights but did not widen the perspectives and critiques of gender as such, and, as a result, many of the previous initiatives were incorporated into the agenda of the regime. This is how the Atameken 'Women in Business' or even the earlier Union of Businesswomen of Kazakhstan initiatives were formed, for example. Their agenda did not even start addressing the intersectional aspect of discrimination and was still operating within the stagnant female–male paradigm silencing and erasing non-binary people and their agenda.

Where do non-binary groups have to turn to in order to find their platform and their voice in the patriarchal-authoritarian agenda of the regime? Neither the Concept on Gender Policy nor major state policy on gender equality has provision for non-binary people, acting as if these groups do not exist. This is why the rise of such organizations as Feminita, KazFem, Kok.Team, and FemAgora, who directly address the rights of LGBTQ communities and their visibility in Kazakhstan, is so important. Feminita is 'a grassroots queer-feminist collective that aims to create and strengthen rights of women and activist communities that are able to change the social, political, economic and cultural spheres for the most oppressed groups of the Kazakhstani population'. And by the most oppressed groups they mean lesbians, bisexuals, queer people, disabled women, and women in sex work. Feminita uses the concept of queer to specify who is within their target group – 'inclusive of all women who are left outside all sex and gendered identifications'.[13] KazFem positions itself as a radical feminist group that aims at education, discussion, research, and development of the feminist agenda in Kazakhstan. They work both online and offline with internal work (mainly reading, researching, and activism) and external work (mainly public events). Kok.Team, who did not take part in the organization of the Women's March but who require an introduction in this particular context, is the first LGBT media platform in Kazakhstan. Founded by three activists – Amir Shaikezhanov, Anatoly Chernoussov, and Daniyar Sabitov – in 2017, the platform openly engaged in discussions and raising awareness about the rights, problems, and challenges of LGBT communities in Kazakhstan. I will come back to this paradigm particularly during the discussion of the ways the Women's March was discredited online via their connection to non-traditional values.

However, as they spoke from the podium at the small square behind the Academy of Science and near the Chokan Valikhanov monument – a legendary place in the Almaty civil sphere and open discussions – activists spoke of a future that is queer and free of hierarchies. Their resolution included many voices:

We – women of Kazakhstan:
We – mothers with many children,
We – political prisoners,
And we – women who do not want to have kids,
We – [women] kidnapped and forcefully pushed into marriage, some – while still children themselves,
We – women who are imprisoned for self-defence,
We – lesbians, bisexuals, trans-women and queer women who need to hide this fact,
We – girls, who have been told 'to obey the man and don't argue' since our childhood,

---

[13] Available from the collective's website https://feminita.kz/about-us/.

We – disabled women,
We – *kelin*,[14]
We – survivors of violence,
We – women who have to fear for our lives when we simply return home at night,
Finally, we are feminists![15]

Even though there were many familiar fem-activist faces among almost 500 marching participants, there was a lot of work on the part of the organizers to define and explain their agenda prior to the march and during the speeches. Activists shared news on their personal and collective social media platforms, held live Q&A sessions, and gave interviews to media portals. For example, queer activist Zhanar Serkebayeva, who was interviewed by the Village Kazakhstan media portal just two days before the march, explained what feminism was for her:

Feminism is the fight for fairness, equality and destruction of patriarchy. It means that we are striving to fight any hierarchical practices where someone needs to obey someone else. It is like dreaming about the ideal society where everything is great, and people have achieved absolute equality.[16]

The activists and organizers did not hide the fact that 'women' were their prime group of focus because, in the words of KazFem activist, Ayri Asiyeva,

We are trying to avoid situations, where there would be a skew when men would come and tell us [in reference to mansplaining] how to do things right in feminism. This is why we first of all invite women to the discussion. In general, there is a good rule in activism, 'nothing without us' and 'trying to hear the voices of the oppressed first'.[17]

In Kazakhstan, in a situation where women were constantly targeted by gendered violence, widespread rape culture, and lack of adequate response and victim-blaming from law-enforcement officers, as noted by many activists in gendered-violence assistance initiatives (most

---

[14] From Kazakh: daughters-in-law. Unfortunately, this concept encapsulates a lot of patriarchal values; see 'Project Kelin' on this issue.
[15] 2021 Women's March Resolution.
[16] www.the-village-kz.com/village/city/asking-question/16519-understand-feminism.
[17] Ibid.

notably Ne Molchi), the focus on women's rights at the march was not accidental. This type of alarming tendency of the overall socio-political context that remains hostile to women was also voiced in the official resolution of the march:

We all have the experience of living in a country where we do not feel safe and where laws do not protect us. But we are doing everything possible in order to change this.

Women's feminist March of the 8th of March is a historical date of the fight for the rights of all women and girls. 8th of March is our celebration day [*prazdnik*], it is aimed at achieving equal rights and opportunities for women in the society. In the independent Kazakhstan we are following the agenda [set by] the first Kazakh journalists, teacher and feminist, Nazipa Kulzhanova, who wrote [as early as] in 1923 that free women can develop a country....

We all receive threats, hatred, anger, and aggression. Woman is the base of society but for some reason, woman in Kazakhstan is still not a human [*vse eshe ne chelovek*]. Remember that it is not true, and we are fighting and will continue fighting for our, human rights that are guaranteed to us by the Constitution! We are all different, but we all have equal rights and opportunities. Efforts of every woman are important! Every woman is important![18]

The important background agenda to these slogans, themes, and activism was also the wider idea of inclusivity that many Kazakh fem-activists of this wave have propagated since 2015. In the words of Gulzada Serzhan in her speech at the march, 'Here we are: bisexuals, lesbians, queers'.[19] As rainbow flags, pins, and symbols appeared at the march, the activists, not for the first time but importantly and more visibly, reported about the groups that the regime tries to keep under the radar due to its traditionalist-conservative take on politics. Similarly to Russia, where the anti-LGBTQ propaganda law is in place, many Central Asian politicians are building if not an exact then at least not a radically opposite paradigm of heteronormativity.[20]

---

[18] 2021 Women's March Resolution. The text was drafted in both Russian and Kazakh.
[19] https://mediazona.ca/online/2021/03/08/marsh.
[20] See Shoshanova 2021 and notably two MA dissertations from Nazarbayev University on this theme, Ilyassov 2020 and Ten 2020, both from the MA in Eurasian Studies. See also Kudaibergenova 2019, where I compare the issue of gender non-binary approaches in Russia and Kazakhstan.

The idea of inclusivity is a crucial point for this new generation of fem-activists in Kazakhstan, who no longer ask for women's recognition in business, politics, or the public sphere (as their predecessors did). Instead, this recognition goes without saying, but the old problems and challenges – harassment, gendered and domestic violence, the gender pay gap, lack of security, and discrimination against women in the labour market – are now also combined with the acute understanding of the need to provide equality and human rights to all regardless of their gender or sexual identity. This inclusivity is something that significantly shapes the diverse voices and opinions of fem-activists and their choices to participate in certain political initiatives and movements or not. It is not a secret that many of those who came to or organized the 2021 Women's March in Almaty had been in close connection or vicinity to both the Oyan, Qazaqstan movement and the Qazaq Koktemi field. And here is where the complexity arises. As a field of opportunities, Qazaq Koktemi is a lot more open and inclusive to various ideas of democratization, pluralism, and often pluriversality, and inevitably the inclusion of all human rights. Fem-activists who took active part in the formation of the Qazaq Koktemi field argued for the crucial role of feminism and queer approaches in shaping the democratic future of Kazakhstan and making it a country where all rights matter and are honoured regardless of ethnicity, age, sexuality, or gender identity. This axiom is so important and widespread among fem-activists that many of them cite it as a reason to leave movements, collectives, and initiatives that they believe do not support these values. In the words of one of the activists,

I am a feminist, and it was important for me to talk about inclusivity, but for some people in the [given political] movement LGBTQ rights and fem-agenda were not primary. They said that first we needed to achieve changes in the political system, and then we can deal with everything else after we have achieved this one goal. But how can we do anything without inclusivity and constant empowerment of all? It was unclear to me, and this was why I left [the movement].[21]

On the other hand, other fem-activists decided to stay in the political movements to continuously develop their inclusivity agenda further. There is a shared ethos among the activists forming the Qazaq Koktemi

---

[21] Author's interview with fem-activist, June 2021 (anonymous).

field that all human rights should be respected, and there is a strong agenda for inclusivity, feminist rhetoric, and queer activism in this field.

Visibility of LGBTQ rights in particular became a significant and more vocal point for many fem-activists after the Women's March and following the discrediting of LGBTQ activists and the harassment of Feminita leaders Zhanar Serkebayeva and Gulzada Serzhan in Shymkent and Karaganda during meetings with their supporters in the summer of 2021. Both Serkebayeva and Serzhan are among the most visible and vocal figures of the LGBTQ movement but also of political protest in Kazakhstan. Their organization, Feminita, strived for the equality and visibility of LGBTQ people in Kazakhstan; they researched and published their findings that LGBTQ people go through double discrimination in many spheres of employment and education as well as private lives in Kazakhstan.[22] Almost half of the respondents to their survey reported that they had experienced or knew someone in their circles who had experienced violence and harassment due to their sexual orientation. On top of that, when 'LBK-women' (lesbian, bisexual, and queer women) report these crimes to the police, 'the police officers do not even take these statements', until these women are subjected to the 'the circle of offence':

> When a lesbian comes to the police to report that she was beaten up, almost all police officers (at the station) would stare at her. And all of them would ask the same questions: 'You seem to look *normal*, why were you walking around this club?', 'Well-deserved [that you got beaten up], didn't you know that pedophiles go to this club?', 'You have such long hair, how did you become a lesbian?'. Policemen allow themselves a lot more than a father or mother would. As an activist, I want to declare that we would not stand this attitude from the police. None of the other countries have the same levels of obnoxiousness, physical violence, and blackmail.[23]

Feminita activism was dedicated to public outreach in different cities and regions of Kazakhstan, not just the central cities of Almaty and Astana. This is why Serkebayeva and Serzhan organized regular meetings with their supporters in places such as Shymkent, Karaganda, Kyzylorda, and other regional cities and towns. However, in 2021 alone they experienced unprecedented violence against and discrediting of their activism in Shymkent, where they

---

[22] Reports available at https://feminita.kz/проекты/lbq-needs-assessment/.
[23] From Zhanar Serkebayeva's interview with Radio Azattyq, 2 July 2017.

were violently removed by the police officers 'for their own safety' in June. Another alarming precedent happened during their planned meeting with LGBTQ audiences in Karaganda at the end of July 2021, when a mob of around 150 to 200 angry men came to the pre-planned meeting hall and demanded the violent ousting of the 'gay concert'. It remained unclear who had misinformed the mob participants and even more unclear as to why police and special forces (SOBR) were not used to arrest the violent men who were ready to beat up the group of activists. Instead, the police escorted all the LGBTQ activists, including Serkebayeva and Serzhan, out of the building onto a special bus and left the Feminita founders at the train station to depart back for Almaty. The meeting eventually had to be held online on Zoom in early August 2021 under unprecedented security measures.

The alarming situation around the Feminita activists and law enforcement's inadequate response to the anti-LGBTQ mobs in both Shymkent and Karaganda was reflective of continuing anti-LGBTQ attitudes and oppression all over Kazakhstan. Several Kazakh-speaking bloggers, among them Kairat Kudaibergen,[24] started an unofficial campaign on social media calling out all visual and public expressions of 'anti-traditional' behaviour as 'anti-Kazakh' representation. The absurdity of this campaign started with burning toys with rainbow colouring or assaulting a Kazakh illustrator, who works under the pen name of Qantars, for her paintings of girls kissing in Kazakh dresses. However, these claims of anti-LGBTQ 'propaganda' mask a deeper contradiction and the authoritarian-patriarchal nature of the regime that created deep cleavages in Kazakhstani society along the lines of 'traditionalist', nationalist, and 'unacceptable' values and behaviours. The situation is even more alarming because these divisions and calls to censor the LGBTQ agenda online, discriminating against and attacking LGBTQ activists,[25] openly infringed human rights but left law-enforcement agencies deaf to calls to investigate the hate speech. In the conditions of the authoritarian-patriarchal discourse of the regime, the LGBTQ agenda more often is associated with the political discrediting of

---

[24] Not related to the author. Kudaibergen is actually a very popular name in Kazakhstan especially after the fame that the Kazakh singer Dimash Kudaibergen achieved worldwide.
[25] This open discrimination has forced many LGBTQ activists to leave Kazakhstan for good or to seek opportunities to do so in the future.

movements, activists, and opposition rather than with inclusivity, human rights, and democratization. I discuss this problem in the next section.

The LGBTQ Agenda in the Conservative Dictatorship: Between Discrediting and the Fight for Human Rights

In the context of authoritarian-patriarchal discourse where the dominant role is taken by the heterosexual family and the values associated with conservative heteronormativity, homophobia quickly became the trademark of open traditionalists. Some of the politicians openly engaged in this discourse, including the presidential candidate who ran in the 2019 elections, Sadybek Tugel, allowing himself to openly talk about fighting with 'dirty' gay propaganda[26] without facing any significant consequences. Meanwhile, Kazakhstan did not pass an anti-gay propaganda law like those which already exist in Russia and in neighbouring Kyrgyzstan. Anti-gay propaganda laws prohibit any information (even educational) about 'non-traditional sexual relations' and prevent activists in this sphere from interacting and engaging with young people. The draft of this law was approved by the Kazakh parliament in 2014 but was not signed by then-president Nazarbayev, which made the law void. According to the Kazakhstani constitution at that time, a law is approved and comes into force only after it is ratified by the two chambers of the parliament and signed by the president himself. But even in the absence of the gay propaganda law, which Human Rights Watch labelled the 'classic example of political homophobia', anti-LGBTQ harassment is still a great problem in Kazakhstani society.

Conservative political forces and commentators, among them the Namys group, which is closely associated with the regime, try to brand LGBTQ activism as something 'alien' to Kazakh culture and Kazakhstani socio-cultural contexts. They also use this traditionalist rhetoric to blame pro-democracy forces and movements as being closely associated with the 'West' and aiming to destroy the well-being and 'health' of the nation. Thus, Oyan, Qazaqstan activists'

---

[26] Tugel speaking against homophobia and sex work: https://informburo.kz/novosti/kandidat-v-prezidenty-sadybek-tugel-predlozhil-borotsya-s-gryaznoy-gey-propagandoy.html.

rallies in Astana were often branded as a 'gay parade', and several activists were accused of promoting the LGBTQ agenda or being gay themselves. In the words of these conservative commentators, being gay was considered as one of the lowest and most degrading positions and identities. This situation is even more alarming since discreditation, hate speech, public comments, and calls to ban any LGBTQ symbols (including the rainbow) often go beyond just absurd public comments. The attacks on Feminita activists and harassment of LGBTQ people in everyday circumstances pose a serious danger to them. Growing disinformation, conspiracies, and intolerance of LGBTQ communities without understanding their needs, rights, contexts, and the way they are discriminated against on a daily basis in Kazakhstan fuel this conservative divide and provide more space for harassment, discreditation, hate speech, blame, and criticisms.

Female activists in particular fall under this category of criticism because, for conservative politicians and the authoritarian-patriarchal discourse alike, women and especially ethnically Kazakh women remain the main target of traditionalization. As activist Fariza Ospan underlined, according to this discourse Kazakh women are told what their role is under the patriarchy – mainly as a mother, an obedient daughter-in-law (*kelin*), and a woman who selflessly follows all the rules of the patriarchal society without questioning what is right or wrong. What is hidden in this discourse of the obedient 'Kazakh woman' is the level of physical and emotional violence she has to endure and a kind of normalization of this violence, often under the banner of 'true Kazakh traditions'. For example, scandals broke out in numerous Kazakh social media and pop culture accounts over normalizing gendered violence, when one blogger claimed that she was hit by her husband because she beat him at chess, and she laughed it off by claiming that 'men should always win'. In another instance, one music video depicted a physical brawl between a husband and wife that looked more like a boxing match. Further re-traditionalization under the auspices of what some people dress up as 'Kazakh traditions' can be significantly dangerous for all actors involved, but women, in particular, remain more vulnerable. Women in Kazakhstan are the main targets for domestic violence, hidden and open labour discrimination, harassment, rape, and stigmatization and shaming (*uyatization*).

My interview sample revealed that female activists are targeted and blamed for their unmarried status, sexual orientations, and physique and physical appearance; they receive hate mail online and hate speech while being detained at unsanctioned rallies. Female activists also more often than their male counterparts are labelled by conservatives as gay and as LGBTQ activists, as if there is something wrong with being either. In the words of Assem Zhapisheva, she was especially targeted and received hate comments for her LGBTQ activism and her stance that all rights should be respected and provided:

> *Assem Zhapisheva*: I am blamed for being 31 and unmarried.
>
> *Diana T. Kudaibergen*: Does this concern anyone?
>
> *Assem Zhapisheva*: Well, for them [pro-regime forces] this [seems to be] a big problem. And before that bots wrote that I was the [Western] agent ... Do you know Kok.Team [an LGBT community and media portal in Kazakhstan]? Kok.Team have an annual award, and they gave it to me because in their opinion, I contributed the most for the provision of the LGBT rights. I received it last year and of course, bots started writing, 'that's it, here she is! Now we understood everything – she is LGBT! She was sent by the *Gosdep* [US State Department] and she wants to organize the sexual revolution here!' ... I constantly receive a lot of [negative comments] for it [Zhapisheva's LGBT activism]. I also have my partner Dima and he has his *Za Nami uje Viehali* [social media channel] in the Russian language, and there was the case when Khamitov, the MMA fighter started offending LGBT [community] and he [Dima] created content about it, we wrote it together – it was about why it is important to value and respect LGBT rights. Because if you do not value their rights, then your rights will also be discriminated at some point [because all human rights should be respected equally] – simple things like that. We placed this content on Dima's channel and later I also published a large text on my own channel about the necessity of human rights and the respect for all rights [including LGBT rights in Kazakhstan] and that you should fight for your rights and that you shouldn't discriminate other people's rights and I tried to explain it somehow. But Dima and I we both received a lot of [negative comments] (*mnogo vsego priletelo*) – for LGBT and against. It's the usual story [in Kazakhstan].[27]

In mentioning the Kok.Team web portal, Zhapisheva referred to a well-known Kazakhstani LGBT media portal whose producers are involved in creating media and cultural content about the rights of the LGBT community in Kazakhstan. Daniyar Sabitov, Anatoly Chernoussov, and Amir Shaikezhanov have run Kok.Team's

---

[27] Author's interview with Assem Zhapisheva.

Russian- and Kazakh-language content online since they founded the organization in 2017. Yulia Ten in her study on queer discourses in Kazakhstani contemporary visual culture wrote that 'apart from this important immediate work with the community, Kok.team also devotes considerable time to talking about more abstract ideas of queerness in order to formulate an idea of the place of gay people in contemporary Kazakhstan'.[28] Kok.Team's name is formed from the combination of the Kazakh word for 'blue' – *kok* (which is also often green) – and English 'team', but it also sounds like Kazakh 'Koktem' – spring. This coincidence allowed many bots and critics of the Kazakh Spring and Oyan, Kazakhstan movement to associate the two with the LGBTQ agenda in Kazakhstan. The members of the Qazaq Koktemi field were unbothered by this connection – after all, many of the activists within the field are queer activists themselves and openly support the queer agenda and fight for its visibility and inclusion. To the majority of those I interviewed from this field, a queer future is inevitable in Kazakhstan, and that is a fact. Thus, the work of such organizations as Kok.Team, Feminita, and Femagora is invaluable in creating content that makes the LGBTQ community more visible in the Kazakhstani context. Daniyar Sabitov's collages call into question the idea that Kazakh history did not have LGBTQ communities in the past and also challenge the whole authoritarian-patriarchal discourse that Nazarbayev's regime was so tireless in constructing, focusing only on the heteronormative agenda. Through their podcast 'Valikhanov's Pony', Sabitov and Chernoussov tried to open a discussion about possible ways to normalize the existing queerness in Kazakhstan and fight off disinformation, discreditation, homophobia, and shameful practices:

Sabitov and Chernoussov's approach towards the Kazakhstani queer voice is thus state- and nation-centered and not cosmopolitan one. They are not concerned with writing local queers into the global history as such, but rather are focusing on the incorporation of their memory into the national history as it would be presented in Kazakhstan's textbooks at school.[29] In this way, they recognize the primary importance of state institutions such as schools, universities, and museums in changing national identity discourse, in which queers would not be seen as contradicting to other cultural marks of identity (connected to ethnicity, religion, and so on). Thus, Sabitov and Chernoussov insist on the idea that queerness can (and should) be contextualized in

[28] Ten 2020: 35.   [29] Sabitov and Chernoussov, 'Queer Archive' [Kvir Arkhiv].

Kazakhstan, and that it is important to emphasize that queerness and Kazakhness (as a basis for national identity) can be seen as complementary and non-contradictory to each other.[30]

To Kazakhstani queer activists, the only way to fight off the regime's patriarchal vision is to challenge it in its normative and narrative core – by placing queer families in dialogue with the conceptual core of 'family relations in Kazakhstan', by normalizing queerness in everyday contexts and in labour relations, and by openly fighting for the rights of the LGBTQ communities. A lot of the work also involves education, sharing of information, and public discussions in both languages (Kazakh and Russian) – in short, giving voice and visibility to these communities and forming a space for them in the 'normalized' Kazakhstani gendered discourse.

However, this type of activism is continuously discredited in the political field, and more time is needed to change the frames and approaches to understanding queerness and queer rights as part of universal rights for all the citizens. The workings of the authoritarian-patriarchal discourse are too rooted in Kazakhstani society, and growing traditionalist fears that the LGBTQ agenda could destroy some 'traditions' are still strong. Unfortunately, the shadow of this discrediting also influences political activism. Only one person among my respondents in the Oyan, Kazakhstan movement felt that the disinformation that their rallies were 'gay parades' was harming the movement's agenda, since it was losing the votes of an electorate that was still 'unsure' about their conservative values and could have seen an open support for an LGBTQ agenda as shocking. This is, however, the view of several political forces currently standing in sharp opposition to the regime. Their position on an open LGBTQ agenda is cautious because they believe that majority of the Kazakhstani electorate and their potential audiences and supporters are still not ready to criticize any potential discreditation of queer activism. Even though opposition leaders are not openly critical of or opposed to the LGBTQ rights agenda, their silence on this question is quite telling. If political entrepreneurs are to continue to play according to the rules set by Nazarbayev's regime, including the rules of the strict authoritarian-patriarchal discourse on gender order, very little will change in the political atmosphere and competition.

[30] Ten 2020: 52.

This is why Qazaq Koktemi's queer activism and the field's close connection to and solidarity with queer and feminist activists in Kazakhstan is so important. More efforts to highlight issues of inclusivity, human rights, and the visibility and rights of LGBTQ communities outside the central cities of Almaty and Astana will be able to shape the political field in Kazakhstan and democratize it further. The queer future that many activists of the Kazakh Spring propose is a future free from the authoritarian domination that can regulate people's lives as far as their sexual-orientation preferences and identities, which they currently have to hide if these identities do not fall under the dominant view of the regime's gender concept. The queer future is the future of inclusivity and the protection of all rights, irrespective of ethnic, sexual, or any other differences. The cornerstone of this activism is the idea of the equality of all and the central focus on the provision of all human rights under the working constitution and legal-political system, which is currently completely dominated by the reign of the authoritarian regime. Thus, the queer future is the fight against authoritarianism.

Can Feminism Save Kazakhstan?

One of the slogans that was on many banners at the 2021 Women's March in Almaty read 'Feminism will save Kazakhstan' (*Feminizm spaset Kazakhstan*). This was no accidental slogan. In the context of the patriarchal dictatorship, where the locus of visible and physical power was located quite literally in the numerous male bodies of the regime figureheads and the most potent male body of the president, the question of true gender equality was silenced, erased, moved away from the forefront of the major political arena. Patriarchy was the synonym of the old dictatorial system where those who represented some sort of 'equality' were used as short-term fixes for the purposes of reporting – the female ex-minister of social affairs who was fired after yet another outburst over major social inequality, the silent but 'pretty' (female) members of a newly elected 'pocket parliament' or an occasional female head of large educational and health institutions. The major questions for the third or current wave of Kazakhstani feminism are diverse – decreasing the gender pay gap, addressing the major structural problem of domestic violence, ubiquitous rape culture, and the normalization of gendered violence per se, but also a further fight for the provision of human rights for all, beyond the regime's rigid 'male–female' spectrum. This current wave of Kazakhstani feminism can be successful because it is the first wave within this field to emerge with an acute understanding that any civic expression or any agenda for fighting for equality and against everyday violence, discrimination, and harassment has to go hand in hand with vast democratization and the change of values. A lot of this work has to do with institutional change and the active participation of civic actors in the changing law-making atmosphere but also, importantly, in the spheres of education, media, culture, and art.

With no sustainable resources for their activist work, Kazakhstani feminists have to win the fight against the multi-million budgets the regime spends annually on formal media (television, republican print media, web portals) and informal media (sponsoring popular bloggers, social media celebrities). In these conditions, fem-activists turn to social media and depend on prolonged periods of often-voluntary work. Social media portals such as BatyrJamal – the opposite of *Bakytsyz Jamal* (unhappy Jamal), the heroine of the first Kazakh novel written by Myrzhakyp Dulatov[31] – allow the creation of a space for alternative discussions and the spread of information. BatyrJamal, unlike her namesake, is warrior – *batyr*. As one of the co-founders of this media public and a fervent political activist (also a member of the Oyan, Qazaqstan movement), Aisana Ashim, said in an interview with The Village Kazakhstan, the mission of BatyrJamal:

Is to create the society where [every] woman has rights and is protected by the law enforcement system and by the laws. [To create the] society with zero-tolerance to violence and sexism. [To create the] society where [every woman] is respected and where she is not considered an object, where she is free to deal with her body and destiny without fearing unfair court trials or public shaming. And our mission also [reflected] in fostering confidence in young women and [teaching them] not to fear anything and to self-realize themselves.

The goal of *BatyrJamal* is to research and to be able to make sense of concepts, situations, and stories, and then to educate the audiences in order to raise awareness about the disorder and inequalities in the country but also

---

[31] Written in 1910, the novel tells the story of an educated Kazakh woman Jamal, who is forced into a marriage with a violent and patriarchal man after her first husband dies. Unable to survive her unhappy married life, she tries to escape to the city but dies on the road, caught by a snow blizzard.

to equip [people] with knowledge, widen their perspectives and strengthen their self-confidence.[32]

Similar initiatives that focus on educating people about the rights and concepts of gender equality and inequality are also represented by the annual feminist festival Femagora, the web portal Masa, and the social media accounts of all the fem-activists discussed in this chapter. Their main aim is to facilitate further discussion and to educate people – often at the level of how feminism 'is NOT about killing or harassing all the men'[33] but about equality across all types of gendered and non-gendered identities, positions, and discourses. The feminist activism field in Kazakhstan remains diverse, often fragmented, proving its natural striving for pluriversality rather than a singular dominant view on a given category, theme, or debate. The field is volatile, and many activists themselves are part of diverse movements, groups, and dialogues. Many fem- and queer activists freely fluctuate in the Qazaq Koktemi field, and some of the most fervent Kazakhstani feminists continuously shape the fem-agenda within Oyan, Qazaqstan, and other pro-democratic movements.

While I am not a proponent of structuring or ordering the fem-activist or queer-activist space in Kazakhstan, nor do I believe that such structuring is possible (instead it is a lot more fruitful to focus on specific initiatives, discourses, battles, and voices), my research into political movements shows that the fem- and queer-activist agenda is at its strongest point in the political field, even compared to five to seven years ago. Queerness allows for diverse alternative views, to strive for freedom and the importance of providing human rights for all. It also stands in sharp opposition to the regime's heteronormativity and its obsessive desire 'to control the message', as many of my respondents also note. The Kazakhstani authoritarian context is defined by a specific paradox. While some elites within the regime might be aware of the fact that neither their nor anyone else's power is particularly abundant, over-reaching, or total, at the same time their internal legitimacy is rooted in the constant reconstruction of the myth that it is.

---

[32] From the full interview available at www.the-village-kz.com/village/weekend/best-of-web/17565-women-life-in-kazakhstan.

[33] Unfortunately, this slogan remains a ubiquitous message spread by those opposing feminist activism and the fem-agenda in general in Russia, Kazakhstan, and the former Soviet space.

In this paradox, the individual's body, particularly the female body or the queer body, becomes the ideal space for performing this myth by enabling control and harassment, arresting fem-activists, and telling them that the police officers would 'get away with anything', as was the case with Fariza Ospan's unlawful detention (see Chapter 5). Widespread rape culture and consistent (albeit not on formal media channels) normalization of gendered violence, calls for *rape victims*[34] to reconcile with their rapists,[35] are also part of this myth of regime control, the spread of the type of heteronormative values coupled with lawlessness and the idea of 'getting away with anything'.

Thus, because Kazakhstani feminism stands in sharp opposition to these normalizations and the type of informal values of corrupt law-enforcement systems where rapists and vicious perpetrators of gendered violence have endless opportunities to avoid legal punishment, it is more optimistic to think that feminism could, in fact, save Kazakhstan. The activists' direct agenda to battle with unfairness (*nespravedlisvost'* in Russian and *adilsizdik* in Kazakh) and inequality, which are rooted in authoritarian-patriarchal system of Kazakhstani dictatorship, is a possible alternative way out. Their acute understanding that this battle is far from ending and that it would require a prolonged period of intense resistance, public politics and political engagement in general (including through active and direct work with other political forces and social movements) is possibly even more reassuring.

---

[34] Feeling uneasy about the language used and the type of stigma that follows many survivors, I unfortunately have to use the legal-normative language at this stage and thus highlight it in italics. Elsewhere it should be written as 'survivors'.

[35] In the autumn of 2020, a popular Kazakh-language TV Show 'Kel, Tatulasayuq' (Come, Let's Reconcile!), airing on 31 Channel, featured a story of an eighteen-year-old female survivor who was raped by three men at the age of fourteen. The show producers invited the eighteen-year-old woman to the studio where she was forced by the people in the studio (so-called experts and other participants) to reconcile with her rapists, none of whom served a sentence for their crime. Their victim meanwhile got pregnant and gave birth to the child. The show received a lot of attention and was followed by several media scandals, making it even more popular and visible. Some commentators stressed the sexist language and harassment against the female protagonist, who was sexually objectified and victim-blamed for what had happened to her. Following the scandal, many Kazakh fem-activists protested against the legal provision that allows *rape victims* to reconcile with their rapists.

Figure 7.2 Feminist artist Zoya Falkova at the 2021 Almaty Women's March with her legendary art object 'Evermust' protesting against domestic violence. © Zoya Falkova

The 2021 Women's March in Almaty brought together very diverse voices among its participants, which can be seen not only in the familiar and even famous faces of those 300 people who marched but also in their posters and demands. Some called directly on President Tokayev and other political institutions of the current dictatorship while others radically and symbolically attacked the overall culture of violent patriarchy. The feminist artist Zoya Falkova appeared on the streets with her object 'Evermust' –a punching bag in the form of a female body (see Figure 7.2). Other participants came to the march with posters asking the regime to 'imprison those who are involved in corruption and not the [female] activists', as harassment of activists is still ongoing in Kazakhstan. Feminita activists Gulzada Serzhan and Zhanar Serkebayeva reported on their social media throughout the summer months of 2021 that they had been harassed equally by unknown individuals as well as some unidentified law-enforcement actors. In August 2021, they received death threats and messages about searching for their addresses and more personal details. They openly reported their endangerment and further harassment for their activism.

The anti-violence agenda, when violence plays a significant role in any dictatorship, was also the biggest part of the march's demands and slogans. Directed at the body as a space of freedom rather than of regime control, the message of the march was diverse but clear – we are not here to endure the violent and unfair status quo. While this manuscript was under final preparation, the news broke that the local municipality (*akimat*) in Almaty refused to grant permission for the 2022 peaceful Women's March rally.

8 | Making Sense of the Bloody January 2022 Mass Protests

WITH MARLENE LARUELLE

The January 2022 protests in Kazakhstan (known locally as Bloody January – *Qandy Qantar*) were unprecedented both in their scale and in the rapidity with which they spread across the country's major cities. But the drivers behind these protests had long been plain to see: economic inequality, rampant corruption, and the regime's failure to deliver on its promises of good governance and economic growth. Indeed, they were rooted in the Nazarbayev regime itself. The authoritarian regime's systemic penetration of the very fabric of state–society relations throughout President Nursultan Nazarbayev's thirty-year rule produced conditions where the regime's political decision- making was largely divorced from society. As the gap between the two widened during the challenging last decade of Nazarbayev's rule (2011–21), exacerbated by the economically disastrous effects of the pandemic, socio-economic grievances intensified. In the absence of contested elections or accountable governance, and given the spread of patronal politics, citizens had no way to influence political decision-making. Protests were thus the only way for them to be heard.

The regime made promises of vast economic developments (Matveeva 2009; Olcott 2010; Kudaibergenova 2015; Tutumlu 2019) that ordinary people rarely saw brought to fruition in their everyday lives (Junisbai 2010; Kudebayeva and Barrientos 2017; Kerimray, De Miglio, Rojas-Solórzano, and Ó Gallachóir 2018; Kudebayeva 2019; Sanghera and Satybaldieva 2021). This prepared the ground for widespread social unrest against the authoritarian 'system' – all that was needed was something to spark it. The regime's

---

This chapter is a modified version of Diana T. Kudaibergenova and Marlene Laruelle (2022), Making sense of the January 2022 protests in Kazakhstan: Failing legitimacy, culture of protests, and elite readjustments, *Post-Soviet Affairs*, 38(6), 441–459, DOI: 10.1080/1060586X.2022.2077060 reproduced with permission from Taylor & Francis, https://www.tandfonline.com/.

success at using discursive pre-emption (Schatz 2009) to undercut opposition has gradually decreased, up to the inability of the elites to read the protest-oriented mood of a growing part of the population.

The January 2022 protest wave emerged as a direct response to the crisis within the regime. Since it did not allow for the institutionalization of a new opposition after the failures of the old opposition and its almost total disappearance by 2015–16, the protests were not homogeneous or well planned. Instead, they involved a variety of protesting groups, some of which were organized in informal political and labour union networks and others of which were not organized at all but simply groups of citizens who came together spontaneously due to their shared rage at the fact that the regime was 'robbing' them of opportunities for a better life.

There are many holes in the official narrative about the 'failed coup', which claims that '20,000 terrorists' raged around and burned down Almaty – the country's largest city and the unofficial stronghold of the network of oligarchs surrounding Nazarbayev's family and closest friends. What is clear is that regime dynamics, mistakes and failures of governance, and intense power struggles that miscalculated the level of contentions on the ground led to a major protest wave and unprecedented violence against Kazakhstani citizens, hundreds of whom were killed, injured, or repressed.

In this chapter, it is argued that the peaceful mass protests and their hijacking by organized violent groups (criminals or alleged terrorists)[1] from the south of Kazakhstan are best understood through the framework of regime–society relations. We posit that a key failure of the regime built by Nazarbayev is its inability to reconcile its neoliberal prosperity rhetoric with citizens' calls for a welfare state. We then explore how the tradition of protests that culminated in Bloody January had been building since 2011 and discuss the major layers of power interactions and power struggles that produced both protests and violence.

---

[1] As of the time of this writing, these violent groups have not officially been identified. President Tokayev insisted in his official speeches to the Kazakhstani public and at the CSTO meeting that the 'attack' was organized by 'trained terrorist groups' that staged a failed coup. He tweeted about '20,000 terrorists' and hinted that these were mainly foreigners, but he later deleted the tweet.

Regime–Society Relations No Longer Work

The Nazarbayev regime built a system of authoritarian neoliberalism whereby every group within the society was 'promised' according to its socio-economic position. The discourse directed at ordinary citizens was one of a prosperous Kazakhstan: Nazarbayev's economic modernization, it claimed, was bound to bring a miracle one way or another (see the 1997 Kazakhstan 2030 Strategy). Meanwhile, the president's loyal elites and inner circle, known as the 'Family', obtained their wealth through corruption (McGlinchey 2011; Cooley and Heathershaw 2017). This state-level corruption, which exacerbated growing socio-economic inequality in society, led to a problematic status quo that was masked by the society's supposed consent to the authoritarian neoliberal system. The regime largely developed this idea under the banner of 'harmonious social relations', 'stability', and 'unity' of all Kazakhstanis. While 1 per cent of the population had somehow amassed a significant amount of wealth in a relatively short period of time (see Table 8.1), the mass of the population lived under increasingly impoverished conditions (Yessenova 2010), unable to voice their concerns through elections or any viable political institutions.

Officially, the poverty level in Kazakhstan is a low 5.8%. The poverty wage, which is calculated as 70 per cent of the living wage, stood at a mere 55 USD (24,011 KZT) per month as of January 2021. Yet the official statistics hide the reality that a significant proportion of the country's inhabitants are struggling to make ends meet; they are the 'invisible poor'. The comments of Olzhas Baidildinov, an advisor to the sacked energy minister, Magzum Mirzagaliev, at a press conference about liquefied petroleum gas (LPG) prices in Astana on 3 January 2022 thus sparked social outrage by revealing that the elites were no longer aware of the impoverished conditions in which their citizens lived. Baidildinov had suggested that 'those unhappy with the LPG price hikes' should take public transport instead of private cars, even as he bragged on his social media account about his expensive shopping trips and lavish lifestyle.

Adding to the deteriorating economic conditions, household debt in Kazakhstan hit 23.7 billion USD in October 2021.[2] This helps explain

---

[2] CEIC Global Economic Data on Kazakhstan: www.ceicdata.com/en.

why so many ordinary Kazakhstani citizens responded positively to the populist idea of writing off their consumer debts, which has been proposed by such opposition politicians as Zhanbolat Mamay. Mamay and his unregistered Democratic Party of Kazakhstan (DPK) called for a number of protests and rallies in Almaty throughout the difficult 2020 pandemic year, demanding that all citizens' consumer debt be written off (KazTag.kz, 12 October 2021).

Furthermore, this type of moral economy and normative claims were confined within the regime's promises of economic prosperity and open bragging about the economic might of the state. In Nazarbayev's rhetoric, which became a mantra for many citizens, the state was prosperous and able to give every citizen the type of 'good life' for which they hoped:

> Our country's declared mission was to build an independent, flourishing and politically stable Kazakhstan with intrinsic national unity, social justice, and economic prosperity enjoyed by the entire population. To cite my words from the address, security and increasing prosperity for all Kazakhstanis defined the Kazakhstan we all wanted to build.[3]

While politicians played with this populist idea of 'prosperity for all' and failed to fully deliver on their promises to those outside Nazarbayev's inner circle (see Figure 8.1), ordinary citizens had deeply internalized the calls for fair distribution of the country's resources. This led some of them to demand such changes as direct financial support (i.e., not mediated through the institutional infrastructure of the state):

> I am entitled to my share of land because our constitution guarantees 10 acres for each citizen. Kazakhstan is rich in land and ranks the ninth largest country in the world. Surely, the state has the capacity and has obligation to provide its citizens with the land. (Bakai informal settlement leader quoted in Sanghera and Satybaldieva 2021: 155)

Those who did not demand the populist redistribution of the country's rich resources formed into movements such as Oyan, Qazaqstan and called for political reforms and democratization instead.

The demands of both groups reflected their engagement with the regime's discursive framework and power dynamics and were shaped by regime–society relations. Those claiming entitlement to a share of the country's wealth were responding to the widely shared public transcripts

---

[3] Nazarbayev 2008: 25.

of mass-scale corruption at the highest elite level, especially among members of the Nazarbayev 'Family', who hold at least the top four places on the *Forbes* list of the richest Kazakhstanis (see Table 8.1). As Sanghera and Satybaldieva explain, 'the privatization of valuable assets established a powerful class of rentiers' (Sanghera and Satybaldieva 2021: 45) who are sharply separated from the mass of ordinary citizens surviving on extremely low salaries and contending with unequal labour conditions. Meanwhile, the groups calling for significant political change envisioned a Kazakhstan free of corruption and based on the rule of law, which would allow for more transparent socio-economic competition. Both groups, in their own ways, were advocating for the 'good life' the Kazakhstani way. Their clash of values and lack of organized mobilization on the ground led to a situation where their protest was used by regime elites to stage a coup against President Tokayev in January 2022.

The 2011–2022 Decade: Building a Tradition of Protests

Scholars of post-Soviet contentious politics observe that contentions often emerge around elections and transform into 'colour revolutions' (Way 2008; Bunce and Wolchik 2009; Kalanadze and Orenstein 2009; Greene 2013; Smyth 2018). However, Kazakhstan's protests do not fit the model of the 'colour revolutions': they should be analysed not as one-off eruptions, but as having gradually developed and become connected over prolonged periods of contention (see Figure 8.1 for the latest data). Indeed, the contentions grew out of grievances that came to be shared by a growing number of socially and economically vulnerable citizens over the years. Many of them organized grassroots movements and protest groups: these include the semi-organized mothers' protests in 2019 and more structured political movements like Oyan, Qazaqstan, which emerged during the Kazakh Spring (Qazaq Koktemi) protests immediately following Nazarbayev's resignation from the post of president in March 2019 and the transition of power to Tokayev, who – after serving as interim president – was elected in June of that year.

The many contentions that occurred over the course of the last decade of Nazarbayev's rule (see Figure 8.1 for the 2018–21 data) demonstrated the cracks inside the 'system'. We can identify four major nodal points for these protests: the 2011 Zhanaozen massacre; the 2014 'Black Tuesday' protests against the devaluation of the local currency, the

Table 8.1 Forbes' *ten richest people in Kazakhstan, 2021*

Name	Personal Wealth (million USD)	Source/economic sector of wealth
Vladimir Kim	4,700	Metals, minerals (KazMinerals), finance, KazakhMys corporation
Bulat Utemuratov	3,500	Banking, telecoms, RG Gold (65%), hotels, 'Burger King' franchise, media, hotels/real estate, minerals
Timur Kulibaev	2,900	Energy, minerals, real estate market, banking (previously also Almaty airport – sold in 2020)
Dinara Kulibaeva (Nazarbayeva)	2,900	Diverse business, finance, energy, real estate, banking, and education holdings
Rashit Sarsenov	810	Banking, retail, petroleum/energy, insurance, hotel, vinery
Kenes Rakishev	950	Banking, finance, insurance, gold mining, private education (with wife Asel Tasmagambetova)
Bakhytbek Baiseitov	270	Banking, investment, oil and energy, service
Nurlan Smagulov	710	Large car dealing, real estate, shopping malls rentier, two factories assembling cars, Almaty hotel
Aidyn Rakhymbayev	610	Real estate, hotels, construction sector, Chocofamily Holding (service), involved in the Hilton Tashkent construction project
Vyacheslav Kim	4,200 (215 in 2012)	Kaspi.kz (25%) within the Kaspi bank group, finance, retailing

Source: Authors' compilation based on https://forbes.kz/leader/50_bogateyshih_biznesmenov_kazahstana_-_2021_1621273818/.

tenge; the 2016 mass land reform protests; and the Qazaq Koktemi political protests that started in March 2019 and continue to this day.

Nazarbayev's last decade of rule was thus not as 'stable' as the regime attempted to portray it. According to the Armed Conflict Location and

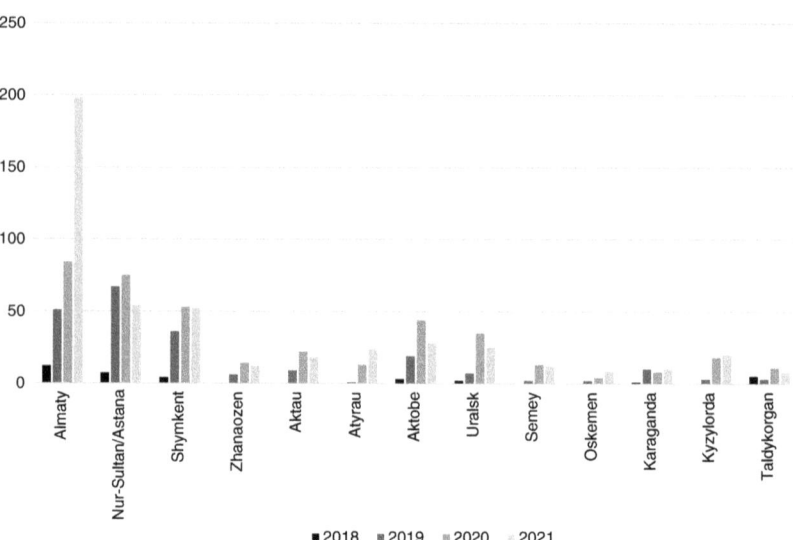

Figure 8.1 Geographical distribution of protests in Kazakhstan, January 2018–June 2021
Source: Authors' compilation based on data from the Oxus Society Protest Tracker

Event Data Project database on protests, there were at least 2,559 protests, 65 riots, and 61 reported fatalities between January 2010 and January 2022.[4] The Oxus Society Protests Tracker lists at least 1,328 total protests from January 2018 to June 2021, most of which (1,126) were rallies (see Figure 8.1). What matters in these protest waves is not only the number of rallies or the number of their participants (usually fewer than 100), but their agenda and legacy. For example, the 2014 'Black Tuesday' protests in Almaty created the precedent for larger rallies without organizational help from the institutional opposition, which had begun to disappear under the weight of political competition and the repressions following the 2011 Zhanaozen tragedy.

The 2011 Zhanaozen protests started as labour disputes in the oil-producing town of Zhanaozen in Mangystau region, western Kazakhstan. The general strike started at the end of May and turned

---

[4] The official numbers of fatalities in the January 2022 protests in Kazakhstan is 227 people, 19 of whom were law enforcement officers. Across Kazakhstan, more than 4,000 people were injured.

into a peaceful stand-off between the major companies and the workers, who occupied the main square. The contentions arose over local workers' inability either to protect their collective rights through labour unions or to rely on a labour code that could protect them from the precarious working conditions in Kazakhstan's industrial hub, a region vaunted for its energy wealth. As Sorbello argues:

> inequalities in pay and conditions, limitations of freedoms, and neoliberal corporate practices were gradually introduced by TNCs [Transnational Corporations] in the oil sector and had a direct effect on the relationship between labour and capital and indirectly aided the government's authoritarian project, because precarisation of work is ultimately also an instrument of control. (2021: 16–17)

The protestors thus peacefully demanded improvements to their working conditions, the right to organize into independent labour unions, and an increase in their salaries (with equal pay for foreign and local workers) amid growing inflation in the region (Satpayev and Umbetaliyeva 2015).

The workers' calls for higher salaries were branded 'greedy' by the regime and their protests deemed illegal on the grounds that 'the strike actions did not follow the exact procedure stipulated in the Kazakh Labour Code' (Satpayev and Umbetaliyeva 2015: 126). Violence broke out on 16 December – Independence Day and the day of the December uprisings in Soviet Almaty that had been tragically suppressed (Fierman 1998; Kudaibergenova and Shin 2018; Shelekpayev 2021). A group of violent provocateurs started demolishing the stage that had been constructed on the main square, where the peaceful protestors had stood their ground for six months without any violence. These violent groups 'reportedly later set fire to the city hall, the headquarters of the local oil company OMG [local OzenMunaiGas], a hotel, several other buildings and vehicles. Eyewitnesses said police fired on unarmed protestors, but the authorities claimed they were forced to defend themselves' (Satpayev and Umbetaliyeva 2015: 127). Shocked local residents related how armed police and other armed officers had aimed at unarmed protestors, killing many. The official death toll was sixteen, but unofficial reports count at least sixty civilian casualties.[5]

---

[5] The *Novaya Gazeta* investigative journalist Elena Kostuchenko, who was on the ground, claimed that there were at least sixty-five victims and possibly more, given the unidentified bodies buried at the cemetery. See her second report in Russian at https://batenka.ru/protection/war/zhanaozen/.

The trauma of the violent suppression of the Zhanaozen protests in 2011 and the subsequent trials of the leaders of the unofficial labour unions and the activists who had been involved left a lasting mark on Kazakh society. It has produced sustained symbolism and solidarity: every year on 16 December, different groups of protestors commemorate the victims of Zhanaozen – and the 1986 violence – with rallies.[6] New groups of political activists have mobilized around this cause for the past ten years. In western Kazakhstan specifically, the legacy of the protests has been an understanding that protest presents a 'possibility' for dialogue with the regime and local authorities in the absence of any other viable institutions or channels for engagement.

The Zhanaozen protests marked the crest of the first wave of collective discontent with the regime's socio-economic provision. Before Zhanaozen, there had also been clashes in 2006 on the outskirts of Almaty between informal settlers seeking affordable housing in the Shanyrak and Bakai settlements; one policeman was killed when the frenzied crowd set him on fire. The 2008 global financial crisis, which froze real estate projects across the country, had also led to localized protests by people who had invested their money in the apartments that were stuck under construction (*dol'shiki*) (Sanghera and Satybaldieva 2021).

Even if the dream of the 'good life' promised by the regime was starting to disintegrate, the regime managed to maintain some control by dismissing key elites (all close to Nazarbayev) who had been involved in these tragedies. Imangali Tasmagambetov, who had been the mayor of Almaty during the demolition of the Shanyrak and Bakai informal settlements, and Timur Kulibayev, Nazarbayev's powerful son-in-law who had been the head of the National Fund Samruk-Kazyna at the time of the Zhanaozen 2011 tragedy, both lost their political capital as the

---

[6] Right after the tragic December 2011 Zhanaozen events, different political formations and groups from the institutional opposition started rallying in support of the western Kazakhstan's workers and victims of police violence. These rallies continued and became a tradition for various opposition groups, which commemorated the 'victims of the regime' (among them assassinated political leaders Zamanbek Nurkadilov and Altynbek Sarsenbayev) every year on 16 December. Even after the formalized institutional opposition was defeated after the post-2011 repressions, when the majority of leading oppositional politicians left the public scene, the tradition of commemorating 'victims of the regime' on 16 December persisted.

result of their 'mismanagement' of these crises. This allowed Nazarbayev to continue convincing citizens that prosperity was coming to them.

However, the sharp devaluation of the Kazakh tenge in February 2014 crushed these hopes and betrayed these promises. Outraged citizens who had lost their savings went out into the streets of Almaty with a clear message to Nazarbayev: '*Shal, ket!*'[7] (Go away, old man). The 2016 land protests in western Kazakhstan and Almaty fuelled protest culture further. But it was the Kazakh Spring in the wake of Nazarbayev's resignation that inspired citizens' hopes for 'true' political reforms but then 'crushed them overnight',[8] spurring a consistent protest culture and demands for political change and reforms.

The Kazakh Spring protests erupted sporadically in different forms and waves of contentions: lone picket; Banksy-type anonymous banners with political messages; online activism and resistance; the mushrooming of social media channels, chats and 'publics'; and consistent protests and activism on the streets of Almaty and Astana (Nur-Sultan). The Kazakh Spring is a political field without a single leader but with a unified agenda for political reforms and democratization. The different movements have demanded the opening-up of the political sphere to independent parties and non-regime politicians; open and contested elections at all levels of governance, including local *akims* (governors and mayors of major cities), who are currently appointed directly by the president; and the gradual transition from a presidential republic to a parliamentary one. The consistent waves of protests and the networked nature of the Kazakh Spring protest culture provided the space for young, educated Kazakhstanis not only to claim political agency and become informed about the corrupt and unfair nature of the Nazarbayev regime, but also to openly protest against the regime in the streets and online.

The Structure of the January 2022 Protests

The mass mobilization in January 2022 received an impetus from three important structural changes in regime–society relations. First, Nazarbayev's 2019 resignation led to the emergence of widespread

---

[7] The slogan was first voiced by Kazakh feminists Zhanara Serkebayeva and Guldana Serzhan during the 'Black Tuesday' mass protests in Almaty in February 2014 and subsequently became iconic and widespread across different rallies.

[8] Author's interview with Kazakh Spring activists, June 2020.

grassroots initiatives united under the Kazakh Spring banner and mass street protests that made many citizens aware of the possibility of contentious politics. Second, the economic inequality exacerbated by the pandemic crisis and corruption scandals[9] in the vital healthcare system increased the rifts between elite groups who were divorced from the impoverished social groups and failed to understand their demands. Finally, and perhaps most significantly for the 'riot of the marginal groups' (as they have been dubbed in the local press), the consistent impoverishment of different parts of the Kazakhstani population and unbearable economic inequality opened space for discourses of unfairness that the regime failed to address.

As Sanghera and Satybaldieva write, economic inequality and 'the commodification of money, land, labour and basic services (such as education and health) can be a source of multiple grassroots movements, galvanizing a wide range of protesters from rural migrants, farmers and pensioners to public sector workers and urban mortgage-holders' (2021: 43). Feelings of injustice and inequality can cause spontaneous leaderless protests where grievances are expressed in very distinct groups. 'But this very diversity can produce divisions within and between social movements, preventing the formation of a broad-based countermovement capable of exerting effective pressure on the state' (2021: 43).

In order to understand the events that unfolded into the unprecedented mass protests in Kazakhstan, we first need to specify the complexity of different groups involved in each region. Protests were comprised of very diverse and disjointed groups that happened to be on the streets at the same time. Each city, with its own socio-economic conditions and legacies of previous social movement formations and protests, makes this layout even more complex. For example, the 2011 Zhanaozen labour disputes left deeply structured and embedded networks of informal mobilization and informal labour unions in western Kazakhstan (Sorbello 2021).

---

[9] See www.caravan.kz/news/pandemiya-ne-stala-pomekhojj-dlya-korrupcii-v-kazakhstane-a-sovsem-naoborot-700734/. Just in the first six months of 2021, the country's anti-corruption committee officially announced more than 100 cases of corruption dealing with the state resources directed to pandemic-related projects (https://kz.kursiv.media/2021-07-09/antikorrupcionnaya-sluzhba-vyyavila-bolee-sta-narusheniy-pri-realizacii/). See also Ruzanov and Zharlygasinov 2021.

The January events in Kazakhstan started in Zhanaozen and spread quickly to the neighbouring city of Aktau, making the Mangystau region the hub of the rapidly growing peaceful protests as of 2 January. This prompted Tokayev to form a special government commission, which travelled to Aktau to establish a dialogue with the peaceful protestors. He also quickly lowered LPG prices to 85–90 KZT (0.20 USD). But this did not calm the protestors, who then demanded the ouster of the government, calling for parliament, local governors, and even the president to step down in favour of 'new faces' who would implement political reforms.

The protests quickly spread to the major city of Almaty in the south of the country, where local activist groups began calling for peaceful protestors to come out into the streets across Kazakhstan 'in solidarity' with the Zhanaozen and Mangystau protestors. The violence, which evolved most dramatically in Almaty and other cities in the south (Taldykorgan, Taraz, Kyzylorda, and Shymkent), has to be separated from the initial peaceful mobilization in terms of both its claims and the structure of the protest.

The protests in Almaty started on the evening of 4 January, when the political groups Oyan, Qazaqstan (Wake Up, Kazakhstan!) and the unregistered Democratic Party of Kazakhstan (DPK), chaired by Zhanbolat Mamay, called for their supporters to gather and peacefully protest around the First President's Park and the Almaty Arena – two distinct points in the city located far from each other. The columns of protestors then reached[10] Respublika Square[11] in central Almaty, where they clashed with the police, who were awaiting them with tear gas and stun grenades.[12] The clashes continued throughout the night as the groups of protestors occupied the main square on Satpayev Street (uptown) and the Old Square (downtown) on Tole bi Street, where the Soviet and post-Soviet parliaments had been located before the capital was moved to Akmola-Astana-Nur-Sultan. Both squares are

---

[10] Protestors walked for eighteen kilometres singing the anthem, raising flags, and shouting slogans like '*Alga, Kazakhstan!*' (Go, Kazakhstan!) and '*Shal, ket!*' (Down with the old man!) – a slogan promoted by Kazakh feminists Zhanara Serkebayeva and Guldana Serzhan in the 2014 Black Tuesday protests in Almaty calling for then president Nazarbayev to resign.

[11] Respublika Square, formerly known as Brezhnev Square, was where the December 1986 protestors were brutally suppressed.

[12] See Mazorenko and Kaisar 2022, Nusimbekov 2022, and Moldabekov 2022 for the published eye-witness reports on the ground.

imbued with historical and contemporary symbolism: every protest since 1986 has occurred in one of the two, bringing together members of the old – and now completely diminished – formal opposition. Those protestors who gathered in Almaty from 4 January, however, represented highly disorganized groups of spontaneous actors without a single leader.

The leaderless nature of Almaty's contentious cycles among the peaceful protestors clearly differed from the organized peaceful protests in western Kazakhstan, where previous links and informal leaders allowed for self-mobilization and even a tribune with an open microphone. However, the Almaty protestors did not lack solidarity; indeed, this formed the backbone of the peaceful protests. People held flags and called for 'significant' political changes and 'Kazakhstan without the Nazarbayev family'; they called for anti-corruption measures and a better life, clearly referencing the socio-economic inequality in which many found themselves. There were also populist calls for the redistribution of wealth: many in the crowds continued to see the state as the owner of assets and regulator of the specific economic relations that benefited some privileged groups of elites.[13]

These groups did not unite or form a singular leadership. Indeed, the conditions of authoritarian rule had led to the political disintegration of the formalized opposition: the DVK movement in 2001, the Ak Zhol party in 2005–6, and the Azat Social-Democratic Party in 2006–12. The remaining opposition figures – exiled former banker Mukhtar Ablyazov and his circle of mostly exiled activists – are highly marginalized in Kazakhstan. The developing parties – those of Zhanbolat Mamay, for example, and movements such as Oyan, Qazaqstan – have only gained force since 2019. The latter initiated a social media campaign for peaceful rallies in solidarity with the Zhanaozen and Mangystau protestors on 2 January, and the two groups organized the largest peaceful rallies for the cause in Almaty on the evening of 4 January. Yet these activists were quickly identified by the police and detained or beaten, with the result that they had little chance to participate in the subsequent days of protest. Meanwhile, the streets of Almaty were taken over by socio-economically diverse groups of people, united in their grievances, who seized the tremendous window

---

[13] See Mazorenko and Kaisar 2022, www.opendemocracy.net/en/odr/what-really-happened-kazakhstan-protests-january/.

of opportunity that the evening and night of 4 January opened up. Unprecedented peaceful rallies thus took over the major public squares.

Previous contentions in the industrial areas and the unequal legal conditions of the labour disputes directly provided by the regime to tame the revolts in the industrial cities played out completely the opposite way and united the protestors. The existence of informal networks and smaller cities where people had stronger bonds through work, families, and similar socio-economic conditions of everyday life, like those in western Kazakhstan, allowed for the protests to remain peaceful throughout and sustain themselves thanks to a growing sense of solidarity. The increasingly unequal living conditions in big cities like Almaty led to the disintegration of the protestors, who were united by fairly similar demands for a better life and better political governance but saw different ways to achieve these demands depending on their class background and access to such privileges as a stable income, housing, and education. Almaty's legacy of protests in the past decade clearly separated those fighting for survival and those fighting for a better quality of life within the 'golden square' (the centre of the city). As Sanghera and Satybaldieva write, the divisions of the grassroots movements in Almaty were embedded in the localized conditions and the demands of those within the specific class-spatial locale of the cities:

Almaty might have the largest informal settlements in Central Asia. The informal residents have been locked in legal struggles with local authorities, which have enacted brutal measures to eradicate the sites. The ongoing encounters with the city administration have turned the informal settlements into permanent sites of grassroots struggles for legality. (2021: 152)

In essence, the development of Kazakhstani regime–society relations is imbued with complex layers and understandings of illegality and inequality. Dwellers in informal settlements, who come from the lowest classes, remain illegally housed due to their lack of institutional access, even as the regime's abundant access to and appropriation of state institutions allows it to spread its own illegality, which is rooted in the political system itself.

The violence that evolved most dramatically in Almaty and other cities in the south (Taldykorgan, Taraz, Kyzylorda, and Shymkent) has to be separated from the initial peaceful mobilization in terms of both its claims and the structure of the protest. The first reports and eyewitness accounts from Almaty and Taldykorgan identified some of the violent groups as meticulously organized, taking orders from specific 'curators' and acting with a clear plan in mind: occupation, destruction, unprecedented violence. Since many of these groups of men were dressed in ordinary clothing that did not distinguish them from other protesters, it was hard to separate the two groups.

However, the organized violent groups employed several tactics to hide their identities. They drove cars without plates, attacked and killed anyone who tried to film or identify them, broke street surveillance cameras to be sure they would not be recorded, followed orders, and worked in groups. This behaviour distinguishes them from the groups of sporadic and completely disorganized protesters who met on the streets for the first time while participating in the mobilization (see Table 8.2). The crowd that occupied the main square in Almaty in front of the burning administrative *akimat* building on 5 January included a diverse range of participants, all with distinct interests and reasons for mobilization.

Qantar Online Activism and the Long Post-January

When the protesters had left the streets, many still imprisoned and tortured by the secret police to confess to crimes they did not commit, a major online campaign known as Qantar (January) emerged to help the victims of the January 2022 mass violence. The volunteers joined forces almost sporadically and opened several online groups on platforms such as Facebook and Instagram. They wanted to give names to the heroes – the man who was seen waving the national flag and walking through the thick smog of grenades (and who was called the Flag Runner), for example, and they wanted to help these families recover, pay for the needed medical aid, and collect the names of those who were killed. Campaigns in support of January 2022 protesters immediately emerged in the diaspora where two hubs – one in Paris and one in Berlin – became pivotal for collecting funds for the survivors and seeking justice for the killed. In this section, we dwell on these initiatives to explain the aftermath of the major traumatic events that Bloody January (known locally as *Qandy Qantar*) and to focus on the ways the Kazakh Spring activists recuperated in the face of the regime's mass violence but also with the increased support base.

Table 8.2 Preliminary findings on the January 2022 protest groups

	In Almaty	In the regions
Peaceful	<ul><li>previously formed political groups (Oyan, Qazaqstan, and Zhanbolat Mamay movement)</li><li>individual political activists</li><li>ad hoc self-organized protest groups led by known opposition figures (e.g., Zhasaral Kuanyshalin)</li><li>public intellectuals</li><li>spontaneous protestors out on the street with their own grievances</li><li>journalists and eyewitnesses</li><li>protection squads (*narodnaia druzhina*)</li><li>neighbourhood watch</li></ul>	<ul><li>peaceful protestor groups (spontaneous or organized)</li><li>informal labour unions (especially in industrial cities)</li><li>groups built on previous social networks</li><li>groups united by other (non-professional and non-familial) interests</li><li>journalists and local activists</li><li>protection squads (*narodnaia druzhina*)</li><li>neighbourhood watch</li><li>in western Kazakhstan also specific groups of 'workers' wives'</li></ul>
Violent	<ul><li>organized crime groups</li><li>violent group elements (organized or spontaneous)</li><li>violent protestors (spontaneous)</li><li>potential terrorist groups</li><li>other violent groups (yet to be identified)</li><li>random looters (disorganized)</li><li>spontaneously organized looters</li></ul>	<ul><li>destructive elements</li><li>localized looters (random)</li><li>in some regions, organized violent groups and potential terrorists (especially in Kyzylorda and Taldykorgan), according to the official data</li></ul>

Source: Authors' compilation based on independent reports by Orda.kz, Vlast.kz, The Village Kazakhstan, Masa Media, official information from the Prosecutor General's office, and numerous (confidential) eyewitness reports.

Kazakhstanis are no strangers to social media, where they share information and use trusted chats and Telegram channels to discuss politics, but it was Instagram that became a game-changer for those seeking justice and help after the January violence. When the Internet was restored in Kazakhstan, the first days were filled with smog from the grenades, fears and uncertainty, disbelief and distrust in the state narrative about what happened, and the painful search for the loved ones who had disappeared after they left their homes in different cities of Kazakhstan during the first week of January. The Qantar 2022 platform was registered on 14 January first as a voluntarily based helpline to search for the people who went missing. But the organizers immediately realized that they had to form lists of those who were killed separately from the lists of those who were detained and tortured.

The news about tortures and violence at the police stations started pouring in like a massive rainstorm, but fewer of these stories received as much media attention as the case of the Kyrgyz jazz musician Vikram Ruzakhunov, who appeared on Kazakh state television in early January with a doctored 'confession'. In the video, he claimed that he had received 200 USD from unspecified group of people to participate in the mass protests. The video clip showing the bruised and beaten Kyrgyz national was supposed to fit into the state narrative of 20,000 foreign (and local) extremists who were paid to organize mass protests, burn down administrative buildings in major Kazakh cities, and target the police. The same narrative fed the public with videos from the protests demonstrating violent protestors wearing ordinary clothing clashing with law-enforcement officers dressed up in identifiable uniform. Ruzakhunov's relatives recognized him from the state television video and called on the embassy and the public to save him. On 10 January, Ruzakhunov arrived in his native Bishkek in Kyrgyzstan and gave lengthy interviews about his false statement, which he agreed to videotape to make his relatives and friends aware of the situation.[14] In Kazakhstan, Ruzakhunov's imprisonment had started a major anti-misinformation campaign against the regime's version of events. But instead of making the investigation process transparent and open to foreign and local civic activist observers, the regime decided to play on the ambiguity of the whole situation and cited the 'lengthy' investigation processes.

---

[14] www.rferl.org/a/kazakhstan-kyrgyz-musician-severely-beaten/31668455.html.

The regime's ambiguity and misleading claims about the nature, structure, and organization of the protests led to diverse and often radically opposite views about the events of January 2022. This is a tactic used by many authoritarian regimes to divert and misguide the public about the actual events and hide the visible effects of illegal tortures of the protestors that Instagram helped to spotlight through the Qantar 2022 platform. As Lisa Wedeen writes (1999: 41), ambiguity is crucial for autocracies because 'the production of spurious claims and counterfactual statements operates to *communicate* the regime's power by dominating public space and by providing the formulas for acceptable public speech and conduct'.

The Tokayev regime in post-January Kazakhstan quickly solidified their domination of the public space by first shutting down all alternative sources of information during the first crucial days of protests and clashes. Coupled with sounds of exploding grenades, gunfire, and scenes of defeated police, the regime's ambiguity about the exact number of 'foreign terrorists, momentarily created the sense that the regime itself was not in full control of the situation. Many Almaty and Taldykorgan dwellers mentioned in Telegram chats that they felt as if it was the start of a civil war; some even feared the creation of Islamic caliphate in southern Kazakhstan where the most heated clashes happened. The regime then quickly acquired an authoritative position on the situation, demonstrating that Tokayev was 'in control'. This was achieved by two strategies. First was the imprisonment of Karim Massimov, the former head of security and Nazarbayev's closest ally, and the removal of Nazarbayev himself from the chairmanship of the country's Security Council – the position once guaranteed to him for life under the Law of the First President. Then Tokayev demonstrated that he was in control when Russian and Belarusian troops and elite forces arrived to 'clean up' the streets of Almaty and other major cities under the Collective Security Treaty Organisation (CSTO),[15] which in itself was an unprecedented move under the Charter of the organization. Just weeks before Russia's invasion of Ukraine, the deployment of their troops in Kazakhstan was still seen by many local observers as a potential threat to Kazakhstani sovereignty, but President Tokayev insisted on the necessity of this move. He required the geopolitical turn

---

[15] See Catherine Putz's report: https://thediplomat.com/2022/01/csto-deploys-to-kazakhstan-at-tokayevs-request/.

to start solidifying his rule against the alleged *coup d'état* against him. This was another narrative that emerged in state reporting immediately after Massimov's imprisonment. The deployment of foreign forces in the face of local security forces' complete abandonment of the major security structures in Almaty, Taraz, and Taldykorgan – the key cities in the southern and south-eastern parts of Kazakhstan – was also a move that allowed Tokayev to demonstrate to Nazarbayev loyalists in law enforcement that the rules were changing.

The message was loud and clear for those who spoke the regime language, and local police followed Tokayev's orders with mass arrests of practically anyone who happened to be on the streets of major Kazakh cities in the second week of January. One pretext for arrest was presence of protest videos on people's phones. For example, a police officer could stop any citizen on the street, demand their phone, and check the gallery or messengers; if they found videos of the clashes, they claimed that the citizen participated in the protests and filmed them. Hundreds of people were arrested based on this pretext and were tortured to make them sign the forced confessions claiming that they were terrorists. The police also illegally raided hospitals in search for injured protestors and brought them to police stations, where they were tortured. The Qantar 2022 Instagram group had to swiftly change their agenda as they were swamped with requests to report tortures and deaths of people in custody. Instagram became a feed full of faces of ordinary citizens (predominantly male), their bruised, burnt, beaten bodies, and their stories.

The volunteers posted messages from the relatives of those protestors and ordinary people who were arrested, tortured and sometimes killed in two languages – Kazakh and Russian. They posted and continue posting (at the time of this manuscript's completion) photos and videos of their relatives; they also post photos of handwritten letters and final words of those who did not return from the police station. The post-January violence was unprecedented for Kazakhstan and served as a quiet theatre of intimidation, sending the clear message that no one was safe on the streets and that anyone could be detained and tried as a terrorist.

On the wave of these reports and stories told by the tortured, famous Kazakh journalist Dinara Yegeubayeva started her Instagram live streams where she interviewed activists and political commentators about the situation and violence post-January. As her virtual audience grew, she started inviting those people who were unknown to the majority of Kazakhstanis but who knew what was going on in the detention centres, prisons, and hospitals where the injured and tortured protestors were held. Her channel opened a space for the horrifying accounts of physical and emotional violence.

The intimidation, torture, and killing of protestors was the strategy of the new regime to intimidate its opponents among the existing regime elites, who now had to pledge allegiance to Tokayev. However, in the conditions of violent intimidation, insecurity, and people's distrust in the regime, this strategy could backfire and threaten Tokayev's rule. This is why the new constitutional amendments, and the state programme *Zhana Kazakhstan* (New Kazakhstan) were introduced as part of Tokayev's presidential address to the nation in March 2022. The Long Post-January identifies the prolonged period from the start of the mass protests until the public and activists are satisfied with the results of the investigations, which could potentially provide more clarity and unite the deeply fragmented Kazakhstani society and the regime.

The Fluidity of the Kazakhstani Political System

It is still unclear whether certain elite groups from the regime itself infiltrated the mass protests in an attempt at what Tokayev openly declared to be a 'failed coup', or whether that is simply a narrative constructed by the regime to discredit the protests and protestors. The violence that erupted on 5 January and which both interacted with and hijacked the peaceful protests has to be understood through the lens of the regime's own inner dynamic. The Kazakhstani political regime has been described as patronal, neo-patrimonial, kleptocratic, nepotic, soft authoritarian, and so on. The three decades of Nazarbayev's sole rule – which has widely been described as neo-patrimonial (Laruelle 2012; Hale 2014; Isaacs 2014; Peyrouse 2016; Isaacs and Frigerio 2018; Junisbai and Junisbai 2019; Tutumlu 2019), clan-based (Schatz 2004; Collins 2006), and highly personalized (Isaacs 2010; Laruelle 2019, 2021; Kudaibergenova 2020) – have produced a dynamic system where the regime functions as a regulator of relations and power struggles. Two notions are particularly relevant to decipher the supposed failed coup: the division of power between different teams, and the existence of parallel states inside the state structure.

A Multiplicity of Loyalties

Russian/Soviet and Western scholarly debates on the 'nature' of the regimes in Central Asia have long been shaped by the notion of clans. These debates often conflated the genealogical clan, with its (often mythologized) anthropological sense of kinship, and the political clan, understood from a political science perspective (Schatz 2004; Jacquesson 2012).

This is not to say that the genealogical clan is entirely absent from the political clan: it seems, for instance, that the *shaprashty* clan (of which the Nazarbayev family is part) has been particularly politically influential since the Soviet era (*Novaya Gazeta*, 17 January 2020). But the political clan is much better understood as a 'team' (*komanda* in Russian) – that is, as a group of people inside the high-level state administration united under a leader. The components of their loyalty are diverse, including personal friendship, shared professional formation (having graduated from the same university, for instance), institutional dependence, shared vested financial interests, and so on. This multiplicity of loyalties means that people may belong to several *komandy* at the same time, often in concentric circles (sub-*komandy* that report to a higher *komanda*), and these *komandy* may simultaneously cooperate and compete in different contexts. This results in a fluid system of loyalty that is uncertain to the actors themselves: they are never entirely sure that other members of their *komandy* will not shift their loyalty to a competing group when tensions arise. Actors therefore have the agency to prioritize one loyalty over another and make decisions in a very undetermined environment.

This fluidity guarantees that the regime can adapt to rapidly evolving contexts. Tokayev, for instance, has always been part of the circles around Nazarbayev, but there were in fact several competing *komandy* revolving around 'Elbasy', including one loyal to former prime minister Karim Masimov that seems to have been in conflict with Tokayev's. Once a large part of the presidential powers shifted to Tokayev in spring 2019 after Nazarbayev's resignation, the new president brought with him a new *komanda* whose loyalty was greater to him than to Nazarbayev's inner circles as such. When popular pressure coming from the protests pushed Tokayev to distance himself from Nazarbayev's legacy and cement his presidential status by promoting his own *komanda*, the competing groups may have reacted by withdrawing their loyalty from the president.

Several 'States' within the State

This multiplicity of *komanda* loyalties should be articulated with another institutional complexity, namely the existence of several parallel 'states' within the state. At least three of these can be identified: the formal civilian bureaucracy, the security services, and the corporate sector.

The higher echelons of the formal bureaucracy, embodied by the term Ak Orda – the 'White Horde', the name of the building of the presidential administration in Astana – is constituted by those whose power resides in the bureaucratic, technocratic status they have inside the official state structure (for instance, heads of departments within a ministry). They belong to one or several *komandy*, but their power resides in their institutional titles, which they regularly lose during administrative reshuffles. These powers are not purely symbolic; they have also a financial side, allowing the power-holder to make money through corrupt practices. Because Kazakhstan has invested a lot of its state-building symbolic politics in becoming a 'modernizing' state (Kudaibergenova 2015; Insebayeva 2022), bureaucratic power is strong, even if it alone is not sufficient to secure a political career.

The security services are a central institution in all post-Soviet states. Even in Soviet times, they had their own autonomy that could compete with decisions taken by the Party or the civilian state. The Kazakhstani security services do not enjoy as much power as their Russian counterparts (unlike Putin, who came from the KGB, Nazarbayev came from the civilian Communist Party structure, while Tokayev came from the diplomatic world) and do not benefit from the same symbolic prestige in the current nation-building programme. Nor can they be compared to the Uzbek security services, which during Islam Karimov's presidency were able to become the backbone of the Uzbek state, controlling all the key economic sectors (Lewis 2015; Zakirov 2021). In the Kazakhstani case, it seems the security services have been a weaker component of the 'system', competing on more equal terms with other state structures.

Nevertheless, the Kazakhstani security services have their own loyalty mechanisms and autonomous realm, shaped – as everywhere in the post-Soviet space – by overseeing a large part of the criminal world (Galeotti 2018). The boundaries between criminal groups and the private-security business, which is itself connected to law-enforcement agencies – many businessmen working in the flourishing private-security business are former law-enforcement or army officers – are likewise ambivalent. Several of the so-called terrorist attacks on court buildings, KGB buildings, and police checkpoints that Kazakhstan witnessed in 2011 and 2016 seem, for instance, to have been closer to criminal groups settling the score with law-enforcement agencies than to jihadist actions (Karin 2016; Beysembayev 2016).

The Islamist realm constitutes another subculture whose boundaries permeate the criminal world and the security-services system. The role of Nazarbayev's nephew Karait Satybaldy in protecting Islamist cells and trying to launch a traditionalist religious party – blocked by the authorities in 2019 – has been well documented (Exclusive.kz, 19 November 19 2019; Exclusive.kz, 24 March 2020).

Yet the official storyline of violence being mostly the result of Islamist groups remains largely unproven. The authorities have officially mentioned two policemen being beheaded – a killing technique usually associated with jihadism – and a Kazakh Syria-based jihadist group, the Soldiers of the Caliphate, made a social media video post on 5 January calling on the population to transform the protests into jihad. While there is abundant video footage showing people with arms in the street, there are no signs of flags or slogans that might pertain to any form of radical Islam. It can therefore be inferred that the authorities' emphasis on Islamic violence: (1) was necessary to justify CSTO involvement (ECFR 2022); (2) is part of a classic propaganda effort on the part of the Central Asian states to label enemies as Islamists (Lenz-Raymann 2014; Montgomery and Heathershaw 2016); and (3) is designed to divert the public debate from the more sensitive question of dissent among ruling elites and the role of the security services in the violence.

Indeed, numerous sources report that both army and law-enforcement officers left Almaty and Taldykorgan on the night of 5 January, allowing violence towards official buildings and massive looting. While it is still unclear whether this was part of a plan to allow violence and then engage in repressions or (more likely) a sign that the law-enforcement sector had shifted its loyalty to those elites opposed to

Tokayev, it confirms that this 'state within the state' functions according to its own informal law. The new government's announcement of a deep reform of the law-enforcement sector (TASS, 11 January 2022) seems to weigh in favour of the need to retake control of that realm.

The corporate world constitutes the third of these 'states within the state'. It emerged in the 2000s during the recentralization process launched by the regime to recapture economic sectors that were both commercially viable and served as a potential incubator for opposition (Duvanova 2013). Since then, this corporate world has grown in power as the symbol of the neoliberal paradigm of the Kazakhstani regime and of the country's brand for export. Kazakhstan's foreign policy is heavily shaped by the need for foreign investment, of which the corporate world is the backbone. That corporate world has been captured by Nazarbayev's sons-in-law (the most famous of whom, Timur Kulibayev, Dariga's husband, controls Almex Holding Group and through it a large number of the most profitable energy-related businesses) and entourage (as with the two huge mining holdings ENRC and Kazakhmys). This capture by the 'Family' has contributed to the calcification of Kazakhstan's dynamic market economy and its growing dysfunctionality in terms of redistribution capacity.

Nazarbayev's sons-in-law lost their main symbolic positions during these events: Kulibayev resigned from the chairmanship of the Presidium of the National Chamber of Entrepreneurs Atameken (the main industrial lobby in the country), Dimash Dosanov from the national oil transporter KazTransOil, and Kairat Sharipbayev from the national gas company QazaqGaz. Yet it remains to be seen if the de-oligarchization of the economy will be able to progress beyond these purely symbolic gestures.

The fluidity of the Kazakhstani regime highlights how difficult it will be for scholarship to decipher the elite-level component of Bloody January. The detention of security strongman and Nazarbayev's close ally Karim Massimov, consistent reshuffles in the powerful realm of the security services, as well as the array of resignations of key members of the Nazarbayev family, caused some experts to jump to conclusions about a grand rearrangement of power within the regime itself. But the multiplicity of loyalties, both personal and institutional, and the ongoing transition of power from Nazarbayev to Tokayev make the political system particularly liquid. Even elite-level actors likely have only a partial vision of how events unfold and make decisions based on their own positionality and what they interpret has happened.

Several narratives will thus likely continue to coexist: one is that Nazarbayev's family and Masimov's *komanda* tried to use the protests to weaken Tokayev and avoid him placing his own *komanda* at the reins of power; a second suggests that Tokayev took advantage of the protests to liquidate the 'Old Guard' around Masimov and the 'Family'; and a third posits that Nazarbayev and Tokayev bargained peacefully behind the scenes and that the supposed 'failed coup' was nothing more than a cover story to justify the violent repression of the protests.

Whatever the 'reality' may be – and it may be portions of all three stories – the January 2022 events reflect the fact that transition in 'hybrid' post-Soviet regimes more often happens through a succession of gradual changes than in a radical, one-time manner. Gurbanguly Berdymuhamedov in Turkmenistan needed almost two years to push out of power those who had been too close to the first president, Saparmurat Niyazov, and install his own people. Shavkat Mirziyoyev in Uzbekistan may have made rapid and highly visible changes within the first few weeks and months, but it took him a long time to finalize the turnover of elites in the more hidden sections of the state, such as the security services (Anceschi 2021).

The Kazakhstani transition seems more complex than these, as the first president did not die in power but decided to supervise the transition himself. A first formal transition at the presidential level happened in March 2019. However, Nazarbayev only partially relinquished power and very little changed politically, economically, or in terms of symbolic nation-building. A second, more chaotic transition took place in January 2022, when Nazarbayev stepped down from his 'lifetime' position as head of the Security Council, his *komanda* left two 'states within the state' – the security services and, to a lesser and more superficial extent, the corporate world – and de-Nazarbayevication began (the depth of this trend has yet to be decided and will be adjusted depending on the balance of power). The parliamentary decision to scrap Nazarbayev's symbolic positions was the biggest transformation in the country's modern history since the 1991 declaration of independence. Yet the transition is far from complete, as the 'Family' is still in control of substantial assets and seems thus far to have avoided any legal challenges. A third transition will happen upon Nazarbayev's death, potentially with more damaging effects for members of the Nazarbayev family.

Is There a Missing Ethnic Component to the Discussion?

Western and Russian scholarship on Kazakhstan has historically focused too heavily on the ethnic component of Kazakhstan's political and social life due to the memory of the early 1990s, when the country's sovereignty seemed at risk and activists from the Russian minority were showing signs of secessionism. The 'Russian minority' prism has continued to haunt media reporting, as well as, to a lesser extent, scholarship, even if the literature has increasingly stressed that the 'Russian minority' is in fact a constituency supportive of the Nazarbayev status quo (Laruelle 2016; Diener 2015, 2022). Since the 2019 Kazakh Spring, the still largely Russian-dominated cities of the north and the east, such as Petropavl and Ostkemen, appear to have remained quite calm and loyal to the regime; notably, the January protests were not as prolonged there as in other cities.

Tokayev's call for help from the Russia-led Collective Security Treaty Organization (CSTO) was also read by Western observers as carrying the risk of an 'invasion' by Russian troops that would endanger the country's sovereignty. Yet the intervention was handled extremely well by both sides. Russia showed for the first time that CSTO Rapid Forces could indeed deploy within a few hours; the troops were sent to secure official buildings, mostly in Nur-Sultan, as well as key industrial assets, and did not interact directly with the protestors, so there was no image of Russian soldiers repressing Kazakhstani citizens, which would indeed have created a very negative image for both Moscow and Nur-Sultan; and they left very rapidly, after just over a week in Kazakhstan (*Foreign Policy*, 13 January 2022). Thus, while the intervention was at first decried on some local social media as a sign of Russian colonialism and something that would taint Tokayev's legitimacy in the long term, it seems that the well-managed and short-lived CSTO presence had fewer damaging effects than were predicted.

It remains unclear what price Kazakhstan will have to pay Russia for the intervention. The country's multi-vectoralism, the centrepiece of Kazakhstani foreign policy, has been already damaged by Kazakhstan's accession to the Eurasian Economic Union (Kudaibergenova 2016) and Russia's growing strategic domination of the Kazakhstani military and military-industrial sector – even if Kazakhstan retains a significant part of its agency (Akhmetova, Terzhanova, Akhmetova, et al. 2017; Laruelle, Royce, and Beyssembayev 2019). Local observers have suggested two possible symbolic gestures that Kazakhstan might make: recognizing Crimea as part of Russia – which the Kazakhstani authorities have never officially done – and postponing the shift to the Latin alphabet, planned for 2031 (Shakhanova 2018; du Boulay and du Boulay 2021), which could have repercussions within Russia, as Tatarstan has often expressed a desire to make this move.

The ethnic component of Bloody January to be explored is therefore related not to Russian minorities and their relationship to Russia, but to the Kazakh nation itself. If narratives of the risk of the ethnic and linguistic disappearance of the Kazakh nation and the Kazakh language are still common references in the Kazakh-speaking nationalist media realm, sociocultural changes on the ground seem to reflect the contrary, pointing to the blossoming of the Kazakh nation both demographically (ethnic Kazakhs now comprise around 68 per cent of the population, compared to 40 per cent in the last Soviet census in 1989) and linguistically (the share of the population with mastery of Kazakh has risen sharply, with between 80 and 90 per cent of teenagers now saying they write, speak, and/or understand it) (Statistical Agency of the Republic of Kazakhstan, 2010). The economic boom years of the 2000s contributed to the birth of new Kazakh-speaking urban and upper-middle classes, embodied by the rise in power of a new generation of political figures and grassroots activists who call for more ethnonationalist state-building. Tokayev's new State Secretary – with impressive extended powers (*New Times*, 31 January 2022) – Erlan Karin (born 1976) personifies the trend of nationalist 'nation-builders' who are now in the higher echelons of power. One might also mention Aidos Sarym, a nationalist formerly in the opposition who has been co-opted as a deputy for the presidential party, Nur Otan.

But the successful Kazakhification of Kazakhstan has also resulted in a very contrasted socio-economic and sociocultural picture. The official statistic that less than 5 per cent of rural dwellers live in poverty, as calculated by the World Bank in 2019, is the tree hiding the forest of deep regional discrepancies that mostly affect the Kazakh-speaking rural population. The western region of Mangystau, as well as the southern regions of Shymkent and (to an even greater degree) Almaty perform the worst on almost all indicators in the sphere of primary and secondary educational attainment, have the highest rate of NEET youth (those not in education, employment, or training), feature a poor situation for women generally (with higher levels of early marriage, for instance; Kopeyeva 2019), and are viewed with condescension by the urban population, both Russian- and Kazakh-speaking (Koch and White 2016). The fact that the protests began in western Kazakhstan and were most violent in the Almaty region (Almaty city and Taldykorgan) confirms that the significant socio-economic gaps between regions and between urbanites and rural dwellers are driving social unrest in the country.

It seems that many of the most violent protesters – whether spontaneous or 'hired' to loot and destroy properties – were young, ethnic Kazakh males from the rural regions around Almaty. This phenomenon of rural anger against the urban way of life – with rural dwellers seeing themselves as 'losers' compared to the urban 'winners' from the neoliberal changes of the last three decades – is not specific to Kazakhstan; indeed, it has been well documented in neighbouring Kyrgyzstan (Sanghera and Satybaldieva 2021). A large part of the local narrative about the violence therefore stresses the sociocultural gaps between 'newcomers' (*priezhie*) and urbanites (*gorozhane*), inscribing the Bloody January events into a *longue durée* discourse on the post-Soviet transformations of the urban fabric and strong urban xenophobia: many urbanites, both Russian- and Kazakh-speaking, complain about the cultural disruptions caused by the 'newcomers' (Jašina-Schäfer 2019).

This trend is anchored into broader transformations of the Kazakh nation in which internal lines of division are becoming more emotionally loaded. This is the case, for instance, with the supposed division between *nagyz* ('real') Kazakhs, a term used to describe those who have successfully preserved their national identity, and *shala* ('half') Kazakhs, Russophone and urban Kazakhs who are considered too detached from their Kazakhophone and rural roots (Bohr, Mallinson, Brauer, et al. 2019). Another division operationalized during the protests was the one between urbanites and *mambety*, a very derogatory term used to brand the rural population as 'rednecks'. This urban/rural divide is also reflected in widespread xenophobia against Oralmans, ethnic Kazakhs repatriated from abroad. Those who come from outside the Soviet realm (mostly Mongolia), in particular, have been decried as culturally retrograde and unable to adapt to modern Kazakhstan. Oralman leaders insist, on the contrary, on their own cultural purity and ability to restore national traditions long lost by their modernized brethren in the homeland (Beysembayev 2015).

The January 2022 protests will, no doubt, constitute a turning point in the history of independent Kazakhstan due to the mass character of the protests, the violence that erupted, and the ongoing – at least symbolic – de-Nazarbayevication that followed. The country's image abroad will be transformed: the brand of a stable Kazakhstan with no intra-elite struggle and based on popular consensus has been damaged and will take time to rebuild. The Tokayev government will be closely monitored as it attempts to reform power hierarchies and redress socio-economic grievances: as of the time of writing, it is unclear whether any de-oligarchization of the economy can happen or if the changes will remain superficial, as with the launch of redistribution mechanisms such as the new Social Fund. The pandemic has obviously aggravated the economic situation for many social groups, and it is not certain that the current rise in oil and gas prices will help the regime to compensate for the structural dysfunctionalities the national economy faces.

The regime is sending mixed signals in terms of regime transition. A high level of violence was avoided; the Nazarbayev family also remains in the country and has kept its assets. This suggests that the regime change is limited and can therefore be seen as a success for Nazarbayev and other autocrats who may be looking for a model for stepping down from their formal roles without losing informal power. However, the general feeling is that the protests symbolize the failure of the Nazarbayev era, which is finishing on a note tainted by violence, Russian military intervention, and repression.

More importantly, a culture of protests has developed and consolidated, especially on the wave of the Kazakh Spring development since spring 2019. Not only will this not vanish in the years to come, but it is likely to strengthen: even without a unifying leadership, this new culture shares a common imaginary (December 1986, Zhanaozen in 2011, Kazakh Spring in 2019) and has been able to invest in new fields of action such as urban activism, environmental awareness, land- and property-related issues, and so on. The atmosphere in Kazakhstan thus parallels that of Belarus: in both countries, the time of authoritarian 'fathers of the nation' seems to be coming to an end – a phenomenon also visible in Russia, albeit to a lesser extent.

At the same time, the country entered a new phenomenon of its own development that can be termed the Long Post-January. Unlike other scenarios of regime change, such as the revolutions of the Arab Spring, which happen swiftly via coups and internal regime take-over, radically and within an established time frame, or the long muddle through regime consolidation as with Turkey's failed coup, the Kazakhstani situation represents a completely different scenario. The Nazarbayev regime fell immediately after the first clashes in the first week of January 2022, but his slow removal from Kazakhstani politics, including the 6 June 2022 Constitutional vote to remove mention of him from the constitution and the potential dismissal of the Law on the First President, blurs his departure. He clearly lost his political and institutional powers but continues to bargain for his economic capital with the new Tokayev regime. Tokayev took time to consolidate his powers after the bloodshed of the January protests, and he will be remembered as the bloody dictator who ordered the shooting of civilians 'without warning'. From his first moves in installing the new government and imprisoning the old guard from the Nazarbayev inner circle (including Nazarbayev's nephews and deceased brother, who used to control the whole Almaty region), it is clear that he is slowly restructuring the regime, seeking to get rid of disloyal elites and cement his rule. This happens against the backdrop of the population's consistent demands for a more effective economic governance and the existing potent protest moods as well as consistently growing fears of uncertainty over Russia's aggression in Ukraine.

In many ways, the unexpected and violent war in Ukraine plays well for Tokayev. Kazakhstanis for years shared fears of Russian aggression and lived in the shadows of its potential on the pretext of the protection of ethnic Russian compatriots living in Kazakhstan (Diener 2015). The protesting days of early 2022 demonstrated that Russia can install its troops in Almaty, in the heart of Kazakhstan, within hours, not even days. This factor of Russia's looming danger and influence continues to shape openly nationalistic movements but also helps Tokayev to divert focus and attention from the internal rifts and traumatizing effects of the January violence and tortures that followed to the geopolitical dangers and Kazakhstan's foreign policy towards the Russo-Ukrainian conflict. However, the regime's authoritarian myopia in addressing the post-January traumas will cost them dearly in the longer run.

After all, the January 2022 protests went up like a match struck in a room full of gas and on the wave of solidarity for the Zhanaozen 2011 trauma and support for the Zhanaozen 2022 protests. These same solidarities will tend to fire up if not addressed properly by the regime.

But Tokayev's biggest mistake is his decision to build his regime on the existing structure of regime–society relations that has already proved ineffective and resulted in mass protests and violence. His first steps with the 'cosmetic repairs' to the old Kazakhstan with the 'New Kazakhstan' state programme are still weak in the face of the greater social problems, widening gaps of economic inequality, and citizens' growing civic culture and protest moods. While this book is not designed to make political predictions, the framework of regime–society relations it offers demonstrates that if Tokayev continues with the old ways of dealing with societal problems by promising and not delivering, his regime is doomed.

Conclusions

In March 2019, then seventeen-year-old artist Medina Bazargali organized the first walking protest against the authoritarian power transition. As they walked on Panfilov Street in downtown Almaty and broadcast their lone march live on their Instagram stories, they kept on saying 'I have a choice!' (*U menya est' vybor!*) and 'My vote was stolen' (*Moi golos ukrali*) in connection to the hasty announcement of new presidential elections. Thousands of Kazakhstanis watched the video and repeated the slogans that later gave impetus to the process of awakening and claiming the right to open and contested elections and democratization, and to protest against the old authoritarian regime. When I interviewed Medina Bazargali months later, in the summer of 2020, they told me that there was only one fear they felt acutely at the time of their walking picket in March 2019 and throughout the development of the Kazakh Spring:

There is this *big fear* that you would spend your whole life in this totalitarian state, and you won't be able to change anything; and then when you are 40 years old, you'd still realize that nothing had changed [in the political atmosphere of the country]. This is the biggest fear, this is the type of fear that is wrapping everything; this type of fear is necessary in order to continue the fight against it all because you cannot fight against something is you are not afraid of it. Because the only thing you can do is to face your fear, to do everything possible to destroy or at least diminish the possibility for your most fearful scenario to happen. What is this fear? [What are we fearing?] It is the fear of the possibility; the fear that some sort of scenarios that you don't want to allow to happen, would actualize in reality and that it would be the way [you have imagined in the worst conditions]. And then you are not the same, you no longer can feel happiness in your life or do things and think that everything will be great. This is the real fear [of totalitarianism]. And then there is the *small fear*, it's a short-term fear, the type of fear for losing your life [due to protests or activism].

There is an incredible force and power in Bazargali's account: the fear of a totalitarian future overpowering the immediate fear for one's safety and even life. Some of my respondents openly expressed their sadness that their rallies did not attract hundreds of thousands of protestors (before January 2022) precisely due to this latter or 'smaller' fear of coercion or due to their lack of information. What makes one protest in an authoritarian state? How much injustice has to be concentrated in one society to make people take to the streets and fight for their rights in the least conventional but possibly the only available way? These are the questions many activists in Kazakhstan ask themselves on a daily basis, while others do not and instead invest all their time and effort in making changes elsewhere – fighting regime propaganda, advocating for full inclusivity and human rights for all, waging war against disinformation, educating those who fall into the traps of re-traditionalization.

In this book I did not aim to look at the Qazaq Koktemi phenomenon as a failed or quiet or unfulfilled revolution. The Kazakh Spring's emergence and rapid development into a new field that allowed it to rethink the rules of the game of doing politics in Kazakhstan and topple the once-powerful regime of Nazarbayev's sole rule requires a field of studies on its own right. The case of the Kazakh Spring and the changes it brought offers a new way of studying, analysing, and thinking about authoritarian politics and regime–society relations, their durability, and resilience. This book demonstrated that the demise of the regime can be a prolonged affair, where a new autocrat uses the window of opportunity – in our case, mass protests and major geopolitical conflict – as a space to consolidate his rule, even though he is doing so in a completely new reality. Kazakhstan is a peculiar case for the study of authoritarianism, even a surprising one.

First, it surprised political observers and scholars with the sudden and voluntary resignation of the long-term dictator; then, it surprised observers with its major protest waves, when the regime's conventional wisdom was that Nazarbayev's cult enjoyed wide popularity. The Kazakh Spring demonstrated that revolutionary change might not happen overnight, nor is it always designed to do so. Indeed, the definition of revolution that I intentionally avoided throughout the book is of the sweeping current, a type of the storm that swallows everything and brings extensive, radical changes to the core of the system, often by destroying it. Indeed, the discourse of the post-Soviet revolutions frames them as rapid, spectacular in the abundance of the protesting masses, violent, hopeful yet almost never successful enough. Qazaq Koktemi or the Kazakh Spring is not the typical revolution that some outside observers were hoping to see. The Qazaq Koktemi field calls for structural changes of the mind; their battles are grounded in the change of perceptions and values, and the change of the dominant discourses about what is possible and impossible under a given authoritarian rule, and this different approach is the only way to inspire democratic changes through tedious everyday work, not just sporadic and mass protests. In fact, when mass protests happened and brought mass violence, many in the Kazakh Spring field spent a long time considering how the transformations could be less violent and traumatic for the whole society. January, or *Qantar* in Kazakh, became a strong discourse of trauma, of feelings of insecurity, and of low trust in political institutions. In the most difficult two years of the long post-January – the post-traumatic syndrome that all society continues to live with – the Kazakh Spring activists managed to sustain their activism by fighting for transparent investigation of the violence, by peacefully protesting at the courts where many innocent people were accused of terrorist acts, and by creating social media networks monitoring torture compiling lists of victims and their families, and raising money for them. In the conditions of the long post-January, the Kazakh Spring activists reveal more clearly how regime and society continue to live in completely parallel realities, almost divorced from one another.

The Kazakh Spring, with its diverse actors, offers an alternative view about the political, social, and cultural development of Kazakhstan in the future. In doing so, the activists of the Kazakh Spring also tore open the inadequacies, inequalities, and cracks within the authoritarian system. Their protest revealed and will continue to reveal even more and often unexpected findings. One example is how law works according to the rules of the regime but how at the same time the regime is not as omnipresent and omnipotent as it tries to portray itself. One of the biggest achievements of the Kazakh Spring is that it set a precedent and made many of its participants (public or anonymous) realize that their contribution can bring a change that they did not believe it could. The processes of the protesting spring are also historic for Kazakhstan and will remain part of the larger and potentially very long discourse of the 'post-Nazarbayev' era that is still in progress while this book is being finalized. Yet Nazarbayev's dictatorship fell, and the Kazakh Spring protestors had a lot to do with inspiring the demise of the regime. Now their work is engaged with changing the new regime of Tokayev.

The authoritarian regime in Kazakhstan has proven to be a lot more fragile than we, the citizens, had thought, yet its reach – in institutional ownership of the police and judiciary as well as access to welfare distribution and the totalization of ideological production through media and local bureaucracy – is significant. No other opponent can reach as far as the 'state', to address the vast majority of citizens in some of the most remote parts of the country as the regime can. This lack of access to further institutionalization pushes protest movements to restricted class and urban domains that turn into hubs of political activism. These are not just the people who have access to the digital network, which might be seen as a lot more limited than the reach of the regime (through bureaucracy, media, and education) but nevertheless plays as important a field dimension for creating alternative thinking. But these are networks of people who feel that they can get a platform to voice their concerns. As a case in point, Oyan, Qazaqstan, which was formed as a movement during the Kazakh Spring (Qazaq Koktemi), allowed its participants to feel part of the larger collective anonymously, publicly, actively, or on a voluntary basis, where everyone chose their own workload and time commitments. This flexible approach added to the self-perception of 'making the change' that many of these participants felt they were lacking. Thus, collective participation and collective identity formation on the basis of the same values of liberation from authoritarianism have not only empowered these activists but also made them feel like significant contributors to tangible and real political dialogue.

Many of the activists felt that their engagement with the Kazakh Spring was the first time that they were able to participate in the political field at all. Thus, the word 'activism' was rethought and given a new meaning. It moved away from being a marginal or peripheral activity for a few NGO-connected, institutionalized people or volunteers and became a type of 'fashionable' or trendy position for urban dwellers. The Kazakh Spring importantly brought about a kind of collective solidarity that can remain anonymous, when people do not always need to meet in person or to know each other in order to remain part of the same field and share pro-democratic values with each other. Contrary to the regime's provision of authoritarian values and shared perceptions (e.g., the belief in political and other type of 'stability' that is dominant in groups who support the regime), the type of solidarity that the Kazakh Spring brought about is more about rule of law and the possibility of fighting for one's rights. And as research has shown, even for people who were not directly connected to the specific movements that emerged on the wave of the Kazakh Spring, the slogans and messages they produced provoked great support in different types of social groups. 'Kazakhstan without Nazarbayevs' or *'Shal, ket!'* became widely shared slogans across the whole country, and images of toppling Nazarbayev's monuments will forever remain of significant historical and symbolic value for the Kazakhstani people.

The development of the Kazakh Spring in the first two years from its inception is crucial for the understanding of how the political field will develop in post-Nazarbayev Kazakhstan. As a completely distinct and new field of protest politics, it gave rise to the new horizontal movement, but also a new language, approaches, methods, processes, and understandings of activism. It has empowered the first post-post-Soviet generation and thus was termed by many commentators as a 'youth protest' that for the first time declared on their banners and posters the demand for 'Kazakhstan without Nazarbayevs'. The Spring protestors' vision and understanding of how they frame their political protest is also very new. Their demands for 'Constitution instead of Revolution' brought back the powerful agenda of the rule of law that has been diminished in the Kazakhstani political language of the past five to seven years, when the political opposition has been significantly weakened and disintegrated. The Kazakh Spring also brought new shifts in the understanding of the nationalizing regime that rarely saw significant competitors or potent voices in this sphere before. The possibility of incorporating a decolonial framework into further political and social activism (including in the contemporary art field where it emerged initially) provides new and exciting venues for rethinking the legacies and dominant frameworks of post-Soviet nation-building, categorization, and inequality they reinforce.

The Kazakh Spring also for the first time incorporated strong voices of feminist and queer activists and brought in a gender-equality agenda that was not as prominent or visible in the political or opposition field in Kazakhstan before. Why is this agenda so important for the Kazakhstani or any other non-democratic context? Because gender equality and queer activism bring about the ideas and values of the inevitability and the entirety of human rights, respect for differences, freedoms, and rights for all regardless of their identifications or the type of labels and concepts that society or anyone else tries to apply to them. The convergence of the Kazakh Spring activists with this important field of gendered and queer activism in Kazakhstan is thus a sign of further democratization and the expansion of the political field to become more inclusive and more attentive to the rights, freedoms, and representations (in the total and not theatrical 'window-dressing' sense of the word) of all citizens. It is the sign and signal of an important shift in the type of 'opposition' politics that no longer just concentrated, openly or subversively, on the same patriarchal and traditionalist values propagated by the regime and its supporters. That said, to many of the aggressive supporters of traditionalist values, the so-called *uyat*-men (shaming men) or the groups of activists who continuously harass queer activists, this agenda and shift is highlighting the 'Westernization' of the Kazakhstani political field and values. This is a typical agenda and discreditation used by many other groups, movements, and even regimes (e.g., the Putinist regime in Russia) that deny or disregard the fact that these rights and identifications, choices, and freedoms have existed and continue to exist all over the world and are not an exclusively 'Western' agenda. And thus, these rights and representations can no longer be ignored and require further inclusion into the political field, debates, and activism. Before the Kazakh Spring, this type of 'gendered' activism remained isolated on the margins of political activism and did not enter other political movements or the 'opposition' field. The problem with this type of positioning and marginalization of the gendered agenda was that it left the field in its own niche, away from the 'bigger' agenda of political debate.

In this book, I have argued that Qazaq Koktemi, the Kazakh Spring, was able to shape ideas and concepts, citizens' perceptions of the state and regime, and their own position and participation in this paradigm of power relations that I analysed as regime–society relations. The Kazakh Spring activists can be credited with exposing the ineffectiveness of this paradigm of political relations, which only inspires further shaky and undemocratic developments.

In the end, what I have attempted to demonstrate is (1) how the protest wave reveals the hidden or less visible ways of doing authoritarian politics under certain regimes; (2) how these new protest waves emerge and what makes them possible; (3) what are the ways, contexts, and other local factors that make such radically visible and sudden waves of protests as those of the Kazakh Spring possible; (4) how the relations and discourses are produced and worked in this particular field; and finally, (5) how this protest wave pushes the regime and makes it change its tactics. I believe that the example of Qazaq Koktemi as a field that has changed the way the political is understood and practised in Kazakhstan is a very useful and illustrative manifestation of this change.

To the vast majority of outsiders, Qazaq Koktemi simply represents the period of continuous protests and the formation of different protests groups, all of which remained deinstitutionalized, unregistered, and sometimes even spontaneous – a quality that is not unusual for many social movements all around the world.[1] I propose a different perspective on the ways protest movements operate within this new field, while still battling with authoritarianism's core elements – lack of political competition, of pluralism, of transparency, of open and contested elections, and opacity over political decision-making and citizens' resulting apathy regarding political processes. Rather than encapsulating the analysis only in the structure of social movements themselves, I focus on the interplay of the different protest actions (including social movements like Oyan, Qazaqstan) among themselves and with regime politics. Using context and the temporal development of the Kazakh Spring, I focus on the way the interplay between the repressive regime and democratization struggles defines and shapes each of them. This is a complex picture of the way the regime frames opposition (old and new) but also the way the protest wave pushes the regime and makes it change its tactics. In the end, this interplay leads to a slow but consistent change in the ways the political is done in Kazakhstan.

Lessons Learned

It is unquestionable that the inception of the Kazakh Spring was swift and, in many ways, sudden, though expected. The makers of the Kazakh Spring were ready to organize movements, like those of Oyan, Qazaqstan, and to start the type of political art activism that

---

[1] See Flesher Fominaya 2015, for example.

was well developed in the generation of their parents.² The Kazakh Spring left a lasting effect on those who participated and made a mark on Kazakhstani politics as one of the stages for its further and real democratization (not from above but from below). But the first stages of the Spring require some reflection, and thus I want to finish the book in the words of the makers of the Kazakh Spring. What changed for them? How did they evaluate the important changes? In the words of Beibarys Tolymbetov speaking to Adamdar.ca, the Kazakh Spring became a critical point of a new era:

People became estranged from the truth. But luckily, history has a tendency to keep moving and to resolve its contradictions. The product of this contradiction was the youth who had not lived under the Soviet Union and were too young to remember the social situation of the '90s. This generation is like the Israelites in the desert – free of the negative memories of global transformation and the attraction to a 'stable' life. And it was these youth who became the engine of the new protest. The first blow was to the values imposed by the authorities, who for all these years stubbornly tried to create a new cult justifying typical authoritarianism. The youth showed that they live according to their own values, which run contrary to the efforts of the powers that be. This is how the slogan 'Nur-Sultan is not my capital' came to be. History did not stop on its path after that, and the authorities had to endure another blow to their double standards. People began paying greater attention to the fact that the official statements of the masters, the servants of the people, weren't quite lining up with their actions. The youth were inspired by 'you can't run away from the truth'.³

For Tamina Ospanova, another participant in 'You cannot run away from the truth', the historic Almaty marathon protest art, the Kazakh Spring became the 'point of no return':

Life is no longer the same, undoubtedly. We witnessed an unjust court, waited for our friends to come back, saw Beibarys off to the army; I remember all of this like a dream. This year I met great, brave people; we learned from each other and supported each other in every way; I learned a lot of new things about politics, about our rights, how important it is to understand all of this and deal with it. Even if it seems like it has nothing to do with you. After the snap election was announced, the 'You can't run away

---

² In many ways, my earlier research into the political art of Central Asia was the a necessary precedent for me to start writing about the Kazakh Spring.
³ From the interview with Adamdar.ca, available at https://adamdar.ca/en/post/y ou-can-t-run-away-from-the-truth-one-year-later.

from the truth' protest became a kind of point of no return in the minds of citizens. We saw support from Kazakhstanis all over the country and outside its borders and a subsequent wave of protests. There were a great many solitary pickets; at some point they stopped arresting people – it seemed like we were breaking through a thick, invisible wall. But then a new spring came, beginning with the 'abduction' of activists on the first of March.[4]

Other activists have worked for the empowerment of the Kazakh Spring as a field and for the consistent working of its movements; for example, Oyan, Qazaqstan noted that, while the fight is ongoing, there have already been many lessons that have shaped and changed the way people view the authoritarian regime and how the regime views those who openly oppose it on the streets. One of them is the necessity to continuously raise awareness about the civil sphere and civic culture. And another is the necessity for activists to sustain horizontal movements instead of falling into the abyss of hierarchical fights. In the words of two anonymous Oyan, Qazaqstan activists:

We do not have leaders. Maybe some people consider some of us [more publicly known members] as leaders – I understand some people's attitudes to me personally, but it just explains that some activists initially were more public than others. For example, Asya [Tulesova] was already a known public person before [the Spring]. But within the movement, many non-public people do so much work [that is unseen to the wider public]. I constantly talk about it – we do not have leaders! But in return I hear that 'you won't get anywhere without the leaders, you won't get [elected] to the parliament'. "tell [our critics] that *we* [Oyan, Qazaqstan] d" not want to get to the parliament, and what we hear back is, 'then why are you doing all of this [activism]? Why do you need it?'. Then you start explaining how [activism] is so important [without political institutionalization] but they [critics] just disregard it as something unimportant because for them it is such a complex idea. But for me this is precisely not a difficult, but a very simple idea.[5]

Other members of the movement continuously question how to make the movement truly horizontal. My sample of interviews included those activists who for some reason have left Oyan, Qazaqstan but" remained active within the Kazakh Spring field and in diverse networks

---

[4] Tamina Ospanova's interview with Adamdar.ca, available at https://adamdar.ca/en/post/you-can-t-run-away-from-the-truth-one-year-later.
[5] Author's interview with an anonymous Oyan, Qazaqstan activist.

of activists. Thus, their political activism and communication with many *oyanovcy* (members of the Oyan, Qazaqstan movement) remained ongoing and, in some cases, very active. The harsh lessons they have learnt through their bitter experiences left them wondering how to sustain a horizontal approach to activism. In the words of one anonymous activist:

> I think that for me, Oyan, clearly demonstrated how hard it is to build some sort of horizontal movements because it is not always clear how the horizontal approach works in movements because there are not many examples of it working [locally]. It is unclear what is horizontal [sometimes] and you have to use different sources and references, use some vertical systems as an example to see how decision-making is done – who is more authoritative, what is the right decision, and that you cannot finalize the discussion so quickly but allow it to be sustained without forgetting how [collective decision-making] is so important. It is still hard to incorporate these things [to the local context] because we live in this country [Kazakhstan] ... and regardless how you would approach this context, we still live in these highly authoritarian and exclusive structures, and it is hard to move away from them and the way of thinking they impose. This is why it is so important for me to take this experience and horizontal approach to other movements I participate in ... I think that we need to do everything to make the process [of activism] inclusive and horizontal. That's it. That's the only way. And then we will see the [positive] results.[6]

In analysing contentious politics in Kazakhstan and other post-Soviet states, we should avoid several fallacies. First, there is no one-template-fits-all or magic cookbook for successful revolutions – all contentious politics are context-dependent and do not always lead to similar outcomes. Class and access to resources (state welfare, education, positions, opportunities in one's career, and the 'good life') play a crucial role in the way activists work with contentions. This book discussed Qazaq Koktemi as one phenomenon, but there are other competing and overlapping phenomena as well – the populist and the nationalist, and the old guard, and soon there will be many more unexpected players whom we cannot control but need to anticipate.

Second, we need to change our evaluation of the 'success' of a specific movement and adjust expectations in the post-Soviet space where the legacies of the 'colour revolutions' continue to influence expectations

---

[6] Author's interview with an anonymous source, August 2021.

and the ways different protest movements are framed. Not every movement ends in the complete overthrow of the ruling elites or a total change from a super-presidential republic to a parliamentary one. For many movements, it would take years of consistent and mundane *protest work*, which often escapes the headlines and might be marginalized as 'unsuccessful' or stagnant over longer periods of time. Yet changes on the discursive level and more adequate political mobilization and the formation of solidarities are important at these micro- and meta-levels of actions. In Kazakhstan, where it felt like 'Nazarbayev was forever' (*Nazarbayev navsegda*), even a slight change in the political imagination and the opening of the political field for more engagement turned into a crucial and for some even radical point in their revolutionary attitudes. In this book, I tried to follow this method to study the detailed changes in attitudes and approaches to civic engagement that were not as popular in certain age and class groups. For example, the very formalized appeal of the Protestor Körpe on Instagram was an example of the significant shift in practices that the activists behind this initiative did not call on before. For many of the activists involved in the Kazakh Spring or Oyan, Kazakhstan, formal rules and letters addressed to the president presented a type of activism they did not previously consider worthwhile.

Finally, this shift in attitudes and practices of protest and civic engagement also demonstrates how, in all types of protest and social-movement contexts, activists and participants are using diverse formal (or traditional) and informal channels of communication, action, and engagement. While the use of social media in the study of protests and social movements is not new in academia, some researchers still find it unconventional and perhaps even ineffective in evaluating or validating certain data, attitudes, and influences. Yet in conditions of almost-total regime control of all 'conventional' media channels and when the confidentiality of communication is crucial under repressive regimes, protestors are pushed to the online space simply because it becomes the only space for opportunities, communication, and engagement. Belarusian protestors mainly communicated through a number of Telegram channels, whose audiences grew exponentially from the first days of the protest because of the demand for *real* information about the protests in different cities. In the post-January reality of Kazakhstan, we are seeing the same developments. Many citizens are disappointed with the lack of transparency around the official investigation into the causes and main actors of the violence that overtook the peaceful protests in southern parts of the country during Bloody January. In the first few months after the tragedy, there was very little information about the number of the victims, injured, and arrested. Activists had to build up the lists of the dead, injured, and tortured protestors and ordinary citizens by themselves using social media and word of mouth. The same happened with commemoration of those protestors who had died and contesting fabricated court hearings of protestors who were tortured to plead guilty. People had to fight for their right to commemorate the victims, and some of them continue to be arrested for what the regime views as 'unsanctioned rallies', when families and activists gather on the squares where people were killed to remember them on 5 and 6 January. Those are the unofficial days of the heightened violence when most people died. As the colloquial saying goes, even if President Tokayev has announced his 'reforms' for New Kazakhstan, the ways of authoritarian governance remain as in Old (read Nazarbayev's) Kazakhstan.

And a final word on methods: in one of our series of interviews, Medina Bazargali noted with a type of curatorial and art-activist language, that 'fixating' (*fiksatsiya*) certain events as they happen in sequence, in connection to each other, embedded in specific interconnected and interdependent contexts, is equally important as organizing or participating in them. The voices and historical re-enactments of significant events and waves within the Kazakh Spring that are shared on the pages of this book are thus crucial for future and perhaps past understandings of what is going on in Kazakhstan, in the wider post-Soviet space, and in the field of protest and social movements in general.

The chapters of this book, thus, were intentionally planned as a type of 'living archive' or snapshot of the crucial moment when the Kazakh Spring emerged. This focus was intentional, since my own experience with working with authoritarianism and its systems demonstrates again and again the fundamental truth of the phenomenon that Hannah Arendt captured so well in the *Origins of Totalitarianism*. She noted that 'nothing is more characteristic of the totalitarian movements in general and of the quality of fame of their leaders in particular than the starting swiftness with which they are forgotten and the startling ease with which they can be replaced'.⁷ Indeed, the totalitarian and authoritarian temporality is such that it is rarely fully anticipated, calculated but also very rapid when it changes, especially when the Spring is here. *Көктем жақындап қалды.*⁸

---

⁷ Arendt 2007: 407.
⁸ One of the slogans of the Oyan, Qazaqstan rallies that translates from Kazakh as 'Spring is near', 16 December 2019.

References

Agaidarov, A., Izvorski, I. V., and Rahardja, S. 2020. *Kazakhstan Economic Update: Navigating the Crisis*. Washington, DC: World Bank Group.

Akhmetova, K. A., Terzhanova, A., Akhmetova, A. A., Saduakassova, A. B., and Smailova, G. K. 2017. Economic integration: Advantages and risks for the Kazakhstan economy. *Journal of Advanced Research in Law and Economics*, 8(26), pp. 1047–55.

Akhrarkhodjaeva, N. 2017. *Instrumentalisation of Mass Media in Electoral Authoritarian Regimes: Evidence from Russia's Presidential Election Campaigns of 2000 and 2008*. New York: Columbia University Press.

Alexander, C. 2018. Homeless in the homeland: Housing protests in Kazakhstan. *Critique of Anthropology*, 38(2), pp. 204–20.

Alexander, J. 2006. *The Public Sphere*. Oxford: Oxford University Press.

Amanzholova, D. A. 2013. *Alash: Historical Meaning of Democratic Choice*. Almaty: Taimas Publishing House. [Алаш: исторический смысл демократического выбора. Издательский дом" Таймас".]

Ambrosio, T. 2015. Leadership succession in Kazakhstan and Uzbekistan: Regime survival after Nazarbayev and Karimov. *Journal of Balkan and Near Eastern Studies*, 17(1), pp. 49–67.

Anacker, S. 2004. Geographies of power in Nazarbayev's Astana. *Eurasian Geography and Economics*, 45(7), pp. 515–33.

Anceschi, L. 2017. Kazakhstani neo-Eurasianism and Nazarbayev's anti-imperial foreign policy. In M. Bassin and G. Pozo (eds.), *The Politics of Eurasianism: Identity, Culture and Russia's Foreign Policy*, pp. 283–300. London: Rowman & Littlefield International.

Anceschi, L. 2021. After personalism: Rethinking power transfers in Turkmenistan and Uzbekistan. *Journal of Contemporary Asia*, 51(4), pp. 660–80.

Arendt, H. 2007. *The Origins of Totalitarianism*. Durham, NC: Duke University Press.

Becker, J. 2004. Lessons from Russia: A neo-authoritarian media system. *European Journal of Communication*, 19(2), pp. 139–63.

Bekus, N., and Medeuova, K. 2017. Re-interpreting national ideology in the contemporary urban space of Astana. *Urbanities*, 7(2), pp. 10–21.

Bernhard, M., Edgell, A., and Lindberg, S. I. 2016. Suicide by competition? Authoritarian institutional adaptation and regime fragility. Authoritarian Institutional Adaptation and Regime Fragility (October 1, 2016). V-Dem Working Paper, 37, pp. 1–44. https://papers.ssrn.com/sol3/papers.cfm?abstract_id=2851432.

Bernstein, A. 2013. An inadvertent sacrifice: Body politics and sovereign power in the Pussy Riot affair. *Critical Inquiry*, 40(1), pp. 220–41.

Beysembayev, S. 2015. *Fenomen kazakhskogo natsionalizma v kontekstste segodniashnei politiki: ot otritsaniia k ponimaniiu*. Almaty: Fond Soros-Kazakhstan, www.soros.kz/wp-content/uploads/2015/09/kazakh_nationalism.pdf.

Beysembayev, S. 2016. Violent extremism in Kazakhstan: The fertile soil of gang culture. Seminar at the Central Asia Program, The George Washington University, Washington, DC (12 January).

Bissenova, A. 2017. The fortress and the frontier: Mobility, culture, and class in Almaty and Astana. *Europe-Asia Studies*, 69(4), pp. 642–67.

Blum, D. W. 2016. *The Social Process of Globalization: Return Migration and Cultural Change in Kazakhstan*. Cambridge: Cambridge University Press.

Bohr, A., Mallinson, K., Nixey, J., et al. 2019. Kazakhstan: Tested by transition. Report. www.chathamhouse.org/2019/11/kazakhstan-tested-transition/5-identity-politics.

Boix, C., and Svolik, M. W. 2013. The foundations of limited authoritarian government: Institutions, commitment, and power-sharing in dictatorships. *The Journal of Politics*, 75(2), pp. 300–16.

Botoeva, G., 2019. Use of language in blurring the lines between legality and illegality. In A. Polese, A. Russo, and F. Strazzari (eds.), *Governance beyond the Law*, pp. 67–83. Basingstoke: Palgrave Macmillan.

du Boulay, S., and du Boulay, H. 2021. New alphabets, old rules: Latinization, legacy, and liberation in Central Asia. *Problems of Post-Communism*, 68(2), pp. 135–40.

Bourdieu, P. 2014. *On the State: Lectures at College de France*. Cambridge: Polity.

Bunce, V., and Wolchik, S. 2009. Debating the color revolutions: Getting real about 'real causes'. *Journal of Democracy*, 20(1), pp. 69–73.

Caron, J. F., and Malikova, V. 2021. Understanding anti-regime activists' failures during the 2019 Kazakhstan presidential election. In J. F. Caron (ed.) *Understanding Kazakhstan's 2019 Political Transition*, pp. 79–100. Singapore: Palgrave Macmillan.

Castells, M. 2015. *Networks of Outrage and Hope: Social Movements in the Internet Age*. Hoboken, NJ: John Wiley & Sons.

Cohen, R., Newton-John, T., and Slater, A. 2017. The relationship between Facebook and Instagram appearance-focused activities and body image concerns in young women. *Body Image*, 23, pp. 183–7.

Collins, K. 2006. *Clan Politics and Regime Transition in Central Asia*. Cambridge: Cambridge University Press.

Cooley, A., and Heathershaw, J. 2017. *Dictators without Borders: Power and Money in Central Asia*. New Haven, CT: Yale University Press.

Cummings, S. (ed.) 2004. *Power and Change in Central Asia*. Abingdon: Routledge.

Cummings, S. 2006a. Legitimation and identification in Kazakhstan. *Nationalism and Ethnic Politics*, 12(2), pp. 177–204.

Cummings, S. 2006b. *Kazakhstan: Power and Elite*. London: IB Tauris.

Dave, B. 2007. *Kazakhstan: Ethnicity, Language and Power*. London: Routledge.

Del Sordi, A. 2018. Sponsoring student mobility for development and authoritarian stability: Kazakhstan's Bolashak programme. *Globalizations*, 15(2), pp. 215–31.

Della Porta, D., and Diani, M. 2001. *Social Movements: An Introduction*. Oxford: Blackwell.

Denzin, N. K., Lincoln, Y. S., and Smith, L. T. (eds.) 2008. *Handbook of Critical and Indigenous Methodologies*. London: Sage.

Diener, A. C. 2015. Assessing potential Russian irredentism and separatism in Kazakhstan's northern oblasts. *Eurasian Geography and Economics*, 56(5), pp. 469–92.

Diener, A. 2022. Multiscalar territorialization in Kazakhstan's northern borderland. *Geographical Review*, 112(1), pp. 125–46.

Dubuisson, E. M. 2017. *Living Language in Kazakhstan: The Dialogic Emergence of an Ancestral Worldview*. Pittsburgh, PA: University of Pittsburgh Press.

Dubuisson, E. M. 2020. Whose world? Discourses of protection for land, environment, and natural resources in Kazakhstan. *Problems of Post-Communism*, 69(4–5), pp. 410–22.

Duvanova, D. 2013. *Building Business in Post-Communist Russia, Eastern Europe and Eurasia: Collective Goods, Selective Incentives, and Predatory States*. Cambridge: Cambridge University Press.

ECFR. 2022. CSTO Intervention in Kazakhstan: What Is It About and What Is Russia's Agenda? YouTube video. www.youtube.com/watch?v=hrqf9tyNIg4.

Edgar, A. 2006. *Tribal Nation: The Making of Soviet Turkmenistan*. Princeton, NJ: Princeton University Press.

Fairclough, I., and Fairclough, N. 2013. *Political Discourse Analysis: A Method for Advanced Students*. London: Routledge.

Faranda, R., and Nolle, D. B. 2011. Boundaries of ethnic identity in Central Asia: Titular and Russian perceptions of ethnic commonalities in Kazakhstan and Kyrgyzstan. *Ethnic and Racial Studies*, 34(4), pp. 620–42.

Fauve, A. 2015. Global Astana: Nation branding as a legitimization tool for authoritarian regimes. *Central Asian Survey*, 34(1), pp. 110–24.

Fierman, W. 1998. Language and identity in Kazakhstan: Formulations in policy documents 1987–1997. *Communist and Post-Communist Studies*, 31(2), pp. 171–86.

Fierman, W. 2009. Identity, symbolism, and the politics of language in Central Asia. *Europe-Asia Studies*, 61(7), pp. 1207–28.

Fisun, O. 2012. Rethinking post-Soviet politics from a neopatrimonial perspective. *Demokratizatsiya: The Journal of Post-Soviet Democratization*, https://ssrn.com/abstract=2645304, pp. 1–11.

Flesher Fominaya, C. 2015. Debunking spontaneity: Spain's 15-M/Indignados as autonomous movement. *Social Movement Studies*, 14(2), pp. 142–63.

Foucault, M. 1977. *Discipline and Punish: The Birth of the Prison*. New York: Pantheon.

Galeotti, M. 2018. *The Vory: Russia's Super Mafia*. New Haven, CT: Yale University Press.

Gandhi, J. 2008. *Political Institutions under Dictatorship*. Cambridge: Cambridge University Press.

Gandhi, J., and Przeworski, A. 2007. Authoritarian institutions and the survival of autocrats. *Comparative Political Studies*, 40(11), pp. 1279–1301.

Gapova, E. 2015. Becoming visible in the digital age: The class and media dimensions of the Pussy Riot affair. *Feminist Media Studies*, 15(1), pp. 18–35.

Geddes, B., Wright, J. G., and Frantz, E. 2018. *How Dictatorships Work: Power, Personalization, and Collapse*. Cambridge: Cambridge University Press.

Gehlbach, S., Sonin, K., and Svolik, M. W. 2016. Formal models of nondemocratic politics. *Annual Review of Political Science*, 19, pp. 565–84.

Gel'man, V. 2015. *Authoritarian Russia: Analyzing Post-Soviet Regime Changes*. Pittsburgh, PA: University of Pittsburgh Press.

Gel'man, V. 2016. The vicious circle of post-Soviet neopatrimonialism in Russia. *Post-Soviet Affairs*, 32(5), pp. 455–73.

Gerschewski, J. 2013. The three pillars of stability: Legitimation, repression, and co-optation in autocratic regimes. *Democratization*, 2(1), pp. 13–38.

Giddens, A. 1986. *Durkheim on Politics and the State*. Stanford, CA: Stanford University Press.

Glasius, M. 2018. What authoritarianism is … and is not: A practice perspective. *International Affairs*, 94(3), pp. 515–33.

Gómez-Barris, M. 2018. *Beyond the Pink Tide*. Oakland: University of California Press.

Greene, S. A. 2013. Beyond Bolotnaia: Bridging old and new in Russia's election protest movement. *Problems of Post-Communism*, 60(2), pp. 40–52.

Hale, H. E. 2011. Formal constitutions in informal politics: Institutions and democratization in post-Soviet Eurasia. *World Politics*, 63(4), pp. 581–617.

Hale, H. E. 2014. *Patronal Politics: Eurasian Regime Dynamics in Comparative Perspective*. Cambridge: Cambridge University Press.

Heinrich, A., and Pleines, H. 2018. The meaning of 'limited pluralism' in media reporting under authoritarian rule. *Politics and Governance*, 6(2), pp. 103–11.

Huntington, H. E. 2016. Pepper Spray Cop and the American dream: Using synecdoche and metaphor to unlock internet memes' visual political rhetoric. *Communication Studies*, 67(1), pp. 77–93.

Ibadildin, N., and Pisareva, D. 2020. Central Asia in transition: Social contract transformation in Nazarbayev and post-Nazarbayev Kazakhstan. In A. Mihr (ed.), *Transformation and Development: Studies in the Organization for Security and Cooperation in Europe (OSCE) Member States*, pp. 101–16. Cham: Springer.

Ilyassov, D. 2020. (De)construction of queer identities based on their queer discourse in Kazakh. MA diss., Nazarbayev University, Astana, Kazakhstan.

Ince, J., Rojas, F., and Davis, C. A. 2017. The social media response to Black Lives Matter: How Twitter users interact with Black Lives Matter through hashtag use. *Ethnic and Racial Studies*, 40(11), pp. 1814–30.

Insebayeva, N. 2022. *Modernity, Development and Decolonization of Knowledge in Central Asia: Kazakhstan as a Foreign Aid Donor*. Basingstoke: Palgrave Macmillan.

Insebayeva, S., and Insebayeva, N. 2021. The power of ambiguity: National symbols, nation-building and political legitimacy in Kazakhstan. *Europe-Asia Studies*, 74(4), pp. 660–82.

Isaacs, R. 2010a. Informal politics and the uncertain context of transition: Revisiting early stage non-democratic development in Kazakhstan. *Democratization*, 17(1), pp. 1–25.

Isaacs, R. 2010b. 'Papa'–Nursultan Nazarbayev and the discourse of charismatic leadership and nation-building in post-Soviet Kazakhstan. *Studies in Ethnicity and Nationalism*, 10(3), pp. 435–52.

Isaacs, R., 2011. *Party System Formation in Kazakhstan: Between Formal and Informal Politics*. Abingdon: Routledge.

Isaacs, R. 2013. Nur Otan, informal networks and the countering of elite instability in Kazakhstan: Bringing the 'formal' back in. *Europe-Asia Studies*, 65(6), pp. 1055–79.

Isaacs, R. 2014. Neopatrimonialism and beyond: Reassessing the formal and informal in the study of Central Asian politics. *Contemporary Politics*, 20(2), pp. 229–45.

Isaacs, R. 2019. The Kazakhstan Now! Hybridity and hipsters in Almaty. In M. Laruelle (ed.), *The Nazarbayev Generation: Youth in Kazakhstan*. Lanham, MD: Lexington Books, pp. 227–44.

Isaacs, R., and Frigerio, A. 2018. *Theorizing Central Asian Politics: The State, Ideology and Power*. Basingstoke: Palgrave Macmillan.

Jacquesson, S. 2012. From clan narratives to clan politics. *Central Asian Survey*, 31(3), pp. 277–92.

Jäger, P. F. 2014. Flows of oil, flows of people: Resource-extraction industry, labour market and migration in western Kazakhstan. *Central Asian Survey*, 33(4), pp. 500–16.

Jardine, B., Khashimov, S., Lemon, E., and Kyzy, A. U. 2020. Mapping patterns of dissent in Eurasia: Introducing the Central Asia protest tracker. The Oxus Society for Central Asian Affairs.

Jašina-Schäfer, A. 2019. Everyday experiences of place in the Kazakhstani borderland: Russian speakers between Kazakhstan, Russia, and the globe. *Nationalities Papers*, 47(1), pp. 38–54.

Junisbai, B., and Junisbai, A. 2005. The Democratic Choice of Kazakhstan: A case study in economic liberalization, intraelite cleavage, and political opposition. *Demokratizatsiya*, 13(3), pp. 373–92.

Junisbai, B. 2010. A tale of two Kazakhstans: Sources of political cleavage and conflict in the post-Soviet period. *Europe-Asia Studies*, 62(2), pp. 235–69.

Junisbai, B., and Junisbai, A. 2019. Are youth different? The Nazarbayev generation and public opinion. In M. Laruelle (ed.), *The Nazarbayev Generation: Youth in Kazakhstan*. Lanham, MD: Lexington Books, pp. 25–48.

Kabatova, K. 2018. Overcoming a taboo: Normalizing sexuality education in Kazakhstan. In M. Laruelle (ed.), *The Nazarbayev Generation: Youth in Kazakhstan*. Lanham, MD: Lexington Books, pp. 289–304.

Kalandadze, K., and Orenstein, M. 2009. Electoral protests and democratization beyond the color revolutions. *Comparative Political Studies*, 42(11), pp. 1403–25.

Karin, E. 2016. *The Soldiers of the Caliphate: The Anatomy of a Terrorist Group*. Astana: Kazakhstan Institute for Strategic Studies.

Kendirbai, G. T. 2020. *Russian Practices of Governance in Eurasia: Frontier Power Dynamics, Sixteenth Century to Nineteenth Century*. New York: Routledge.

Kerimray, A., De Miglio, R., Rojas-Solórzano, L., and Ó Gallachóir, B. P. 2018. Causes of energy poverty in a cold and resource-rich country: Evidence from Kazakhstan. *Local Environment*, 23(2), pp. 178–97.

Koch, N. 2014. Bordering on the modern: Power, practice and exclusion in Astana. *Transactions of the Institute of British Geographers*, 39(3), pp. 432–43.

Koch, N. 2018. *The Geopolitics of Spectacle: Space, Synecdoche, and the New Capitals of Asia*. Ithaca, NY: Cornell University Press.

Koch, N., and White, K. 2016. Cowboys, gangsters, and rural bumpkins: Constructing the 'other' in Kazakhstan's 'Texas'. In M. Laruelle (ed.), *Kazakhstan in the Making: Legitimacy, Symbols, and Social Changes*, pp. 181–207. Lanham, MD: Lexington Books.

Kopeyeva, A. 2019. Understanding factors behind regional inequality in education in Kazakhstan. *CAP Paper* 224, July.

Kosnazarov, D. 2018. #Hashtag activism: Youth, social media, and politics. In M. Laruelle (ed.), *The Nazarbayev Generation: Youth in Kazakhstan*, pp. 247–68. Lanham, MD: Lexington Books.

Kudaibergenova, D. T. 2015. The ideology of development and legitimation: Beyond 'Kazakhstan 2030'. *Central Asian Survey*, 34(4), pp. 440–55.

Kudaibergenova, D. T. 2016. The use and abuse of postcolonial discourses in post-independent Kazakhstan. *Europe-Asia Studies*, 68(5), pp. 917–35.

Kudaibergenova, D. T. 2017a. *Rewriting the Nation in Modern Kazakh Literature: Elites and Narratives*. Lanham, MD: Lexington Books.

Kudaibergenova, D. T. 2017b. Contemporary public art and nation: Contesting 'tradition' in post-socialist cultures and societies. *Central Asian Affairs*, 4(4), pp. 305–30.

Kudaibergenova, D. T. 2018. Punk shamanism, revolt and break-up of traditional linkage: The waves of cultural production in post-Soviet Kazakhstan. *European Journal of Cultural Studies*, 21(4), pp. 435–51.

Kudaibergenova, D. T. 2019a. The body global and the body traditional: A digital ethnography of Instagram and nationalism in Kazakhstan and Russia. *Central Asian Survey*, 38(3), pp. 363–80.

Kudaibergenova, D. T. 2019b. Compartmentalized ideology and nation-building in non-democratic states. *Communist and Post-Communist Studies*, 52(3), pp. 247–57.

Kudaibergenova, D. T. 2020. *Toward Nationalizing Regimes: Conceptualizing Power and Identity in the Post-Soviet Realm*. Pittsburgh, PA: University of Pittsburgh Press.

Kudaibergenova, D. T. 2021. Power, knowledge, and the 'self' in everyday normalization of the political truth. *Problems of Post-Communism*, 68(2), pp. 151–62.

Kudaibergen, D. T. 2024. *What Does It Mean to Be Kazakhstani?* London: Hurst Publishers.

Kudaibergenova, D. T., and Shin, B. 2018. Authors and authoritarianism in Central Asia: Failed agency and nationalising authoritarianism in Uzbekistan and Kazakhstan. *Asian Studies Review*, 42(2), pp. 304–22.

Kudebayeva, A., and Barrientos, A. 2017. A decade of poverty reduction in Kazakhstan 2001–2009: Growth and/or redistribution? *Journal of International Development*, 29(8), pp. 1166–86.

Kulsariyeva, A. 2014. National idea 'Mangilik El' (eternal nation) and concept 'zheruiyk' (promised land) in the ideological discourse of modern Kazakhstan. *Science and Society*, 2(2), pp. 92–100.

Kuttykadam, S. 2010. *Kazakhskaia Drama: Na scene i za Kulisami: Istoria Sovremennogo Kazakhstana*. Almaty: Knizhnyi klub.

Kuzio, T. 1988. Nationalist riots in Kazakhstan. *Central Asian Survey*, 7(4), pp. 79–100.

Laruelle, M. 2004. The two faces of contemporary Eurasianism: An imperial version of Russian nationalism. *Nationalities Papers*, 32(1), pp. 115–36.

Laruelle, M. 2012. Discussing neopatrimonialism and patronal presidentialism in the Central Asian context. *Demokratizatsiya*, 20(4), pp. 301–24.

Laruelle, M. 2014. The three discursive paradigms of state identity in Kazakhstan. In M. Omelicheva (ed.), *Nationalism and Identity Construction in Central Asia: Dimensions, Dynamics, and Directions*. Lanham, MD: Lexington Books, pp. 1–20.

Laruelle, M. 2016. Which future for national-patriots? The landscape of Kazakh nationalism. In M. Laruelle (ed.), *Kazakhstan in the Making: Legitimacy, Symbols, and Social Changes*, pp. 155–81. Lanham, MD: Lexington Books.

Laruelle, M. 2018. Why no Kazakh Novorossiya? Kazakhstan's Russian minority in a post-Crimea world. *Problems of Post-Communism*, 65(1), pp. 65–78.

Laruelle, M. 2020. Making sense of Russia's illiberalism. *Journal of Democracy*, 31, pp. 115–29.

Laruelle, M. 2021. *Central Peripheries: Nationhood in Central Asia*. London: UCL Press.

Laruelle, M., Royce, D., and Beyssembayev, S. 2019. Untangling the puzzle of 'Russia's influence' in Kazakhstan. *Eurasian Geography and Economics*, 60(2), pp. 211–43.

Laszczkowski, M. 2016. *'City of the Future': Built Space, Modernity and Urban Change in Astana*. New York: Berghahn Books.

Ledeneva, A. V. 2013. *Can Russia Modernise? Sistema, Power Networks and Informal Governance*. Cambridge: Cambridge University Press.

Lenz-Raymann, K. 2014. *Securitization of Islam: A Vicious Circle. Counter-Terrorism and Freedom of Religion in Central Asia*. Bielefeld: Transcript Verlag.

Linz, J. 2000. *Totalitarian and Authoritarian Regimes*. Boulder, CO: Lynne Rienner Publishing.

Loewe, S. 2015. When protest becomes art: The contradictory transformations of the Occupy Movement at Documenta 13 and Berlin Biennale 7. *FIELD: A Journal of Socially-Engaged Art Criticism*, 1, pp. 185–203.

Lucento, A. 2017. Care outside the comfort zone: Maternal aesthetics, Katrin Nenasheva and the new politics of performance art in Russia. *Performance Research*, 22(4), pp. 79–88.

Magaloni, B. 2008. Credible power-sharing and the longevity of authoritarian rule. *Comparative Political Studies*, 41(4–5), pp. 715–41.

Marat, E. 2018. *The Politics of Police Reform: Society against the State in Post-Soviet Countries*. Oxford: Oxford University Press.

Matveeva, A. 2009. Legitimizing Central Asian authoritarianism: Political manipulation and symbolic power. *Europe-Asia Studies*, 61(7), pp. 1095–121.

Mazorenko, D., and Kaisar, A. 2022. On the ground in Kazakhstan's protests: What really happened? Open Democracy, 27 January 2022, www.opendemocracy.net/en/odr/what-really-happened-kazakhstan-protests-january/.

McGlinchey, E. 2011. *Chaos, Violence, Dynasty: Politics and Islam in Central Asia*. Pittsburgh, PA: University of Pittsburgh Press.

McKee, Y. 2016. *Strike Art: Contemporary Art and the Post-Occupy Condition*. London: Verso Books.

Milner, R. M. 2013. Pop polyvocality: Internet memes, public participation, and the Occupy Wall Street movement. *International Journal of Communication*, 7, p. 2357-2390.

Moldabekov, D. 2022. Dostoinstvo [Dignity], Adamdar.ca, available online at https://adamdar.ca/en/post/dostoinstvo-2/279.

Montgomery, D. W., and Heathershaw, J. 2016. Islam, secularism and danger: A reconsideration of the link between religiosity, radicalism and rebellion in Central Asia. *Religion, State & Society*, 44(3), pp. 192–218.

Murphy, J. 2006. Illusory transition? Elite reconstitution in Kazakhstan, 1989–2002. *Europe-Asia Studies*, 58(4), pp. 523–54.

Nazarbayev, N. 2008. *The Kazakhstan Way*. London: Stacey International.

Nazarbayev, N. 2014. Kazakhstan's Way–2050: Common Aim, Common Interests, Common Future. *Address of the President of Kazakhstan to the Nation*.

Nusimbekov, T. 2022. The night: About the events on January 4–5 in Almaty, Adamdar.ca, available online at https://adamdar.ca/en/post/the-night/278.
Olcott, M. B. 1990. Perestroyka in Kazakhstan. *Problems of Communism*, 39, pp. 65–77.
Olcott, M. B. 2010. *Kazakhstan: Unfulfilled Promise*. Washington, DC: Carnegie Endowment for International Peace.
Orakbaeva, S. 2011. Government regulation of housing. *Vestnik KazNU. Seriya Ekonomicheskaya*, 84(2), pp. 127–9.
Østbø, J. 2017. Demonstrations against demonstrations: The dispiriting emotions of the Kremlin's social media 'mobilization'. *Social Movement Studies*, 16(3), pp. 283–96.
Quijano, A. 2007. Coloniality and modernity/rationality. *Cultural Studies*, 21(2–3), pp. 168–78.
Paksoy, H. B. 2016. Alma-Ata, December 1986. In H. B. Paksoy (ed.), *Central Asia Reader: The Rediscovery of History*, pp. 160–4. Abingdon: Routledge.
Pearce, K. 2014. Two can play at that game: Social media opportunities in Azerbaijan for government and opposition. *Demokratizatsiya*, 22(1), pp. 39–66.
Peyrouse, S. 2016. The Kazakh neopatrimonial regime. In M. Laruelle (ed.), *Kazakhstan in the Making: Legitimacy, Symbols, and Social Changes*, pp. 29–62. Lanham, MD: Lexington Books.
Pink, S., Horst, H., Postill, J., et al. 2016. *Digital Ethnography: Principles and Practice*. London: Sage.
Poell, T. 2020. Social media, temporality, and the legitimacy of protest. *Social Movement Studies*, 19(5–6), pp. 609–24.
Prozorov, S. 2014. Pussy Riot and the politics of profanation: Parody, performativity, veridiction. *Political Studies*, 62(4), pp. 766–83.
Przeworski, A., 2022. Formal models of authoritarian regimes: A critique. *Perspectives on Politics*, pp. 1–10.
Radnitz, S. 2021. *Revealing Schemes: The Politics of Conspiracy in Russia and the Post-Soviet Region*. Oxford: Oxford University Press.
Reuter, O. J., and Szakonyi, D. 2015. Online social media and political awareness in authoritarian regimes. *British Journal of Political Science*, 45(1), pp. 29–51.
Rorlich, A. A. 2003. Islam, identity and politics: Kazakhstan, 1990–2000. *Nationalities Papers*, 31(2), pp. 157–76.
Ross, A. S., and Rivers, D. J. 2017. Digital cultures of political participation: Internet memes and the discursive delegitimization of the 2016 US presidential candidates. *Discourse, Context & Media*, 16, pp. 1–11.

Rottier, P. 2003. The Kazakness of sedentarization: Promoting progress as tradition in response to the land problem. *Central Asian Survey*, 22(1), pp. 67–81.

Ruzanov, R., and Zharlygasinov, T. 2021. Corruption in the healthcare sector during the COVID-19 pandemic: Causes, consequences and responses. *Economics: The Strategy and Practice*, 16(3), pp. 217–26.

Salimjan, G. 2017. Debating gender and Kazakhness: Memory and voice in poetic duel aytis between China and Kazakhstan. *Central Asian Survey*, 36(2), pp. 263–80.

Sanghera, B., and Satybaldieva, E. 2021. *Rentier Capitalism and Its Discontents*. Cham: Springer International Publishing.

Satpayev, D., and Umbetaliyeva, T. 2015. The protests in Zhanaozen and the Kazakh oil sector: Conflicting interests in a rentier state. *Journal of Eurasian Studies*, 6(2), pp. 122–9.

Shakhanova, G. 2018. Being in close neighborhood with Russia: The Kazakhstan's state-framed identity and Latinization of the script. An attempt for Westernization or creating own subalternity? *Journal of Central Asian Studies*, 25(1), pp. 1–24.

Sharipova 2019. Youth organizations and state–society relations in Kazakhstan: The durability of the Leninist legacy. In F. Caron (ed.), *Kazakhstan and the Soviet Legacy*, pp. 139–54. Basingstoke: Palgrave Macmillan.

Sharipova, D., and Beissembayev, S. 2021. Causes of violent extremism in Central Asia: The case of Kazakhstan. *Studies in Conflict & Terrorism*, 46(9), pp. 1702–24.

Schatz, E. 2004. *Modern Clan Politics: The Power of 'Blood' in Kazakhstan and Beyond*. Seattle: University of Washington Press.

Schatz, E. 2009. The soft authoritarian tool kit: Agenda-setting power in Kazakhstan and Kyrgyzstan. *Comparative Politics*, 41(2), pp. 203–22.

Shelekpayev, N. 2021. Rethinking transfers of power and public protest in Kazakhstan, 1959–1989. *Europe-Asia Studies*, 74(5), pp. 857–71.

Shilton, S. 2021. *Art and the Arab Spring: Aesthetics of Revolution and Resistance in Tunisia and Beyond*. Cambridge: Cambridge University Press.

Shoshanova, S. 2021. Queer identity in the contemporary art of Kazakhstan. *Central Asian Survey*, 40(1), pp. 113–31.

Smith, L. T. 2021. *Decolonizing Methodologies: Research and Indigenous Peoples*. London: Zed Books.

Smyth, R. 2018. Considering the orange legacy: Patterns of political participation in the Euromaidan revolution. *Post-Soviet Affairs*, 34(5), pp. 297–316.

Sorbello, P. 2021. Industrial relations in Kazakhstan's oil sector (1991–2019). Doctoral dissertation, Unversity of Glasgow.

Sultanbayeva, Z., and Nuryeva, A. 2016. *Art Atmosphere of Almat-Ata*. Almaty: TOO Service Press.
Suny, R. G. 2001. Constructing primordialism: Old histories for new nations. *The Journal of Modern History*, 73(4), pp. 862–96.
Svolik, M. W. 2012. *The Politics of Authoritarian Rule*. Cambridge: Cambridge University Press.
Svolik, M. W. 2013. Contracting on violence: The moral hazard in authoritarian repression and military intervention in politics. *Journal of Conflict Resolution*, 57(5), pp. 765–94.
Tarrow, S. 1998. *Power in Movement: Social Movements and Contentious Politics*. Cambridge: Cambridge University Press.
Ten, Y. 2020. Gender nonconformity and homosexuality in Kazakhstan's contemporary visual culture. MA in Eurasian Studies dissertation. Nazarbayev University, Astana.
Tlostanova, M. 2018. *What Does It Mean to Be Post-Soviet? Decolonial Art from the Ruins of the Soviet Empire*. Durham, NC: Duke University Press.
Totaro, M. 2021. Nightmarizing states: Affective encounters with counter-extremism in Kazakhstan. *Problems of Post-Communism*, 68(2), pp. 141–50.
Tutumlu, A., 2019. Governmentalization of the Kazakhstani state: Between governmentality and neopatrimonial capitalism. In R. Isaacs and A. Frigerio (eds.), *Theorizing Central Asian Politics: The State, Ideology and Power*, pp. 43–64. Basingstoke: Palgrave Macmillan.
Tutumlu, A., and Imyarova, Z. 2021. The Kazakhstani Soviet not? Reading Nazarbayev's Kazakhstani-ness through Brezhnev's Soviet people. *Central Asian Survey*, 40(3), pp. 400–19.
Tutumlu, A., and Rustemov, I. 2021. The paradox of authoritarian power: Bureaucratic games and information asymmetry. The case of Nazarbayev's Kazakhstan. *Problems of Post-Communism*, 68(2), pp. 124–34.
Udod, X. 2018. Feminisms in Kazakhstan: On the intersection of global influences and local contexts. MA in Eurasian Studies dissertation. Nazarbayev University, Astana.
Urinboyev, R. 2020. *Migration and Hybrid Political Regimes*. Berkeley: University of California Press.
Urinboyev, R., and Svensson, M. 2013. Living law, legal pluralism, and corruption in post-Soviet Uzbekistan. *The Journal of Legal Pluralism and Unofficial Law*, 45(3), pp. 372–90.
Uyama, T. 2000. *The Geography of Civilizations: A Spatial Analysis of the Kazakh Intelligentsia's Activities, from the Mid-Nineteenth to the Early Twentieth Century*. Sapporo: Slavic Research Center.
Wacquant, L. J., and Bourdieu, P. 1992. *An Invitation to Reflexive Sociology*. Cambridge: Polity Press.

Way, L. 2008. The real causes of the color revolutions. *Journal of Democracy*, 19(3), pp. 55–69.
Wedeen, L. 1998. Acting 'as if': Symbolic politics and social control in Syria. *Comparative Studies in Society and History*, 40(3), pp. 503–23.
Wedeen, L. 1999. *Ambiguities of Domination. Politics, Rhetoric, and Symbols in Contemporary Syria*. Chicago: University of Chicago Press.
Wedeen, L. 2009. *Peripheral Visions*. Chicago: University of Chicago Press.
Wedeen, L. 2019. *Authoritarian Apprehensions: Ideology, Judgment, and Mourning in Syria*. Chicago: University of Chicago Press.
Wolfel, R. L. 2002. North to Astana: Nationalistic motives for the movement of the Kazakh (stani) capital. *Nationalities Papers*, 30(3), pp.485–506.
Yablokov, I. 2018. *Fortress Russia: Conspiracy Theories in the Post-Soviet World*. Cambridge: Polity.
Yemelianova, G. M. 2014. Islam, national identity and politics in contemporary Kazakhstan. *Asian Ethnicity*, 15(3), pp. 286–301.
Yessenova, S. 2005. 'Routes and roots' of Kazakh identity: Urban migration in postsocialist Kazakhstan. *The Russian Review*, 64(4), pp. 661–79.
Yessenova, S. 2010. Borrowed places: Eviction wars and property rights formalization in Kazakhstan. In D. C. Wood (ed.), *Economic Action in Theory and Practice: Anthropological Investigations*. Leeds: Emerald Group Publishing Limited.
Yurchak, A. 2013. *Everything Was Forever, Until It Was No More: The Last Soviet Generation*. Princeton, NJ: Princeton University Press.
Zakirov, B. 2021. Authoritarian stability in Uzbekistan under patronal president Islam Karimov. *Central Asian Affairs*, 8(3), pp. 273–96.

Index

#cancelElbasy
  hashtags, 39
#QazaqKoktemi
  hashtags, 52, 212
#shalket
  hashtags, 39

19 March 2019
  Nazarbayev's resignation, 17

Abay, 79, 156, 164
adil sailau ushin, 78
Agadil, Dulat
  activist, 37, 196
Ak Orda
  presidential palace, 18, 36, 38, 44, 61, 121, 128, 191, 200
Akhmediyarov, Askhat
  artist, activist, 54, 55, 65
Akimat Astany, 51
Alash, vii, 32, 33, 60, 83, 123, 169, 175, 177, 180, 182, 183, 185, 186
Alash Orda, 5, 60, 83, 183, 186, 187
Almaty marathon, 46, 52, 56, 57, 66, 282
Alzhanov, Dimash, 64, 68, 86, 95, 96, 97, 113, 126, 130, 131, 132, 181, 190, 210, 211
Arab Spring, 13, 14
Ashim, Aisana
  media owner, activist, 54, 116, 182, 186, 239
Astana (formerly Nur-Sultan), viii, 6, 14, 22, 23, 36, 37, 47, 48, 51, 55, 60, 61, 62, 79, 80, 88, 92, 93, 94, 107, 108, 116, 119, 122, 123, 124, 128, 130, 148, 150, 154, 177, 180, 184, 210, 211, 231, 234, 238, 246, 253, 255, 288, 289, 291, 292, 294, 295, 299, 300

authoritarian myopia, 16, 48, 117, 118, 188, 273
authoritarian resilience, 8, 9, 21, 38

BatyrJamal, 116, 127, 153, 154, 239
Bazargali, Medina
  artist, activist, x, 68, 70, 73, 99, 101, 113, 168, 192, 275, 286
Belarus, 27
Belarus protests 2020, 81, 106, 208, 285
Bloody January, 7. *See* January 2022 mass protests

Cancel Elbasy, viii, 71, 167, 212, 216, 218
coffee shops, 121, 126, 219
corruption, 5, 6, 21, 23, 31, 32, 36, 51, 63, 73, 74, 84, 102, 106, 115, 125, 138, 141, 143, 149, 152, 211, 242, 244, 246, 248, 254, 256, 299
court hearings, 10, 55, 65, 68, 71, 72, 79, 85, 136, 137, 140, 156, 157, 159, 160, 162, 168, 176, 206
Covid-19
  pandemic, lockdown, 43, 72, 118, 148, 149, 150, 151, 158, 168, 298
CSTO, 14
  Collective Security Treaty Organization, 7, 14, 245, 261, 266, 269

December 1986 protests, 40
  Zheltoqsan, 33, 40, 56, 97, 123, 127, 197, 198, 255
December 2011 protests
  Zhanaozen, 2, 33, 97, 127, 197, 252
Democratic Choice of Kazakhstan (DVK), 3, 22, 39, 40
  Zhanbolat Mamay, 42, 44, 45, 55, 61, 142, 156, 247, 255, 256, 259

301

Ten, Denis
  Olympic ice skater, 75, 76, 81
digital ethnography, 29
Dulatov, Myrzhaqyp, 33, 60, 83, 177

elbasy, 2, 21, 36
electoral observers, 88, 91, 111, 112, 113
Euromaidan, 27
EXPO-2017
  corruption, 76, 126

Facebook
  Social Media, 49, 50, 51, 67, 80, 90, 93, 112, 140, 142, 154, 158, 161, 162, 165, 210, 258, 290
Facebookstan, 49, 50, 84
Femenita, 231, 232, 234, 236, 242

Hale, Henry, 16, 20, 98, 99, 263, 292
hipster, 65, 110, 113, 117, 121, 126, 183, 196
Hong Kong protests, 155, 207

Instagram, 8, 29, 32, 38, 46, 47, 50, 57, 60, 67, 68, 72, 81, 84, 85, 90, 93, 94, 116, 126, 140, 141, 142, 148, 150, 153, 154, 157, 158, 159, 160, 161, 162, 166, 168, 184, 188, 205, 210, 216, 217, 224, 258, 260, 261, 262, 275, 285, 290, 294

January 2022 mass protests (Qandy Qantar), vii, 1, 2, 3, 5, 6, 7, 13, 14, 21, 25, 26, 30, 34, 35, 43, 117, 118, 135, 137, 139, 193, 196, 244, 245, 246, 248, 250, 253, 258, 259, 261, 268, 272, 273
June 2019 protests, 42, 48, 72, 84–96

Kazakhstan 2030
  strategy, 246, 294
Kazakhstan without Nazarbayevs, 24
KazFem, 220, 223, 224, 225, 226, 228
kettling
  riot police tactics, 33, 82, 194, 196, 209
kosanovshina, 41, 42, 44
Kunaev, Dinmukhamed, 40, 197

Laruelle, Marlene, vii, x, 9, 18, 37, 61, 63, 119, 170, 172, 185, 193, 263, 269, 293, 294, 295
law enforcement, 8, 10, 21, 32, 57, 73, 74, 75, 82, 99, 101, 105, 106, 114, 116, 133, 134, 135, 136, 137, 138, 149, 158, 160, 161, 162, 163, 164, 165, 194, 207, 208, 218, 228, 232, 239, 241, 242, 250, 260, 262, 266, 267
Law on the Father of the Nation, 36
Law on the First President, 25
LGBTQ, 44, 222, 225, 226, 231, 232, 233, 235, 236, 237, 238

Mamay, Zhanbolat, 42
Masa
  independent media, 54, 116, 127, 153, 168, 176, 182, 183, 186, 240, 259
Men Oyandym
  campaign, 120, 121, 122
mnogodetnie materi
  mothers with multiple children, *kop balaly analar*, 120, 126, 128
mothers' protests, 6, 128, 200, 222, 248
mothers with multiple children, 129
  mnogodetnie materi, kop balaly analar, 18

nationalizing regime, 18, 32, 169, 172, 173, 174, 175, 187, 192, 214, 279
national-patriots
  Kazakh nationalism, 119, 170, 171, 172, 174, 185, 200, 295
Nazarbayev's resignation, 46
neopatrimonialism, 16, 291
NKVD
  Soviet, 80, 180
Nur-Otan, 6
  party, 6, 61, 153, 222
Nur-Sultan. *See* Astana
Nur-sultanization
  cult of personality, 36

Okrestina
  Belarus Protests 2020, 208
Osinovskaya, Arina
  activist, 220, 223

Index 303

Ospan, Fariza
  activist, x, 89, 90, 114, 115, 126, 159, 160, 161, 205, 206, 208, 220, 234, 241
Oyan, Qazaqstan, vii, 1, 14, 15, 22, 23, 24, 28, 29, 31, 33, 44, 45, 46, 47, 48, 50, 52, 53, 55, 60, 61, 63, 64, 65, 67, 68, 70, 71, 76, 82, 84, 86, 87, 88, 89, 92, 94, 95, 96, 97, 98, 102, 103, 108, 109, 110, 112, 113, 114, 115, 116, 117, 120, 124, 126, 127, 129, 130, 131, 142, 143, 144, 145, 146, 147, 155, 159, 160, 161, 162, 175, 179, 181, 182, 183, 185, 187, 190, 191, 200, 201, 202, 205, 207, 210, 213, 218, 230, 233, 239, 240, 247, 248, 255, 256, 259, 278, 281, 283, 287

parliament, 6, 22, 36, 41, 45, 62, 64, 123, 125, 174, 199, 210, 217, 221, 233, 238, 255, 283
parliamentary republic, 62, 201
Peremen
  performance, 80, 212, 214
poster wars, 39, 168, 212
post-Nazarbayev, 7, 11, 13, 20, 21, 50, 60, 71, 176, 277, 279
Protest Körpe, 157
Putin, Vladimir, 3, 9, 19

Qandy Qantar. *See* January 2022 mass protests
queer, 10, 27, 45, 191, 225, 226, 227, 228, 230, 231, 236, 237, 238, 240, 241, 279, 280, 292, 298

rally permit, 37
regime–society relations, 19, 24
resignation, 1, 15, 21, 30, 31, 36, 37, 38, 40, 47, 50, 51, 59, 61, 62, 65, 102, 126, 217, 248, 253, 264, 276
revolution, 1, 2, 7, 13, 26, 27, 28, 29, 32, 39, 70, 71, 97, 127, 139, 166, 211, 215, 235, 276, 277, 298
riot police, 2, 127

Sagutdinov, Aslan
  activist, 79, 80

Senate, 5, 51
Serkebayeva, Zhanar
  activist, 220, 228, 231, 232, 242, 253, 255
seruens
  walking protests, 92, 109, 110, 111, 115, 201, 202
Serzhan, Gulzada
  activist, 220, 229, 231, 232, 242, 253, 255
Shal, ket!, 2, 3, 7, 10, 46
Shanyrak, 25
Shymkent, 23, 92, 124, 126, 128, 131, 149, 159, 160, 184, 205, 220, 231, 232, 255, 257, 270
SOBR
  special forces, riot police, 194, 232
Soviet Nationality Policy, 172
Suleimenova, Suinbike, 57
  activist, artist, 52, 54, 66, 68, 70, 71, 77, 79, 82, 113, 126, 192, 206, 207, 220

Taldykorgan, 6, 36
Tansari, Dina
  Activist, 220, 224
Telegram, 23, 29, 44, 67, 76, 90, 93, 116, 142, 145, 147, 150, 153, 162, 183, 190, 210, 260, 261, 285
social media, 23
Tlostanova, Madina, 177, 178, 179, 192, 299
Tokayev, Kassym-Zhomart, 2, 4, 5, 6, 7, 14, 25, 30, 38, 41, 42, 48, 51, 52, 62, 89, 91, 100, 139, 142, 159, 177, 193, 209, 214, 218, 242, 245, 248, 255, 261, 262, 263, 264, 265, 267, 268, 269, 270, 272, 273, 274, 278
Tolymbetov, Beybarys, 57
  activist, viii, 52, 57, 66, 67, 71
torture, 2, 14, 28, 134, 137, 180, 194, 196, 209, 258, 260, 261, 262, 263, 273
Tulesova, Asya
  activist, viii, 29, 32, 44, 52, 57, 58, 66, 67, 71, 72, 73, 74, 75, 76, 77, 82, 87, 111, 113, 116, 126, 136, 140, 155, 156, 157, 160, 205

Ukraine, 26, 138, 193, 261, 273
  war in Ukraine, 9
Umyltymas 1986/2011
  slogans, 197
Umytpa
  project, 116, 149, 150, 151, 152, 153, 168
Ungarova, Mira
  activist, 60
unsanctioned rallies
  rally permit, 37
Usenovshina
  corruption, 74
Uyabayeva, Nesipkul
  Citizen, viii, 79, 107, 108
uyat, 78

vlast', vii, 1, 31, 43, 68, 98, 99, 100, 101, 103, 104, 105, 109, 114, 120, 132, 134, 135, 145, 150, 152, 153, 161, 170, 187, 202, 214
VPN-stan
  censorship, 49, 154

Wedeen, Lisa, 11, 19, 21, 143, 144, 163, 169, 203, 204, 214, 215, 261, 300
Western Kazakhstan, 25

WhatsApp, 46, 89, 90, 93, 94, 95, 107, 140, 144, 152, 154
Women's March, viii, 33, 44, 45, 220, 223, 224, 225, 226, 227, 228, 229, 230, 231, 238, 242, 243

You cannot run away from the truth, 46, 52, 56, 57, 58, 65, 66, 67, 72, 73, 78, 79, 213, 282
Yurchak, Alexei, 26, 119, 138, 185, 186

Zaitov, Rinat
  Aityschi, 93, 94, 95
Zakharov, Roman
  artist, activist, 58, 59, 67, 68, 69, 70, 71
Zhanaozen, 2, 33, 35, 118, 127, 139, 195, 196, 197, 200, 201, 216, 248, 250, 252, 254, 255, 256, 272, 273
  protests, 35
  2011, 2, 6
Zhapisheva, Assem 6, 1, 86, 113
  activist, 46, 68, 71, 82, 86, 101, 116, 121, 126, 142, 150, 151, 153, 181, 182, 183, 184, 187, 203, 235
Zheltoqsan
  December 1986 protests, 40, 123, 199, 201

www.ingramcontent.com/pod-product-compliance
Ingram Content Group UK Ltd.
Pitfield, Milton Keynes, MK11 3LW, UK
UKHW020046240125
453910UK00021B/409